West Wind, Flood Tide

West Wind, Flood Tide

THE BATTLE OF MOBILE BAY

JACK FRIEND

NAVAL INSTITUTE PRESS
Annapolis, Maryland

The latest edition of this work has been brought to publication with the generous assistance of Marguerite and Gerry Lenfest.

Naval Institute Press
291 Wood Road
Annapolis, MD 21402

First Naval Institute Press paperback edition published in 2013
ISBN 978-1-61251-487-1 (paperback)
ISBN 978-1-61251-351-5 (eBook)

The Library of Congress has cataloged the hardcover edition as follows:
Friend, Jack, 1929–
 West wind, flood tide: the Battle of Mobile Bay / Jack Friend.
  p. cm.
 Includes bibliographical references and index.
 ISBN 1-59114-292-x (alk. paper)
1. Mobile Bay, Battle of, Ala., 1864. I. Title.
 E476.85.F75 2004
 973.7'5—dc22

                                                          2003017844

♾ Print editions meet the requirements of ANSI/NISO z39.48-1992 (Permanence of Paper).
Printed in the United States of America.

28 27 26 25 24 23   11 10 9 8 7 6

For Venetia

CONTENTS

➤➤ ◄◄

PREFACE

IT TAKES A GREAT LEAP OF THE IMAGINATION TO STAND ON THE BEACH at Fort Morgan and picture in the mind's eye the violent scene that occurred there more than a century ago. The serenity and beauty of the place make it difficult to reconstruct the images and sounds of the Civil War's bloodiest naval battle. Gone is the smoke, the smell of burnt powder, the swish and whine of missiles, the crash of splintering wood—and the human sounds: shouts, screams, oaths. Except for the fort's great mass of brick and earth and the lone buoy that marks the grave of the ironclad *Tecumseh*, nothing is visible to suggest the horror of that fateful day.[1] This book is an account of the naval action at Mobile Bay on 5 August 1864, which was described by Adm. David Glasgow Farragut, commander of the Union fleet, as the "most desperate battle I ever fought."[2]

In the spring of 1864, as dogwood blossoms heralded the end of winter throughout the Confederacy, independence was almost a certainty—the Southern heartland was still intact from the Shenandoah Valley to the red-clay hills of Georgia. Richmond, Atlanta, and the seaports of Mobile, Charleston, and Wilmington were thriving despite the blockade and the inconveniences of a wartime economy. West of the Mississippi, the situations was much the same; except for New Orleans and a few small Union garrisons on the coast, Louisiana was firmly in Confederate hands.[3]

Following the Confederacy's crushing defeats at Vicksburg and Gettysburg in 1863, there was a pause in the fighting, followed in the early spring of 1864 by Union defeats in Louisiana and Tennessee, and by two bold raids: one as far north as Chambersburg, Pennsylvania, and the other to the outskirts of Washington, D.C., within sight of the Union capital. In Virginia, Robert E. Lee had Ulysses S. Grant stalled outside Richmond, with little hope of advancing, and in Georgia—seven hundred miles to the south—Joseph E. Johnston was contesting William Tecumseh Sherman's move toward Atlanta with skill and sagacity.[4]

In the North, the hope that had followed Vicksburg and Gettysburg had now turned to despair. Tired of the slaughter and the burden of total war—conscription, heavy taxes, and dictatorial government—the northern electorate blamed Abraham Lincoln for his mismanagement of the war. If the Confederacy could "deny the North a major military triumph" before the November presidential election, the South was certain to achieve its independence, not on the battlefield, but by a negotiated peace.[5]

Even Lincoln believed that the war was lost. During the summer he wrote himself a memorandum and filed it away: "This morning, as for some days past, it seems exceedingly probable that this Administration will not be reelected. Then it will be my duty to so cooperate with the President-elect as to save the Union between the election and the inauguration; as he will have secured his election on such ground that he cannot possibly save it afterwards."[6]

Much was at stake for both sides. A Union victory at Mobile would break the battlefield stalemate and help Abraham Lincoln win the presidency; it would also provide Sherman with a safe base after the capture of Atlanta, should he choose to head for the Gulf of Mexico instead of the Atlantic. A Confederate victory, on the other hand, would strengthen the Peace Democrats' bid for the presidency and the chances of a negotiated peace, which would result in Southern independence.[7]

The Battle of Mobile Bay was fought 5 August 1864, in the fourth year of the war. With numerical superiority in vessels and firepower several times that of the Confederate forces, Farragut's killed and wounded exceeded his combined losses at New Orleans, Port Hudson, and Vicksburg. Mobile Bay was a hard-earned strategic success for the Union and an important political victory for President Abraham Lincoln. For the Confederacy, Mobile Bay was another example of the price the Union would have to pay for victory.[8]

The battle was also a "contest between the wills of two great fighting admirals:" Farragut, conqueror of New Orleans and the Mississippi River, the most popular sailor in the Union navy; and Franklin Buchanan, ranking officer of the Confederate Navy, and commander of the ram *Virginia* when it sank the Union warships, *Cumberland* and *Congress*. "Both were American, both had been raised and trained in the same naval tradition, both had fought under the same flag, and each was a hero to the people and government he now served."[9]

Fortunately, a plethora of eyewitness accounts from both sides and from all ranks tell us in vivid detail what that day was like. Life aboard a mid–nineteenth-century warship was harsh and demanding, yet with few exceptions morale was high and courage abundant. From the opening gun of the battle to the surrender of the *Tennessee*, three hours later, eighty-two Union sailors earned the medal of honor. The historical record does not tell us how many heroic acts occurred in the Confederate squadron; the South did not have such a medal. However, judging from the after-action reports of Confederate officers, acts of heroism and sacrifice were just as prevalent.[10]

Capt. A. T. Mahan, in his biography of Farragut, praised both Farragut and Buchanan for the way they conducted the battle. He wrote of Farragut: "there seems to be much to praise and very little to criticize in the tactical dispositions made by the admiral on this momentous occasion." As for Buchanan's tactics, Mahan felt they were "well devised," that the Confederate admiral made the "best use of the advantages of the ground possible to so inferior a force."[11]

But rare is the combat commander who makes no mistakes on the battlefield, and Farragut and Buchanan were no exceptions. Although Farragut's decision to lash his vessels in pairs was tactically sound, he would be criticized later for placing the fleet's most powerful sloops in the van. Lacking the firepower to effectively suppress Fort Morgan's batteries, his smaller, rear vessels were severely punished as they passed Fort Morgan. A more serious mistake was his signal ordering the *Brooklyn* to "Go on!" as the van of the fleet drifted helplessly under a galling fire. As will be seen later, the command was ambiguous, and Capt. James Alden of the *Brooklyn* eventually took the rap. He would not be promoted to rear admiral until 1871, ten months after Farragut's death.[12]

Throughout the narrative, I have described only what was known and believed at a particular point in time, even if erroneous. I have been careful, however, to correct these misconceptions as new information became available during the normal course of events. In the words of Karl von

Clausewitz, "War is the province of uncertainty; three-fourths of the things on which action in war is based lie hidden in the fog of greater or less uncertainty"—and the Battle of Mobile Bay was no exception.[13]

In later years, the battle would be immortalized by the apothegm "Damn the torpedoes," mentioned for the first time by Foxhall Parker in an 1877 speech after the admiral's death. These were not Farragut's exact words, although they capture the spirit of the order he gave when the outcome of the battle hung on a slender thread.[14]

ACKNOWLEDGMENTS

THIS PROJECT COULD NOT HAVE BEEN COMPLETED WITHOUT THE assistance of others. At the outset, I would like to thank those who helped put the book together. Their devotion to the effort—the long hours and attention to detail—are indeed appreciated. These include my chief assistant Sara Lamb, Anne Gibbons, Karen LaSarge, Bill Barkley, Jeff Darby, and Chuck Torrey. I also would like to include in this group Jim Stokesbury of Remsen, Iowa, for his help with research, and my son Danner, whose computer analysis of ships' logs was invaluable.

I am also indebted to those who offered suggestions, as well as criticisms, when discussing the various theories proposed in the book. To the following, my sincere thanks for your help. And to those whose names I have inadvertently omitted, my heartfelt apologies: writing this book has been a long voyage.

Mike Bailey, Alabama Historical Commission, Fort Morgan, Alabama; Dan Basta, NOAA, Rockville, Maryland; Dufour Bayle, Metairie, Louisiana; Ray Bellande, Ocean Springs, Mississippi; Blanton Blakenship, Alabama Historical Commission, Fort Morgan, Alabama; Col. George Brooke Jr., Lexington, Virginia; Dr. Bob Browning, historian, U.S. Coast Guard, Washington, D.C.; Walt Burden, U.S. Corps of Engineers (retired), Mobile, Alabama; Beverley Dabney, Norfolk, Virginia; Caldwell Delaney, Mobile, Alabama; Dr. Bill Dudley, director, Naval Historical Center, Washington, D.C.; Grace Bestor DuValle, Mobile, Alabama; Bob Edington, Daphne, Alabama; Dr. Sam Eichold, Mobile,

Alabama; Richard Ely, Harrington, Delaware; Charles Enslow, Bloomington, Delaware; Tom J. Freeman, Ocean Springs, Mississippi; Chuck Haberlein, Naval Historical Center, Washington, D.C.; Mike Henderson, Historic Fort Gaines, Dauphin Island, Alabama; Jay Higgenbotham, director, Mobile City Archives (re-tired), Mobile, Alabama; Bob Holcombe, Confederate Naval Museum, Columbus, Georgia; Jan Joseph, Mobile, Alabama; Dr. Harold Langley, Smithsonian Institution (retired), Washington, D.C.; Dr. Robert Latorre, University of New Orleans, New Orleans, Louisiana; Becky Livingston, National Archives, Washington, D.C.; Mary Livingston, Bloomington, Delaware; Kevin Lynaugh, David Taylor Model Basin, Bethesda, Maryland; Marjorie McNinch, Hagley Museum and Library, Wilmington, Delaware; Dean Mosher, Fairhope, Alabama; Mike Music, National Archives, Washington, D.C.; Norman Nicolson, Mobile, Alabama; Warren Norville, Mobile, Alabama; Charlie Perry, Charleston, South Carolina; Ernest Peterkin, Camp Springs, Maryland; Roger Pineau, Bethesda, Maryland; Bill Roberson, Mobile, Alabama; Syd Schell, Mobile, Alabama; Adelaide Trigg, Mobile Alabama; Mary Van Antwerp, Fairhope, Alabama; Mel Wiggins, Mobile, Alabama; Steven Wise, Beauford, South Carolina; and Clifford Young, Boston, Massachusetts.

PROLOGUE

→> <←

THE TRAIN RIDE FROM NEW YORK TO WASHINGTON, D.C., GAVE CAPT. David Glasgow Farragut plenty of time to mull over how he would steam up the Mississippi River, force his way past two forts, and capture New Orleans. He had been selected as a candidate to command the operation and was on his way to be interviewed by Gideon Welles, secretary of the navy. Welles had picked Captain Farragut because of his "great superiority of character, clear perception of duty, and firm resolution in the performance of it," with full knowledge that the captain's other abilities could not be determined until tested in the crucible of war.[1] The idea excited Farragut, and he wanted the job. If all went well today, 21 December 1861, he would be presented with the greatest challenge of his career.

Arriving in Washington, Farragut was met at the train station by Gustavas V. Fox, assistant secretary of the navy, who took him to the home of Postmaster General Montgomery Blair, where Fox described the plan of attack, the force to be employed, and the object to be obtained. When asked for his opinion, Farragut answered without pause that it would succeed. Fox then handed him a list of vessels and asked if they were enough. Farragut replied he would "engage to run by the forts and capture New Orleans with two-thirds the number." Smiling at the captain's optimism, but impressed with his confidence, Fox told him that additional vessels would be added and that Secretary Welles was prepared to give him the command when they met later in the day.[2]

Farragut, now a flag officer, assumed command of the West Gulf Blockading Squadron on 21 February 1862. The command extended from Saint

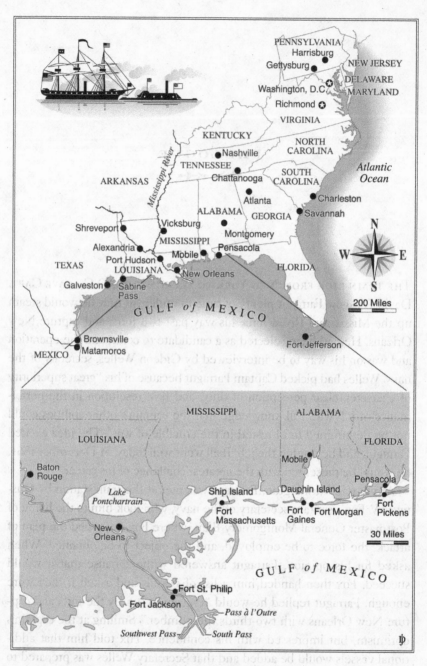

The seat of war, 1862–1864.

Andrews Bay in West Florida to the Rio Grande and included the coasts of Mexico and Yucatan. His orders were to "proceed up the Mississippi River and reduce the defenses which guard the approaches to New Orleans[;] ... appear off that city and take possession of it under the guns of your squadron, and hoist the American flag thereon, keeping possession until troops can be sent to you. If the Mississippi expedition from Cairo shall not have descended the river, you will take advantage of the panic to push a strong force up the river to take all their defenses in the rear. You will also reduce the fortifications which defend Mobile Bay and turn them over to the army to hold."[3]

In March, when the admiral arrived at Ship Island off the Mississippi coast to take command of his squadron, Welles warned him that the rebels were building armored vessels at New Orleans and Mobile, and that "no unclad ship can contend, except at great odds, with even a moderately armored vessel." He also said he did not believe there was "any vessel so formidable as the *Merrimack* in the Mississippi, but we have pretty authentic accounts of some, and that one or two are building at Mobile."[4]

During the early morning hours of 24 April 1862, as he had predicted, Farragut's fleet of eighteen vessels passed Forts Jackson and St. Philip and the small Confederate squadron that stood between the Gulf and New Orleans. The next day he took possession of New Orleans, and by 12 May had captured Baton Rouge and Natchez, with Vicksburg next on the agenda. In the meantime, Farragut had sent Welles an account of his brilliant victory, closing with the words: "I trust ... that it will be found by the Government that I have carried out my instructions to the letter and to the best of my abilities, so far as this city is concerned."[5]

Later that day, having learned that the rebels had eighteen gunboats at Memphis and a ram under construction, Farragut wrote a second letter to the secretary explaining that without additional vessels he could not confront this force and also, as directed, attack Mobile, where the rebels were "building an ironclad ram there of great dimensions."[6] Confident that Welles would approve, Farragut had ordered Capt. David Porter to take his mortar boats to Ship Island, fifty miles from Mobile, but not to attempt any operations "until we are ready to support you, as we have a knowledge of at least two rams or ironclad batteries at Mobile, and they might destroy the small vessels if they entered the bay. But I do not think they will venture outside."[7]

On 7 May, having received Farragut's order, Porter steamed for Fort Morgan with his mortar flotilla to reconnoiter where the vessels should be anchored during the initial bombardment, and where buoys should be planted "for the ships to run in by" when they arrive. He would later report that "great excitement" existed within the forts when his steamers appeared. Three days later, fearful that Pensacola would be next, the rebels evacuated the navy yard; and by 12 May, Union troops had occupied Pensacola, making available to Farragut one of the finest deep-water ports on the Gulf, only sixty miles from Mobile Bay, his immediate objective.[8]

The appearance of mortar boats off Fort Morgan was not the only reason for the Confederate evacuation of the Pensacola Navy Yard; Farragut's vessels merely hastened a process that was already under way: Abandonment of the yard had started sixteen days earlier, following the capture of New Orleans. In a report to his commanding officer, Confederate brigadier general Thomas M. Jones wrote: "On receiving information that the enemy's gunboats had succeeded in passing the forts below New Orleans with their powerful batteries and splendid equipments, I came to the conclusion that, with my limited means of defense, reduced as I have been by the withdrawal of nearly all my heavy guns and ammunition, I could not hold [the enemy] in check or make even a respectable show of resistance. I therefore determined, upon my own judgement, to commence immediately the removal of the balance of my heavy guns and ammunition."[9] With the Union in possession of Fort Pickens, and the want of sufficient troops to defend the navy yard, the only option available to the Confederacy was to abandon the yard and leave behind a smoldering ruin.

With Pensacola in Union hands, Farragut reasoned, the groundwork for an attack on Mobile was in place, thus allowing him to temporarily turn his attention back to the Mississippi and the Confederate "fortress" of Vicksburg. On 18 May, four hundred miles up the Mississippi River, Cdr. Samuel P. Lee arrived off Vicksburg with six gunboats and two steamers, carrying fourteen hundred troops, and in Farragut's name, demanded that the town surrender, which was refused outright by the local military governor, Col. James L. Autrey, in terms that could not be mistaken: "Mississippians don't know, and refuse to learn, how to surrender to an enemy. If Commodore Farragut or Brigadier General Butler can teach them, let them come and try."[10]

When Farragut arrived at Vicksburg two days later, he assessed the situation and concluded that the place could not be taken without additional help from the army. He was told that the town's garrison of eight thousand troops could be reinforced very quickly by twenty thousand, should the need occur. Furthermore, the "guns of his ships could not effectively reach the defenses on the bluffs," and "his military force was not large enough either to take or to hold the town."[11]

On 23 May, Farragut and Lee's flotilla returned downriver to Grand Gulf, where the Union fleet was anchored. Exasperated and still fuming over Colonel Autrey's arrogance, he had decided on the way down to return to Vicksburg with the fleet and give all his captains an opportunity to assess the situation. The next day at 4:00 P.M., the *Hartford, Richmond, Brooklyn*, eight gunboats, and the two transports arrived four miles below Vicksburg. As the flagship's anchor splashed down, signal 2139 was hoisted, ordering all commanding officers to report aboard; Farragut wanted a second opinion before he decided not to attack. By 5:00 P.M. all were aboard the *Kennebec*, which moved up within two miles of the town. In sight were three or four guns, mounted one hundred feet above the water, that commanded the river for four miles up and down. Below the town were four guns with fields of fire across and up the river; and on the bluffs above, two hundred feet high and three hundred yards back, were several more large guns.[12]

The next day, Farragut was not feeling well; he was in his cabin when Captain Bell, Gen. Thomas Williams, and the general's staff made another reconnaissance aboard the *Kennebec*. When they returned at sunset, Farragut again summoned all his captains for a council: Should Vicksburg be attacked? When the vote was counted, there were nine nays, two yeas, and one undecided, the latter cast by Capt. James Alden of the *Richmond*. Farragut, still smarting over Autrey's arrogance, "wanted to punish the enemy by destroying the town, but was restrained by his better judgment and acquiesced in the opinion of the majority."[13]

Farragut ordered six gunboats to stay behind and blockade the river; they were to prevent supplies from reaching Vicksburg by water and occasionally to shell the defenses. The other vessels would return to New Orleans. Rumor had it that Farragut would now attack Mobile.[14] When Farragut arrived at New Orleans on 30 May, he found a letter waiting from Assistant Secretary Fox, who was bristling with anger. Fox had read in a

New York newspaper that Farragut's squadron had "returned to New Orleans, instead of continuing up the river to Memphis." He wrote, "Mobile, Pensacola, and, in fact, the whole coast, sinks into insignificance compared with this."[15]

A second letter, written two days later by Welles, continued where Fox's letter left off. The secretary began by saying: "A dispatch, in triplicate, has been sent to you by the *Dacotah, Ocean Queen,* and *Coatzacoalcos,* directing you to carry out your instructions of 20 January in relation to ascending the Mississippi so soon as New Orleans should be in your possession." Continuing, he dropped a bombshell: "Another vessel being about to sail from New York, probably to-morrow, I avail of that opportunity to say to you that the President of the United States requires you to use your utmost exertions (without a moment's delay, and before any other naval operations shall be permitted to interfere) to open the river Mississippi and effect a junction with Flag-Officer Davis, commanding (pro tem) the western Flotilla."[16]

Farragut answered Welles with a long letter explaining the difficulties he faced keeping his vessels operational, but now he had no choice but to follow orders and join Davis above Vicksburg. However, without troops to attack and hold Vicksburg, he told the secretary, little would be accomplished.[17]

On 24 June, shaken by Welles's letter, Farragut was back at Vicksburg with an imposing show of strength. Included were the sloops *Hartford, Richmond, Brooklyn, Iroquois,* and *Oneida;* and the screw gunboats *Wissahickon, Winona, Sciota, Pinola, Kennebec,* and *Katahdin.* In addition, Porter's mortar flotilla and the two transports, carrying a brigade of infantry, were standing by.

At 2:00 A.M. on the twenty-eighth, the fleet got under way in two columns: the *Richmond, Hartford,* and *Brooklyn* to starboard; the *Iroquois, Oneida,* and six gunboats to port. At 4:00 A.M. the mortars opened, and by 4:30 the *Richmond* was under heavy fire from the enemy's batteries. "The hills seemed ablaze with the batteries; shots came crashing through the bulwarks and exploded among the men crowded about the guns, sending 'brains and blood flying all over the decks.'" At 5:00, as the sun rose "red and fiery," the lead vessels were passing out of range of the batteries and by 6:15 had anchored above the town. During the morning, Farragut wrote Welles and asked for assistance from the army: "I passed up the river this morning, but to no purpose" unless twelve or fifteen thousand men are sent to attack and hold Vicksburg. The same request was sent to General Halleck and Flag Officer Davis.[18]

On 1 July, much to Farragut's gratification, Davis arrived with a fleet of four ironclads, four mortar boats, four river steamers, and two hospital boats, but no troops. Two days later, Halleck answered Farragut's letter with a reply that was halfway expected: "The scattered and weakened condition of my forces renders it impossible for me at the present to detach any troops to cooperate with you at Vicksburg."[19] Eleven days later, Welles wrote Farragut, conceding that it was time for him to return to the Gulf: "The army has failed to furnish the necessary troops for the capture of Vicksburg. . . . Under these circumstances it is thought that greater objects can be accomplished by your proceeding to the Gulf and operating at such points on the Southern coast as you may deem advisable"— which, of course, would be Mobile Bay.[20]

Before Farragut received Welles's letter, an event occurred that embarrassed the flag officer and caused him to be censured by Welles. On the fifteenth, the rebel ram *Arkansas* descended the Yazoo River, forced its way through Farragut's and Davis's fleets, raining carnage and death as it passed, and came to anchor under the guns of Vicksburg. Coincidentally, the day Welles wrote Farragut ordering him to the Gulf, Maj. Gen. Earl Van Dorn, the Confederate commander at Vicksburg, sent a dispatch to Jefferson Davis informing him that he had ordered the *Arkansas* "to run the gantlet, and, if successful, sweep the river below and run to Mobile as soon as out."[21]

On 26 July, the *Hartford* weighed anchor and steamed down river— its ultimate destination: Pensacola, fifty-five miles from Mobile. A few days later, Flag Officer Davis withdrew his squadron to Memphis, leaving Vicksburg and the *Arkansas* firmly in the hands of the rebels. During a brief stop at New Orleans, humiliated that the *Arkansas* had been allowed to escape, Farragut learned that he had been promoted to rear admiral— news that must have soothed his wounded pride.[22]

Arriving at Pensacola on 20 August, Farragut inspected the yard and reported to Welles its condition and suitability as a depot. "It is the most perfect destruction or wilderness you can conceive of," he told Welles; but with repairs, which he enumerated, he would be able to move against Mobile "as soon as possible." On 21 August, at last free to attack Mobile, Farragut wrote the secretary from Pensacola that he was preparing his vessels "as fast as I can for operations against Mobile, but I find my force is small." True to form, Welles now had changed his mind about Farragut's operating at "such points" he deemed advisable. He told the admiral that the "unsettled state of affairs on the Mississippi, the want of a sufficient military force to make all secure, and the present condition of your vessels, do not seem to admit of the expediency of attempting the concentration of an adequate force at Mobile for the reduction of that place."[23]

The navy department's strategic priorities obviously differed from Farragut's: The energetic and competent Fox was given the task of explaining the situation to the new rear admiral. He wrote Farragut that the war was going badly for the Union, and the new *Passaic*-class monitors, soon to be launched, were earmarked for Charleston. Left unsaid was the administration's belief that a victory at Charleston—the symbol of secession—would have a much greater impact on Northern morale than a victory at Mobile Bay. Not wanting to admit that nonmilitary considerations were at play here, he added. "We don't think you have force enough, and we do not expect you to run risks, crippled as you are. It would be a magnificent diversion for the country at this juncture. . . . We only expect a blockade now and the preservation of New Orleans."[24]

Farragut must have taken the department's admonition against attacking Mobile as a suggestion, rather than an order, for he responded aggressively, saying that with only a little effort Forts Morgan and Gaines could be taken. All he needed was two more sloops, one monitor, and help from the army. He explained that the army was needed "to take Fort Gaines, as the ships can not get sufficiently close to it, and it must be taken to secure an entrance for our supplies, as we have no vessels of light draft to get up Grant's Pass to take Cedar Point."[25]

In October, Farragut told Maj. Gen. Benjamin Butler, commanding officer of the Department of the Gulf at New Orleans, "I am now determined to go ahead upon the forts at Mobile." He said that he would never again be in better condition to attack and would have to "go it alone if you don't hurry up a small force for me." This was a bluff: Having explained to the department the role of the army, if the navy were to run past the Mobile forts, it is doubtful the admiral would have gone in alone.[26]

After returning to the Gulf, Farragut spent the next eleven weeks at Pensacola, overseeing the affairs of his forty-vessel squadron, stretched out around the Gulf from the Rio Grande to a point ninety-five miles east of Pensacola. Except for failing to capture the Confederate raider *Florida* when she eluded the blockade at Mobile Bay, there was little excitement. There was plenty of action, however, on the battlefields of the East, mostly favoring the enemy—and on the Mississippi, where the rebels were fortifying Port Hudson. Recognizing the apparent hopelessness of obtaining help from the army for an assault on the Mobile Bay forts, as well as signs of increased rebel activity on the Mississippi, Farragut decided to move his headquarters to New Orleans. Leaving Pensacola on 7 November, he arrived there two days later.[27]

Although now in New Orleans, faced with increasing rebel activity on the river, Farragut could not get Mobile off his mind. He consequently called on General Butler at his plush headquarters on Canal Street to ask once more for troops to attack Fort Gaines—this time only a thousand. He told Butler, somewhat testily, that he could run into Mobile Bay without his help, but he did not want to risk having his communications cut off from the outside. A politician to the core, old "Spoons" offered Farragut a deal: He would help if Farragut would join him in attacking Port Hudson first. Farragut, however, was not blind to some of Butler's own problems. The general needed at least twenty thousand more men for operations on the Mississippi and in Texas, but considering the advantages that would be gained by reducing the Mobile forts, one thousand men represented excellent economy of force.[28]

Farragut's reference to going it alone was again a bluff. He knew that Forts Morgan and Gaines could not be captured and held without assistance from the army, and conversely, the army could not take the forts without help from the navy. Unopposed, the enemy's vessels could lay off the beach and enfilade the army's trenches at will. In a letter to Commo. Henry Bell, a fellow sailor, the admiral candidly admitted that he would not "take another place without troops to hold it."[29]

For the next eight months, the Mississippi River occupied Farragut's time. With the fall of Vicksburg and Port Hudson in July 1863, he knew the time had come when his larger vessels, particularly the *Hartford, Richmond,* and *Brooklyn,* had to be overhauled. The *Hartford* needed her masts, bowsprit, and lower rigging replaced, as well as repairs to numerous shot holes and shell damage. On 1 August 1863, after turning over command to Bell, the admiral bid farewell to his squadron and sailed north. Despite the flagship's injuries, she reached New York on the twelfth, taking only eleven days to make the cruise.[30]

It had now been seventeen months since Welles had ordered Farragut to capture New Orleans, push up the Mississippi, then "reduce the fortifications which defend Mobile Bay." Two of these objectives had been achieved; the third—an attack on Mobile Bay's lower defenses—was still awaiting ground troops and ironclads, which where absolute necessities considering the enemy's defenses. But now Farragut had an ally, Maj. Gen. Ulysses S. Grant, the victor of Vicksburg. Coincidentally, on the same day that Farragut wrote Welles informing him that the *Hartford* needed an overhaul, Grant wrote Halleck, then the army's general in chief, and suggested that the army's next move should be the capture of Mobile. In the months to come, Farragut and Grant would work hand in hand to achieve this objective.[31]

In October, anticipating his return to the Gulf, Farragut wrote Fox, again pleading that monitors be sent to Mobile. Any day now, the rebels would have the *Tennessee* and other ironclads in the lower bay, and the federal advantage in numbers would be lost. On 30 December, confirming Farragut's fears, Welles sent him an intelligence report indicating that Adm. Franklin Buchanan intended to steam out and raise the blockade, no later than January. His squadron would comprise six vessels: the ram *Tennessee*, three other ironclads, and two wooden gunboats, the report indicated. Welles had reason to believe the information was credible, and he urged Farragut to hasten his departure. On 5 January 1864, in a blinding snowstorm, the *Hartford* left New York for Pensacola.[32]

AT NAVAL HEADQUARTERS IN MOBILE, ADMIRAL BUCHANAN WAS BURNING both ends of the candle. He had few experienced officers to man the squadron's vessels and no flag captain, flag lieutenant, or midshipmen to assist with administrative duties. He would work in his office from early morning until 3:00 P.M. attending to duties "from the grade of midshipman up," then visit the navy yard, ordnance department, or wherever his presence was needed, ending his day well into the night. The Mobile Squadron now numbered eleven vessels. Only six, however, were operational: the wooden gunboats *Selma*, *Morgan*, and *Gaines;* the ironclads *Tuscaloosa* and *Huntsville*, and a partially armored ram, the *Baltic*. But with speeds of only a few knots, the latter three were scarcely more than floating batteries. Launched but unfinished were the large ironclads *Tennessee*

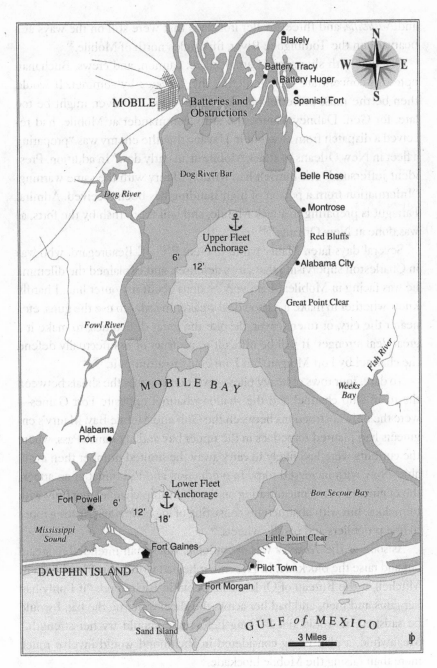

Mobile Bay, 1864

and *Nashville*, and three smaller ironclads that were still on the ways at a boatyard on the Tombigbee River, fifty miles north of Mobile.[33]

Plagued with shortages of armor plate, cannon, and crews, Buchanan opted to concentrate on completing the *Tennessee* by summer. It would then be the most powerful ironclad afloat. This, however, might be too late, for Gen. Dabney Maury, the army commander at Mobile, had received a dispatch from an agent in Havana that the enemy was "preparing a fleet in New Orleans to attack Mobile at an early day." In addition, President Jefferson Davis himself had written Maury with the same warning: "Information from a person of high standing has been received. Admiral Farragut is preparing to attack Mobile, and will try to rush by the forts, as was done at New Orleans."[34]

Several days later, Maury wrote to Gen. P. G. T. Beauregard, who was in Charleston supervising that city's defenses, and explained the dilemma he was facing in Mobile: "I am very anxious about my outer line. I hardly know whether to make it a good deal weaker in order to use the guns, etc., nearer the city, or to endeavor, despite the great difficulties, to make it a great deal stronger. It will be difficult to obstruct or to effectually defend the channel by Fort Morgan, but I am going to attempt it."[35]

To date, four rows of heavy piles—extending across the shoals between the main ship channel and the shallow channel opposite Fort Gaines— were the only obstructions between the Gulf and Mobile Bay. Maury's engineers had planted torpedoes in the upper bay and at Grant's Pass, where the currents were less likely to carry away the limited number then available. Now with increased torpedo production and the threat of an attack, the engineers were concentrating on the main ship channel, not only with torpedoes, but with obstructions consisting of log booms and floating ropes to foul propellers and paddle wheels.[36]

As soon as the *Tennessee* was operational, Buchanan intended to steam out and raise the blockade. In December he had written his friend John K. Mitchell at the Bureau of Orders and Detail in Richmond: "if I only had her guns and men, and had her across the shoal water on the bar, I would be satisfied, it would not be long before she should try her strength." Meanwhile, a plan being considered in Richmond would involve much more than raising the Mobile blockade.[37]

In early January 1864 Lt. Gen. Leonidas Polk, commanding the Department of Alabama, Mississippi, and East Louisiana, received a letter from Col. Custis Lee, an aide-de-camp to Jefferson Davis. Attached to the letter was a plan for the recapture of New Orleans, submitted by Col. T. J. Reid Jr., who had collected detailed information concerning the city's defenses while imprisoned there after the fall of Port Hudson. Colonel Lee told Polk that the president was "sure that you will agree with him in considering the prize aimed at worth great efforts and corresponding risks, and as the feasibility of the undertaking can be better determined upon from your position than at this distance from the field of operations, the subject is committed to your most earnest consideration and best judgment. It is needless to call your attention to the necessity for the utmost secrecy, if anything is to be done, and for the greatest expedition in getting the troops into position after the movement is commenced." Lee then added: "It will probably be necessary to have the cooperation of the naval authorities at Mobile, and authority is herewith transmitted to call upon Admiral Buchanan to give you all the aid in his power."[38]

Part One

EVOLUTION OF A BATTLE

CHAPTER 1

➤➤ ◄◄

Ram Fever

THE NEWS WAS DEPRESSING. ON 17 JANUARY 1864, AS THE *Hartford* dropped anchor in Pensacola Harbor twelve days after leaving New York, Farragut was met with "ram fever," confirming Secretary Welles's belief that Buchanan was about to steam out and raise the blockade. As soon as the boarding ladder was lowered, Capt. Thornton Jenkins, commander of the Mobile blockade, came aboard and reported to Farragut that the rebel squadron at Mobile was now superior to his own and was indeed making plans to attack the blockade.[1]

In a letter written three days before to Commo. Henry H. Bell, commander pro tem of the West Gulf Blockading Squadron during Farragut's absence, Jenkins had informed him that Buchanan was making active preparations to attack the squadron. He then enumerated the dire results should the attack be successful, concluding with the following admonition: "The raising of this blockade by driving off or totally destroying all of our vessels . . . is too great a temptation to an active and enterprising enemy, not to say a desperate one, to be fully disregarded by us." Jenkins then took a jab at Napoleon III of France, whose troops had occupied Mexico, purportedly to settle an overdue national debt. "Whatever may be the intention of the enemy inside Mobile Bay or of their friends elsewhere who have threatened to come to their assistance at this point," he wrote Bell, "it certainly is our duty to be well prepared to act, not only on the defensive, but to attack with the assurance of possible, if not probable, victory in case the opportunity is presented."[2]

Nine vessels, including the *Richmond*, were assigned to the Mobile blockade: three small screw steamers, "only better than none"; three small screw gunboats with "inferior armaments," and two side-wheel gunboats, having "fair armaments" but much in need of repairs. Furthermore, as many as three of these vessels were usually away coaling, procuring supplies, or undergoing repairs. In Jenkins's opinion, the total firepower of the gunboats and steamers on blockade should at minimum be equal to that of all the enemy's wooden vessels, plus at least two wooden vessels of heavy armament for each of the enemy's ironclads.[3]

Having received Jenkins's letter, Bell followed up with a dispatch to Welles, which included additional details about the proposed attack: "Although we have frequent reports of the rams in Red River and Mobile being failures, we do not confide in them, and are prepared to meet them with every prospect of success on our side, if they shall come, although the *Pensacola* and river boats are the only available vessels; the machinery of all other steamers here being apart and undergoing repairs."[4]

Assessing the situation, and believing it to be credible, Farragut ordered the *Hartford* to proceed to Mobile as soon as her bunkers were topped off. He also directed the frigate *Colorado* to leave the mouth of the Mississippi and steam for the same destination. With this done, he penned a note to Commodore Bell in New Orleans announcing his arrival at Pensacola and informing him that he was going to Mobile to see firsthand the situation, then on to Ship Island and New Orleans. "I should go direct to New Orleans," he added, "but for the report that it is Buchanan's intention to come out with the rams and attack the blockaders."[5]

By 10 February, having visited the Mobile blockade, Ship Island, and New Orleans, Farragut was back in Pensacola, convinced that the rebel squadron was still in Mobile. However, while in New Orleans, he learned of a plan by Gen. William T. Sherman to "strengthen the Union position in Vicksburg by destroying the two primary railroads of central Mississippi," which converged in Meridian. Sherman wanted Farragut to keep troops tied down in Mobile while he moved toward Meridian with an army of twenty-five thousand.[6] After returning to Pensacola, the admiral informed Welles that he intended to assist Sherman by feigning an attack on Mobile, "unless the ironclads should come out, as the refugees all say they will, so soon as the *Tennessee* and the *Nashville* are ready. I shall continue to keep a good lookout for them, and whenever the army can give us 5,000 men we will see what can be done with the forts."[7]

On 11 February, Farragut wrote Maj. Gen. Nathaniel Banks, commander of the Department of the Gulf, and told him that he was "going ahead with my part of the programme to assist General Sherman. I will have six mortar boats pounding away at the fort in Grant's Pass by the time this reaches you, as they all leave here to-day for the Mississippi Sound." The bombardment of Fort Powell commenced 16 February and continued intermittently through the twenty-ninth, the last day of the month, throwing "near 2,000 shot and shell" at the little fort. The next day, however, Farragut brought the operation to an abrupt stop: The *Tennessee* had crossed the bar and was "in full view in the bay opposite Grant's Pass," or so he thought.[8]

On 1 March, prodded by Maj. Gen. Jeremy Gilmer, the Confederacy's chief engineer, Buchanan had ordered the ironclads *Huntsville* and *Tuscaloosa*—both smaller versions of the *Tennessee*—and the ram *Baltic* to proceed down the bay and take positions in the rear of Fort Powell. If Farragut were planning to assault Fort Powell and enter the bay, these vessels would serve as a deterrent, despite their unsuitability for operations in the lower bay.[9]

By now, however, it had become apparent to General Maury that the attack on Fort Powell was a feint to draw Confederate troops from Sherman's front in central Mississippi. Others, however, were not so confident. Kate Cumming, a visitor in the city, attributed the concern to rumor: "While I was in Mobile the cry that 'the enemy is coming' was raised two or three times. There was a report that an immense army was coming through Florida, another through Mississippi, and another by Pascagoula, and at the same time the fleet was to attack the forts down the bay. For a while, poor Mobile seemed as if it was going to be gobbled up all at once but the enemy have found a few stumbling blocks in their way."[10]

When the ironclads left Mobile, the *Tennessee* was still trapped above Dog River Bar. Buchanan had tried to solve the problem with "camels," the name given to boxlike structures used to lift a vessel and decrease its draft. By attaching camels, partially filled with water, to both sides of the *Tennessee*'s hull, then pumping them free of water, the *Tennessee* was raised a mere "twenty-two inches, a good three feet short of what would be necessary" to cross the bar. Disappointed, but not discouraged, Buchanan wasted little time in ordering a new set of larger camels.[11]

FARRAGUT WAS DESPONDENT. HE HAD BEEN EXPECTING THE *Tennessee* to make an appearance in the lower bay since returning from New York. On 2 March he wrote his son, Loyall, that the *Tennessee* had come down the bay the day before and appeared very formidable, adding that a "norther was blowing" at the time and he would take a better look when the weather cleared. The same day, Farragut wrote Banks and told him the bad news: The *Tennessee* was "full in sight of us off Grant's Pass, lying in the middle of the bay." Despairingly, he added that an attack on Mobile would now have to be postponed until the arrival of ironclads, and "God only knows" when that will be.[12]

Four days later, still believing he had seen the *Tennessee*, Farragut wrote Commo. James S. Palmer, the commander of the squadron's First Division in New Orleans: "We are in the dark as to the fate of the ram *Tennessee;* some say she has not yet crossed Dog River Bar; some that she has come down, I among the latter; those who were looking at her when the norther struck her say (some of them) that she went down, others that she went up the bay in tow of the other steamers. The deserters I send you will say that she never came over the bar, but I saw a vessel that I do not believe could be anything but the *Tennessee*."[13]

On 9 March, Farragut admitted to Welles that he was wrong. An intelligent refugee—an engineer—had confirmed that the *Tennessee* was in Mobile at the time, her camels a failure. The admiral now believed that he had seen either the *Tuscaloosa* or the *Huntsville*.[14]

Two months later, Farragut reported to Welles: "All the late accounts from Mobile agree in representing Buchanan as making exertions to get camels large enough to float the ram *Tennessee* over Dog River Bar, and no doubt is felt of his success." Expressing his anxiety, the admiral told Welles that he was in "hourly expectation of being attacked by almost an equal number of vessels, ironclads against wooden vessels, and a most unequal contest it will be." He closed with a sobering thought: "should we be unsuccessful, the panic in this part of the country will be beyond all control. They will imagine that New Orleans and Pensacola must fall."[15]

When Buchanan hurriedly left Mobile on 29 February to personally command the vessels supporting Fort Powell, the *Tennessee* was anchored at the mouth of the Spanish River opposite the city, where camels were being attached to her hull. When the camels were pumped free of water, it was hoped that the ram would ride high enough to cross Dog River Bar, several miles down the bay. Unfortunately, the effort was a failure, lifting the *Tennessee* two feet short of the required four.[16]

In a letter dated 13 March, Buchanan described the challenge to John Mitchell, his friend in charge of Office Orders and Detail in Richmond: "I am doing all I can to get the *Tennessee* over the bar. You will see by Myer's report of the *Huntsville* how difficult it is to get over that bar drawing only 9 feet 4 inches, her draft. She was nearly a week before we could get back after getting over. You may judge how difficult it will be to take a heavy flat vessel over drawing more than 13 feet. I hope Farragut will not get here before I am ready. If he does the *Tennessee* must meet him when she is ready. Everybody has taken it into their heads that one ship can whip a dozen, and if the trial is not made, we who are in her are d—d for life, consequently the trial must be made, so goes the world."[17] Never one to waste time bemoaning a setback, Buchanan ordered a new set of six camels to be constructed, but bad luck struck again. On 3 April an accidental fire destroyed two of the six. Reacting with greater determination than ever, the admiral ordered another pair to be constructed and attached to the *Tennessee* by mid-May. In the meantime, he would continue looking for experienced seamen and artillerymen to man the *Tennessee*'s guns.[18]

On 6 April, to facilitate attachment of the new camels to the ram's hull, the ship was moved from the Spanish River back to a mooring on the Mobile River opposite the navy yard. Several days later, Buchanan wrote Cdr. Thomas ap Catesby Jones, commandant of the Naval Gun Factory and Ordnance Works at Selma, that he was "driving on" with the two new camels because he believed Farragut would attack Mobile any day now. "He is in Pensacola with a large force. Page thinks Forts Morgan and Gaines very weak. I don't agree with him. They might be stronger, but still they are very strong, I think." Shifting to the national scene, he then expressed a belief that was gaining in popularity throughout the South: "A battle on the Potomac is inevitable, 'tis said, and if we whip them the war will soon close. God speed."[19]

Three weeks later, Buchanan reported that the camels had been completed and were being attached to the *Tennessee*'s hull at the navy yard. By 16 May they had been pumped free of water, decreasing the ram's draft of thirteen feet to nine, barely enough to clear the bar's nine and a half feet. The next day, he came aboard and ordered the *Tennessee* to proceed to Spanish River and anchor just inside the row of piling that obstructed the approaches to the city.[20]

On 18 May, as the sun edged above the eastern shore of Mobile Bay, the *Tennessee* weighed anchor and passed hawsers to the gunboat *Morgan* and the steamer *Magnolia*. At 4:00 P.M., having successfully cleared the bar, the

Tennessee came to anchor about six miles north of Fort Morgan, where workmen began to remove the camels. By daylight the next morning, the camels had been set adrift, but Commander Johnston, the ram's captain, reported to Buchanan that the tide had fallen so much that the *Tennessee* was "hard and fast aground." What was worse, the enemy was now aware of her presence. "Here was an insurmountable and most unlooked-for end to the long-cherished hope of taking the enemy by surprise, dispersing the blockading fleet, and capturing Fort Pickens at the entrance of Pensacola Bay."[21]

On the twenty-second, confirming the rumor that he still intended to attack the blockade, Buchanan came aboard the *Tennessee,* still aground above Fort Morgan, and addressed the crew. He told them that tonight the *Tennessee* would steam out and attack the enemy, that he expected every man to stand by his guns until death and never surrender "for the eyes of the people of the Confederacy were turned upon them and they expected much." Three cheers from both officers and men echoed across the wind-swept waters of the lower bay, indicating their willingness to follow him wherever he led. At sundown, however, the *Tennessee*'s pilots reported that the weather had been worsening and it now was too rough to go out. Disappointed, but agreeing with the assessment, the admiral canceled the attack. A night sortie amid the numerous shoals off Mobile Bay, risky enough in calm waters, was unthinkable in a running sea, especially when the enemy was anticipating an attack.[22]

The next morning, as the *Tennessee*'s crew was preparing the ram for another attempt to raise the blockade, the lookout reported that a steamboat was approaching from the north. Much to the astonishment of the crew, the steamer *St. Nicholas* came alongside with a large party of ladies, purportedly to watch the battle. Recognizing the inappropriateness of such a venture, after a most polite explanation by Commander Johnston, the steamer turned around and returned to Mobile.[23]

At 3:30 P.M. the pilots returned from Fort Morgan and reported that conditions were favorable for an attack, which set off a frenzy of activity clearing for action. The admiral, however, who knew as much about the weather as his pilots, had some misgivings about the report; the wind was picking up and waves could be seen breaking over the shoals off Fort Morgan. Nevertheless, aware of the pressure that was building to raise the blockade, he ordered Johnston to start the engines and prepare for action, only to find the ram was once more hard aground.[24]

On the twenty-fourth the *Tennessee* was finally floated and, accompanied by the *Morgan, Gaines, Selma,* and *Baltic,* she steamed to an anchorage just north of Fort Morgan. With eleven enemy vessels off the bar and the advantage of surprise lost, Buchanan would now have to rethink his strategy. At daylight, he went ashore to Fort Morgan and telegraphed Secretary Mallory to report the situation and ask for advice. Three days later he received a reply: "Use your own discretion."[25]

In a letter to Commander Catesby Jones at the Selma Gun Foundry, General Page, who had been a captain in the U.S. Navy, expressed his feelings concerning Buchanan's aborted attempt to raise the blockade. "Buchanan looks humbled and thoughtful. The movements of his ship and squadron were, in my judgment, delayed and made unnecessarily public after she came down. She should have been kept alone, and the moment she was released from the camels she should have gone out. This was my opinion at first. The secretary has let B. off easier than I expected."[26]

As soon as reports reached Pensacola that the *Tennessee* was over the bar with a flotilla of ironclads and gunboats, Farragut boarded the *Metacomet* and steamed to Mobile for a firsthand appraisal of the situation.[27] Arriving off Mobile, Lt. Cdr. James Jouett steamed up the main ship channel and edged the *Metacomet* into Sand Island Channel, well within range of Fort Morgan's heavy batteries. From the deck of the *Metacomet,* the admiral steadied his telescope and focused on the massive casemate of the world's most powerful warship. He could make out the blue flag of Admiral Buchanan waving above the casemate, which was pierced with four gun ports on each side. He also saw what he thought was a torpedo fixture attached to her bow. At last the *Tennessee* was in full view and she appeared to be as formidable as deserters and other informants had described.[28]

That afternoon, 25 May 1864, Farragut wrote Welles and reported the dreaded news. He told the secretary that with three thousand men and one or two ironclads he would not hesitate to attack Buchanan and the forts. The admiral then explained that if he were to run in, "it would be in his [Buchanan's] power to retire to shoal water with his ironclads (in fact, all their vessels draw much less water than ours), and thus destroy us without our being able to get at him." He added that the bows of Buchanan's ships were being reinforced with iron and equipped with torpedo spars, then subtly reminded Welles that the department had not yet responded to his call for ironclads, which he had made more than a year ago.[29]

In a letter to his friend Rear Adm. Theodorus Bailey, commander of the East Gulf Blockading Squadron, Farragut wrote, in a show of bravado, that Buchanan was preparing to come out and attack him and then raid New Orleans. "Let him come; I have a fine squadron to meet him, all ready and willing. I can see his boats very industriously laying down torpedoes, so I judge that he is quite as much afraid of our going in as we are of his coming out, but I have come to the conclusion to fight the devil with fire, and therefore shall attach a torpedo to the bow of each ship and see how it will work on the rebels—if they can stand blowing up any better than we can."[30]

On 30 May, Farragut wrote Brig. Gen. Alexander Asboth at Pensacola that he agreed with his intelligence reports, except for the number of rams the rebels had near Fort Morgan. Asboth had reported that the *Tennessee* was "lying above Fort Morgan, with three other smaller ironclads and five wooden vessels, ready to come out at any moment." After the arrival of two more gunboats, they intended to raise the blockade and steam to New Orleans and farther up the Mississippi. Farragut told Asboth that the *Tennessee* and *Baltic* were the only ironclads near Fort Morgan at present. The other two, the *Tuscaloosa* and *Huntsville*, had returned to Mobile, along with the three wooden gunboats, adding: "I have a beautiful fleet to meet them, ready and willing on any day of the week; he may hurt us a good deal but be assured we will hurt him a little."[31]

Farragut was convinced that Buchanan was preparing to sortie out and attack him; it was only a matter of time. Refugees were reporting that the ironclads *Tuscaloosa* and *Huntsville*, as well as three wooden gunboats, were across Dog River Bar. These would soon be joined by the *Nashville*. In addition, three more ironclads were either at or near Mobile—a formidable force.[32]

On 1 March, the same day that Farragut thought he had seen the *Tennessee*, Grant was given three stars and appointed general in chief of all Union armies. Four days later, the Red River campaign commenced. Militarily unsound and poorly led, it was doomed to failure. Grant recognized that possession of Mobile was important to General Sherman as a supply depot and secure base if he chose to move south after the capture of Atlanta. Consequently, the new general in chief had wasted no time ordering Banks to finish the Red River expedition and "assemble all his available force at New Orleans as soon as possible, and prepare to receive orders for the taking of Mobile."[33]

Grant and Farragut, the ranking officer in the navy, were now moving toward a common goal: an attack on Mobile. Both recognized the importance of capturing the city and the advantages to be gained. Within a few days after his appointment, Grant directed Halleck, who had reverted to chief of staff, to contact the secretary of the navy and ask him to "order two of the iron-clads from Charleston to report to Admiral Farragut, with instructions to the latter not to attack until the army is ready to operate with him." Grant, of course, had no authority over Welles; requests from the nation's ranking general and admiral, however, could not easily be ignored.[34]

On 7 June, now acting with a sense of urgency, Welles ordered Cdr. J. W. A. Nicholson, captain of the new ironclad *Manhattan*, to "proceed with all possible dispatch to Pensacola with the U.S.S. *Manhattan* and report for duty to Rear Admiral Farragut. You will report at New York to Commander Mullany, who, with the *Bienville*, will accompany the *Manhattan* to Pensacola." The secretary then followed with an order to Rear Adm. David Porter, commanding the Mississippi Squadron at Cairo, Illinois: "It is of the greatest importance that some of the new ironclads building on the Mississippi should be sent without fail to Rear-Admiral Farragut. Are not some of them ready? If not, can you not hurry them forward?"[35]

At last the long-awaited Mobile attack was now on the table.

CHAPTER 2

→→ ←←

A New General in Chief

BOTH FARRAGUT AND GRANT HAD WANTED TO ATTACK MOBILE EARLIER in the war—Farragut in 1862, after the fall of New Orleans, and Grant in 1863, following the surrender of Vicksburg. A major obstacle, however, stood in the way: A French army had occupied Mexico in early 1862, ostensibly to force payment of a delinquent debt, but in reality to establish a foothold in North America while the United States was distracted by a bloody war.[1]

The Union commander whose department included Texas was Maj. Gen. Nathaniel Banks, one of Lincoln's political appointees—a former governor of Massachusetts and Speaker of the U.S. House of Representatives. When Banks assumed command of the Department of the Gulf in the fall of 1862, Henry W. Halleck, then general in chief of the Union armies, gave him his marching orders: "The first military operations which will engage your attention on your arrival at New Orleans," Halleck wrote, "will be the opening of the Mississippi River and the reduction of Fort Morgan or Mobile City, in order to control that bay and harbor. In these expeditions you will have the cooperation of the rear-admiral commanding the naval forces in the Gulf of Mexico and the Mississippi River." Continuing, Halleck then prioritized the objectives:

The President regards the opening of the Mississippi River as the first and most important of all our military and naval operations, and it is hoped that you will not lose a moment in accomplishing it. This river being opened, the question will arise how the troops and naval forces there can be employed to the best advantage. Two objects are suggested as worthy of your attention:

First, having captured Vicksburg, send a military force directly east to destroy the railroads at Jackson and Marion, and thus cut off all connections by rail between northern Mississippi and Mobile and Atlanta. The latter place is now chief military depot of the rebel armies in the West.

Second, ascend with a military and naval force the Red River as far as it is navigable, and thus open an outlet for the sugar and cotton of northern Louisiana. Possibly both of these objects may be accomplished, if circumstances should be favorable.

Appended as an afterthought, Halleck added the following: "It is also suggested that, Red River being in our possession, it will form the best base for operations in Texas." Having read Halleck's operational objectives, it was clear to Banks that Mobile—initially cited as an important objective—was now subordinate to affairs west of the Mississippi. Lacking the training and experience of a professional soldier, Banks's tactical skills would soon prove wanting. As a politician, however, he was not altogether lacking in strategic insight; to him, the capture of Mobile was far more important than the occupation of Texas.[2]

Aware of Mobile's economic and strategic importance to the Confederate heartland, Grant, then commander of the Department of Tennessee, also felt that Mobile should be attacked. After the surrender of Vicksburg in July 1863, he wrote Halleck. "It seems to me now," he began, "that Mobile should be captured, the expedition starting from some point on Lake Pontchartrain." Coincidentally, the day that Grant wrote Halleck, Banks wrote Grant with the same recommendation: "The capture of Mobile is of importance second only . . . to the opening of the Mississippi. . . . I can aid you somewhat by land and sea, if that shall be your destination. Mobile is the last stronghold in the West and Southwest. No pains should be spared to effect its reduction."[3]

A few days later, Grant received a reply from Halleck defending his belief that the Trans-Mississippi should be next. "Before attempting Mobile," he began, "I think it will be best to clean up a little. Johnston should be disposed of; also Price, Marmaduke, etc., so as to hold the line of the Arkansas River. This will enable us to withdraw troops from the Missouri, Vicksburg, Port Hudson, remodeled so as to be tenable by small garrisons;

[this will] also assist General Banks in cleaning out Western Louisiana. When these things are accomplished there will be a large available force to operate [against] Mobile or Texas. The navy is not ready for co-operation. Should Fort Sumter fall, iron-clads can be sent to assist at Mobile."[4]

Frustrated that the president and Halleck were opposing a move against Mobile, Banks wrote the general in chief, exhorting him to attack the place. "We have outlines of their works," he said, "and can estimate very well their strength. I am confident a sudden movement, such as can be made with 20,000 or 25,000 men . . . will reduce it with certainty and without delay."[5] In a second letter, Banks told Halleck that the "co-operation of the naval force now here is all that is required."[6]

On 6 August, annoyed with Banks's and Grant's continued insistence that Mobile be attacked first, Lincoln ordered Banks, via Grant, to go ahead and occupy Texas "with the least possible delay. Do this by land, at Galveston, at Indianola, or at any other point you may deem preferable. If by sea, Admiral Farragut will co-operate. There are reasons why the movement should be as prompt as possible." At the same time, the president ordered Grant to give Banks "all necessary assistance for its execution."[7]

Aware that he was dealing with the army's most popular general, Lincoln told Grant that an attack on Mobile was tempting but recent events in Mexico made it necessary to show the flag in west Texas as soon as possible. Grant, of course, was well aware of why the president was concerned with Texas. In 1862 France, England, and Spain had occupied Mexico to collect delinquent foreign debts. Napoleon III, however, had greater ambitions: He wanted to annex Mexico as part of the French empire.[8]

Still convinced that Lincoln was missing an opportunity by not moving against Mobile, Grant again wrote the president. Agreeing that the situation in Mexico required attention, he still believed Mobile "could be taken with but little effort, and with the rivers debouching there, in our possession, we would have such a base to operate from on the very center of the Confederacy as would make them abandon entirely the states bound West by the Mississippi."[9] Grant was convinced the war would be won in the east, not across the vast stretches of the Trans-Mississippi, and he was frustrated that he could not get this point across to the president.[10]

Concerned that his order to occupy Texas had not yet been carried out, Lincoln wrote Secretary of War Edwin Stanton and directed him to build a fire under Halleck. "I believe," the president wrote, "no local object is

now more desirable."[11] Halleck preferred a combined army-navy operation up the Red River to Shreveport, but the river would not be navigable
until the spring thaw, and the president wanted quick action. Halleck
gave Banks the choice of moving by land or sea, and Banks chose the latter: In his opinion, an amphibious landing on the coast provided the best
solution. Banks's first attempt failed, however. After a bloody repulse at
Sabine Pass, he managed to capture Brownsville, Brazos Santiago, at the
mouth of the Rio Grande, as well as several points farther east with about
sixty-two hundred troops. Texas had been occupied.[12]

Later in the year, Grant again proposed that Mobile be attacked. He
now was the commander of all Union troops between the Alleghenies
and the Mississippi, excepting Louisiana, and his star was rising. His subordinates were Maj. Gens. William T. Sherman, A. J. Smith, and Frederick Steele. In a letter to Halleck dated 7 December 1863 from Chattanooga, Grant suggested that an army move on Mobile by way of New
Orleans and Pascagoula, and capture it by the end of January. "Should the
enemy make an obstinate resistance at Mobile," he wrote, "I would for-
tify outside and leave a garrison sufficient to hold the garrison of the town,
and with the balance of the army make a campaign into the interior of
Alabama, and possibly Georgia."[13]

Grant wanted to embark an army of thirty-five thousand at Nashville,
as if going to West Tennessee or Vicksburg, drop down the river to New
Orleans, and from there make an amphibious landing at Pascagoula, forty
miles southwest of Mobile. Washington, however, did not want him to
withdraw troops from Tennessee and expose Knoxville to the Confederate army of Lt. Gen. James Longstreet, encamped forty miles to the
northeast. Also aware of the threat Longstreet posed to East Tennessee,
Grant had no intention of embarking on the campaign until this problem
was resolved. He was determined, however, to keep Mobile on the front
burner.[14]

Faced with Grant's determination to attack Mobile, Halleck responded,
making clear that an attack on Mobile would be subordinated to the objectives stated in Grant's dispatch, dated 7 December, namely: "to expel the
enemy from East Tennessee, and to provide against his return into the valley: second, to either force the rebels farther back into Georgia, or to provide against their return by that line into Tennessee: third, to clean out
West Tennessee, and, fourth, to move a force down the Mississippi and
operate against Mobile. The importance of these objects is considered to

be in the order above stated. It is thought that the fourth should not be definitely determined upon until the other three are accomplished, or their accomplishment made reasonably certain." Halleck then ended true to form: "Moreover, circumstances may be such by the time that your spare forces reach Port Hudson or New Orleans as to require their services west of the Mississippi; if so, the latter part of the plan would be somewhat varied or its execution delayed."[15]

As the new year opened, preparations for the invasion of Texas were gaining momentum. In a letter dated 4 January 1864, Halleck informed Banks that he had directed Grant to provide the campaign with "all the aid in his power." He also had ordered Maj. Gen. Frederick Steele, commander of the Department of Arkansas, to participate. In addition, several regiments and batteries had been ordered to New Orleans, as well as a naval flotilla under the command of Rear Adm. David Porter.[16]

Halleck's interest in Texas went beyond Napoleon III and Mexico. The Trans-Mississippi, he believed, held the key to victory. By occupying the population centers there and cutting off the flow of supplies to the east, the Confederate armies across the river would wither on the vine. There were also several other advantages that even Banks was beginning to appreciate. In northwestern Louisiana, a hundred million dollars of baled cotton was waiting to be seized, as well as millions of dollars of contraband such as lumber, sugar, salt, cattle, and livestock. In addition, a few thousand more loyal citizens on the rolls might enable the state to reenter the Union under Lincoln's 10 Percent Plan.[17]

In Grant's opinion, Halleck was obsessed with the Trans-Mississippi Theater. Possession of Louisiana, Arkansas, and Texas "seemed to possess more importance in [Halleck's] mind than almost any campaign east of the Mississippi." Grant, on the other hand, believed the war would be won in the east, not across the vast stretches of the Trans-Mississippi— and there was not much time left to win it before the November presidential election. It would be a mistake, therefore, to be sidetracked by events in Texas. The Trans-Mississippi needed attention, but not at the expense of losing the war by a negotiated peace.[18]

Meanwhile, events were taking shape that would have a profound effect not only on the Red River expedition but also on Mobile and the entire course of the war. In December a bill had been introduced in Congress to revive the rank of lieutenant general, and rumors were circulating that Grant would be nominated. On 8 January, Halleck wrote Grant a letter, the tone of which suggests that he may have been covering his tracks in the event Grant should become his boss. He explained: "In regard to General Banks' campaign against Texas, it is proper to remark that it was undertaken less for military [reasons] than as a matter of State policy." He then confessed that the proposed Red River campaign had less advantages than a movement on Mobile; politically, however, it was necessary that the Union "occupy and hold at least a portion of Texas."[19]

Halleck's letter was clearly an attempt to justify his support of operations west of the Mississippi over those in Alabama and Georgia. Hoping to mollify Grant, he may, however, have gone too far when he reminded him, in a chiding manner, that the president had made the decision to occupy Texas "for reasons satisfactory to himself and his cabinet, and it was, therefore, unnecessary for us to inquire whether or not the troops could have been employed elsewhere with greater military advantage." Having scolded Grant for questioning the president's decision to occupy Texas, the general in chief followed with an explanation of the rationale behind the decision: "Keeping in mind the fact that General Banks' operations in Texas, either on the gulf coast or by the Louisiana frontier, must be continued during the winter," he wrote, "it is to be considered whether it will not be better to direct our efforts for the present to the entire breaking up of the rebel forces west of the Mississippi River, rather than to divide them by also operating against Mobile and Alabama."[20]

Ignoring Halleck's logic, Grant replied that since the Red River was still too low for navigation, he had ordered Sherman to make a raid on Meridian, Mississippi, and destroy the rail lines between it, Mobile, Selma, and all points north. Having done this, he would then return to Vicksburg, "unless the opportunity of going into Mobile with the force he has appears perfectly plain." Of course this was a long shot, and Grant knew it, but it provided him with an opportunity to again remind Halleck that he had not forgotten about Mobile. Grant told Halleck, "I do not look upon any points except Mobile, in the south, and Tennessee, in the north, as presenting practicable starting points from which to operate against Atlanta and Montgomery."[21]

By the end of January 1863 preparations for the Red River campaign were in full swing. Banks was assembling an army of forty-two thousand. Seventeen thousand would come from his Department of the Gulf; ten thousand from Sherman; and fifteen thousand from Steele's Department of Arkansas, now under Grant's operational control. The enemy strength was estimated at twenty-five thousand, giving Banks a near two-to-one advantage. The navy would contribute thirteen ironclads, four tinclads, and six gunboats for removing obstructions, gunfire support, and convoying transports; the army would provide the transports. The navy and two army columns would move up the Red River, while a third would leave Little Rock, Arkansas, all to converge on Shreveport by 25 April. With Grant's concurrence, however, Sherman had demanded that his troops be returned thirty days from the time they embarked up the Red River.[22]

On 9 March 1864, the rumors proved true; Grant was appointed general in chief of the army, with Halleck as his chief of staff. Three days later the van of Banks's army—Porter's flotilla and A. J. Smith's troops—began moving up the Red River. The campaign to occupy Texas was under way.[23]

In a letter dated 25 March, Grant ordered Banks to "finish his present expedition, and assemble all his available force at New Orleans as soon as possible, and prepare to receive orders for the taking of Mobile." Grant did not want to be misunderstood. He had previously prepared Banks for this order by telling him "if Shreveport were not to be taken by the 25th of April, at latest, then A. J. Smith's corps was to be returned to Vicksburg by the 10th even if it leads to the abandonment of the expedition."[24]

On 26 March, after the capture of Fort de Russy and several skirmishes along the way, Banks's two southern columns and the naval flotilla reached Alexandria, 105 miles from Shreveport. Low water in the river and the difficulty of transporting supplies and hauling cannon over narrow, rutted roads, created problems, but the land columns and naval flotilla continued to push ahead. Steele's Arkansas column, however, was running into trouble from Confederate forces in northern Louisiana and would not be able to converge on Shreveport as planned.

Grant wrote Banks on 31 March, ordering him to abandon Texas entirely, except for the Rio Grande garrisons, go on the defensive, and free up twenty-five to thirty thousand troops for an attack on Mobile in conjunction with Admiral Farragut who would be provided with "two or more" ironclads before the campaign commenced. Grant then recommended that Pascagoula be his base of operations, and added: "It is intended that your movements shall be co-operative with movements elsewhere, and you cannot now start too soon."[25]

Sherman also sent a letter to Banks: "All is well in this quarter and I hope by the time you turn against Mobile our forces will again act to the same end, though at distant points." He closed by hoping that Shreveport would be in Banks's possession by the time he received his letter. Sherman would be depending on Banks, with the aid of the navy, to divert troops from his front as he pushed across Georgia.[26]

During the afternoon of 8 April, at a road junction called Sabine Crossroads forty miles downriver from Shreveport, the rebels struck. Before sundown, the Union army and navy were in serious trouble: The army was in full retreat, and the river was falling, threatening the Union flotilla fifty miles upriver. Had it not been for the building of a dam, leaving an opening through which the vessels could pass, all would have been lost.

By 19 May the army had reached the safety of Simsport, having crossed the Atchafalaya River on a makeshift bridge of steamboats. Two days later, the gunboats and transports entered the Mississippi River, bringing the campaign to a close. Lt. Cdr. Thomas O. Selfridge, captain of the river monitor *Osage*, believed the Red River expedition was one of the Union's "most humiliating and disastrous" defeats of the war.[27]

After staggering Confederate defeats at Vicksburg and Gettysburg, the Red River disaster sent a message to the Northern electorate that the war was far from over. Much of the South was still intact. Richmond, Atlanta, and the seaports of Mobile, Charleston, and Wilmington were thriving, despite the blockade. In Virginia, Grant was stalled outside Richmond; and in Georgia, Joseph E. Johnston's Army of the Tennessee was poised to contest every foot of Georgia's soil as Sherman moved toward Atlanta. If the South could hold onto its heartland for another six months, Northern discontent with the war would defeat Lincoln at the polls, and the South would gain its independence through a negotiated peace.[28]

Grant did not learn of Banks's repulse at Sabine Crossroads until 22 April. Three days later with additional information in hand, Grant told Halleck that A. J. Smith's division would have to stay with Banks until the expedition was out of difficulty. He added, "General Banks, by his failure, has absorbed 10,000 veteran troops that should now be with General Sherman and 30,000 of his own that would have been moving toward Mobile, and this without accomplishing any good result." Grant now had no choice but to put the Mobile attack on hold.[29]

On 29 April, Grant and Halleck exchanged four telegrams concerning Banks, with Grant telling his chief of staff, "On due reflection I do not see that anything can be done this spring with the troops west of the Mississippi, except on that side." This meant that Sherman would not be supported by an attack on Mobile, thus allowing the rebels to reinforce Atlanta at will. The solution, Grant said, was to replace Banks with a "good officer," and consolidate the Trans-Mississippi into one military division. Halleck cautioned Grant that Lincoln would be hesitant to fire Banks outright, "as it would give offense to many of his friends, and would probably be opposed by a portion of his Cabinet." Grant responded with a face-saving suggestion: He would "leave General Banks in command of his department, but order him to the army's headquarters in New Orleans." In other words, Banks would be subordinated to the commander of a newly formed military division and relegated to a desk job.[30]

The man Grant selected to replace Banks was Maj. Gen. E. R. S. Canby, a competent, experienced soldier who had seen combat in the Seminole and Mexican wars, and had fought Confederates and Indians in 1862 as commander of the Department of New Mexico. A West Point graduate, Canby excelled in administration, resulting in his appointment to the War Department as assistant adjutant general, where his skills were sorely needed to straighten out the chaos and confusion resulting from the Red River fiasco.[31]

Canby's appointment as commander of the new Military Division of West Mississippi would become effective on 7 May. The division included all of Texas, Louisiana, Arkansas, Missouri, and the Gulf Coast as far east as St. Andrew's Bay, Florida. Speaking for Grant, Halleck wrote Canby a lengthy letter telling him to consolidate his forces and straighten out Banks's mess. He also told Canby that the Mobile campaign had been temporarily canceled.[32]

On 4 May, Grant's strategy to end the war was executed. In Virginia, the Army of the Potomac, supported by subsidiary thrusts from the James River and in the Shenandoah Valley, moved against Lee's Army of Northern Virginia; and in Georgia, Sherman's troops advanced against Gen. Joseph E. Johnston's army, minus the critical support that would have been provided by an attack on Mobile. Three weeks later both Union armies were meeting stiff resistance. From the field in Georgia, Sherman wrote Halleck proposing that the decision not to attack Mobile be reconsidered. He told the chief of staff that Johnston was opposing him with "every man he can scrape," and that Mobile was at their mercy. The next day Sherman wrote again, asking that the troops he had loaned to Banks be used to attack Mobile instead of remaining in Louisiana. He proposed that these troops be reinforced and "sent to Pascagoula to act against Mobile, in concert with Admiral Farragut, according to the original plan of the campaign."[33]

Recognizing the need to divert troops from Sherman's front, Grant ordered Halleck to comply with Sherman's request, if enough troops could be found west of the Mississippi. Still shackled by his Trans-Mississippi mentality and his misreading of Grant's order as a suggestion, Halleck replied that Canby had sent forces to Memphis to protect Sherman's communications and doubted that much could be done to help Mobile at present. He then added that the movement would be too late to help Sherman, since he was in possession of Allatoona Pass and now was moving against Marietta. Annoyed by Halleck's persistent failure to recognize the importance of Mobile, Grant shot back: "The object of sending troops to Mobile now would not be so much to assist General Sherman against Johnston as to secure for him a base of supplies after his work is done. Mobile also is important to us and would be a great loss to the enemy." Knowing Grant's feeling about Mobile and Canby's willingness to cooperate, Sherman already had ordered A. J. Smith, who by now had returned to Memphis, to join with Admiral Farragut and make "a strong feint or demonstration on Mobile by way of Pascagoula. Even if you make a landing it will draw troops from Georgia, but I know there is little or nothing left at Mobile, and if you move rapidly you can take the city and hold it. Show this to General Canby, and General Slocum may take a copy and construe it into an order to make up your command to 10,000 men if possible. What is done should be done at once."[34]

Having received Grant's letter explaining why Mobile should be attacked, Halleck wrote Canby and told him the general in chief's wishes: "General Grant suggests that, if troops can be spared from West Mississippi, a force be sent, under General Reynolds or General Franklin, against Mobile."[35]

Canby arrived in New Orleans on 9 June, having spent a month traveling up and down the Mississippi familiarizing himself with his new command. In keeping with Grant's strategy, Canby viewed activities in his division as subordinate to operations east of the Mississippi. One of his first decisions, therefore, was to send a division of seven thousand men into northern Mississippi to keep the rebel general Nathan Bedford Forrest from attacking Sherman's rear. Then, recognizing the importance of

Mobile to Sherman's success in Georgia, Canby began to organize a force at Morganza, Louisiana, to make the attack. On 16 June he appointed Maj. Gen. Joseph R. Reynolds to command the expedition, and ordered depots in Natchez and Vicksburg to "furnish promptly any supplies or materials" that Reynolds needed. That night he boarded a fast dispatch boat for a visit with Admiral Farragut off Mobile: The navy's support would be critical to the mission's success.[36]

The attack on Mobile was now imminent. All that remained was to flesh out the details and order its execution.

CHAPTER 3

→→ ←←

The Decision to Attack

THE SEVENTEENTH OF JUNE 1864 WAS A FINE DAY OFF THE COAST OF
Alabama: a calm sea, a gentle southwest breeze, the temperature still under 80 degrees. Nothing in the scene suggested that bloody battles were
raging in Virginia and Georgia—battles that were eroding Northern support for a war with no end in sight.[1]

The black smoke on the horizon had now been identified as the dispatch boat *Glasgow* from Lake Pontchartrain. Aboard was General Canby,
bound for the sloop of war *Hartford*, flagship of the West Gulf Blockading
Squadron off Mobile. As new commander of the Military Division of
West Mississippi, he needed to meet with Rear Admiral Farragut to discuss plans for an immediate attack on Mobile. Pressed with the demands
of his new job and the urgency of the message he carried, Canby had not
had time to inform the admiral that he was coming; the blue flag with two
white stars flying from the peak of the *Hartford*'s mainmast, however, told
him he was in luck.[2]

From the *Hartford*'s anchorage seven miles off shore, Canby could see
the shimmering dark line that marked the coast of Alabama, and where it
was broken by Mobile Bay. The distance was too great to see the two rebel
forts on either side of the entrance or the small fortification that guarded
Mississippi Sound. What he could see, however, was Sand Island, halfway
in, and the ruins of a lighthouse, destroyed earlier in the war by the rebels.

As the general and two aides stepped through the *Hartford*'s wide gangway onto her spotless deck, they were greeted by the admiral, who had

been alerted that an important visitor was coming aboard. Wasting no time on formalities, Farragut ushered Canby to his spacious day cabin, located under the poop deck. Before getting down to business, the general told Farragut that he was pressed for time and needed to get back to New Orleans early the next morning. The *Glasgow*, a captured blockade runner, was fast: thirteen knots. But in darkness it would take fifteen hours to cover the 150 miles to Lakeport on Lake Pontchartrain, a thirty-minute buggy ride from New Orleans.[3]

Canby opened the meeting by explaining that he had just arrived in New Orleans after spending almost a month on the Mississippi River familiarizing himself with the military situation in his new command. He told Farragut that he had just received a letter from General Sherman, requesting that a "strong feint or real attack be made on Mobile from Pascagoula in connection with Admiral Farragut's fleet," and that Grant supported Sherman's request. Sherman would give Canby an army of ten thousand, an adequate force since reports indicated that all the troops in Alabama had been sent to Georgia.[4]

Farragut must have smiled as Canby continued, for the admiral had just written Gustavas Fox that a move on Mobile now would result in an easy victory. With Grant, Sherman, and Farragut calling for an attack on Mobile, the matter was settled; nothing remained but to formulate a plan and give the order. In compliance with Grant's strategy of prioritizing operations in Virginia and Georgia, Canby viewed his role in the coming Mobile campaign as subordinate to Sherman. His relationship with Farragut, however, was that of a partner: The army and the navy needed each other.[5]

Farragut was elated. For nearly two years he had wanted to attack Mobile—or if not Mobile itself, then Forts Morgan and Gaines. It could now be done, although the cost and risk would be much greater.

The plan that began to take shape consisted of an overland attack on Mobile from Pascagoula and a joint army-navy assault on the two forts. Because of its location on an island, Fort Powell would be left to the navy. All agreed, however, that a force larger than ten thousand would be needed. Having consolidated his command and gone on the defensive, as Grant had directed, Canby said he could free up twenty thousand men for the attack. In fact, he already had alerted the 19th Corps, stationed at Morganza, Louisiana, to stand by for orders. With the operation outlined in concept, orders were given for the development of detailed information concerning the various approaches to Mobile: landing sites, road conditions, availability of water, and so on. Once these studies were completed, an operational plan would be drawn up and a date selected for the attack.[6]

As 3:00 P.M. approached, Farragut explained to Canby that the army could count on his support, but he needed two or three ironclads, one of which was reported to be on the way. To attack without armored vessels would risk the destruction of his squadron. The enemy's most formidable warship, the ram *Tennessee*, lay just inside the bay, waiting to engage Farragut's wooden vessels as they entered. Possibly the general might use his influence to help acquire two or three ironclads. An hour later, after an early dinner, Canby and his aides reboarded the *Glasgow* for a night run back to Lake Pontchartrain. As the general crossed the deck, Capt. Charles Heywood's forty-four-man marine guard gave him a snappy salute. Heywood had a score to settle with the rebels: He had been on the *Cumberland* in 1862 when Admiral Buchanan sank her at Hampton Roads. Although knowledge of the impending attack was confined to Farragut's staff and senior officers, word spread rapidly throughout the fleet that something unusual was afoot. J. C. Gregg, a marine private aboard the *Brooklyn*, wrote in his diary, "Preparations are being made for a fight here and we are daily expecting it to commence."[7]

DAVID GLASGOW FARRAGUT WAS A CONSUMMATE SOUTHERNER. BORN in Knoxville, Tennessee, and raised in New Orleans, as a child he often visited Pascagoula where his father, a sailing master in the navy, had invested in property. His sister, Mrs. Nancy Farragut Gurlie, was still living there. When Farragut's mother died, his father had arranged for him to live in New Orleans with the family of Commo. David Porter, who was instrumental in obtaining a midshipman's warrant for the boy. The future admiral first came under fire during the War of 1812 when Porter, then captain of the frigate *Essex*, engaged two British ships, the *Phoebe* and the *Cherub*, off Valparaiso, Chile, in 1814. In the ensuing battle, the *Essex* was sunk.

For the next forty-one years, Farragut's career followed a steady but less than meteoric rise to the rank of captain, which he attained while in command of the navy yard at Mare Island, California. At no time, not even during his Mexican War service, did fate and chance combine to expose those traits that would propel him into the spotlight as a great fighting admiral.

His exploits at New Orleans and on the Mississippi increased his fame and stature but did not guarantee success at Mobile, where the rebels possessed many advantages. His star could fall faster than it had risen.[8]

Canby had hardly returned to his headquarters on Julia Street in New Orleans when details of the impending attack reached Mobile. A city of mystery and intrigue, spies, double agents, and Confederate sympathizers, Union-occupied New Orleans was continually besieged with rumors. By 26 June word had reached Brig. Gen. Richard Lucian Page, commander of Mobile's Lower Defense Line, that the city was to be attacked "by land and water very soon." Similar hearsay had not been uncommon in the past, but the number of vessels off the bar, as well as vessel traffic, had nearly doubled since May, an indication that the enemy might be preparing to attack. Admiral Buchanan had reported in mid-June that seventeen vessels were off the bar and that he expected an attack any day. Gen. Dabney H. Maury, Confederate commander in Mobile, also expected an attack.[9]

Located at the head of Mobile Bay, thirty miles from the Gulf, and the terminus of a large river system that penetrated the interior, Mobile was first and foremost a seaport. Before the war, the city was the nation's third-largest exporter, primarily of cotton. As such, Mobile's economy was dominated by trade-related enterprises, with manufacturing accounting for only 15 percent of employment. The rivers and railroads that had once brought cotton to the presses and warehouses of Mobile now made a hub for the movement of troops and supplies to and from the heartland of the Confederacy. This, combined with Mobile's importance as a blockade-running port, also made the city important to the enemy, particularly now that Sherman was meeting stiff resistance in Georgia.[10]

Since Farragut's bombardment of Fort Powell in February, much had been done to improve Mobile's defenses. During the attack, General Gilmer, chief of the Confederate Engineer Bureau, had been ordered to Mobile to consult with General Maury. After inspecting the fortifications that encircled the city, he felt that although improvements were needed, with continued effort the city's defenses could be "pressed forward soon to a state of efficiency." His evaluation of the harbor defenses was the same. "If a little more time be allowed us," he wrote after returning to Richmond, "it will be a hopeless task for the Yankees to undertake the capture of Mobile by way of the Harbor."[11]

Also in Mobile at the time of Farragut's attack on Fort Powell was

Fitzgerald Ross, an Englishman with Southern sympathies. During his stay, he was given a tour of the city's defenses, which he found to be very impressive. Not wanting to tip off the enemy with too much information, he wrote: "Though I must not say much more about them, I may mention, as proof of the solidity of these works, that the parapets are 25 feet wide, the traverses against splinters of shell are 18 feet wide, [and] against enfilading fire, 32 feet wide. Beside these Forts there are two other lines of defense at Mobile, which will soon be one of the most strongly fortified places in the world."[12]

In the months that followed, efforts to strengthen Mobile's land and water defenses were pushed forward with great urgency. In April the assistant inspector general of the Confederacy, Col. George Hodge, was sent to Mobile to report on progress. In glowing terms, he reported his findings: The works "evince a scientific proficiency in engineering unsurpassed . . . by anything on this continent, and are themselves the most eloquent evidence of the educated skill of the engineer in charge, Lt. Col. Von Scheliha."[13]

Mobile's harbor defenses were situated so as to prevent enemy vessels from coming within effective shelling range of the city. A system of pile obstructions—sunken hulks, and torpedoes, covered by shore batteries, and the fire of six water batteries—effectively served this purpose. Across Mobile Bay, torpedoes, obstructions, and two strong batteries on the Appalachee and Tensaw Rivers prevented the enemy from using the waterways of the great delta north of the bay to approach Mobile from her unguarded rear.[14]

Thirty miles to the south, defending the water approaches to the bay from the Gulf and Mississippi Sound, were Fort Morgan and Fort Gaines, large brick-casemated structures, and Fort Powell, an earthwork, located on an island between Fort Gaines and the mainland. The Gulf entrance to the bay was blocked by four rows of piling and a triple line of torpedoes. Grant's Pass, where Fort Powell was located, was also obstructed by piles and torpedoes.

The naval forces at Mobile numbered eight vessels: the ram *Tennessee*, the rams *Tuscaloosa* and *Huntsville*, the ironclads *Baltic* and *Nashville*, and the wooden gunboats *Selma*, *Morgan*, and *Gaines*. In addition, three rams were under construction on the Tombigbee River. The effective force, however, was limited to six vessels—the three rams and three gunboats—and of these, only the *Tennessee* and the gunboats were capable of operating

Union flagship USS Hartford
NAVAL HISTORICAL CENTER

in the lower bay. The *Tuscaloosa* and *Huntsville*, although well armed and armored, were too slow and cumbersome to venture there for any length of time; and the *Baltic* and *Nashville*, although impressive in appearance, were poorly designed and due to be scrapped. The *Tennessee*, however, was a powerful man-of-war, her firepower and armor compensating for the squadron's small size.[15]

The *Tennessee* had been launched in Selma, Alabama, during the winter of 1863, and towed downriver to Mobile for completion. The vessel was 209 feet long, had a beam of 48 feet, and a draft of 13 feet. Approaching the *Tennessee* in a small boat, a visitor would have been awed by the size of the ram's huge casemate, her gray paint now streaked by iron rust. Apart from the vessel's unsightly color, her bulky appearance was a far cry from the graceful lines of a wooden sloop of war. She was, however, the world's most powerful warship, and sleek lines and fresh paint would count for little in the battle that was sure to come.

Boarding the ram's afterdeck, the visitor would pass between two twenty-nine-foot boats, suspended from davits, and four massive ventilators that funneled air into the lower decks. Also in this area were the steering chains that led from the wheel to the tiller. Observing these, an expe-

Confederate flagship CSS Tennessee
NAVAL HISTORICAL CENTER

rienced naval contractor would detect a serious defect in the way they were arranged: each lay in a shallow, open groove in the iron deck, rather than under it. An effort to prevent jamming by covering the grooves with one-inch sheet iron was being considered, but there was little that could be done at this late date to correct the situation. Nevertheless, Buchanan was extremely proud of the vessel and eager to test her strength. He acknowledged the *Tennessee*'s obvious weaknesses but felt certain that, gun for gun, her rifled cannon could match anything in the federal fleet, even their big 15-inch Dahlgren smoothbores.[16]

The casemate was entered through the aft gun port. Inside the *Tennessee*'s casemate, one could see the ram's battery of six Brooke rifles, ready-racks where shot and shell were kept for immediate use, and an assortment of tools and implements for loading and running the guns in and out of the ports. The *Tennessee*'s casemate was pierced with ten gun ports: four on each side, one forward and one aft, positioned so that the bow and stern guns could be pivoted to fire in broadside. The three pivot-gun ports, fore and aft, had eight-inch-thick wrought-iron shutters that swung pendulum fashion, allowing the shields to be closed when reloading. The center ports were identical to the bow and stern ports, except that the shutters slid up and down in tracks along the wall of the casemate. This arrangement made jamming highly probable in battle, but like the ram's tiller-chain grooves, nothing could be done now to correct the situation.[17]

Moving toward the bow, a visitor would pass the *Tennessee*'s large smokestack and massive windlass before reaching the forward pivot gun, which would have been withdrawn from the gun port and secured to the deck. Visible through the bow gun port was the forward deck, where the vessel's anchor, anchor hoist, and two large ventilators were located. The *Tennessee*'s famous ram, a large tapered protrusion, fifteen feet long, twelve feet deep, and twelve feet wide, was partially submerged. Immediately behind the bow gun, a ladder ascended to the pilothouse, where the vessel was commanded and conned.

The *Tennessee* had three decks—the gun deck, berth deck, and orlop deck. The galley, crew's quarters, and a storage compartment were located in the forward section of the berth deck; the officers' quarters, wardroom, and stateroom were in the aft section. The orlop deck, the next deck down, contained the engine room, fire room, magazine, shell room, and several storage compartments. The vessel's complement numbered 169—22 officers and 147 men.

The vessel was powered by two noncondensing engines that were connected to the propeller shaft by an idler shaft and bevel gearing. The cylinders, which came from the river steamer *Alonzo Child*, were twenty-four inches in diameter and had a seven-foot stroke. The poppet valves were arranged similar to those on western river steamers. With these engines the *Tennessee* was deplorably underpowered, her top speed being only six knots. Ladders forward and aft on the gun deck connected with the berth and orlop decks. In addition, various hatches and scuttles enabled ammunition and other heavy objects to be moved between decks.[18]

One of the first visitors to the *Tennessee* after the ram was launched was Kate Cumming, a hospital nurse, who later earned the sobriquet the Florence Nightingale of the Confederacy. Miss Cumming wrote in her diary that "Lieutenant Jordan, one of the officers, kindly showed us all over. It is a ram, and has many a dark-looking corner, where the men are to be stowed away in case of a battle. All looked very mysterious. I certainly felt I should not like to be one of the crew."[19]

WITH STEEL-BLUE EYES AND A CLEAN-SHAVEN FACE, BUCHANAN AT sixty-two was "strikingly handsome." Of medium height with a trim waist, he had the appearance and physique of a much younger man. Although upright in carriage, he walked with a halting limp, a reminder that here was a fighting admiral who had been close enough to the enemy to be shot by a musket. His ruddy complexion and snow-white hair spoke of decades on the quarterdeck; his high forehead and aquiline nose, of breeding and intelligence. But it was the set of "Buck's" mouth that best described his resolute character. "When full of fight," his fleet surgeon wrote, "he had a peculiarity of drawing down the corners of his mouth until the thin line between his lips formed a perfect arch around his mouth."[20]

Buchanan was one of the old navy's ablest officers, and his forty-nine-year career had been filled with intriguing assignments. He had seen action in the Mexican War, was the first superintendent of the U.S. Naval Academy, and served as Commo. Matthew Perry's fleet captain when "Old Bruin" opened Japan to American trade. In 1861, after much agonizing, Buchanan resigned as a captain in the U.S. Navy and joined the Confederate Navy with the same rank. Six months later, as commanding officer of the ram *Virginia*, he sank the frigates *Cumberland* and *Congress* and fought the *Monitor* to a draw at Hampton Roads in one of the most famous naval battles in history. In August 1863 Buchanan was promoted to admiral and became the ranking officer in the Confederate Navy. He was then sent to Mobile to take command of the naval force there, an assignment that would bring him one step closer to his nemesis, Adm. David Farragut.[21]

Having waited so late in the war to attack Mobile, the Yankees would now be confronted by a massive system of fortifications, a powerful ram, and a first-class, fighting admiral.

CHAPTER 4

✦✦ ✦✦

The Plan

CAPTAIN DRAYTON'S LARGE CABIN WAS BUSTLING WITH ACTIVITY.
Located on the gun deck below the admiral's cabin, it was the administrative center of the West Gulf Blockading Squadron. Alluding to the paperwork required by the sixty-eight vessels of the squadron, he had jokingly
remarked that if the *Hartford* were to be sunk by the *Tennessee*, "down will
go at the same time a mass of papers and reports that is disgusting to look
at, and which it would almost be a relief to get rid of even at such a cost."[1]

Following Canby's visit, the burden had increased. On this day, however, Drayton had managed to find a few minutes to write his friend S. M.
Hoyt: "Gen'l Canby paid us a visit yesterday to see the Admiral on business," he began; "he must be undeniably clever or he could scarcely be
placed in this way all of a sudden in supreme Command." Drayton then
expressed his belief that the general faced a tough challenge: "If half of
the stories however are true which are told of the utter state of demoral-
ization to which Banks brought his present army I should think some
time required before any fight could be got out of it." Canby was not a
complete stranger to Farragut; they had met in New York when the *Hartford* was being overhauled, and Farragut was already aware of the general's many talents. Grant would not have selected Canby to replace
Banks had he not been aware of the general's reputation for "coolness
and sound judgement."[2]

Back in New Orleans, Canby wasted no time in writing Halleck and
informing him that preparations for an attack on Mobile were under way.
Admiral Farragut had agreed to cooperate and was "quietly conducting

some preliminary examinations that are necessary." The number of troops, however, would be greater than the ten thousand suggested by General Sherman. "I will be able to send a force twice as great without endangering anything," he wrote.[3]

No sooner had Canby written Sherman than he received a report from Farragut, describing landing sites at Pascagoula, Portersville, and Pensacola, and offering the use of two lighters at Ship Island and some tinclads, now at New Orleans. He also volunteered the services of Captain Jenkins, one of his most experienced captains, should Canby's engineers need help. The admiral's Mississippi Sound pilots had told him that vessels could "carry 8 feet water up to [the] Pensacola wharf, or 6 feet up to within 100 yards of the shore at Portersville. The road is good from Portersville up to Mobile; the Pascagoula road is also good, except in two or three places in wet weather."[4]

An overland attack from Pensacola, forty-five miles from the eastern shore of Mobile Bay and fifty-five miles from Mobile itself, had the advantages of a secure base served by a deep-water port. The major disadvantages were the distance to be covered and the complications of transferring troops and supplies across Mobile Bay. A landing at Portersville, although only twenty-five miles from Mobile, would be hampered by shallow water and the marshy nature of the coast at that location. Pascagoula, on the other hand, had sufficient depth to land an army, and was not that much farther away from Mobile—forty miles compared with twenty-five.

A report prepared for the Navy Department earlier in the war described the approach from Pascagoula to Mobile as a country of "hard, level, sandy roads through pine woods, clear of underbrush, and easily known by the telegraph poles." Six miles out of Pascagoula, a "rough bridge of 30 feet" crossed a "deep, muddy stream" bordered by thick bushes. For the next thirty miles, the country was flat and sparsely populated with a "scattering of log houses." Nine miles from Mobile the road crossed Dog River, forty feet wide, muddy, and unfordable. A "well-worn" bridge crossed the river, but the report speculated that the bridge might have been replaced by something more substantial. Just beyond was a deep ravine, which gave way to gently rolling land, "sparsely settled by uncultivated people." The road terminated at Government Street, "two miles west of the Mobile wharves." Both Grant and Sherman had indicated a preference for this approach.[5]

On 22 June, Gen. Joseph Reynolds left New Orleans to take command of the forces at Morganza. Canby ordered the supply depots at Natchez, Vicksburg, and Memphis to "furnish promptly any supplies or materials" requested by Reynolds. Canby also planned to visit Morganza, as he wanted to be on hand when the expedition departed.[6]

As planning for the land attack progressed, Farragut still held to the conviction that he could not go in without ironclads. Drayton, who had commanded the ironclad *Passaic* at Charleston, agreed: "If they don't send us down some iron clads, there seems nothing left for us except to wait quietly until the enemy comes out. For to run the gauntlet of the forts, only to come in on an iron fleet of certainly double our power in smooth water, would not seem quite sensible, and I don't believe that even Farragut would venture on such a step."[7] Canby also had not forgotten the one serious obstacle standing in the way of an attack on Mobile: Farragut's need for ironclads. From the way the admiral talked, he would not go in with fewer than two. On the twenty-fourth Canby wrote Porter and told him that in an operation about to begin in Farragut's command, "two or three lightdraft monitors would be very useful." Anticipating Porter's argument against sending the vessels, he added that Commodore Palmer, Farragut's commander on the lower Mississippi, believed that "monitors like the *Winnebago* and *Chickasaw* can be sent into the sound or into Mobile Bay without danger." He closed by asking Porter to send the vessels as soon as possible, if they could be spared.[8]

The next day, Secretary Welles wrote Porter from Washington and gave him a direct order to transfer the *Winnebago* and *Chickasaw* to Farragut. Welles had previously told Porter to send the vessels, but the admiral had written back and asked him to reconsider—the Mississippi River monitors were not designed for open water and might founder in a sea. In a 25 June dispatch to Farragut, Welles notified him to expect the river monitors, and also included more good news: The ironclad *Manhattan* had left the capes of Delaware on 20 June to join Farragut's squadron, and her sister ship, the *Tecumseh*, would be sent in a week or ten days.[9]

Events were moving none too fast. Sherman was having problems in Georgia. His 27 June frontal attack against Johnston at Kennesaw Mountain was a failure. "About 9 A.M. of the day appointed," Sherman later wrote, "the troops moved to the assault, and all along our lines for ten miles a furious fire of artillery and musketry was kept up. At all points the enemy met us with determined courage and in great force. . . . By 11:30 the assault was in fact over, and had failed." Five hundred miles to the north, across the heartland of the Confederacy, the news was not much better: Lee was holding Grant and the Army of the Potomac at bay outside Petersburg in what appeared to be the beginning of a protracted siege.[10]

The army, of course, could attack Mobile by land and bypass the lower forts. This, however, would leave Mobile's back door open through which supplies could be brought in by blockade runners. Planning, therefore, continued for a two-pronged attack: The army would march overland and lay siege to Mobile, and a joint army-navy force would attack the lower forts and seal off the bay.

Farragut's experience on the Mississippi River had convinced him that shore batteries could not stop the passage of a determined squadron of steam vessels. Torpedoes, however, were a different matter. Almost daily the enemy could be seen planting these "infernal machines" across the channel. He would have to find out more about their location and plan his tactics accordingly. There was also the problem of floating obstructions, for in addition to planting torpedoes, the rebels had been observed obstructing the channel with *chevaux de frise*—frames of logs tied together and anchored to the bottom.[11]

The plan of attack that began to take shape in the admiral's mind drew heavily on the lessons learned at New Orleans, Port Hudson, and Vicksburg. Conceptually, the plan would include four simultaneous operations: amphibious landings at Pascagoula, Mobile Point, and Dauphin Island, and a "projection operation" into Mobile Bay by the navy. The objective of the three landings would be the capture of Mobile, Fort Morgan, and Fort Gaines. The navy's objective would be to destroy the Confederate naval squadron, capture Fort Powell, and provide the army with gunfire support.[12]

On 27 June, Canby wrote Sherman that he intended to start the expedition against Mobile in a few days to coincide with cavalry raids into Mississippi from Memphis, Vicksburg, and Baton Rouge. He added that a shortage of transports on the river was causing problems but this would soon be rectified. The next day, Canby informed General Steele in Arkansas that the Mobile expedition would begin on 6 July. With twenty thousand troops leaving Louisiana for Mobile, he wanted Steele to make a demonstration in northern Louisiana to keep the rebels from "coming down upon the river while these operations are pending."[13]

By now Canby and Farragut were aware that the Navy Department had ordered four ironclads to Mobile, two from the Mississippi and two from the Atlantic; when they would arrive, however, was uncertain. The need to draw troops from Sherman's front was becoming more critical each day. Canby therefore had decided to land the army at Pascagoula and move overland against Mobile, leaving the lower forts to be attacked when Farragut received his ironclads, which, he hoped, would be any day now. The *Manhattan*, which Welles had reported at sea and off the coast of Delaware on the twentieth, had now reached Port Royal, South Carolina, fifteen hundred miles from Mobile. Off Fort Monroe at Hampton Roads, Virginia, Cdr. Tunis A. M. Craven, captain of the *Tecumseh*, telegraphed Welles that he would be ready for sea in six days. "Have projectiles been sent to my place of destination?" he asked. On the Mississippi, however, Porter had not yet ordered the *Winnebago* and *Chickasaw* to report to Farragut.[14]

At brigade headquarters in the large, two-story house just outside Fort Morgan's southeast bastion, J. W. Crowell, the fort's telegraph operator, had just tapped out a message to Confederate army headquarters in Mobile: "Twelve vessels off the bar this morning." Noting that the number of blockading vessels had dropped from a high of seventeen in early June to twelve, Page was not convinced that the prospect of an attack had lessened. More than likely, he reasoned, the vessels were returning to Pensacola and Ship Island for ammunition, coal, and supplies before going into battle.[15]

Not all Page's officers, however, interpreted the change as a sign of impending action. Lt. Robert Tarleton, a Yale graduate, had written his fiancée, Sallie Lightfoot, that the general had stopped all leaves and was in "daily, almost hourly expectation of an attack. Where he gets his information from I can't imagine. The fleet outside is not so large as it was some weeks ago."[16]

BRIG. GEN. RICHARD LUCIAN PAGE, FIFTY-SEVEN, WAS A FIRST COUSIN of Robert E. Lee. This, however, was not why he had been transferred from the Confederate navy, commissioned a brigadier general in the army, and given command of the lower defenses of Mobile Bay. Page's qualifications were his knowledge of warships, heavy ordnance, and seacoast fortifications. The coming struggle for control of Mobile Bay, so the authorities in Richmond reasoned, would require a naval mentality. To defeat the Union's best admiral, one would have to think like a sailor, and old "Ramrod," Page's nickname, was a sailor to the core.

Commissioned a midshipman in 1824, Page had reached the rank of commander by 1845, having served almost continually at sea, except for a tour as ordnance officer at the Norfolk Navy Yard. He saw action during the Mexican War, after which he returned to Norfolk as executive officer of the yard. From there he was given command of the sloop of war *Germantown* of the East Indian Squadron. His next assignment had brought him back to Norfolk, once again as an ordnance specialist.[17]

In April 1861, after thirty-six years of service, Page resigned as a commander in the U.S. Navy, was given the same rank in the Virginia navy, and was assigned to the Norfolk Navy Yard as ordnance officer. A month later, he was transferred to the Confederate States Navy but remained at Norfolk, salvaging heavy guns and supplying them to the gunboats and fortifications that defended Virginia's rivers and coastal waters.

Page's next assignment took him to Port Royal, South Carolina, as second in command of the Confederate naval forces in South Carolina and Georgia. There, during the Battle of Port Royal, he narrowly escaped death. While he was superintending the working of the forward gun on the *Savannah*, flagship of the Confederate squadron, a shell fired by a Union warship smashed the *Savannah*'s pilothouse, missing Page by inches.

Arriving in Mobile, Page was given command of the department's Third Brigade, which was responsible for the defense of lower Mobile Bay and the protection of Alabama's coast from the western end of Dauphin Island to the Perdido River, fifty miles from Pensacola. His command included Fort Morgan, Fort Gaines, Fort Powell, an infantry camp that protected the saltworks on the Bon Secour River, and two cavalry camps in southeastern Baldwin County that watched the coast and the inland approaches to Mobile from Union-occupied Pensacola. The June returns of the brigade listed 1,027 men and 70 officers present for duty. The 1st Alabama Battalion of Heavy Artillery and the 1st Tennessee Heavy Artillery manned Fort Morgan and Camp Anderson; the 21st Alabama Volunteer Infantry, serving as artillerymen, garrisoned Forts Gaines and Powell; and the 7th Alabama Cavalry and 15th Confederate Cavalry, Camps Withers and Powell.[18]

Mobile Bay was the key to Mobile's defense, and the main channel opposite Fort Morgan was the key to the bay's defense. Once Farragut's fleet entered the bay, the battle would be lost. A triple row of torpedoes, the guns of Fort Morgan, and Buchanan's squadron were the means by which this would be prevented.

If some of the enemy's lead vessels could be sunk in the channel before entering the bay, the others would withdraw; and if by chance two or three did slip in, Buchanan would dispose of them. At New Orleans, Port Hudson, and Vicksburg, steam vessels had indeed passed land fortifications, but one of war's newest and most deadly weapons, the torpedo, had not been used in these engagements. Page, therefore, had reason to feel optimistic.[19]

Lieutenant Tarleton was also optimistic; he felt the Confederacy would win the war, not just a battle. In a letter to his fiancée, he expressed this belief: "I am more and more convinced every day that this year, possibly this campaign will witness its close. The North is evidently failing in military, financial, and political strength. Their armies and generals are fighting against hope, or rather with the desperate hope that some lucky chance will give them the advantage which numbers do not and counter-revolution is at work at home drying up the sources of their strength."[20]

CHAPTER 5

-★-★-◄★-

The Attack Is Canceled

AS THE FLARE SHOT SKYWARD, IT RESEMBLED A FIERY COMET, RISING rapidly, then slowing in a graceful arc before sputtering out in a shower of sparks. The captain of the three-hundred-ton blockade runner *Ivanhoe* had chosen to enter Mobile Bay through the Swash Channel, directly under the guns of Fort Morgan. By taking this course, he could beach the vessel if threatened with capture and unload its government-consigned cargo of valuable medicines, arms, and ammunition. As the vessel moved slowly along the beach, all eyes on board were scanning the darkness, eagerly straining to detect the Yankee picket boats that usually patrolled a mile or so south of the Swash Channel. The time was 11:00 P.M.; the distance to Fort Morgan and safety, two miles.[1]

Since leaving Nassau four days earlier, the captain and crew of the fast but fragile vessel had dreaded this moment. If discovered, their only advantages would be speed and darkness—at sixteen knots the *Ivanhoe* could outrun anything in the federal fleet—and the moonless night of 30 June provided them with just enough cover to slip in undetected. Suddenly, a flare lit up the night sky. Instinctively, the *Ivanhoe*'s captain gave the command: "Ahead full!" As if booted by some powerful force, the vessel lurched forward, her paddle wheels churning the water into fiery swirls of phosphorous, her bow sending out great fans of salty spray. At top speed it would take five minutes to enter the main channel and pass through the narrow, torpedo-free opening opposite the fort. As the *Ivanhoe* gained speed, it appeared as if the race might be won. But a bright orange flash, followed by the screaming whine of a projectile, indicated otherwise. There, off the port bow, was the murky outline of a federal gunboat. Suddenly a massive jolt, followed by a moaning, scraping sound, told the captain his vessel was aground.

As the gray dawn brightened the next morning, the plight of the stranded steamer was revealed to the blockading fleet. The *Ivanhoe* was a beautiful vessel, her graceful lines reflecting the skill and mastery of the Scottish craftsmen who built her. It would be a pity to destroy such a beauty, but every captain in the Union fleet was eager to try. The job, however, was ideal for the small gunboats; their speed and maneuverability would allow them to run in, fire, and avoid the counterfire that was certain to come from Fort Morgan.

As daylight spread across the Gulf, the rebels already were unloading her cargo, which in value was probably worth more than the vessel. Farragut wanted this stopped and the vessel destroyed. In went the gunboats, their fire scattering the troops that were unloading the stranded vessel. But the shooting was haywire, and counterfire from the fort killed one of the *Metacomet*'s crew. Chagrined, the admiral ordered the gunboats in closer, but still their fire was ineffective.

Later, during the afternoon, Farragut boarded the dispatch boat *Glasgow* and went in for a closer look. This drew fire from the fort, causing concern throughout the fleet for his safety, but he calmly surveyed the scene until satisfied that gunfire alone would not prevent the vessel's cargo from being salvaged. Not one to be diverted from an objective he considered important, Farragut now knew that the vessel would have to be boarded to be destroyed.[2]

The first of July had not been a good day for Farragut; Drayton was also disappointed. He sent a note to Jenkins aboard the *Brooklyn*, confessing that he "could see no signs of the least damage to the blockader, although wonderful stories are told." As Farragut and Drayton were pondering how to destroy the vessel, they were confronted with a much greater problem: events in Virginia had caused the attack on Mobile to be canceled.[3]

Earlier in the day, General Canby had received a dispatch from Halleck that directed him, by order of Grant, to cease offensive operations, secure his lines of communications, and send all available troops in his division to Fort Monroe, Virginia, where they would receive orders. Halleck's dispatch also stated that, in Grant's opinion, the twenty-thousand-man 19th Corps, or its equivalent in numbers, should be sent. Grant's dispatch was an order, not a suggestion, and Canby met it head on by canceling the Mobile operation.[4]

Word had not reached New Orleans about recent events in Virginia, so Canby could only guess that Grant was in trouble. The new general in chief faced two problems. Now that Robert E. Lee had withdrawn his army into the defenses around Richmond and Petersburg, the possibility of a protracted siege and its impact on the November elections cried out for a quick solution. Grant's reaction was to take the offensive—and this required more troops. The other problem was the threat that a Confederate army posed to the national capital. On 22 June, after clearing the Shenandoah Valley of federals, Lt. Gen. Jubal Early and his army of fourteen thousand cut loose from its base near Staunton, Virginia; and, reminiscent of Stonewall Jackson, headed up the valley.

Grant, recognizing the political crisis that a standoff with Lee might precipitate, and sensing the possibility of a move by Early toward the Potomac, had ordered the 19th Corps to Virginia, thus canceling the attack on Mobile and depriving Sherman of a much-needed diversionary attack. Sherman's failure to capture Atlanta before the presidential election—now only four months away—would seriously handicap Lincoln, but a stalemate in Virginia, accented by a bold attack on the national capital, would guarantee his defeat. By his skillful retirement into the strong works that defended Richmond and Petersburg, and his daring order that Early attack Washington, Lee had once more upped the ante on a negotiated peace.

The same day Canby received Halleck's letter, he rushed a dispatch to Farragut, telling him that "operations against Mobile have been suspended. As soon as I am able to leave, and probably in four or five days, I will visit you at the fleet for the purpose of conferring with you upon matters affecting our commands. The demonstrations in the direction of Mobile will be kept up by our preparations and a show of movements until the troops have reached their new destination."[5]

Farragut must have read Canby's dispatch with a heavy heart, although he probably surmised that some pending catastrophe had demanded it. Knowing the importance that Grant and Sherman placed on the Mobile operation, he accepted the news philosophically and directed his attention to the task at hand: the destruction of the stranded blockade runner. He also found time to answer Canby's communiqué and assure him that, although disappointed, he would be standing by when needed. For the next three days, Farragut had little time to reflect on this setback, for he was determined to destroy the beached paddle wheeler. One of his character traits was to "tread down or fight through any obstacles which stood in [his] path," regardless of their nature, and this was no exception.[6] In the meantime, Farragut had ordered the gunboats to move in closer and try for better effect. On the Fourth, the fleet "fired a grand salute in honor of the day and decorated every mast head with a large American flag and Union Jack at the bow," wrote Paymaster Ellsworth Hults in his journal. "I counted upwards of 50 floating at one time. Fort Morgan fired 1 gun, in token of defiance."[7]

Two days later, just before midnight, a boarding party under the command of Flag Lieutenant Watson left the *Hartford* with three boats and managed to board the blockade runner undetected; for some reason, the rebels had opted to defend the vessel from the beach, which was about fifty yards away. Taking advantage of this, Watson's party was able to climb aboard the vessel undetected, set a fire onboard, and leave a keg of powder they did not have time to ignite. As the boats were pulling away, they were subjected to a fusillade of musket fire—but miraculously, no one was hurt. Capt. John Marchand of the *Lackawanna*, an officer who had the admiral's ear, remarked to him the next day: "They set her on fire in the forecastle and cabin and left. She burned for a few hours; but as she is an iron vessel, the conflagration was not very magnificent." In other words, the mission was a failure. Had the powder keg been ignited, it would have been a different story.[8]

Farragut turned sixty-three on 5 July. He had not been in the navy for fifty-four of those years to fail at the seemingly simple task of destroying a two-hundred-ton blockade runner lying immobile in the surf. The gunners on the ramparts of Fort Morgan were a problem, but he would not let this stand in the way of getting the job done. The problem, as he saw it, was to destroy the vessel before it was floated and towed into the bay.

DURING THE EARLY MORNING HOURS OF 7 JULY, THE TELEGRAPH IN General Maury's Mobile headquarters began to click. A message from Fort Morgan was coming in: "There are (18) eighteen vessels off the bar this morning—Page." Soon another followed: "Will you please send down a special steamer to move the goods taken from the 'Ivanhoe.' There are a good many here and I think it advisable to remove them at once, and send them under guard to the City."[9] General Maury was pleased to learn that the *Ivanhoe*'s valuable cargo was in the process of being saved, but the increase of five vessels, up from thirteen a week ago, worried him. Farragut did not need eighteen vessels to destroy a blockade runner.

On 5 July, Maury had wired Gen. Samuel Cooper, adjutant and inspector general of the Confederate Army, that federal monitors were coming to Mobile. As was his custom, he followed up with a letter that explained in more detail the content of the telegram. "I believe it is not improbable that Mobile will be attacked before long. To-day I have received a dispatch from General Jones, at Charleston, sending me statements of Yankee prisoners that monitors are coming out here, are actually on the way. Farragut has a heavy fleet off the bar. Canby has been there in conference with him. General Lee wrote me yesterday that he considers the movements from the Mississippi River may be destined for Mobile, that Canby's army will not again move into West Louisiana very soon. I have reduced my force very much to re-enforce General Johnston." Maury closed by asking that Confederate forces west of the Mississippi River be ordered to make a demonstration that would threaten Canby's rear. The demonstration might also cause A. J. Smith's force, which had left Memphis on the fifth, to return to Memphis, thus allowing troops from Mobile to return to the city.[10]

On 7 July, Maury again wrote Cooper, pleading for troops and ammunition. He said that Canby was preparing to attack Mobile by land with an army of 20,000 to 30,000, against his effective strength of 4,337. Maury had just sent 600 men to Lee in Mississippi "in order to meet an advance of the enemy from Vicksburg" and had alerted a cavalry regiment of 800 to stand by. In Mobile "there are no troops left to me for duty in and about the city, except a few companies of 'local troops,' citizens of Mobile." Although Maury believed he had enough heavy guns, his supplies and ordnance stores, particularly projectiles for the big guns, were insufficient for a siege. The Lower Defense Line had been supplied with three hundred rounds per guns, at the expense of guns nearer the city, few of which now had more than two hundred rounds.

Before closing, Maury mentioned another problem. Because Mobile was a seaport, there were factions among the population that had been hurt economically by the war and would like to see it ended—whether by victory or defeat. Maury alluded to these interests when he told Cooper, "There are a great many people here not at all desirous of the success of the Confederacy, whose machinations are very hard to guard against. They evade the pickets; trade and communicate with the enemy. If arrested, unless testimony is direct and complete, they are very apt to be turned loose by the instrumentality of the lawyers."[11]

Maury's pleas for help were finally getting some attention. As he was writing Cooper, Alabama governor T. H. Watts received a telegram from Jefferson Davis asking that he use his "official and moral power, in the organization of reserves to re-enforce the garrison of Mobile at the earliest possible moment." Meanwhile from Meridian, Mississippi, Lt. Gen. Stephen D. Lee had sent a telegram to Gen. Braxton Bragg informing him that the enemy had occupied Jackson, Mississippi, but with the force at his disposal, he felt "tolerably secure." He added: "Indications from Northern newspapers, and from Mississippi, are that Mobile will be attacked by Canby. Am preparing to aid Maury all in my power." Lee had also written Gen. Kirby Smith asking him to make a demonstration west of the Mississippi to "delay and divert" the forces preparing to attack Mobile.[12]

The sudden increase of traffic on the Mississippi had not been missed by the people of New Orleans, and word soon reached Mobile that commercial steamboats with colorful names like the *Crescent* and the *Creole* had been ferrying troops from Morganza to New Orleans for a week now. A citizen traveling between New Orleans and Baton Rouge on 3 July had observed "seven steamers, two of them of the largest size, all loaded with troops and their camp equipage." An informer who lived on the river just below Baton Rouge had also reported that a "number of transports passed the previous day." Other reports followed: From Algiers, the sudden building of a pontoon bridge for crossing rivers, to be completed by the fifth; the impressment of privately owned horses; and the fitting out of schooners and light-draft vessels with horse stalls. These observations were a sure sign that an expedition was about to depart New Orleans— and rumor identified its destination as Mobile, by way of Pensacola.[13]

General Canby had much to do with perpetuating the rumors. In a letter to Maj. Gen. Cadwallader Washburn at Memphis, Canby explained that although the operation against Mobile had been canceled, he intended to perpetuate the belief that Mobile was the destination. The deception would accomplish two objectives: It would shield the movement's true destination and, at the same time, divert rebel troops from A. J. Smith's front in Mississippi.[14]

On 7 July, eight miles from Atlanta's outer defenses, Sherman replied to Canby's letter of 27 June, in which Canby informed him that an attack on Mobile would be made in a few days. Unaware that the attack had been canceled, Sherman began by acknowledging receipt of the "very agreeable news." "Atlanta is in sight and is defended by a well handled army," he wrote in praise of his opponent, "yet I shall not pause." He said that the cavalry raids into Mississippi from Memphis, Vicksburg, and Baton Rouge were most important and would "keep employed the forces of the enemy that might be mischievous in my rear. . . . But the move on Mobile will be most opportune . . . no matter in what strength, even if confined to a feint." He then informed Canby that he was sending a cavalry force three thousand strong into Alabama to destroy the railroad from Montgomery eastward, which would "separate Alabama from Georgia," and would Canby ask the commanding officer at Pensacola to look out for the column between 20 and 25 July, in the event it should be compelled to go there after the raid.[15]

The Confederate evacuation of Pensacola in 1862 provided the Union with a fine deep-water port, a few hours away from Mobile Bay. Almost totally in ruins when reoccupied, the yard was now capable of undertaking most of the repairs required by vessels of the blockade. Four infantry and two understrength cavalry regiments were stationed at Fort Barrancas and Fort Pickens. From his headquarters at Fort Barrancas, General Asboth, a native of Hungary, commanded the district and its garrison of forty-five hundred.[16]

In the early afternoon of 7 July, the two-thousand-ton ironclad *Manhattan* cast loose from her tow, the gunboat *Bienville*, and anchored off the Pensacola Navy Yard. The captain, Cdr. James Nicholson, wasted no time in writing to Farragut and Gideon Welles that the *Manhattan* had arrived. Farragut had not yet received Welles's letter telling him that the *Manhattan* was on the way, so Nicholson's note, delivered that afternoon, came as a "happy" surprise. In a letter to Welles, Farragut announced the vessel's arrival and his relief that the balance of power was gradually shifting his way. He wrote: "If she [*Manhattan*] is what she is represented, we are all right." Nicholson also wrote Welles: "I have the honor to report my arrival here after a remarkably pleasant passage of eight days from Port Royal. This includes a stoppage of one day at Key West where we put in for coal. . . . I desire to express my thanks to Cdr. Mullany of the *Bienville* for his continual watchfulness and care for all of our wants, his valuable aid in towing and navigating through the Florida Channel and the material assistance both in men and boats given in coaling the vessel."[17]

That night, Acting Master Robert B. Ely, an officer aboard the *Manhattan*, wrote in his diary that several sailboats, "one of them with a lady in it, have been sailing around us since our arrival, their occupants looking at us with all their eyes—as this is the first Ironclad which has ever been so far from home. She is quite a curiosity to the natives. I hope she may prove a thorn in the side of the Rebels."[18]

OFF FORT MORGAN, AS DARKNESS BEGAN TO CREEP ACROSS THE GULF, Farragut decided that Watson should go in again that night and once more attempt to blow up the stranded steamer, a dangerous mission following so closely the previous night's effort. It was not easy for the admiral to ask Watson to risk his life again. Farragut had written his son, Loyall, after Watson's first attempt to destroy the blockader. "I was a little down in the mouth," he began, "because I thought we had not done as well as we ought to, in destroying a blockade runner that tried to force her way by us. But Dyer, in the *Glasgow*, ran her on shore under the guns of Fort Morgan, and I had been trying to get the gunboats to destroy her, but they did bad work, and the rebels were at it night before last, trying to get her off. I determined to send a party to board and set her on fire. Watson volunteered for the work. . . . Well, as you may suppose it was an anxious night for me for I am almost as fond of Watson as yourself."[19]

At Fort Morgan, General Page had issued an order that the *Ivanhoe*'s pickets would now be stationed on the vessel, not on the beach. Lieutenant Tarleton, the officer responsible for guarding the vessel, had originally recommended this, but had been overridden by the post commander, Colonel Jackson. In a letter to his fiancée, Tarleton wrote: "If I had been on board with thirty men, I have no hesitation in saying the vessel could have been defended." Should the enemy attempt to board her again, he implied, they would be greeted with an entirely different reception. In addition to Tarleton's thirty men, a battery of field guns had been located on the beach near the vessel.[20]

Tarleton did not have to wait very long. The next night at 2:15 A.M., two boats were observed approaching, as if expecting the *Ivanhoe* to still be unoccupied. As the boats neared, not a sound could be heard except the gentle lapping of waves and the call of a night bird somewhere back in the dunes. Fifteen minutes later, when the boats were within musket range, Lieutenant Tarleton gave the command to fire, shattering the night with the roar of musketry and cannon fire. The sound of smashing wood, the shouts, and cries of the wounded told that his fire was striking home. The *Ivanhoe* would not be boarded that night.[21]

CHAPTER 6

➤➤ ◄◄

A New Plan

ABOARD THE *Hartford*, AT HER ANCHORAGE OFF MOBILE'S OUTER BAR, Admiral Farragut was anxiously awaiting news of Watson's expedition. At 4:00 A.M., he was informed that the *Pinola* was returning with the boats in tow. Standing on the *Hartford*'s gangway, it did not take long for the admiral to sense that the expedition had been roughly handled; the wounded being carried up the boarding steps attested to this—but to his relief, Watson had returned unscathed. With daylight less than two hours away, Farragut returned to his cabin. General Canby was coming over to discuss important matters later that day, and the admiral wanted to get some much-needed rest before the meeting.[1]

Farragut was no longer a young man; he had reached the pinnacle of success late in life and, although still remarkably spry, he was feeling his age. The day following his sixty-third birthday, he had written his wife a forthright and revealing letter: "Would to God this war was over that I could spend in peace with you all the few remaining years of my life. . . . Don't you trouble yourself about the war on my account; I am in the hands of a Merciful Providence." This letter was followed by one to his son, describing the lonely burden of command and an officer's responsibility not to reveal his anxieties: "no one knows what my feelings are; I am always calm and quiet."[2]

Down the coast at Pensacola, the weather was oppressively hot, particularly aboard the *Manhattan*. "It is impossible to keep cool," Lieutenant Ely wrote in his diary. The heat, however, did not deter several army officers from coming aboard and marveling at the "size of the guns and the thickness of the turret." Unmindful of the visitors, the crew was hard at work taking in provisions, topping off the coal bunkers, and cleaning decks. The *Manhattan*'s two-thousand-mile sea voyage, the longest ever for an ironclad, had taken its toll. Nevertheless, Ely wrote: "All aboard are impatient to get into action."[3]

By now, off Mobile, Farragut and Canby were setting in motion the action that Ely and the *Manhattan*'s crew were seeking. Canby's party, which included members of his staff, Maj. Gen. Gordon Granger, and Commo. James S. Palmer, Farragut's divisional chief on the lower Mississippi, arrived at 5:00 P.M. This time, Farragut was expecting the general, and the marine guard gave him a proper salute when he came aboard. Once in the admiral's cabin, Canby told Farragut that despite the transfer of the 19th Corps to Virginia, he had found enough troops to invest Forts Morgan and Gaines, possibly four thousand; he would confirm the exact number as soon as possible.[4]

The plan Canby presented included landing three thousand men on the Gulf beach three miles behind Fort Morgan, "simultaneous with the passage of the fleet into the bay." Leaving a rear guard entrenched across the peninsula at Pilot Town, the main force would move to within a mile or three-quarters of the fort, entrench, and open fire with eight 30-pounders, six 3-inch Rodmans, and two mortars as the fleet entered the bay. In Mississippi Sound fifteen hundred troops with rifled field artillery would remain aboard their vessels as a reserve. After the fleet had passed into the bay, a portion of this force, with artillery, would be landed on Dauphin Island from the sound. These troops would then attack Fort Gaines in conjunction with the navy. This plan, the general believed, would not require "regular approaches and breaching batteries." Once Forts Morgan, Gaines, and Powell were "separately and collectively" invested, the rebels would surrender.[5]

Canby told Farragut that Granger would command the army. Granger was a soldier's soldier; he had gotten himself into trouble with General Grant at Missionary Ridge when he impulsively jumped from his horse and began sighting and firing a cannon. The cannoneers were impressed, but not Grant. Grant told Granger he "commanded a corps, not a cannon." In turn, Farragut said that Palmer would stand by to provide the army with whatever assistance it would need from the navy. Although the city of Mobile would be spared, an attack on the lower forts would divert rebel troops from Sherman's front and clear the way for a final push toward Atlanta.[6]

With all in agreement, Canby and his party, anxious to get back to headquarters, reboarded the little steamer for the run back to New Orleans. With two hours of daylight left, Canby and Granger would have had an opportunity to observe the western end of Dauphin Island, where the troops would land—a long, low spit of sand that extended eight miles from the edge of the heavily wooded eastern end of the island, where Fort Gaines was located. As the vessel turned to the north and entered the pass between Dauphin Island and Petit Bois, the next island to the west, they would have seen a huge white cloud of seabirds, feeding in the nutrient-rich waters of Mississippi Sound, just ahead. Once in the sound, the vessel hauled around to the west, the dark green pines on Petit Bois Island now silhouetted against a sky of pale orange. Ten minutes later, the sun would have slipped from sight, giving way to a canopy of bright stars.

The next day, Canby's assistant adjutant general, Maj. C. T. Christensen, wrote Farragut and informed him that the general had just received word from Admiral Porter that the ironclads *Chickasaw* and *Winnebago* were on the way to New Orleans. Also, Canby would let him know as soon as possible how large a force he would send and when it would arrive.[7]

Around midnight of the following day, 10 July, another fast paddle wheeler eluded the blockade, but ran aground as she turned to enter the bay. Captain Marchand, of the *Lackawanna*, wrote in his journal that the vessel "succeeded in passing through our lines, when seven steamers were watching, and in attempting to go through the Swash Channel grounded." At about 7:00 A.M., the *Lackawanna* and three other vessels were ordered to go in and shell the blockade runner. Later, as a rebel steamer attempted to pull the stranded vessel into the bay, the shelling was resumed, but without effect. That night a second attempt was made to float her, this time successfully. Another cargo of much-needed war materials and supplies had reached the rebels.[8]

ONE THOUSAND MILES TO THE NORTH A LARGER DRAMA WAS UNFOLDING on the outskirts of the nation's capital. Lt. Gen. Jubal Early with an army of twenty thousand rebels had reached the outskirts of the city and was pushing down the Seventh Street Road toward the administrative center of government, including the silver and gold of the U. S. Treasury. Raw troops and hospital convalescents manned the massive forts and redoubts that circled Washington, but reinforcements were on the way, including twenty-four hundred men from the 19th Corps. The ease with which General Early got within sight of the capitol after sacking the home of Postmaster General Montgomery Blair did not bode well for the president's reelection.[9]

Off Mobile, events were moving rapidly and Farragut did not have time to lament the escape of the most recent blockade runner. Other matters were on his mind. In Georgia, General Sherman had reached the outskirts of Atlanta. Would he face a long siege, as appeared to be the situation at Richmond and Petersburg, or would he sack the city, then head for the Gulf or the Atlantic, in search of a secure base for his army? In June, General Grant had made Mobile an integral component of the Atlanta Campaign, not only as a means of tying down troops that might otherwise be sent to Atlanta, but as a possible "base of supplies" for Sherman after Atlanta was captured.[10]

Farragut now had three ironclads and a promise from Canby that the army would participate in the attack. This was what he had been waiting for: ironclads and troops to attack the forts. With the army's role defined, the admiral now began to develop a detailed plan for the navy.

On 12 July, Farragut published General Order No. 10, which began with the dramatic phrase: "Strip your vessels and prepare for conflict." Specific instructions followed: send down superfluous spars and rigging; trice up or remove whiskers; put up splinter nets on the starboard side; barricade wheels and steersman with sails and hammocks; lay chains or sand bags on the deck over machinery; hang sheet chains over the side; land starboard boats or tow them over the port side; lower port boats to the water's edge; place the pilot and a leadsman in a location convenient to the commander. To avoid stifling initiative, the order gave commanders the authority to "make any other arrangements for security that your in-genuity may suggest."[11]

Next, the order addressed the admiral's tactical plan. The vessels would enter the bay in couples, lashed side by side, the flagship leading. When approaching the fort, each couple would keep on the starboard quarter of the pair ahead to give the bow guns a clear field of fire. Opposite the fort, the column would straighten out; and after passing, would echelon to port, allowing the stern guns a clear field.

Then came the Farragut touch: "It will be the object of the fleet to get as close to the fort as possible before opening fire." The fleet, however, would open the "moment the enemy opens." The admiral also directed that "short fuzes" be used for shell and shrapnel, and that grape be used when within three hundred to four hundred yards of the fort. The order instructed that if a vessel were disabled, its partner should carry it through. If this could not be done, the next astern should assist. But as the fleet would be moving with the flood tide, "it will only require sufficient power to keep the crippled vessels in the channel." The larger vessels were now ordered to "place guns upon the poop and topgallant forecastle and in the tops on the starboard side." If, however, the enemy fired grape, the men should be removed from the topgallant forecastle and poop deck to the gun deck below. Barring this, the howitzers should keep up a constant fire while within shrapnel range.

The work of preparing the vessels for combat began as soon as General Order No. 10 was issued. While the *Galena* was still off Mobile, Paymaster Hults wrote in his diary: "Active preparations are going on in the fleet & new vessels [are] constantly arriving to participate in the attack on Mobile. We are constructing splinter netting all around the ship['s] bulwarks, out of strong manila rope & expect to cover the boilers with heavy cable, & inside with sand bags." In a letter dated 26 July to Admiral Farragut, Capt. John Marchand, the *Lackawanna*'s captain, wrote from Mobile that since "sails have but little effect except in strong winds, I respectfully desire to send down the yards and upper masts as you suggested. With the above exception, the landing of two boats, and getting the Sheet Chains on the ship's side (which can be done in a few hours), preparations for battle are completed."[12]

The freedom to improvise that Farragut had allowed his captains was spawning many innovations and arrangements not mentioned in the battle order. For example, hammocks and sails were stacked on the poop deck to protect the officers from sharpshooters; boiler iron shields were installed around the fore and main maintops, where howitzer crews would be stationed; railings and stanchions were removed to clear fields of fire and prevent injuries from metal fragments; bags of coal were placed around "steam drums"; and wooden bulwarks filled with sand were constructed in coal bunkers to protect the boilers.[13]

Captain Jenkins was converting the *Richmond* into a floating fortress. As he explained to Farragut, he preferred to go in without masts, but sensing the admiral's dim view of the idea, he would leave his three lower masts up, retaining only the fore and main yards. Masts and spars crashing to the deck during a battle were often the cause of heavy casualties. In addition to this precaution, the space between the berth and spar decks, from the starboard bow to the starboard quarter, was filled with sand bags several feet deep, thus forming an earthen wall between the enemy and the *Richmond*'s vital machinery.

When Jenkins entered the navy as a midshipman in 1828, explosive shells had not been adopted by the world's navies. For hundreds of years, "solid shot had been the mainstay, used to hole an enemy vessel near the waterline, destroy spars and masts, and kill the enemy." The thickness and elasticity of wooden hulls, however, enabled shot holes to be quickly plugged. As a result, few vessels were sunk, although continuous pounding at close range often destroyed an enemy's ability—moral and physical—to continue fighting. In the coming battle, however, powerful guns firing explosive shells with percussion, or time, fuses posed a serious threat to the hull and internal structure of a vessel—not only from the explosion of the projectile but also from fire. Jenkins understood this and was doing all within his power to protect the *Richmond* and other vessels of his division from the heavy guns of Fort Morgan and Buchanan's squadron.[14]

Col. Albert J. Myer, Canby's chief signal officer, sent Farragut two intelligence reports, dated 9 and 11 July. The information was based on statements made by a deserter from Fort Morgan and a refugee from Mobile. The reports covered troop strengths and the armament of various fortifications, including a reasonably accurate description of the number of guns at Fort Morgan and Fort Powell. The report also described, with great precision, the pile obstructions and torpedoes between Fort Morgan and Fort Gaines. From west to east, the line of piles extended from shoal water near Fort Gaines, across Pelican Channel, to the edge of the main ship channel. Beginning where the piles ended, three rows of torpedoes, in staggered order, extended eastward across the channel to a black buoy, which was anchored four hundred yards to one-half mile from the fort.[15]

On 15 July, Farragut wrote Welles that he was "getting ready for coming events. The two monitors in New Orleans are preparing to come round here," he wrote. They were "intended for the river service and require some securities against the sea breaking over their hatches." He also told the secretary that Canby had found enough troops to attack Forts Morgan and Gaines, and mentioned that two days after the *Manhattan*'s arrival at Pensacola a fire broke out but the damage amounted to very little. The vessel would be ready for service in four or five days.[16]

The next day, Farragut penned a letter to his friend Rear Adm. T. Bailey at Key West. Referring to the Mississippi River ironclads, he wrote, "There are some monitors getting down this way, but when they will be ready for their work I can not say, as I have not yet seen them, but as soon as they are, and all things are ready in the army, we will take a look at Buchanan."

Farragut, however, was still fearful that Buchanan would steam out and attack him before the ironclads reached the fleet. "Now is his time," he told Bailey; "the sea is as calm as possible and everything propitious for his ironclads to attack us; still he remains behind the fort. . . . If he won't visit me I will have to visit him. I am all ready as soon as the soldiers arrive to stop up the back door of each fort," he wrote. "I can form no idea when we will make the attack." Farragut then mentioned the sinking of the CSS *Alabama* off Cherbourg, France. "The capture of the *Alabama* is glorious news," he said. "The *Hatteras* would have taken her, but for that unfortunate shot in the boiler." This, of course, was problematical. Farragut was still smarting over Capt. Raphael Semmes's bold incursion into the boundaries of his command. In January 1863 the rebel captain steamed into the Gulf of Mexico, sank the *Hatteras* thirty miles off Galveston, and steamed back out again unscathed. Farragut was humiliated.[17]

Intent on watching Buchanan, Farragut transferred his flag to the gunboat *Tennessee* (not to be confused with the Confederate ironclad) and sent Drayton to Pensacola in the *Hartford* to expedite the *Manhattan*'s departure and, while there, to take on coal and ammunition. No sooner had the *Hartford* dropped anchor off the navy yard than, to Drayton's horror, the *Manhattan* caught fire again. For a second time, the flames were extinguished before the vessel was seriously damaged. Cleaning up the mess and repairing the damage, however, would further delay her departure.[18]

Before retiring, Drayton wrote his friend Hoyt that the admiral had remained with the blockade off Mobile to keep an eye on Buchanan's ironclads. "As we have now an iron clad, Farragut is now becoming very restless, and if the necessities of the army will spare us a few soldiers he wont stay quiet long. Unfortunately just as something is planned, there is an uneasiness about Grant or Sherman, and away go the regiments. I am afraid we shall with difficulty get over the injury caused by Banks' inefficiency and its consequences, but politicians must live, whether the Country does or not."[19]

AS THE SUN ROSE ABOVE THE SCRUBBY PINES AND ABANDONED SHACKS of Harrisburg, Mississippi, 240 miles to the northeast of Mobile, 14 July was already hot. During the night, the Yankees had thrown up breastworks and were now waiting for the Confederates to attack. At 7:30 that morning the gray lines rushed forward, "yelling and howling like Comanches." For three hours, wave after wave charged, fell back, and went forward again. By noon, Confederate casualties totaled almost a third of the force. Although outnumbered nearly two to one and confronted by an entrenched enemy, Gen. Stephen D. Lee, the Confederate commander, was determined to bring the engagement to a quick conclusion so that he could reinforce the Mobile garrison. Intelligence reports from New Orleans and the arrival of an ironclad at Pensacola indicated that Mobile was about to be attacked: Lee had promised Bragg that as soon as he defeated A. J. Smith, Maury's two regiments would be returned, as well as two thousand, possibly three thousand, infantry from Mississippi.[20]

Gen. A. J. Smith had left Memphis the first week in July with fourteen thousand troops, the equivalent of two corps. His objective was to keep Nathan Bedford Forrest away from Sherman's supply lines by harassing the civilian population of north Mississippi and destroying the railroad between Tupelo and Mobile. The Union column had moved from Memphis to LaGrange, Tennessee, and from there to Tupelo, Mississippi, burning and plundering everything in sight. On 12 July, Smith was attacked by Forrest, who was acting in concert with his superior, Lt. Gen. Stephen D. Lee, commander of the Department of Alabama, Mississippi, and East Louisiana. That afternoon Smith entrenched at Harrisburg, a shanty town two miles northwest of Tupelo.[21]

Fearing that Canby was about to move on Mobile, Gen. Stephen Lee wanted to continue the attack so that troops could be sent to Mobile as soon as possible. Forrest, however, preferred to wait, at least for a while. A. J. Smith would soon abandon his fortifications, Forrest reasoned, for want of rations and fodder; and when he moved out, Forrest assured Lee, "I will be on all sides of him, attacking day and night. He shall not cook a meal or have a night's sleep, and I will wear his army to a frazzle before he gets out of the country." Lee, on the other hand, felt that time was critical, and the risk of confronting a superior force behind entrenchments was justified.[22]

With ammunition and supplies running low—which by now had to be a problem for Smith—no commander wanted to be confronted by a determined and dangerous foe, even if inferior in numbers. Surely Smith had not come to Mississippi to be humiliated like Nathaniel Banks in Louisiana. The next morning he abandoned his position and began to withdraw from North Mississippi. That same day, Maj. Gen. J. M. Withers, commander of the Alabama reserves, informed Richmond that "between forty and fifty companies" of Alabama state troops had been ordered to Mobile. Finally the pieces were falling in place for the defense of the city.[23]

Stephen Lee now sent Bragg a telegram announcing that the "raid from Vicksburg was retreating." This crossed a telegram from Jefferson Davis to Lee, ordering him to get word to Kirby Smith in Louisiana to attack Canby, who was apparently preparing to move on Mobile. As directed, Lee dispatched a message to Smith informing him of the president's order to "defeat the plans of the enemy." He added: "There is no doubt the enemy are moving against Mobile or some point east of the Mississippi.[24]

In the meantime, information had reached Lee suggesting that Canby's troops might be destined for some location other than Mobile, but lacking hard intelligence, he would do everything possible to aid Maury should Mobile be Canby's true destination. With the enemy retreating from Mississippi and Kirby Smith mobilizing to attack Canby—not to mention the momentary arrival of reinforcements at Mobile—Lee's spirits rose. Although Mobile's defenses were designed to be defended by ten to fifteen thousand men, as few as six thousand would suffice, if carefully posted and well led. This number now appeared to be within reach.[25]

CHAPTER 7

➤➤ ◄◄

More Delay

AT HIS HEADQUARTERS IN THE NELSON HOUSE, THREE MILES FROM Atlanta's outer fortifications, Gen. Joseph E. Johnston and his chief engineer, Lt. Col. S. W. Prestman, were discussing the city's defenses. Johnston planned to launch a counterattack as Sherman's troops crossed Peachtree Creek. Should the attack fail, he wanted to make certain the fortifications offered a "secure place of refuge" for the troops as they fell back.[1]

Anticipating this, he had ordered the works to be strengthened and reinforced with heavy rifled cannon from Mobile. If Sherman could be "foiled," Johnston believed the Peace Democrats would win the November presidential election and bring the war to an immediate end. For the South to win its independence, all that was needed was to "deny the North a major military triumph" and up the ante in Northern casualties.[2]

Lincoln's personal secretaries, John Nicolay and John Hay, were aware of this and agreed that the North's "military situation was far from satisfactory. The terrible fighting in the Wilderness, succeeded by Grant's flank movement to the left, and the culmination of the campaign in the horrible slaughter at Cold Harbor, had profoundly depressed the country. The movement upon Petersburg, so far without decisive results, had contributed little of hope or encouragement." Continuing, they wrote that, so far, "the campaign of Sherman in Georgia gave as yet no positive assurance."[3]

July 17 had been a long day for Johnston. With his army still outside Atlanta, he had been groping for a way to strike the enemy before withdrawing behind the fortifications. Shortly before 10:00 P.M. a message from Richmond was brought in. Signed by Gen. Samuel Cooper, adjutant and inspector general of the Confederate Army, it read: "Lieutenant General J. B. Hood has been commissioned to the temporary rank of general un-der the late law of Congress. I am directed by the Secretary of War to in-form you that as you have failed to arrest the advance of the enemy to the vicinity of Atlanta, far in the interior of Georgia, and express no confidence that you can defeat or repel him, you are hereby relieved from your command of the Army and Department of Tennessee which you will im-mediately turn over to General Hood."[4]

The next day, Hood and the army's two corps commanders, Lt. Gens. W. J. Hardee and Alex P. Stewart, wrote President Davis and requested that Johnston's dismissal be postponed until the "fate of Atlanta shall be decided. . . . The enemy being now in our immediate front and making, as we suppose, a general advance, we deem it dangerous to change commanders, now especially, as this would necessitate other important changes." Davis refused.[5]

Forty-eight hours after assuming command at Atlanta, true to his reputation, Hood attacked. On 20 July, he hit the enemy at Peachtree Creek, northwest of Atlanta, and was repulsed with 2,500 casualties, compared with Sherman's 1,700. On the twenty-second, he shifted his attention to the east and attacked the enemy's left wing with better results, but again he suffered heavy casualties—5,500 to 3,800—bringing his three-day total to 8,000—2,500 more than Sherman's total of 5,500.[6]

So far, all Hood had accomplished was to force the enemy from a position that it "soon would have departed in any event." Nevertheless, the Battle of Bald Hill, as it came to be known, provided the South with a much-needed boost in morale. The presidential election was only fourteen weeks away, and Hood's exaggeration of his military prowess was exactly what Southerners needed. He must have had this in mind when he notified the secretary of war of his "great victory." General Hardee, he reported, "made a night march and attacked the enemy's extreme left at 1 o'clock to-day; drove him from his works, capturing 16 pieces of artillery and 5 stand of colors. Major-General Cheatham attacked the enemy at 4:00 P.M., with a portion of his command; drove the enemy, capturing 6 pieces of artillery. During the engagement, we captured about 2,000 prisoners, but [our] loss not fully ascertained."[7]

Soon, congratulations began to pour in. In a letter to Jefferson Davis, Robert E. Lee wrote: "If the news of the glorious victory at Atlanta, reported this morning, prove true, it will again open to us Alabama and East Mississippi, and remove a part of the great weight pressing upon us." Lee's letter was followed by one from Braxton Bragg: "The moral effect of our brilliant affair of the 22nd has been admirable on our troops, and I am happy to say our loss was small in comparison to the enemy's. He was badly defeated and completely failed in one of his bold flanking movements, heretofore so successful."[8] Hood knew that, in the long run, a strategy of attrition cannot succeed if the smaller force continually loses the same or more than the larger. He also knew how important it was that Atlanta still be in Confederate hands when the presidential election was held 11 November.

In the Shenandoah Valley, 120 miles northwest of Richmond, Jubal Early was still a thorn in Grant's side. Having returned to the valley after raiding Washington, he remained in the area between Harpers Ferry and Winchester, waiting for a chance to cross the Potomac and strike north again.[9] As Early waited and watched, and Lincoln's popularity sank still further, Richmond was buzzing with talk of the peace mission that had taken place on 17 July. Two Northern gentlemen, supposedly carrying documents from Abraham Lincoln, but without official sanction, met with President Davis and his secretary of state, Judah P. Benjamin. The purpose of the meeting was to explore the possibility of reunion if slavery were allowed to continue as a legal institution. When confronted with the question, Davis said no: "We are fighting for independence, and that, or extermination, we will have." He then, with an acute appreciation of growing political discontent in the North, expressed the following:

> *If your papers tell the truth, it is your capital that is in danger, not ours. . . . Grant has lost seventy-five or eighty-thousand men—more than Lee had at the outset—and is no nearer taking Richmond than at first; and Lee, whose front has never been broken, holds him completely in check, and has men enough to spare to invade Maryland and threaten Washington! Sherman, to be sure, is before Atlanta; but suppose he takes it? You know that the further he goes from his base of supplies the weaker he grows, and the more disastrous defeat will be to him. And defeat may come. So, in a military view, I should certainly say our position was better than yours.*[10]

In Meridian, Mississippi, eight hundred miles to the southwest, Stephen Lee was busy directing the defense of his large department.

Beset by threats from New Orleans, Memphis, and Vicksburg, he had just received a late report on the newest danger: a Union cavalry raid from north Alabama. The column, commanded by Maj. Gen. Lovell H. Rousseau, had reached the small town of Chehaw, thirty miles east of Montgomery, where a battle had been fought. From there the Yankee horsemen headed east toward Opelika, tearing up the railroad as they went. Late reports indicated that the column had now turned north and was approaching the Georgia border.[11]

General Bragg, who had been sent by President Davis to confer with Joe Johnston before his removal, happened to be in Montgomery on 20 July. Shortly after arriving, he telegraphed the president that the railroad east of Montgomery had been "badly damaged," but the enemy was now under hot pursuit by a hastily collected force, mostly of infantry. He also informed Davis that Gen. Stephen D. Lee was on his way to Montgomery with information that the enemy was preparing a large force to operate in Mississippi or possibly to reinforce Sherman at Atlanta. To meet this threat, Bragg recommended that "prompt, decided, and expeditious measures" be taken to bring troops from Gen. Kirby Smith's command, west of the Mississippi, to meet the emergency. "Urge General E. K. Smith to prompt compliance," Davis answered. He also told Bragg to order Gen. S. D. Lee to report to Hood and assume command of the general's old corps. Lee, the president said, should be replaced by Dabney Maury.[12]

At Fort Morgan, Lieutenant Tarleton had written his fiancée that he was "much exercised about the raid from north Alabama, which had just cut the R.R. east of Montgomery." He was concerned about his relatives in Tuskegee, Alabama, he told her, but thought they would be safe, since the town was "six or seven miles from the railroad." He also expressed optimism that Fort Morgan would not be attacked—at least not in the near future; and the arrival of "some ironclads" at Pensacola was not for offensive purposes, but to prevent the *Tennessee* from making a sortie into the Gulf and raising the blockade. His superiors, however, felt otherwise, and preparations for an attack were progressing at a frantic pace.[13]

During the *Ivanhoe* incident, the enemy fleet had scored several hits on Fort Morgan. Concerned with the fort's capability to withstand a protracted siege, General Maury had ordered Lt. Col. Victor von Scheliha to assess the damage. The Prussian did not like what he found. In a report to the general, he stated, "Fort Morgan, in its present condition, cannot withstand a vigorous bombardment." He recommended that the fort be strengthened by traverses and sand-filled cribs, and that the inner citadel be demolished and converted to be bombproof. In addition, von Scheliha suggested that the area inside the fort be filled with five feet of sand and all but a few heavy guns be placed outside on the covered way, where they would not be put out of action if the walls of the fort were breached. He also advised that a partially finished trench across the peninsula be completed and that the planting of torpedoes in the channel be accelerated. In closing, he recommended that Fort Gaines and Fort Powell be strengthened and a telegraph line constructed from Fort Gaines to Cedar Point. The report ended with a plea that "1,500 negroes and 100 carts" be sent immediately to complete the work. With this force and the 120 on hand or in transit, he believed the work could be completed before the end of the month. Von Scheliha was convinced that with the Lower Defense Line strengthened and the upper bay and city defenses completed, "Mobile will hold out as long as our provisions last."[14]

When Maury learned that he had been ordered to assume temporary command of the Department of Alabama, Mississippi, and East Louisiana, in addition to the District of the Gulf, he was not happy. Having been stripped of troops for the defense of Atlanta, the Department of the Gulf now had fewer than four thousand effectives to meet rumored threats at Mobile. Maury was scheduled to meet with General Bragg in Montgomery on 27 July to discuss a number of subjects, the most important of which was a movement by Gen. Kirby Smith's troops to cross the Mississippi.[15]

In the meantime, Maury continued to strengthen the land and water fortifications that encircled Mobile, although the number of impressed slaves fell well below what was needed. On the Lower Defense Line, labor was also a problem, but little by little the forts were becoming stronger, particularly Fort Morgan, and the torpedo field in the main channel more lethal. Pvt. E. B. Presley, however, was not sure what all the fuss was about. An artilleryman at Fort Morgan, he wrote his wife that there were no signs of a fight, at least not more than usual, and he and his companions were getting along "first rate." He recently had a fine time eating watermelons but they had cost a "good price." His little son's lock of hair arrived and he was surprised to see it so dark: "He must be getting grown very fast."[16]

Aboard the Union gunboat *Tennessee*, seven miles south of Fort Morgan,

Farragut was reading an urgent dispatch from Canby. As he continued to read, the curves of his mouth slowly straightened, a sign that he was not pleased: the Mobile attack had been put on hold. This was the third time in two months that an operation against Mobile or its outer defenses had been canceled or delayed. Dated 18 July, Canby's letter read: "I have the honor to state that in consequence of the changes resulting from the transfer of troops to the Army of the Potomac, there will be more delay in collecting the force to be sent to you than I expected when I saw you." The general did not say precisely when the troops would be sent to Mobile, only that he had managed to put together a force of four thousand that would be ready—he thought—before the *Chickasaw* and *Winnebago* left New Orleans for Mobile. Desiring to keep an eye on Buchanan, Farragut had transferred his flag to the gunboat *Tennessee* while the *Hartford* was in Pensacola being readied for the coming battle. Fortunately, the flagship was returning to the blockade that day, and he would be able to discuss the implications of a delay with his fleet captain, Percival Drayton.[17]

Recognizing the importance of attacking Mobile's lower defenses at this time, Canby had informed Sherman that he was about to make a diversionary attack from New Orleans. In the meantime, serious problems were developing west of the Mississippi: The rebels were preparing for a major move. Intelligence reports indicated two possible objectives: an attack against General Steele in Arkansas or an attempt to cross the Mississippi and reinforce Johnston in Georgia. He therefore needed to reassess the deployment of his forces, including the withdrawal of more troops from Brazos Santiago—the Union's sole remaining garrison in Texas—and the use of "colored recruits from the plantations." In any event, he had ordered Col. Miles D. McAlester, his chief engineer, to visit Farragut and coordinate the army's activities with those of the fleet.[18]

Colonel Myers would be responsible for coordinating signals, having already suggested to the admiral that army signalmen be assigned to the vessels—not to replace the navy's method of sending messages but to communicate with the army after the fleet had entered the bay. McAlester would be responsible for selecting landing sites and getting the troops and artillery ashore, a task that could not be accomplished without fire support and landing boats from the navy. Farragut, of course, recognized the complexities inherent in joint army-navy amphibious operations, particularly when landing troops on a hostile shore, and welcomed the involvement of the two officers.[19]

On 20 July, after reviewing the disposition of his forces, Canby wrote Farragut that the troops for Mobile would be ready in about one week. He also informed Sherman that the attack was about to be made and, although not as large as the four thousand originally contemplated, it would have a "good effect." Canby then mentioned that General Asboth was standing by to receive General Rousseau's cavalry column should he choose to head for Pensacola. In closing, he felt obligated to warn Sherman that the diversion of four thousand troops to Mobile would restrict his movements "very materially," but he would do whatever was necessary to help.[20]

The same day that Canby wrote Sherman, Asboth sent him a dispatch stating that on the following day, he would start a column of "1,000 infantry, 2 pieces of artillery, and 50 mounted men" northward to intercept General Rousseau—who, he had been told, might be headed for Pensacola. If the cavalry column was not found, Asboth said, he would destroy the Mobile-Montgomery railroad at Pollard, Alabama, sixty miles northeast of Mobile, and return to Pensacola. He also thanked the general for the promise of a cavalry regiment that "will not lie idle." In the coming battle, Asboth's mission would be to divert rebel troops from Mobile by threatening to destroy the railroad, a challenge the enemy could not fail to meet.[21]

That morning, as gusty winds sent white spray scudding across Pensacola Bay, workmen at the navy yard watched the ironclad *Manhattan* weigh anchor and leave the harbor in tow of a gunboat. She had been at the yard thirteen days repairing the wear and tear of her two-thousand-mile sea voyage and the damage caused by two accidental fires after reaching port. As the vessels left the harbor and turned westward—a sure sign that a fight was near at hand—the sentinels on the ramparts of Fort Pickens could see waves and white spray breaking over the ironclad's decks.[22]

Two hours later, the *Hartford* left Pensacola, having been there a little more than a week preparing for the battle: coaling, taking on ammunition, and replenishing supplies; protecting her machinery with sand bags and chains; and stripping the masts of superfluous spars and rigging—a routine that all vessels of the battle line had been ordered to follow. At 10:00 A.M. the *Brooklyn* and the *Manhattan*, the latter under tow by the *Bienville*, passed each other, the sloop heading for Pensacola, the monitor and her consort for Mobile. Riding low in the water, with waves breaking over her deck, the Manhattan was indeed a novel sight to the crew of a vessel with six feet of freeboard between the water and gun deck. Crowding the port bulwark, the *Brooklyn*'s crew gave the monitor three cheers, which were answered. When the flagship passed a short time later, the ritual of salutes and cheers was repeated. A great battle was in the making. The signs were everywhere. The old salts knew what was coming; they had been there before; the young landsmen, however, had yet to learn. It would not be a picnic.[23]

Aboard the *Manhattan* Lieutenant Ely noted in his diary that the voyage took several hours, raining all the way. Upon arriving, the ironclad was cut loose from the *Bienville* and, under her own steam, came to anchor near the *Hartford*. Noticing black smoke trailing from the *Tennessee*'s smokestack, Ely made several quick entries in his diary. He noted that the *Tennessee* had steam up and appeared to be "quite ready for us." Fort Morgan looked like a "huge pile of sand." The guns were mounted "en barbette," and the casemates protected by a "wall of sand forty feet thick." Ely was most concerned, however, about the three lines of torpedoes said to be sunk across the channel, speculating that "we will probably lose some of our vessels in passing them."[24]

Once the *Hartford* had anchored, Farragut and his staff left the Union gunboat *Tennessee* and reboarded her, pleased to be back in familiar surroundings. During the evening, several army officers, including Colonel Myers and Captain McAlester, came aboard the *Hartford* to discuss the pending attack, although as yet no date had been set. Before retiring, Farragut wrote his son and mentioned the sinking of the CSS *Alabama*, as he had done in his letter to Admiral Bailey earlier in the week. "The victory of the *Kearsarge* over the *Alabama* raised me up," he began. "I would sooner have fought that fight than any ever fought on the ocean." It was like a tournament, in full view of thousands who were confident that the *Kearsarge* would be sunk. He then harked back to the *Hatteras* and how she would have sunk the *Alabama* but for an unlucky shot in her boiler. Apparently, he was still humiliated over losing one of his vessels to the "pirate Semmes."[25]

Seven hundred miles to the southeast, darkness had enveloped the Florida Keys. Off Indian Key, the *Tecumseh* and her two escorts, the *Augusta* and *Eutaw*, had anchored for the night. A light northeast breeze rippled the surface of the water and refreshed the crews, who had been allowed to go topside to escape the oppressive heat belowdecks. Commander Craven was not pleased with the *Tecumseh*'s progress. After leaving Hampton Roads on 5 July, the vessel's engine shaft had overheated, requiring a week's delay for repairs at Port Royal, South Carolina. Now with coal running low, another delay would be necessary at Key West or Dry Tortugas. Even with the best of luck, the *Tecumseh* could not reach Mobile before August. The chances, therefore, of participating in the battle were diminishing almost hourly. While at Port Royal, Craven had learned that the *Tecumseh*'s sister ship, the *Manhattan*, had stopped there three weeks earlier. Certainly by now she had reached Mobile. If so, the battle may have been fought and won, or lost. In any event, he would continue to push on; every hour counted.[26]

Built for the placid waters of the Mississippi River, the double-turreted *Chickasaw* and *Winnebago*, now at New Orleans, were being prepared for the open water of the Gulf of Mexico. There was speculation, however, that neither vessel would make it to Mobile.

CHAPTER 8

➤➤ ◄◄

Manhattan Joins the Fleet

As the first rays of dawn spread across the Gulf on 20 July, the Yankee monitor and her gunboat consort could still be seen at anchor beyond the outer bar. News of the monitor's arrival at Pensacola two weeks ago had not taken long to reach Mobile, and her appearance off Fort Morgan was not unexpected. On 21 July, Lieutenant Tarleton wrote Sallie Lightfoot another long, chatty letter. He began by telling her that rumors of an attack on Fort Morgan were somewhat confirmed the afternoon before when an ironclad, a "regular turretted monster," appeared in the blockading fleet. He was not yet convinced, however, that an attack was imminent, and told her: "The quid-nuncs, of course, are in a great state of excitement and Gen'l. P. is clearing for action by ordering away all ladies, laundresses and non-combatants generally. I need not tell you that it will take more than one monitor to shake my incredulity on the subject of an attack, although I think Gen'l. P. is right to get ready for one."[1]

Tarleton believed that the monitor's presence was a feint to divert Confederate troops from Sherman's front in Georgia, and until a Union army appeared, the enemy would not risk a serious attack. Others felt that the enemy intended to strengthen his fleet, run past the forts, and enter Mobile Bay, thereby cutting water communications with the city. Commander Jones of the Selma Naval Ordnance Works and a nephew of General Page also felt that an attack was not imminent, although the general had done the right thing by sending away all the noncombatants, for a fight was certainly in the making. With only one monitor, Jones did not think Farragut's fleet could pass the fort and enter the bay. Page and Buchanan, however, were taking no chances. The fort's garrison and the naval squadron would remain on the alert until the threat subsided. Intelligence from New Orleans reported that Mobile would soon be attacked. Two Mississippi River ironclads were being readied for the open sea, and troops were waiting for transports—their probable destination: Mobile.[2]

From his elevated position in Fort Morgan's lighthouse, the lookout swept the horizon and focused on the gray smudge trailing a plume of smoke. The Yankee ironclad was no longer in tow of the gunboat; she was coming up the channel under her own power. As the long roll summoned Fort Morgan's six-hundred-man garrison to battle stations, the rattle of anchor chains signaled that Buchanan's squadron was also clearing for action. If the enemy wanted a fight, they would get one. The time was 10:50 A.M.[3]

Peering through the narrow slit in the *Manhattan*'s pilothouse, Commander Nicholson could see thick black smoke trailing from the stacks of the rebel squadron as it moved from behind Fort Morgan into the channel. Ordered to proceed inshore and anchor in the main channel near Sand Island, about three and a half miles from Fort Morgan, he had been told that as soon as Sand Island Channel, the sheltered water north of Sand and West Sand Islands, had been sounded and buoyed, the *Manhattan* would be moved there. Nicholson had been warned, however, that his present anchorage would be within range of Fort Morgan's heavy guns. Not to be caught off guard if a long-range artillery duel should ensue, he had ordered that the *Manhattan*'s cannon be loaded with 35-pound charges and the turret supplied with 3½-, 7-, and 10-second shells.

Before the *Manhattan* cast off from the *Bienville* at 9:30 A.M., Farragut had come aboard and inspected the vessel. This was his first close look at a *Canonicus*-class ironclad, a class much improved over the *Passaic* class, in which his fleet captain, Percival Drayton, had once served. Less than two hundred tons of water in the hull, however, could sink her. From bow to stern the *Manhattan* measured 223 feet, compared with 225 for the *Hartford*. Her beam was 43.4 feet; the *Hartford*'s, 44. The ironclad's draft of 13.6 feet, however, was almost 4 feet less than the flagship's, making the *Manhattan* better suited for shallow water. But what must have impressed the admiral most, however, were the two 15-inch Dahlgrens, weighing 42,000 pounds each, and firing a projectile of 440 pounds.[4]

As the *Manhattan* approached Sand Island, now five hundred yards off her port bow, Nicholson gave the command to "cast anchor." With a great clanging chatter, the eighteen-hundred-pound anchor stripped off six and a half fathoms of chain before reaching the bottom, and this was followed by a second anchor before Nicholson was satisfied it would hold. Lieutenant Ely, who had come on deck from his station in the turret, described the scene: "We can see the rebs at work quite plainly. The *Tennessee* is in full view, and a rather ugly brute she is. The Rebs have not fired at us at all, and we are quite peacefully disposed for present" except for the waves breaking over her sides. "The whole deck is flooded with water and the wardroom damp and filled with foul air," he complained. Despite the excitement, Ely was totally disgusted with "this filthy iron-pot," and would have gladly left her for the comforts of a more conventional vessel.[5]

Out in the Gulf, aboard the screw steamer *Galena*, Paymaster's Clerk E. H. Hults had been watching the drama unfold and was no doubt disappointed when a gunfight failed to materialize. He did, however, see the Confederate squadron deploy for action and later wrote in his diary that the monitor "astonished the inhabitants of Fort Morgan and environs & no doubt they expect active operations shortly upon our part. We will not disappoint them in that."[6]

As darkness spread across the Gulf, a gentle breeze sprung up from the southwest, bringing the temperature down to eighty degrees, a welcome, if meager, respite from the ninety degrees around noon. It had been a good day for Farragut. In a letter to Welles he reported the *Manhattan*'s arrival, to be followed in a week by the *Chickasaw* and *Winnebago*. He had also authorized a landing party from the *Oneida* to examine the Gulf beach four miles east of Fort Morgan to determine its suitability as a landing site for the army. In addition, he had approved an operation to capture a rebel picket that had been observed patrolling the beach near that location. But his boldest decision concerned the stranded blockade-runner *Ivanhoe*, a decision that reflected his unyielding determination to overcome any obstacle that stood in his way.[7]

For the past several days, workmen had been seen on the *Ivanhoe*, apparently plugging the holes in her side. This could mean only one thing: the rebels were preparing to pull her into the bay; a move Farragut would not allow. It had now been three weeks since the steamer had grounded, and the possibility that she still might be salvaged was intolerable. Summoning Lt. Cdr. L. H. Newman, commander of the gunboat *Pembina*, to his cabin, the admiral handed him a set of written instructions that explained, step-by-step, what he wanted him to do. "If there are persons on board, range up as close as you can with safety and fire into her with all your battery on that side, then take a hawser to the vessel and make it fast to the hawser on her port quarter at the water's edge, cut it [the steamer's hawser] below your own, and heave away on board the gunboats and try to get her off. If you do not start her, then fire two broadsides into her and then send a boat with a boarding gang to destroy her with fire, but if you are supposed by force, then run round in a circle, firing in broadside until you are satisfied she is destroyed."[8]

As Farragut and Newman were discussing how to solve the *Ivanhoe* problem, Brigadier General Asboth, the Union commander at Pensacola, had just solved a problem of his own. At daylight that morning, with a mixed force of cavalry and infantry numbering eleven hundred men, he had attacked and captured the rebel outpost at Gonzales, fifteen miles north of Pensacola. As a secondary mission, he had been told by Canby to "look out for" a mounted column from Sherman's army, "which may be compelled to descend to Pensacola about the 20th to 25th."[9]

Although most of the defenders had escaped, eight prisoners, seventeen horses, twenty-three head of cattle, and a large quantity of quartermaster stores, commissary provisions, and ammunition were captured by Asboth's command. The stores and supplies that could not be taken were burned and the fortifications destroyed. Before leaving, the general learned from one of the prisoners that the Union column he had been ordered to "look out for" had—after destroying the Montgomery and West Point Railroad near Pollard—turned around and headed back north.[10]

Hearing this, Asboth decided to push on and destroy the Perdido River trestle—three hundred yards long—west of Pollard. With this accomplished, he would return "between Perdido River and Mobile Bay, and capture the rebel camps (Withers and Powell), and recrossing the Perdido at Nuenece's [*sic*] Ferry, return to Barrancas." However, after advancing several miles on the Perdido Station road, and fighting a small skirmish near Pine Barren Bridge, Asboth sent a dispatch to his assistant adjutant general at Fort Barrancas, informing him that he had received from

three reliable sources positive information that all the available rebel force had been sent from Mobile up the railroad to intercept my command, and that Col. H. Maury with his regiment, the Fifteenth Confederate Cavalry, had already arrived with an additional mounted force, in all 1,300 strong, and a light battery of six pieces, with all of the militia called out along the whole line and at Pollard.

At this juncture, there being no more prospect of meeting Sherman's raiders, and seeing my own small infantry force closely watched in front and right with a superior cavalry force before me, I deemed it proper to return and be contented at present with the success already achieved.[11]

Taking counsel of his fears, Asboth decided to call it a day and return to Fort Barrancas. He would leave destruction of the Perdido railroad trestle for another day.

As Asboth's expedition was returning to Barrancas, sixty-five miles to the west, Cdr. T. H. Stevens was returning from his reconnaissance east of Fort Morgan. He found that the beach there would be well suited for an amphibious landing, depending on the weather and the availability of shallow-draft lighters for the artillery. The troops could be brought ashore in boats and landed within twenty yards of the beach.[12]

At his Julia Street headquarters in New Orleans, Canby had finally come to the realization that he did not have enough troops to attack Mobile and, at the same time, hold the Rio Grande, Arkansas, and Union-occupied Louisiana. In a letter to Halleck, he informed him that with the exception of twelve hundred men at Brazos Santiago, he had ordered Texas to be abandoned. In addition, he told the army's chief of staff that he had "authorized the enlistment of colored troops from the plantations in this department. These men will be taken for garrison purposes and the number taken from each plantation so limited as to interfere as little as possible with its cultivation."

Canby also reminded Halleck that several thousand troops were still at New Orleans waiting to join the 19th Corps in Virginia. "I regret this delay," he continued, "but it is occasioned by circumstances beyond my control. All the seaworthy transportation within reach has been taken up and the transportation ordered by you from New York comes in very slowly." In telling Halleck this, Canby must have recognized that the rebels believed these troops were destined for Mobile and were working day and night to strengthen the city's fortifications, particularly the Lower Defense Line. It was, therefore, important that the Mobile operation be executed as soon as possible.[13]

Off Mobile, Cdr. T. H. Stevens was putting the finishing touches on his plan to capture the rebel picket that patrolled the beach opposite the

Oneida's night blockade station, four miles east of Fort Morgan. After dark, two officers and ten men would be taken ashore with muffled oars. The boats would return to the *Oneida*, leaving the party to conceal themselves behind the dunes, which were about a hundred feet from the water at that point. The officers would be armed with Colt revolvers and swords; the men, with Sharp's rifles, bayonets, swords, and forty rounds of ammunition.[14]

At 9:00 P.M. the *Oneida*'s gig and second cutter landed the party and returned to the ship. Once ashore, Lt. Charles S. Cotton positioned the men behind the dunes and settled down to wait for the patrol, usually a single horseman. Five hours later, the rider, a private in the 7th Alabama Cavalry, had been captured, as well as a lieutenant and three privates whose picket camp he was forced to reveal. By 2:30 A.M. the captors were back on board the *Oneida* with the hapless prisoners, who after interrogation, would be sent to the provost marshal at Pensacola and then to a Northern prison. One of these was Pvt. C. T. Pope who, in a letter to his wife written ten days earlier, told her that he saw the Yankee gunboats "every day when on post," and would "come to see you and the babies soon as I can. Your husband until death. Pray for me every week." At 6:30 A.M. the *Oneida* weighed anchor and steamed for Pensacola with the prisoners.[15]

BY SUNDOWN ON 23 JULY, THE 15TH CONFEDERATE CAVALRY, THE 22D Artillery acting as infantry, and Toben's Battery had moved into a blocking position at the bridge over Pine Barren Creek, six miles north of Gonzales. The enemy's location was thought to be somewhere to the south. A soldier in the 22d later described the confusion: "We arrived at Pine Barren Creek on Saturday, and formed line of battle almost immediately, as the cavalry reported the enemy advancing. All were stripped for a fight, and very anxious to see some free American citizens of African descent come in sight, that we might try our new Enfield rifles."[16]

Back in Mobile, the city had been stripped of troops to meet threats in Georgia, Mississippi, central Alabama, and now from Pensacola. Dabney Maury, who was scheduled to take command of the Department of Alabama, Mississippi, and East Louisiana in four days, would later write: "When I was assigned to command of this department . . . it had been stripped of most of its troops to strengthen the Army of Tennessee. In

Mobile there was not a soldier except the artillery garrisons of the forts and bay batteries."[17]

With the arrival of an ironclad off Fort Morgan, the capture of the beach picket, and the raid from Pensacola, no doubt to cut the railroad between Mobile and Montgomery, Maury sensed that an attack was imminent. He hoped it would be against the Lower Defense Line, which for the moment was in a better position to repulse the enemy than the city. At Fort Morgan, General Page also believed the enemy was about to attack. Accordingly, he put his command on full alert and ordered the evacuation of all women and children. As a precaution, he withdrew the two infantry companies at the Bon Secour saltworks into the fort, and ordered the cavalry at Camps Withers and Powell to deploy and intercept the Pensacola raiders should they attempt to return through Baldwin County.[18]

Within Fort Morgan, the work of building traverses to protect the gunners from shrapnel and enfilading fire was accelerated, a recommendation von Scheliha felt was essential if the fort were to withstand a prolonged siege. In the main channel opposite Fort Morgan, the work of planting torpedoes continued. At Fort Gaines, a shortage of impressed labor had temporarily brought work almost to a halt, although the construction of a new wharf for landing troops and supplies continued. At Fort Powell, however, there was more activity: The front facing Mississippi Sound was being strengthened, and booms and *chevaux de frise* were being placed around the entire work to prevent attacks by boats.[19]

Scheduled to join Hood in four days, Lt. Gen. Stephen D. Lee, who was still in Montgomery, had been directed by the president, through Bragg, to get a message to Kirby Smith, ordering him to mount a diversionary attack in Mississippi. Lee sent the dispatch through Brig. Gen. St. John Liddell, in Woodville, Mississippi, telling him to send it across the river to Smith, or if Smith could not be located, to one of his subordinates, Generals Taylor, Walker, or Polignac. The message read: "Inform General E. K. Smith that the President orders a prompt movement of Lieutenant-General Taylor and the infantry of his corps to cross the Mississippi. Such other infantry as can be spared by General Smith will follow as soon as possible. General Taylor on reaching this side of the Mississippi will assume command of the department."[20]

That same day, S. D. Lee sent Smith a second dispatch, emphasizing the urgency of the movement and the importance of bringing his "horses, mules, and harness" across. Supplies, he said, would be available for Taylor's troops "on this side of the Mississippi." Although Lee did not say what kind or quantity of supplies would be there, he was probably thinking of enough for nine or ten thousand men for a week or ten days, until they could be supplied regularly by the department's quartermaster.[21]

With Sherman knocking at the gates of Atlanta and the enemy preparing to move against northern Mississippi and Mobile, a diversionary strike by a strong force in Sherman's rear might force him to abandon the siege of Atlanta, as well as discourage the attack against Mobile and northern Mississippi.

CHAPTER 9

✦➤ ◄✦

Tecumseh Reaches Pensacola

THE LETTER TO GENERAL CANBY COULD NO LONGER BE POSTPONED. The New Orleans ironclads would arrive in less than a week, and Farragut had heard nothing from the army. Besides, there were signs that the weather would soon be worsening. "Time is very precious with us," he wrote Canby on 25 July, "and I can not urge too strongly upon you the necessity of bringing all your forces up into Mississippi Sound and landing a force in the rear of Fort Gaines." The navy could give the army "perfect protection" during the landing, and if Gaines were attacked first, he surmised only about a thousand men would be needed, compared with four thousand if both forts were besieged simultaneously.[1]

The capture of Fort Gaines, Farragut explained, was needed "to make my communications good." Vessels drawing eight feet could enter the bay from the Gulf through the narrow opening between the fort and the western end of the pile obstructions. Possession of Dauphin Island and Fort Gaines would hasten the fall of nearby Fort Powell and open a second shallow-draft passage into the bay from Mississippi Sound. Once communications with the outside were established, the fleet could assist the army in the reduction of Fort Morgan. The admiral also told Canby that five rebel pickets had been captured on the Gulf side of the fort "near the place we supposed you would land" and the beach there was "very good."

Having learned the day before of Asboth's premature return to Pensacola, and knowing of Canby's promise to provide the general with a cavalry regiment, Farragut expressed his belief that Asboth "would meet with defeat for want of horses and by having traitors in his midst, as we all have." Apparently the rebels knew about the raid before it left Barrancas. This, however, was not unusual; hardly a plan was made that did not get transmitted directly to the rebels, he added. With this said, Farragut closed his letter where it began, with a strong appeal to land a force on Dauphin Island as quickly as possible. At one time, the admiral had considered going in without the army, but this opportunity had passed long ago. The navy was now at the mercy of the army, and time was slipping away.

The navy, however, would be ready when the army finally appeared. Five gunboats, under the command of Lt. Cdr. J. C. P. De Krafft, would cover the landing on Dauphin Island and assist with debarking the troops. With this accomplished, the flotilla—to be known as the Mississippi Sound Division—would move up and shell Fort Powell as the fleet entered the bay. Outside, Lt. Cdr. Edward C. Grafton of the gunboat *Genessee* would cover the Gulf landing east of Fort Morgan with six gunboats and help ferry the troops ashore. His division also would bombard Fort Morgan as the fleet ran in.[2]

On 26 July, Farragut reported to Welles that he was prepared to run in as soon as the army and the New Orleans monitors arrived. Although he did not know when the army would appear, the monitors would be ready in three or four days. All his vessels had been coaled, thanks to the timely arrival of the coal ship *New England*—but coal, as well as ice for the sick and wounded, would be continual problems. His fleet surgeon had been "untiring in getting things prepared at Pensacola, and the army and sanitary commission have been very accommodating to us," he told the secretary. The *Manhattan* was still anchored in the main channel near Sand Island, the admiral told Welles, with "vessels to look out for her." Lieutenant Ely wrote in his diary that a "double-netted gunboat is constantly anchored near us, and at night she takes up a position ahead [so] that if any torpedoes are sent us by the enemy they might blow her up and leave us in safety, at the expense of annihilation of our shield."[3]

For the past several days a stiff wind and rough seas had prevented the sounding and buoying of Sand Island Channel, where the *Manhattan* and other monitors would be anchored. On 27 July the wind abated somewhat, and during the early afternoon Flag Lieutenant Watson and a boat crew from the *Hartford* were towed inshore to sound the Sand Island and Pelican Island channels. By 6:30 P.M. only a third of the area had been covered. Another two days would be needed to finish the work.[4]

Farragut was taking no chances. As recently as two weeks before, a credible informant had reported that "a small torpedo steamer, built upon the latest and most approved plan, very recently left Selma for Mobile. She makes 7 knots an hour, sinks with great facility, and is intended to act upon the blockading squadron." The sinking of the *Housatonic* weeks ago by the *Hunley*, a rebel submarine built in Mobile, added plausibility to this report, and the admiral would much rather lose a gunboat than an iron-clad.[5]

Hardly was the ink dry on Farragut's letter to Welles when he received a dispatch from Canby—what he hoped was an answer to his letter of the previous day pleading for an attack on Fort Gaines. The first sentence must have caused the admiral's hazel eyes to flash with the "fire and spirit" for which he was known. "The troops will be ready to leave here at the same time the monitors do, and I will send them on seagoing vessels, to conceal the destination as much as possible. I will send about 2,000 men, which will be sufficient to secure the occupation of Dauphin Island, and by the time that you are ready I will be able to send an additional force for operations about Fort Morgan." This force, he said, would number about three thousand.[6]

Embarrassed that the army was holding up the Mobile attack, Canby told the admiral that Kirby Smith was moving down the Red River, proba-bly "with a view of crossing the Mississippi." This was indeed a serious threat and Canby apparently wanted the admiral to know why he was hav-ing difficulty scraping up enough troops for the Mobile operation. But the troops had been found and, although small in number, would be ready in a few days.[7]

IN NEW ORLEANS, LT. CDR. GEORGE PERKINS, CAPTAIN OF THE monitor *Chickasaw*, stopped for a few minutes amid the hustle and bustle of activity around him to write his mother. "I shall go to sea to-morrow night, and as soon as the iron-clads arrive off Mobile the fight will come off." He told her that he was very busy and at the moment was writing among a "lot of mechanics who are working as fast as they can to get the ship in order"—everywhere there was pandemonium and confusion. He would, however, write again on the way to Mobile. Perkins then told his mother that the battle would be over when she received his letter, and hoped she would not worry. He then selected his words very carefully, for these might be the last he would ever write: "Remember, if I get killed it will be an honorable death, and the thought should partly take away your sorrow."[8]

While Perkins was writing his mother, another race with time was under way 167 miles southeast of Pensacola. In tow of the gunboat *Eutaw*, the *Tecumseh* sent fans of white spray high into the air as her massive hull smashed through the green swells of the Gulf of Mexico. At 3:00 P.M. the lookout atop the turret noticed that the *Augusta*, one of the gunboats accompanying the *Tecumseh*, had hoisted the *Tecumseh*'s distinguishing numbers, an indication that a signal would soon follow. When it came, Commander Craven knew that he had a serious problem on his hands: The *Augusta*'s engines were pounding violently and could not be repaired at sea.

This problem had plagued the *Augusta* since leaving Hampton Roads and had now grown worse. Recognizing the gravity of the situation, Craven sent John Farron, his chief engineer, to inspect the damage. When Farron returned, he reported that the situation was indeed critical. Without hesitation, Craven ordered the *Eutaw* to continue towing the *Tecumseh* to Pensacola and the *Augusta* to follow along as best she could. Under tow and using her own engines, the *Tecumseh* might be able reach the navy yard in thirty-six hours—with luck.[9] The *Eutaw*'s engines had also been damaged by the long journey and might break down at any time. To Craven, a professional naval officer, the thought of missing the battle was intolerable. Already he knew how he would fight the *Tennessee:* The contest would be at close range, hull touching hull; and if necessary, the *Tecumseh* would "grapple" with the big ram and "capture" her. It could be one of history's great ship-to-ship combats.[10]

Off Mobile, tired and worried, Captain Drayton was winding up the day with a letter to Commodore Palmer in New Orleans. The *Chickasaw* and *Winnebago* were about to leave for Mobile and, as yet, he told Palmer, there was no word from the army. In his letter of 26 July, Canby had told Farragut that the army would leave when the monitors left. "We have heard nothing more of the Army," Drayton wrote, "which as usual moves very slow indeed, not appearing to see the value of time." Continuing, he told Palmer that bad weather would now prevent a successful landing on the Gulf beach in the rear of Fort Morgan, but the plan to attack Fort Gaines from Mississippi Sound was feasible and "would answer our purpose just as well." But without the army, he implied, there would be no battle.[11]

General Maury now had full responsibility for operations in the Department of Mississippi, Alabama, and East Louisiana. After assuming command on 26 July, he had met with General Bragg in Montgomery on 27 July to discuss the strategic situation: the movement of Confederate troops from Kirby Smith's command to Mississippi; the most effective use and dispersion of the department's meager resources; pending attacks on Mobile and North Mississippi; and stepped-up efforts by the enemy to cut Hood's supply lines. At the meeting, he no doubt learned from Bragg the details of Hood's recent foray against Sherman, the second since assuming command ten days ago.[12]

That same afternoon, General Maury boarded the cars for Meridian to meet with Maj. Gen. Nathan B. Forrest but halfway there was called back to Montgomery. Sherman's right flank was moving southward around Atlanta, apparently in an attempt to cut the railroad that connected Atlanta with Montgomery and Macon, and Maury needed to be on hand to monitor the situation. Before returning, he found time to write Forrest, a communiqué that expressed complete confidence in the general's judgment and gave him a free hand to fight the enemy as he saw fit.

> *I hoped to see you to-morrow, but am unexpectedly compelled to return to Montgomery. I wish you to take charge of the defense of the northern part of Mississippi. The prairie country appears to me to be the first object of your care. I know how disproportionate the forces at present under your command are to those which we understand the enemy has, but it will be difficult for him to advance far into the country while you are before him. I would not, if I could, undertake to prescribe to you any plan of operations. I wish you to understand that I entrust to you the conduct of affairs, and desire only to be able to aid you effectively with the means of executing your own views.[13]*

Although affairs were touch-and-go, Maury was not despondent. With Forrest responsible for northern Mississippi and Hood aggressively defending Atlanta, he could turn his attention to Mobile, and the attack that was certain to come. On the Lower Defense Line, Fort Morgan was becoming stronger each day, but at the expense of Forts Gaines and Powell. A temporary shortage of impressed labor had brought work almost to a standstill on Dauphin Island and at Grant's Pass. The loss of Gaines and Powell would be serious indeed, but the loss of Morgan would be catastrophic, for it would end the blockade runner trade and give the enemy control of Mobile Bay, thus bringing the city within range of Farragut's heavy guns and Canby's troop transports.[14]

At the Selma Naval Works, Cdr. Catesby ap R. Jones believed that Farragut would be repulsed if he attempted to run past Fort Morgan. Fire "slowly and deliberately," aiming at the waterline of the wooden ships and the turret base of the ironclads, he wrote Page. "In the present temper of the people," Jones continued, "I am convinced that they would only be content with an obstinate resistance." To stress this point, Jones closed with sobering words for his uncle: "Be assured that in case of accident I will do whatever I can for your family, but trust there will be no occasion and that you may be long spared for them."[15]

IN MAY, DUE TO STRONG CURRENTS, THE FAILURE OF THE ROPE AND timber obstructions in the main ship channel had left only torpedoes to block the thirteen hundred yards between the clear channel opposite Fort Morgan and the West Bank. Although a shortage of labor had slowed the work of strengthening the land fortifications on Dauphin Island and Grant's Pass, the number of torpedoes in the main ship channel had continued to increase, growing from 86 in June to 180 by the end of July. There was a weakness, however: The torpedoes were anchored in three lines in quincunx order, and should the enemy's vessels cross the field at an angle, the distance between torpedoes would increase, allowing some vessels to enter the bay unscathed.[16]

The primary function of the torpedoes was to force the enemy's vessels through the clear channel opposite Fort Morgan, exposing them at point-blank range to thirty-three heavy guns, including the broadsides of the Confederate squadron and the *Tennessee*'s ram. This channel also served a second important purpose: it allowed blockade runners to enter and leave the bay, and the Confederate squadron to enter the Gulf and engage the enemy fleet.

On 26 July, Godfrey, captain of the blockade runner *Denbigh*, had edged his vessel through the clear channel and into the Swash Channel off Mobile Point. From there he crept eastward along the Gulf beach, the blackness of the night and the vessel's gray color allowing him to clear the last blockader undetected. Having done this, Godfrey rang four bells, the signal for full speed. Below in the engine room, as the throttle valves were opened, the *Denbigh* lunged forward and was soon making fifteen knots.

Fort Morgan today (Dauphin Island in the distance).
ANDY DEES

On 28 July, Godfrey would mark his seventh run from Havana to Mobile and back, the regularity of his trips winning the *Denbigh* a sobriquet: the Packet. With luck, he would reach Havana in two days and with more luck would be on his way back to Mobile in a week or ten days with another cargo of war material for the South's embattled armies.[17]

In Georgia, another battle was raging—the third since Hood had relieved Johnston. Fierce fighting was reported southwest of Atlanta, as the enemy attempted to cut the city's rail communications there. Although the fighting was still developing, Hood had apparently once again foiled an attempt to flank his army. In Virginia, the situation was even better. Lee had Grant stalemated outside Richmond and Petersburg, and Early was again preparing to ford the Potomac and spread havoc. Sherman's invasion of Georgia and the possible loss of Atlanta had depressed the Southern people, but Hood was now holding Atlanta as Lee was holding Richmond. If the South's two largest cities could be held until November—only three months away—the North might replace Lincoln with a peace president, and the South would gain independence.[18]

The failure to capture Atlanta, however, would increase the probability of an attack on Mobile, an axiom understood by Maury, Page, and Buchanan, but not by the citizen soldiers at Fort Morgan, who lacked the experience of the professionals. Maj. James T. Gee, the post commander at Fort Morgan and a practicing surgeon before becoming an artillery officer, was one such doubter. He thought General Page overreacted by ordering all noncombatants away from the Lower Defense Line when the Yankee monitor arrived. "We are just as quiet as if the Monitor had never arrived," he wrote his wife on 28 July. "Captain Cary . . . comes down every day to join in condemning the stupidity of Old Gen. P. in causing us to send our wives off."[19]

Young Lieutenant Tarleton was also critical of Page, who had been a professional officer in both the old navy and the Confederate Navy before being transferred to the army as a brigadier general. "We have given the navy [referring to General Page] a pretty fair trial," he wrote his fiancée, "and it is time to send us someone who does not think a Federal ship of war invincible. I have noticed one peculiarity about our naval men here, from Admiral Buchanan down to the last midshipman and that is an unlimited capacity for getting excited. They fly off the handle at the shortest notice and on the slightest pretext."[20]

THE CRY "LAND HO!" BROKE THE MONOTONOUS SPLASH OF THE *Eutaw*'s paddle wheels. To the north, a bright sheen hovered above the sugar-white sand of Santa Rosa Island. Soon the dark, low silhouette of Fort Pickens was visible; across the bay, the buildings and machine shops of the Pensacola Navy Yard slowly appeared. The approaching pilot boat, however, was the center of attention: Had the battle been fought? If so, had the Union won or lost? The pilot would know. Commander Craven had not come this far nor pushed his crew this hard to spend the rest of the war anchored in Pensacola Bay. It would, of course, take three or four days to prepare the vessel for combat, considering the wear and tear resulting from an open-sea voyage of two thousand miles. Surely if the fleet had not gone in, the admiral would be willing to wait a few days now that another powerful ironclad was about to join his fleet.[21]

The news was good: the battle had not been fought. By 7:00 P.M. on 28 July, the *Tecumseh* was at anchor in Pensacola Bay, opposite the navy yard. In sight were three sloops of war from the fleet off Mobile—the

Lackawanna, Ossipee, and the screw steamer *Galena,* now without the armor that had originally clad her hull. All were hurriedly dismantling superfluous spars and masts, sand-bagging machinery, loading stores, and topping off bunkers. Everywhere dispatch boats, tugs, coal barks, and lighters threaded their way through the harbor, imparting to the scene a feeling of great urgency. Once the *Tecumseh* was anchored and her fires banked, Commander Craven and Lt. Cdr. Charles Blake of the *Brooklyn* called on Capt. John B. Marchand of the *Lackawanna,* Farragut's senior officer in Pensacola.[22]

Craven and Marchand were old friends, both having served in the navy for almost forty years. No doubt Marchand briefed Craven on the situation off Mobile and cautioned him that the battle was near at hand, possibly within a week, and he should make an effort to join the fleet as soon as possible.[23] That night aboard the *Galena,* Paymaster Clerk Hults recorded in his diary an observation that reflected the feelings of the hundreds of officers and men who had witnessed the arrival of the ironclad as they worked to prepare their vessels for the great battle: "The 'Eutaw' arrived today with the Monitor 'Tecumseh' a one turreted craft carrying two 15 in. guns. The arrival of this monitor & the 'Manhattan,' indicate that the beginning of the end cannot be far off."[24]

Part Two

THE END OF THE BEGINNING

CHAPTER 10

✦➤ ◀✦

Girding for Battle

AT DAYBREAK, 29 JULY, LOW GRAY CLOUDS COVERED THE SKY AND A mild eight-knot wind blew from the northeast. At midafternoon, when the *Richmond* rounded the western tip of Santa Rosa Island and entered the sheltered waters of Pensacola Bay, the surface was as smooth as ice. Dead ahead was the navy yard: a "most miserable appearance," in one officer's opinion. Acting Master Robert Ely of the *Manhattan* had written in his journal:

> *All the most important buildings have been entirely destroyed, and the whole place looks like one vast [pile] of brick and mortar, broken masonry and charred timbers, all lying around in every direction. Only one of the stone houses remains standing. This is now occupied by the Commandant and officers of the Yard as quarters. A large amount of equipment is also stored there. Many of the shade trees are still living and the gravel walks are comparatively uninjured. A large temporary naval hospital has been erected within the limits of the Yard and is now occupied by the sick and disabled of the fleet. The two villages outside the Yard are by all comparison the most miserable and uncomfortable I ever saw. The houses are built of pine wood with no vestige of lath or plaster. Some of them have no windows. The natives are dirty, lazy and contemptible. Most of them are employed in the Navy Yard.[1]*

Ahead, as the *Richmond* passed Fort Pickens and Fort Barrancas, the sloops *Lackawanna* and *Ossipee* and the screw steamer *Galena* could be seen anchored off the navy yard—and beyond, the low, dark silhouette of the *Tecumseh*. Tugs and barges were delivering coal and ammunition to the wooden vessels and returning to shore with "spars, sails, and unnecessary hamper." Aboard the vessels, "chain cables were 'faked' or hung up and down their sides abreast of the engines and boilers, and bags of sand were placed along the decks wherever possible, in order to protect the vitals of the ship. In short every expedient which ingenuity or experience could suggest was resorted to, to protect the vessels and their crews from shot and shell, splinters and falling spars."[2]

But approaching the *Tecumseh* closer, Captain Jenkins noticed a conspicuous lack of activity. He had been sent to Pensacola by the admiral to expedite the departure of the ironclad and the other vessels that were there preparing for the battle. There were problems at the navy yard, and the admiral did not want to leave the responsibility for preparing his vessels solely with Commo. William Smith, the yard's commandant. A stickler for paperwork, understaffed, and beset by threats of attack from the rebels, the commandant was overburdened by the workload and his responsibilities.[3]

Satisfied that the work of stripping and shell-proofing the *Richmond* and other vessels of the fleet was progressing satisfactorily, Jenkins called for a boat to take him to the *Tecumseh*. Having learned of Craven's problems, Jenkins wanted to talk with him and inspect the monitor. He was, of course, familiar with her sister ship, the *Manhattan*, which had been with the fleet off Mobile since 20 July, so he was not unacquainted with her design.[4]

Aboard the monitor, Commander Craven was frustrated; he had not pushed his crew day and night for two thousand miles to be confronted with paperwork and bureaucratic regulations fifty-five miles from Mobile. Alerted that a boat from the *Richmond* was approaching, Craven went topside to greet the visitor. Recognizing Jenkins, he invited him to go below for a frank discussion about the lack of cooperation he was getting from Commodore Smith. The two officers entered the *Tecumseh* through a hatch on the port side of the forward gun deck and descended by a ladder to the berth deck, the next deck down.[5]

From the foot of the ladder, they entered a passageway that led forward into the wardroom, where the thermometer registered ninety degrees. As with all monitors of the *Tecumseh*'s class, the wardroom paint was stained with iron rust and coal tar; everything was dirty and smelled bad; and the crew was demoralized. The officers' cabins were located on either side of the wardroom, with Craven's relatively spacious quarters—cabin, stateroom, and pantry—located between these and the windlass and boatswain's storage rooms in the bow.[6]

Once in his quarters, Craven told Jenkins that the *Tecumseh* was in trouble; his crew was fatigued by the long voyage from Hampton Roads and, without help, could not possibly load the more than two hundred tons of coal needed to top off the vessel's bunkers. Several crewmen, including the chief engineer, had been sent ashore to the hospital and others were likely to follow. After dropping anchor yesterday, he and Captain Marchand had visited Commodore Smith of the navy yard and asked for help, but so far none had arrived.[7]

Aware of the work that remained to be done to prepare the *Tecumseh* for battle, Jenkins asked Craven to give him a quick tour of the vessel. Together they walked aft to the bulkhead that separated the officers' quarters from the turret chamber and passed through an iron bulkhead door. The chamber was filled with machinery that rotated the turret above. In the cramped and dimly lit space, the heat was stifling.[8]

Continuing aft, Craven and Jenkins passed through another bulkhead door and entered the crew's quarters, where many crewmen, fatigued and sick, were sleeping or resting in hammock berths. This compartment also contained the galley, dispensary, officer and crew heads, miscellaneous storage rooms, and the vessel's ready-access powder bin and magazine. A ladder provided access to a hatch on the gun deck.[9] On the orlop deck, below the officers' quarters, turret chamber, and crew's quarters, were more storage compartments: water tanks, shell rooms, powder bins, and turret machinery. The bulkhead door aft of the crew's quarters led to the coal bunkers, fireroom, and engine compartment.

Passing through the door, Craven and Jenkins descended six steps to the orlop deck. From there they entered a passageway, flanked by two coal bunkers, that led to the fireroom, where the boilers were stoked. Continuing, they came to the engine room and the *Tecumseh*'s two 320-horsepower Ericsson steam engines. In the dim light, they could make out a dozen men tending the boilers, reading gauges, and adjusting valves—a skeleton crew, compared with when the vessel was under way. Now, with fires banked and steam pressure down, the temperature was hovering around

100 degrees, well under the 135 to 138 degrees when the vessel was under way. Aft of the engines was the ironclad's massive propeller shaft, a condenser that converted saltwater to fresh, and the pumps that fed water to the boilers and freshwater tanks.[10]

From the engine compartment, Jenkins followed Craven up a ladder and through a hatch to the after gun deck. Walking forward they saw a dinghy, the vessel's huge armored smokestack, two ten-oared cutters, the galley smokestack, ventilator hatch, several coal chutes, ash hatches, the berth deck hatch, and the vessel's enormous turret. Immediately forward of the turret was the wardroom hatch, where they had entered the vessel, and beyond that, near the bow, the anchor hoister.

The turret, twenty-one feet in diameter and nine feet high, was entered or vacated by two roof hatches connected to the deck by a ladder attached to the side of the turret. Climbing one of the ladders to the turret roof, the two officers descended by ladder into the turret, where they saw the *Tecumseh's* two 15-inch Dahlgrens resting on slide carriages. Capable of firing a 440-pound projectile, these guns were indeed impressive. The gun ports through which they fired also could be used to enter and leave the turret, but only if the guns were withdrawn and the port-stoppers lifted.[11]

The two hatches they saw on the turret floor connected the turret with the chamber below. Through these hatches projectiles and powder from the ready magazines and powder bin were hoisted to the turret. Steam from the vessel's boilers powered an engine in the chamber that could rotate the turret 360 degrees around a fixed shaft, providing the guns with an unlimited field of fire. The turret complement numbered twenty men and two officers, one of which was the *Tecumseh's* second-in-command, Lt. John W. Kelley.[12]

Climbing a removable ladder attached to the inside wall of the turret, Craven and Jenkins entered the pilothouse, which was located atop the turret on the fixed shaft that did not rotate. Inside the turret, space was cramped—there was room for only two people. Vision was limited by narrow slits in the pilothouse wall. Also, getting in and out was impossible unless the turret roof was aligned with openings in the pilothouse floor, and the portable ladder was put in place by someone in the turret.

Displacing twenty-one hundred tons, the *Tecumseh* was smaller than the *Richmond's* twenty-seven hundred, but her two 15-inch cannon, her armor, and her revolving turret represented advantages Jenkins's big sloop could not match. The ironclad's lack of reserve buoyancy, however, was cause for concern. A few hundred tons of water in the bilge could sink her.[13]

Returning to the *Richmond*, Jenkins was worried: Much remained to be done before the *Tecumseh* would be ready to join the fleet; her most urgent need was coal and extra men to assist with loading it. Farragut had given Drayton orders to expedite the departure of the fleet's vessels at Pensacola, especially the *Tecumseh*, and time was running out. In a message to Jenkins, dated 3 August, Drayton was brutally frank: "If you can get the *Tecumseh* out tomorrow, do so; otherwise I am pretty certain that the admiral won't wait for her."[14]

THE TWENTY-NINTH OF JULY HAD BEEN A BUSY DAY FOR GENERAL Maury, the commander of the Department of Alabama, Mississippi, and East Louisiana. It had started with a telegram from General Page reporting that sixteen Union vessels were off the bar when the sun came up. Maury was not particularly disturbed about this, since it reflected no substantial increase since the first of the month. What was of concern, however, were the two double-turreted monitors being prepared for sea at New Orleans, and fresh intelligence that another single-turreted monitor had arrived at Pensacola. The question was not would there be an attack, but when.[15]

Elsewhere in the district, the enemy was unusually quiet. Hood had stopped Sherman short of Atlanta and prevented his cavalry columns from cutting the Macon railroad, Atlanta's principal supply route. In north Alabama and western Mississippi, enemy activity was confined primarily to small scouting and foraging expeditions. Lulls such as this, however, often presaged a move by the enemy.[16]

The next telegram Maury received came from the governor of Alabama, T. H. Watts. "Dear Sir" it began, "Please give an order to Col. L. C. Garland, commanding the corps of cadets, to remove the corps to Blue Mountain. I ordered him to report at Selma to commandant of post there. By the 5th day of August he will have 220 or 230. They are well-drilled boys from the University of Alabama."[17] Maury did not want to send sixteen- and seventeen-year-old boys into combat, but the growing shortage of manpower demanded it. Moreover, they had been trained by Capt. Charles H. Lumsden, a graduate of Virginia Military Institute, and reports indicated that the boys were eager to fight. Apparently, Governor Watts was under pressure to station troops at Blue Mountain where they could cover Selma and Montgomery if the enemy should stage another raid from north Alabama. Concurring, Maury wrote on the telegram: "Issue orders in accordance with the wish of Governor Watts" and sent it to his assistant adjutant general, Maj. D. W. Flowerree.[18]

The general now turned his attention to Mobile where he was convinced an attack was imminent. During the past several days, work on the city's fortifications and the Lower Defense Line had intensified due to the temporary impressment of several hundred slaves from various saltworks throughout the state. On the Lower Defense Line, where the first blow was likely to fall, Maury was reasonably satisfied with Fort Morgan's readiness and the strength of the torpedo field across the channel.[19]

He was not pleased, however, with the state of preparedness at Fort Gaines and Fort Powell—and at this critical moment he was under great pressure to return the more than three hundred Negroes who had been impressed from the Bon Secour saltworks. Salt was the primary ingredient for curing and preserving meat, a necessity on the home front as well as the battlefield. Parthenia Hague, a schoolteacher in Huntsville, Alabama, and thousands of other Southern women were now boiling down the brine left in barrels where salted pork had been stored. Even the salty soil under old smokehouses was used to reclaim salt. Maury, therefore, had no choice but to order von Scheliha to return the Negroes to Bon Secour.[20]

Von Scheliha's reports to Maury had indicated steady progress in strengthening Mobile's defenses, particularly on the Lower Defense Line. Regrettably, the obstructions placed in the main channel had been a failure, but the number of torpedoes there was approaching two hundred. A ship passing between the buoy that marked the torpedo field and the shore would be within 250 yards of "seven X-inch Columbiads, three VIII-inch guns, two 8-inch Blakeley rifles, two 7-inch Brooke rifles, some 6.4-inch rifles, several 32-pounders, and the rifle fire of sharpshooters." No vessel, Maury believed, could pass through this channel in daylight, and it was unlikely the enemy would try to navigate it during darkness. As for Forts Gaines and Powell, these could be strengthened once Fort Morgan was ready to withstand a siege.[21]

In New Orleans, Canby's Julia Street headquarters was bustling with activity. The twenty-four hundred troops selected for the attack on Fort Gaines had been scheduled to depart that day, 29 July, but two steamers had broken down, causing the operation to be postponed for twenty-four hours. The delay, however, was not without some benefit, for it would give General Granger, the expedition's commander, another day to oversee the myriad details associated with landing troops and artillery on a hostile shore, always a difficult and dangerous undertaking, even under the best of conditions.[22]

CHAPTER 11

⇥ ⇤

The Troops Embark

AT ALGIERS, ACROSS THE RIVER FROM NEW ORLEANS, CPL. HENRY W. Hart of the 2d Connecticut Light Battery was not sure where the troops were going. Virginia? Some place nearby? Hart believed the latter. "There is much speculation as to our raid or expedition," he wrote his wife. "We are to start on a transport, but one thing is certain, we are to come back for we leave all property and our clothing but what we wear."[1]

Orange Parret of the 77th Illinois Infantry Regiment, also uncertain of the expedition's destination, whiled away the time eating figs. "Was down to our favorite fig tree," he wrote in his diary on 29 July, "[and] filled myself with what I thought at the time was the most delicious fruit I ever went into a tree after." This idyllic scene was interrupted when four companies of the 3d Maryland Cavalry mutinied, protesting the regiment's new status as dismounted infantry. Three regiments, including fifty men from the 77th, were ordered to quell the riot, which was soon brought under control. "There is a convincing logic in the argument of bayonets," wrote a lieutenant of the 77th.[2]

A brigade of six infantry regiments, supported by engineers and artillerymen—two thousand troops—comprised the attack force. Granger's orders were to execute a ship-to-shore amphibious landing on the western end of Dauphin Island and to eventually attack Fort Gaines. Five transports, two barges, and a towed schooner would convey the troops to the island. A sixth steamer would carry supplies, stores, and a telegraph train; a seventh, General Granger's headquarters staff. The expedition would depart from two staging areas: Algiers on the Mississippi River, and

Lakeport on Lake Pontchartrain. After a rendezvous at Ship Island, the vessels would continue up Mississippi Sound to Dauphin Island, where the navy would cover the landing with gunfire and provide boats for getting the troops ashore.

Canby had assured Granger that three thousand more troops would be available as soon as they arrived from Texas. This would increase the expedition's strength to nearly five thousand; the number needed to invest Fort Morgan. In the meantime, he would have to manage with half that number. The capture of Fort Powell would be Farragut's responsibility, once the fleet entered the bay. With both Gaines and Powell in Union hands, his smaller vessels would have access to and from New Orleans and the logistical and maintenance facilities at Pensacola and Ship Island, each less than two days steaming time.[3]

Six weeks had passed since Canby first met with Farragut to plan an attack against Mobile. The objective then had been to move against the city with an army of twenty thousand, capture it, and thus provide Sherman with a secure base should he choose to strike out for the Gulf Coast after leaving Atlanta. This did not preclude a move into the interior of Alabama or Georgia in support of Sherman if the situation appeared favorable. However, as a result of Grant's order to Canby to send twenty thousand troops to the Army of the Potomac—at a time when the rebels in Louisiana were threatening to cross the Mississippi or move into Missouri—an attack on Mobile was not possible. Canby believed, nevertheless, that he could scrape up enough troops, in conjunction with Admiral Farragut's fleet, to attack the city's Lower Defense Line. If successful, this would close the bay to blockade runners and pin down troops that might otherwise be sent to reinforce Hood in Atlanta. In addition, a victory would give Union morale a much-needed boost. He wanted Farragut to know, however, that the rebels were concentrating "in considerable force along the west bank of the Atchafalaya" but did not know their intentions. Not wanting to be diffident now that Mobile was finally about to be attacked, he left to Farragut's imagination the consequences should the rebels cross the Mississippi and reinforce Hood.[4]

The war was not going well for the North. The presidential election was only three months away, and Abraham Lincoln was in trouble. If he should be defeated, the rebels would win the war by default. Hood's defense of Atlanta had many in the North worried. Since Johnston's removal Sherman had attacked Hood on three occasions, without success.

Apparently, the rebel general was defending Atlanta with the same resolve and skill with which Robert E. Lee was defending Richmond and Petersburg. The prospect of another stalemate did not bode well for Lincoln in the coming election. A victory at Mobile Bay could reverse the tide of despair now spreading throughout the North, or at least indicate that the tide had begun to turn.[5]

With the army ready to depart momentarily for Dauphin Island, Commodore Palmer, Farragut's divisional chief at New Orleans, had no choice but to order the *Chickasaw* and *Winnebago* to sea; the work of preparing the river monitors for open water would continue, if necessary, while en route to Mobile. By daylight, 29 July, both vessels had left New Orleans and were steaming for the mouth of the Mississippi River, where they would be towed by the gunboats *Metacomet* and *Tennessee* across the Gulf to Ship Island, and from there up Mississippi Sound to the fleet off Mobile.[6]

However, no sooner had the *Chickasaw* departed New Orleans than her wheel ropes parted, prompting Lieutenant Commander Perkins, to send a dispatch back to Palmer: "I would respectfully report the steering gear of this vessel unsafe and unapplicable. I have been compelled to anchor in consequence of the wheel ropes stretching and allowing the propeller to strike the rudder. The whole steering gear, in my opinion, is wrong." Perkins then added: "I will remedy the evil, as far as possible, in an hour or two and proceed to my destination." Controlling his anger, he closed with a request: "May I beg that you will forward the spare wheel ropes as soon as possible."[7]

Off Mobile, Farragut had given Drayton the go-ahead to publish General Order No. 11, the second general order pertaining to the forthcoming attack. Included were three items not covered in General Order No. 10.

So soon as the vessels have passed the fort and kept away N.W., they can cast off the gunboats at the discretion of the senior officer of the two vessels, and allow them to proceed up the bay to cut off the enemy's gunboats that may be attempting to escape up to Mobile.

There are certain black buoys placed by the enemy from the piles on the west side of the channel across it toward Fort Morgan. It being understood that there are torpedoes and other obstructions between the buoys, the vessels will take care to pass to the eastward of the easternmost buoy, which is clear of all obstructions.

So soon as the vessels arrive opposite the end of the piles, it will be best to stop the propeller of the ship and let her drift the distance past by her headway and the tide, and those having side-wheel gunboats will continue on by the aid of their paddle wheels, which are not likely to foul with the enemy's drag ropes.

A fourth item, included in General Order No. 10, was repeated and clarified:

Should any vessel be disabled to such a degree that her consort is unable to keep her in her station, she will drop out of line to the westward and not embarrass the vessels next astern by attempting to regain her station. Should she repair damages, so as to be able to reenter the line of battle, she will take her station in the rear as close to the last vessel as possible.[8]

Having approved General Order No. 11, Farragut turned his attention to Sand Island Channel, the protected harbor where the monitors would be anchored. Having little reserve buoyancy, these vessels were vulnerable to heavy seas, particularly when at anchor. The spar buoys needed to mark the harbor had arrived from Pensacola and would be placed that day. The *Manhattan*, which was still anchored in the main channel, would be moved to the new anchorage the next day, where she would be joined by the other monitors as they came in.[9]

At 9:30 the next morning, Martin Freeman, the *Hartford*'s pilot, boarded the *Manhattan* and climbed into the pilothouse with the vessel's captain, Commander Nicholson. As the monitor weighed anchor and moved up the channel under her own power toward the anchorage, Lieutenant Ely wondered why the rebels did not fire on the vessel. "I certainly expected that they would open on us this morning as we steamed leisurely toward them," he wrote in his diary, "but not a shot was fired. The Rebel gunboats got under weigh when they saw us coming and moved about a mile up the bay, out of reach."[10]

Having received Canby's dispatch of 29 July that the troops had embarked for Dauphin Island, Farragut now learned from Commodore Palmer that the monitors were also on the way. The admiral was elated: everything was falling into place. In a letter to the commodore he wrote: "I am delighted to learn that the monitors have left New Orleans. I have the other in a snug harbor inside the Light-House Island. She went in this morning very handsomely, so that my fears are quieted. The *Tecumseh* has also arrived in Pensacola and will be ready by Monday for service. I am all ready so soon as the monitors arrive from New Orleans."[11] As of midday 30 July, though, the Dauphin Island landing force had not left New Orleans, nor had the *Chickasaw* and *Winnebago* left the Mississippi River. It had taken Canby an extra day to find replacements for the transports that had broken down, and the *Chickasaw*'s crew had taken longer than Perkins had estimated to repair the defective wheel ropes.[12]

Upriver at Algiers and Lakeport, however, the troops had been given orders to strike camp and were now preparing to embark for a still unidentified destination. Orange Parret recorded in his diary these last hours ashore: "Before leaving we went down the lane to our favorite fig tree. Steam Boats and Ships were running up and [down] the river in front of the city seemingly all in a hurry as though the errand of each was of much importance. We feel sad because we have to leave our fig grove perhaps forever."[13]

At Fort Morgan, Lieutenant Tarleton was disappointed that General Page would not fire on the monitor that came inside Sand Island earlier in the day. "She now lies there in a secure harbor," he wrote his fiancée, "attended by several wooden vessels which Gen'l P. will not fire on, though they are all in easy range of our guns." For some reason the general was not particularly worried about the monitor's change of anchorage even though she had moved menacingly up the main channel for more than a mile before turning to port and entering Sand Island Channel.[14]

During the past several days, Page had seen boats sounding the waters immediately north of Sand Island and surmised that the federals were planning to move the monitor there. To have fired on the monitor at a range of two and a half miles would have wasted ammunition. Although the 7-inch Brooke rifles at Fort Morgan and aboard Buchanan's squadron had a maximum range of between four and five miles; the effective range was two miles or less, depending on the force and direction of the wind. At maximum range a target could be missed by several city blocks.[15]

Nor was Commander Johnston, the *Tennessee*'s captain, overly concerned with the monitor's movements, although he did signal the gunboats to weigh anchor and await further orders. Johnston was more troubled about the *Tennessee*'s unprotected tiller chains, a vulnerability that needed to be corrected before Farragut attempted to enter the bay with his entire fleet. The chains ran across the afterdeck in uncovered grooves from the casemate to the tiller head—a distance of fifty-six feet—an arrangement highly susceptible to jamming in battle, which would render the *Tennessee* unmanageable.

Johnston, having written Buchanan about the problem, had just received a reply from the admiral informing him that Henry D. Bassett, a Mobile shipbuilder, would be down to correct the problem. "Constructor Bassett has instructions to examine the steering gear of the *Tennessee* and to remedy the defects you speak of if possible." Buchanan's "if possible" reflected his belief that the problem was indeed serious. Short of immobilizing the *Tennessee* for extensive hull alterations, little could be done quickly except to cover the grooves with one-inch iron sheathing, a remedy that would provide little protection against a 100-pound missile. But time was running out. The Union vessels were now removing their topmasts and upper yards, a sure sign that an attack was near.[16]

With the Northern presidential election turning on the question of "immediate peace or continued war," the defense of Atlanta and the Southern heartland was now the focus of Confederate strategy. Richmond and the Shenandoah Valley appeared safe, as did the Trans-Mississippi; holding on to Atlanta and the heartland was a substantial challenge. The key, President Davis believed, was a diversionary attack across the Mississippi River in Sherman's rear by troops from the Trans-Mississippi Department.[17]

During the period 18–23 July, Gen. Kirby Smith received three telegrams from the president directing him to send his subordinate, Lt. Gen. Dick Taylor, across the Mississippi with a force of nine to ten thousand and to assume command of the Department of Alabama, Mississippi, and East Louisiana. In turn, Maury would resume his old job in Mobile as commander of the District of the Gulf. Ordering Taylor to execute the crossing, Smith wrote: "You will proceed to Alexandria forthwith, and take command of the two Infantry Divisions in the Dist. of West La.; with these Divisions you will cross the Mississippi river with as little delay as possible. Upon reaching the nearest telegraph Station you will report to Richmond for further instructions."[18]

If successful, Taylor's movement could end the war. Diverting troops from the siege of Atlanta would enable Hood to hold on until the November election; also, Mobile might be spared an attack. Knowing that the effort would be a long shot, Smith made a passionate appeal to his western troops, aware that some would be reluctant to leave their native soil and go east: "Your president appeals to you," he began. "Your comrades east of the Mississippi River call to you for aid. Events are transpiring. A campaign is there progressing which is to decide the destiny of our country. It is up to you to give success to that campaign and to restore peace to our beloved land. Your mission is a holy one."[19]

Meanwhile, twenty-five miles north of the Potomac River, Chambersburg, Pennsylvania, was burning. Unlike the Mississippi River, the much smaller upper Potomac could be forded at numerous places. Having raided Washington and subsequently cleared the Shenandoah Valley of Yankees, General Early sent Brig. Gen. John McCausland back across the river with two brigades of cavalry and a horse artillery battery, a total of twenty-eight hundred men. Their destination: Chambersburg. Their mission: to collect reparations for the destruction of property in the Shenandoah Valley by Yankee general David Hunter. One such property was the Virginia Military Institute in Lexington, McCausland's alma mater. Also included were the home of Stonewall Jackson and Washington College, down the road from VMI. Having reached Chambersburg at daybreak on 30 July, McCausland demanded five hundred thousand dollars in currency, or one hundred thousand dollars in gold. When the demand was not met, McCausland set fire to the town, which soon turned into a roaring inferno. Satisfied that his mission had been accomplished, he gave the order to retire and headed for the Potomac.[20]

When Robert E. Lee detached General Early's corps from the Army of Northern Virginia during the second week of June, he had two objectives in mind: clear the Shenandoah Valley of the enemy and, if possible, cross the Potomac and threaten Washington. This would not only secure the valley's bountiful harvest of agricultural products but also force Grant to either divert troops from Richmond and Petersburg, or attack the fortifications there, hoping that Early would be recalled. Confident that he could repel such an attack without Early's corps, Lee would be satisfied with either move; bringing the war to Northern soil, however, would have the greater impact on the November presidential election. An editorial in the *Philadelphia Ledger*, published in the *Times Picayune* on 10 August, reflected the enemy's growing concern with the management of the war and the apparent ease with which the "loyal States above the Potomac have been invaded and plundered. It is not credible to a vigorous prosecution of the war that in its fourth year Maryland and Pennsylvania should be liable to invasion; nor is it necessary, with the means at our command, that it should be."[21]

Recognizing the effect that Early's diversionary raids were having on Northern morale and the defense of the Confederate capital, Jefferson Davis was anxiously awaiting news that Taylor had crossed the Mississippi and was threatening Sherman's rear. Not only would his presence in northern Mississippi, bolstered by Forrest's cavalry, divert troops from the siege of Atlanta, but it also might cancel or postpone an attack on Mobile, the loss of which would open the interior of Alabama to invasion, thus severing Atlanta's rail links with Meridian and Montgomery.

Davis, however, had reason to be optimistic as the summer came to an end, as did Sgt. Maj. Joseph McMurran of the 4th Virginia. "Now the prospect of peace encourages all," he wrote in his diary, "and even the people of Maryland say that Lincoln will now have to make a proposition for an armistice." Referring to Early's daring incursion across the Potomac in June, he called it "the boldest and most successful move of the war."[22]

CHAPTER 12

The River Monitors Arrive

As the first rays of daylight spread across the Gulf of Mexico on Sunday morning, 31 July, Fort Massachusetts could be seen dead ahead, a mere speck on the horizon. The twelve-hour open-water crossing from the mouth of the Mississippi River had been made without mishap. But the *Chickasaw* was still plagued with problems; now her engine was giving trouble. On 30 July, an hour below New Orleans, the vessel's tiller rope had parted, to be followed that afternoon by a leak in the condenser. Temporary repairs enabled the *Chickasaw* to join the *Winnebago* late that night above the passes, where they remained most of the thirtieth, waiting for a break in the weather before entering the Gulf.[1]

The break came that afternoon. At five o'clock with the wind dropping and two hours of daylight left, the monitors weighed anchor and steamed toward Pass à l'Outre Bar under their own power. Once in the Gulf they would be taken in tow by gunboats for the passage to Ship Island, a Union coaling and maintenance depot in Mississippi Sound. Midway across the bar an incident occurred that must have convinced Perkins that fate was conspiring to keep him from reaching Mobile. Leaving the pilothouse momentarily, he realized that the vessel had changed course slightly, and was about to run aground. With the agility of a circus acrobat, Perkins sprang back into the pilothouse, seized the wheel, and avoided the danger.

Convinced that the pilot had acted deliberately, Perkins drew his pistol and told him that if the *Chickasaw* "touched ground or anything else, he would blow his brains out." Fearing that the young officer might actually shoot him, the pilot defended himself by saying that the "bottom of the

river was lumpy and the best of pilots were liable to touch sometime."
Undaunted, Perkins told him to choose between trying to "serve the
Confederacy, and saving his life." The fact that the *Winnebago* also hit a
lump while crossing the bar was probably of no great solace to Perkins,
who, under increasing stress, was taking no chances with his reputation.[2]
By six o'clock on 30 July, with only two hours of daylight remaining, the
monitors had crossed the bar under their own power and entered the gulf.
There, the *Chickasaw* was taken in tow by the *Tennessee*, and the *Winnebago*
by the *Metacomet* for the one-hundred-mile crossing to Ship Island.

A lieutenant commander at twenty-seven, Perkins had volunteered for
the Mobile fight and, much to his credit, was given command of the *Chickasaw*. In a letter to his mother before leaving New Orleans, he conveyed
the weight of responsibility he was feeling: "I have a large command for
my rank, a crew of one hundred and forty-five men and twenty officers.
She carries four eleven-inch guns and has two turrets, and you can judge of
her power by the fact that it requires fifteen engines to work her."[3]

At anchor off Ship Island, still fifty miles from Mobile Bay, the *Chickasaw* could not continue until her engine and condenser were repaired,
which might take a full day or more. In the meantime, the *Winnebago* had
last been seen steaming up Mississippi Sound under her own power. At
six knots, she would reach the fleet off Mobile before dark. No one could
blame Perkins for the *Chickasaw*'s problems, but the humiliation of seeing his vessel's sister ship beat him to Mobile must have strengthened
his resolve to make a name for himself once the fighting started. Admiral
Porter's belief that the *Chickasaw* and *Winnebago* would "break to pieces
in the least swell" had been disproved, but the combat effectiveness of
these river monitors against the world's most powerful armored ram remained to be tested.[4]

Elsewhere, the army was at last moving. To the northwest, transports
loaded with troops were steaming across Lake Pontchartrain for a rendezvous at Ship Island with the transports that had gone down the Mississippi River. As the two forces converged, General Canby dispatched a letter from his headquarters in New Orleans to the expedition's commander,
Gen. Gordon Granger, who was with the Lake Pontchartrain task force
aboard his floating headquarters, the steamer *Laura:* "The force under
your command is not in number or appointment as large or as complete as
I designed to send, but I cannot increase it until after the troops from
Texas, or from points above, come within my reach. The present object is

simply that of cooperation with the Navy in the operations about to be undertaken by Admiral Farragut against the Rebel works in Mobile Bay." Canby went on to say that should the attack require a larger force or open the door for more extensive operations, he would support it as far as his means allowed.[5]

Aboard the army transports, the mood resembled a Sunday afternoon picnic rather than an amphibious landing on a hostile shore. One soldier wrote in his diary that the troops left New Orleans with a "holiday lightness of heart." Another, that they left the wharf with "three cheers for Mobile." The mood in the navy, however, was quite different. Lt. Oliver A. Batcheller, an officer aboard the *Lackawanna* off Mobile, wrote his father that the coming battle "may be one of the hardest fights of the war." Likewise, Ellsworth Hults, paymaster aboard the *Galena*, felt that the coming battle would be the bloodiest in naval history. This was seconded by one of the *Conemaugh*'s engineers, who predicted that "when the time comes, there will be a terrible loss of life."[6]

Aboard the *Hartford*, Farragut was informed that the *Chickasaw* and *Winnebago* had reached Ship Island, and the latter was now steaming up Mississippi Sound to join the fleet; the *Chickasaw* would follow the next day. With this good news, the admiral paused to write his son a last letter before the battle. "The monitors have all arrived, except the *Tecumseh*, and she is at Pensacola and I hope will be here in two days," he wrote. Farragut then expressed his belief that Admiral Buchanan and General Page, both of whom he knew personally, were making "great preparations" to receive the fleet, and would do everything in their power "to destroy us."[7]

Acknowledging the possibility of a repulse, the admiral added: "I hope to give them a fair fight, if I once get inside," and recognizing the possibility that he might be killed, he closed with a request: "Take care of your mother if I should go, and may God bless and preserve you both!" With this said, he once again turned his attention to the task at hand: to enter the bay with as many vessels and as few casualties as possible. He would be satisfied, he told his officers, "if the fleet got off with not more than one vessel in every three sunk," but believed the total would not exceed "two or three."[8]

Twenty miles to the west, the *Winnebago* was preparing to get under way for the last leg of her journey. At 1:30 P.M., with the *Hartford*'s pilot, Martin Freeman, at the helm and the dispatch boat *Cowslip* as a tender, the monitor entered the Gulf through Petit Bois Pass and steamed toward the fleet. At 6:00 P.M. the *Winnebago* was snugly anchored in Sand Island Channel near the *Manhattan*. Aboard the *Manhattan*, Acting Master Ely was impressed with the *Winnebago*'s appearance: "She has a temporary house built on deck and appears very much more comfortable than any of the ironclads I ever saw."[9]

The first of August began with rain and strong winds. This did not prevent the *Chickasaw* from leaving Ship Island at 6:00 A.M. in tow of the *Metacomet*, which had been sent back the previous night to hasten her arrival. As they steamed up the sound, Perkins called all hands to general quarters for gun drill. Not satisfied with what he observed, he kept the crews at work for two hours. By 11:00 A.M. the vessels had entered the Gulf through Petit Bois Pass, and by 1:30 P.M. the *Chickasaw* had anchored in Sand Island Channel with the *Winnebago* and *Manhattan*.[10]

During the afternoon, General Granger and his staff came aboard the *Hartford* for a meeting with Farragut. Granger informed the admiral that the army was aboard transports and would land on the west end of Dauphin Island in two days, on 3 August. Mortified, the admiral said the navy would not be able to go in until the fourth. Circumstances beyond his control had delayed the departure of the *Tecumseh* and some of the wooden vessels from the Pensacola Navy Yard, but he had been assured that they would be ready by the fourth. If not, he would go in with what he had.[11]

Following dinner, Farragut, Granger, and their staffs boarded the dispatch boat *Cowslip* and steamed into Sand Island Channel to inspect the *Chickasaw* and *Winnebago*. This was Farragut's first close-up look at the new, double-turreted river monitors. He was impressed, but deeply troubled to find that one of the *Winnebago*'s turrets was jammed. He also realized he would need to replace her commander, an acting volunteer lieutenant, with a more experienced career officer, as he had done with the *Chickasaw*.[12]

Having committed to enter the bay at daylight on 4 August, Farragut now had forty-eight hours to meet the deadline. Much would depend on Captain Jenkins, who was in Pensacola with the twofold mission of preparing his vessel, the *Richmond*, for the coming battle and expediting the departure of other vessels that would make the attack.

On 2 August, Drayton, who was in Pensacola, wrote Jenkins that the fleet was anxiously awaiting the *Richmond* and the other vessels at the navy yard, "especially the *Tecumseh*." "I don't believe the admiral will wait much

longer, but [will] go in with the force he has, which will get in if any can."
In a second letter to Jenkins that day Drayton again exhorted him to hasten the ironclad's departure. "Hurry up the *Tecumseh*, for the army will be
ready on Wednesday to land on Dauphin Island," he wrote. On that same
day, Farragut also wrote Jenkins, "General Granger was here and dined
with me yesterday; [he] expects to be able to land his forces tomorrow
in the sound; so you must all hurry up." Remembering the *Winnebago*'s
jammed turret, he asked Jenkins to send the fleet engineer, Mr. Shock, in
the first available vessel to correct the problem.[13]

During the afternoon, Farragut received a dispatch from Granger stating that all his transports had arrived in Mississippi Sound, with the exception of two. "Should the weather permit," he said, "I will commence to
disembark the troops at daylight to-morrow, provided the above transports
reach here in time."[14]

As DARKNESS DESCENDED ACROSS THE GULF, THE TELEGRAPH AT FORT
Morgan began to clatter again: It had been a frantic day for J. W. Crowell,
the fort's civilian telegrapher. A message from Pascagoula reported that at
6:00 P.M., eight of the transports seen in Mississippi Sound the day before
were now steaming to the eastward. This was the message General Page
had been waiting for. The enemy intended to make a landing on the
Alabama coast, probably on Dauphin Island, but Portersville and Mobile
Point could not be discounted.[15]

Earlier in the day, Page had telegraphed Brig. Gen. Edward Higgins,
Maury's successor at Mobile, that twenty-three vessels, including three
ironclads with steam up, could be counted offshore, and he believed that
an "attack may open at any time." At Fort Powell in Mississippi Sound, Lt.
Col. James M. Williams had written his wife about the arrival of the third
monitor. The "more the merrier—we will have a fine time," he wrote,
adding, "I will continue to write as long as my communications with the
city remain open—and when that is closed listen for the sound of my guns,
and rejoice in the news they bring you."[16]

At department headquarters in Meridian, Mississippi, General Maury
had little cause for rejoicing. He was faced with the difficult task of allo-
cating his limited resources to meet attacks not only at Mobile but also in
Mississippi and north Alabama. At La Grange, Tennessee, just across the
state line, the enemy had a force of fourteen thousand infantry and cav-

alry ready to invade North Mississippi; and in Alabama, three regiments of infantry and two of cavalry were reported moving down from Decatur. Three hundred twenty-five miles to the south, a large fleet, including transports, was poised to attack Mobile's Lower Defense Line.[17]

Maury first notified Secretary of War James A. Seddon of the situation in Alabama and Mississippi, although he expected little assistance from Richmond, except to hasten Kirby Smith's crossing of the Mississippi River. Aware of the plan, the enemy was reported to be concentrating at Morganza to prevent the movement, Maury told the secretary.[18] Having done this, Maury then sent a dispatch to the governor of Mississippi, explaining the enemy's dispositions and apparent intentions, and urging him to "energetically organize and put into the field every available man," adding that he had assigned the defense of north Mississippi to Forrest.[19]

The general then wrote Forrest and repeated what he had stated in a previous letter. "I wrote you from Montgomery," he began,

> but believing you did not receive that letter, write again to say I intrust to you the operations against the enemy threatening an invasion of North Mississippi. . . . By the telegraph this morning I am informed that a heavy column is advancing from La Grange; that a raid is moving down into North Alabama, and that a fleet has appeared off Mobile. You know as well as I the insufficiency of my means at this moment to meet all of these demands upon them as they should be met. But we must do the best we can with the little we have, and it is with no small satisfaction I reflect that of all commanders of the Confederacy you are accustomed to accomplish the very greatest results with small means when left to your own untrammeled judgment. Upon that judgment I now rely.

Maury then told Forrest he was sending him a brigade, and would do his best to increase his force still further.[20]

Maury assigned the defense of central and southern Mississippi to Brig. Gens. Wirt Adams and St. John Liddell, and charged the latter with facilitating Kirby Smith's crossing of the Mississippi River. "Ellis' Cliff suggested as a good point to command the river below Natchez," he told Liddell, adding that rifled guns would he needed, some of which "may come from Mobile." Maury then ordered Liddell to "Act at once on this dispatch." He now turned his attention to north Alabama and ordered

Brig. Gen. Daniel W. Adams, whose cavalry division was headquartered at Opelika, to send a brigade to "watch and check" the enemy column coming down from Decatur.[21] This left only Mobile, the area Maury knew best. Anticipating an enemy landing somewhere on the Alabama coast, supported by cavalry and infantry from Pensacola, he ordered the 1st Louisiana Artillery to Mobile. This unit was instructed to follow the Tuscaloosa Cadets, which he had ordered to Pollard the day before.[22]

Although heavily outnumbered, Maury decided he had made the best possible disposition of the twelve thousand effectives in his department. He now awaited Kirby Smith's nine thousand infantry, which could be used to reinforce Hood in Atlanta or to operate with Forrest in Sherman's rear. With these reinforcements, Hood should be able to hold Atlanta for another three months. By that time, the Democrat's peace candidate, Maj. Gen. George B. McClellan, would be headed for the White House, and the South would have gained its independence. Reasonably certain that Forrest and Adams could check the enemy in Mississippi and North Alabama, Maury now prepared to move his headquarters to Mobile, the area he decided was in the greatest danger.[23]

On Mobile's Lower Defense Line, where the first blow was likely to fall, the garrisons were on full alert. At Fort Morgan the ramparts were being manned throughout the night, anticipating that the enemy might try to enter the bay during darkness, as was done at New Orleans and Port Hudson. Capt. J. W. Whiting of the 1st Alabama Battalion of Artillery would later write that he knew the federals were making preparations for an attack; and for several nights, gun detachments remained at their posts on Fort Morgan's ramparts, expecting the fleet to attempt the passage of the fort.[24]

Pvt. J. L. Lear, a soldier in the 1st Tennessee Heavy Artillery Regiment, wrote in his diary that an order had been given to man "most of the guns of the fort" which "took our whole company." He then added what may have been restricted information: "The torpedo boat blew up a few nights since, killing two and wounding two" of her crew. Cloaked in great secrecy, a Confederate "David" had attempted to go out and sink one of the blockading vessels, but the boiler was not functioning properly, forcing the crew to return. A new boiler was installed, which blew up before the crew could make a second attempt.[25]

The weak links in the Lower Defense Line were Forts Gaines and Powell, where a shortage of labor had left much work undone. At Gaines,

Adm. Franklin Buchanan
NAVAL HISTORICAL CENTER

Rear Adm. David G. Farragut
NAVAL HISTORICAL CENTER

Maj. Gen. Dabney H. Maury
ALABAMA DEPARTMENT OF ARCHIVES
AND HISTORY

Maj. Gen. Edward R. S. Canby
MASSACHUSETTS COMMANDARY, MILITARY
ORDER OF THE LOYAL LEGION, AND THE
U.S. ARMY MILITARY HISTORY INSTITUTE

Brig. Gen. Richard Lucian Page
MASSACHUSETTS COMMANDARY, MILITARY
ORDER OF THE LOYAL LEGION, AND THE
U.S. ARMY MILITARY HISTORY INSTITUTE

Maj. Gen. Gordon Granger
MASSACHUSETTS COMMANDARY, MILITARY
ORDER OF THE LOYAL LEGION, AND THE
U.S. ARMY MILITARY HISTORY INSTITUTE

Confederate
Tactical High Command

Union
Tactical High Command

the guns were without merlons, parados, or traverses for protection of the cannoneers; and at Powell, the southern and eastern faces of the fort were unfinished, offering the cannoneers little protection should the enemy enter the bay and shell the fort from the rear.[26]

Sensing that a battle was imminent, the Confederate naval squadron was also on high alert. Aboard the flagship, Fleet Surgeon D. B. Conrad was convinced that the enemy was about to make an attack: "We noticed a decided increase in the Federal fleet" that was anchored in the Gulf of Mexico off Fort Morgan. The wooden vessels were "stripped to a 'girt line' and clean for action; their topmasts sent down on deck and devoid of everything that seemed like extra rigging. They appeared like 'prizefighters' ready for the 'ring.' Then we knew that trouble was ahead, and wondered to ourselves why they did not enter the bay any day." To Conrad, the monitors were the most ominous: "Strange-looking, long, black monsters, the new ironclads, and they were what the Federals had been so anxiously waiting for."[27]

As 2 August drew to a close, a strange quiet settled over the Gulf, the perennial calm before the storm. Here and there, little red and blue lights pierced the darkness, a sign that the enemy was not idle. The last telegram sent from Fort Morgan that day read: "No special change—vessels signaling tonight probably vessels arriving."[28]

CHAPTER 13

So Daring a Plan

EVENTS WERE NOW MOVING TOWARD A CLIMAX. ON 3 AUGUST THE army would land on Dauphin Island; the next day the navy would enter the bay. At 10:00 A.M. the *Hartford* hoisted General Signal 2139: Captains report aboard flagship. Soon, numerous small boats could be seen gliding across the green swells of the outer bar, each racing to be the first to report. Two army officers, Maj. F. W. Marston and Lt. John C. Kinney of the Army Signal Corps, were already aboard the flagship with a contingent of signalmen to be assigned to the principal vessels of the fleet.[1]

When all were present, Admiral Farragut explained that they had been called together to review the battle plan and receive some additional orders. With the *Tecumseh* scheduled to arrive later in the day, bringing the number of ironclads to four, the fleet would go in the next morning. Captain Drayton, Lieutenant Watson, and other members of the admiral's staff were there to assist with the details.[2]

The signalmen were present to open communications with the army after the fleet had entered the bay. The navy, however, would use its own system for ship-to-ship communications.[3] Army messages were sent by waving a flag to the left and right, each combination of motions representing a letter of the alphabet. The naval signaling system consisted of sending flags aloft, each uniquely colored to represent a number, the meaning of which was determined by reference to a signal book. If a particular sentence or phrase was not listed in the signal book, it would have to be spelled out by hoisting a flag for each letter. The army system, therefore, was much faster, "requiring as many seconds as the other method did minutes, with the advantage of saying precisely what was wanted." The admiral, nevertheless, was reluctant to switch systems on the eve of battle. The army signalmen would stay belowdecks until the fleet had entered the bay.[4]

As the admiral addressed his commanders, the "curves of his mouth bespoke an indomitable resolution," as was his custom when addressing serious matters. With flashing brown eyes and a bold chin, he had the "authoritative appearance of long command" and that ineffable mark of someone accustomed to using it.[5] Aware of his commanders' concern for the torpedoes and obstructions that blocked the channel, Farragut began the briefing by addressing this problem. In May, he began, the enemy's boats could be seen planting torpedoes. By July intelligence reports indicated that the torpedoes were suspended two to four feet under the surface by buoys, which were anchored in three parallel lines in quincunx order. Continuing, he explained that the eastern end of the field, opposite Fort Morgan, was marked by a black can-buoy, and between this buoy and the shoreline, a narrow channel four hundred to nine hundred yards wide had been left clear of torpedoes to accommodate blockade runners.[6]

The timber booms and rope obstructions that had been placed in the main channel earlier in the year, the admiral reported, had been swept away by the currents, and now it appeared that the rebels were again obstructing the channel with drag ropes. He said that a deserter from the rebel gunboat *Morgan* described these as hardwood buoys attached at intervals to a large hawser, moored by railroad iron. Apparently, long strands of loose rope that floated with the tide were connected to the hawser; when caught in a paddle wheel or propeller, the ropes were capable of stopping a vessel dead in the water.[7] To avoid these obstacles, the fleet would enter the bay through the narrow channel east of the black buoy. A blockade runner had entered the bay through this channel as recently as a week ago, evidence that it was clear of torpedoes and obstructions at that time. Considering the importance of blockade runners to the rebels, it would probably remain open.[8]

By going in close to the fort, the admiral explained, the fleet would not only avoid the torpedoes and obstructions in the ship channel but also have a better chance of silencing the enemy's batteries by bringing its own guns to bear at point-blank range in a "well directed fire." The shore there dropped off rapidly, he explained, and could carry twenty-two feet anywhere. "Get closer to your enemy, the nearer the better, the nearer the safer," he reasoned. This would place the fleet's broadsides within two hundred yards of the fort's water battery.[9]

The attack would be made with the advantages of an incoming tide and, with a little luck, a southwest wind. The current would help carry a damaged vessel into the bay, and the wind would blow smoke toward the fort, blinding the rebel gunners.[10] The battle line would consist of two columns: four ironclads to starboard and fourteen wooden vessels, lashed in pairs, to port. The *Tecumseh* would lead the starboard column, followed by the *Manhattan*, *Winnebago*, and *Chickasaw*. The large sloops *Hartford*, *Brooklyn*, and *Richmond*, and their side-wheel consorts, the gunboats *Metacomet*, *Octorara*, and *Port Royal*, would comprise the van of the port column. The smaller screw sloops *Lackawanna*, *Monongahela*, *Ossipee*, and *Oneida* and their partners, the side-wheel gunboat *Conemaugh*, the screw gunboats *Kennebec* and *Oneida*, and the screw steamer *Galena*, would follow.[11]

During the approach, the admiral added, each pair of wooden vessels should echelon to starboard so that their bow guns would have a clear field of fire. When possible, guns should be placed on the poop deck, topgallant forecastle, and starboard side of the tops, where they should keep up a constant fire with grapeshot until out of range. If the enemy fired grape, the gun crews should be removed from the poop and tops to the guns below until out of range. Once past Sand Island, the fleet would bear north by east. When the enemy opened fire, Farragut continued, the fleet would then open with its chase guns and starboard broadsides as soon as they could be brought to bear. Short fuses should be used for shell and shrapnel during the approach. However, when within three to four hundred yards, all guns except the howitzers would switch to grape. The howitzers would keep up a constant fire with shrapnel as long as they were in range. When abreast of the fort, the fleet would steer northwest one-half north until past the Middle Ground, then north by west until ordered to anchor. Once in the bay, each vessel would have to keep a little on the port quarter of the next ahead.[12]

Although the channel east of the black buoy was supposedly clear of torpedoes and obstructions, Farragut did not want to take any chances. Once the vessels were opposite the torpedo field, he instructed those with screws to stop their engines and let the tide and headway take them past the danger area. Those lashed to side-wheelers would continue ahead under their consort's power since paddle wheels were "not likely to foul with the enemy's drag ropes," at least not as likely as a propeller. Should any vessel be damaged or entangled by ropes and unable to maintain its station, she should drop out westward and, if possible, reenter at the rear of the column. After passing the fort, the fleet would bear northwest one-half west, at which time the gunboats would be cast off to prevent the enemy's gunboats from escaping to Mobile. Also, considering the unpredictability of battle—where events seldom go as planned—the fleet, or part of it, might have to use the main ship channel west of the black buoy despite the existence of torpedoes and obstructions.[13]

Because the fleet's ability to maneuver should not be limited, Farragut had ordered Flag Lieutenant Watson to reconnoiter the main channel under cover of darkness, locate the torpedoes and obstructions, and sink or cut loose the buoys to which they were attached. Following the publication of General Order No. 11, in which the vessels were ordered to pass east of the black buoy, Watson had made four nightly excursions into the main ship channel, where torpedoes and obstructions were supposed to exist, but found nothing but buoys moored by anchors.[14]

Watson's failure to locate the torpedoes and obstructions did not prove that the main channel was free of obstacles, the admiral explained. With depths varying from thirty to sixty feet, the current may have forced the buoys to arc downward, pushing them too deep for Watson's grapnels, or possibly many had leaked and sunk, dragged, or broken loose and floated away. Also, Watson was now beginning to suspect that the torpedoes were of the buoyant type, anchored to the bottom and tethered several feet below the surface. Although Watson's unsuccessful attempts to sink or cut loose the torpedoes in the ship channel were disquieting, there was some consolation in the knowledge that, after being submerged in saltwater, many torpedoes were rendered harmless by leakage and marine organisms. The obstructions, if any should be there, also had a defect: although not susceptible to fouling by barnacles and other marine crustaceans, they were prone to be swept away by the current. The admiral was aware of these imperfections, but the hulks of numerous Union vessels rotting in southern bays and inlets dictated prudence. Only in the event of a dire emergency would the fleet enter the bay west of the black buoy. So far, fourteen Yankee vessels, totaling approximately fourteen thousand tons, had been sunk or seriously damaged by torpedoes, and he did not intend to take any chances unless absolutely necessary.[15]

Continuing, the admiral now addressed the role of the monitors. As soon as the fleet began to move, he said, the monitors would leave their anchorage in Sand Island Channel and cross the van of the approaching column, "so as to make it certain that when abreast of the fort we have our ironclads as an offset to those of the enemy, which otherwise might run us down." Overall, the monitors would have three responsibilities, he stressed: first, "neutralize as much as possible the fire of the guns which rake our approach"; second, "look out for the [enemy's] ironclads when we are abreast of the fort"; and third, "occupy the attention of those batteries which would rake us while running up the bay." Once the fleet had passed the fort, the *Winnebago* and *Chickasaw* would follow, and the *Tecumseh* and *Manhattan* would "endeavor to destroy the *Tennessee.*" He then made it clear that the fleet would go in with or without the *Tecumseh.*[16]

Despite precautions, there was no guarantee that the battle would be fought without some vessels being lost to torpedoes, entangled in obstructions, or sunk by gunfire. Everything possible had been done to minimize the cost, which might go as high as one vessel in three—for a total of six vessels out of the entire fleet—but with luck it could be done with the loss of half that number.[17] Two flotillas would support the battle line with gunfire. The Gulf Flotilla would consist of six gunboats under the command of Lt. Cdr. E. C. Grafton. They would shell Fort Morgan from the Gulf as the fleet went in. The Mississippi Sound Flotilla, five gunboats commanded by Lt. Cdr. J. C. P. De Krafft, would fire on Fort Powell.[18]

At this point, several of the captains expressed concern for the admiral's safety, since the flagship was shown leading the wooden column on the diagram previously distributed. The *Brooklyn* had four chase guns and a device for picking up torpedoes, they argued—moreover, the admiral should not be so exposed. Although Farragut believed that exposure was one of the penalties of rank, he "reluctantly consented" to let the *Brooklyn* lead the column.[19] As the briefing came to a close, the commanders of the wooden vessels that would make the attack were instructed to anchor near the flagship, off the outer bar. At 3:00 A.M., "all hands" would be called, the battle line formed, and at first light the sloops, with their consorts lashed to port, should be crossing the outer bar. Three miles ahead, the ironclads would be leaving Sand Island Channel to take position on the starboard side of the wooden ships.[20]

The admiral's plan was bold to the extreme. Lieutenant Kinney, one of the signal officers who had attended the briefing, believed that

> *so daring an attempt was never made in any country. . . .*
>
> *Except for what Farragut had already accomplished on the Mississippi, it would have been considered a foolhardy experiment for wooden vessels to attempt to pass so close to one of the strongest forts on the coast; but when to the forts were added the knowledge of the strength of the ram and the supposed deadly character of the torpedoes, it may be imagined that the coming event impressed the person taking his first glimpse of naval warfare as decidedly hazardous and unpleasant. . . .*
>
> *It was the confidence reposed in him, the recollection that he had not failed in his former attempts, and his manifest faith in the success of the projected movement, that inspired all around him.*[21]

Assured that each of his commanding officers understood the battle plan, Farragut ended the briefing by inviting the group to accompany him aboard the steam tender *Cowslip* for a final look at the forts and the rebel ram, the most powerful ironclad afloat. As the *Cowslip* entered Sand Island Channel, Fort Gaines could be seen about three miles to the northwest—too far away to seriously threaten the fleet. Beyond was Fort Powell, also too distant to be a menace. However, once the fleet entered the bay, this small fort would have to be reduced, for it could prevent supply vessels from passing into Mobile Bay from Mississippi Sound. Three miles to the northeast was Fort Morgan. Lieutenant Kinney described the fort as "one of the strongest of the old stone forts and greatly strengthened by immense piles of sandbags, covering every portion of the exposed front. The fort was well equipped with three tiers of heavy guns, one of the guns, at least, of the best English make, imported by the Confederates. In addition, there was in front a battery of seven powerful guns at the water's edge on the beach. All the guns, of both fort and water-battery, were within point-blank range."[22]

The *Tennessee*, Kinney continued, was "considered the strongest and most powerful iron-clad ever put afloat. She looked like a great turtle; her sloping sides were covered with iron plates six inches in thickness, thoroughly riveted together, and she had a formidable iron beak projecting under water. Her armament consisted of six heavy Brooke rifles, each sending a solid shot weighing from 95 to 110 pounds."[23]

Viewing the enemy's powerful defenses at close range had been a sobering experience for those aboard the *Cowslip*, confirming the admiral's remark that the cost might go as high as six vessels. This was backed up by "several of the coolest officers" in the fleet. The admiral knew Buchanan well, having served with him in the old navy, and believed that "in points of courage, energy and skill he had few equals and no superiors."[24]

As the *Cowslip* approached the *Hartford*, Lieutenant Kinney shifted his attention from the enemy's defenses to the graceful, sweeping lines of the *Hartford* and her three tall masts towering above the deck. He recently had been transferred from the 13th Connecticut Infantry to the Signal Corps and was experiencing his "first practical acquaintance with a man of war."[25]

Circling the *Hartford* before boarding, a first-time visitor would have been impressed with the vessel's elegant figurehead and the elaborately carved trailboards that swept aft along the hull. He also would have noticed the stern's graceful proportions and the carving of an eagle, whose wings were suspended above the vessel's name. Climbing the big sloop's boarding ladder, the visitor would step through the entry port onto the gun or spar deck, where eighteen 9-inch Dahlgren guns were lashed to the deck with their muzzles protruding through openings in the bulwarks. Looking aft, he could see the poop, a small deck raised above the gun deck, mounting a single 100-pounder rifle. Farragut's spacious cabin occupied the space below. Turning toward the bow, the visitor could see the forecastle, a small, elevated deck, mounting two 100-pounder rifles.[26]

Two of the *Hartford's* three masts, the mizzen and main, pierced the gun deck between the poop and forecastle; the third, the foremast, protruded from the forecastle. Each of the masts consisted of three sections and a top, a platform located where the lower and middle sections were joined. During battle, howitzers and sharpshooters were often located in the tops; it also was where the vessel's lookouts were stationed.

The second deck down was the berth deck, which contained—from stern to bow—Captain Drayton's cabin, the wardroom, where the vessel's officers were quartered, the crew's quarters, and the sick bay. The third deck was the orlop deck, which was below the waterline. The vessel's engines, boilers, coal bunkers, shell room, and the magazines were located here, the only part of the vessel reasonably safe from the enemy's guns, but not his torpedoes. During battle, the surgeon's operating compartment, referred to as the "cockpit," was located here. The poop deck and forecastle were connected to the gun deck by ladders, and the gun, berth, and orlop decks by companionways, ladders, hoists, and lifts.

As Kinney was familiarizing himself with *Hartford*, serious problems were developing seven miles to the east off Petit Bois Island. Granger's amphibious operation was falling behind schedule: His brigade would not be ready to land until late afternoon—ten hours behind schedule. It would take that much time to straighten out the confusion resulting from bringing together army and navy units that had neither worked nor trained together.

About midday, satisfied that order was emerging from chaos, Granger sat down in the cabin of the steamer *Laura*, his floating headquarters, and penned a dispatch to his assistant adjutant general, Maj. C. T. Christensen. The report, written from the eastern end of Petit Bois Island, was dated 3 August. It began:

> *I have arrived and anchored off this point with the following transports,*
> *viz.,* Battle, James Brown, Tamaulipas, Clyde, St. Charles, *with barge,*
> *containing in the aggregate about 1,700 men. I shall commence to disembark*
> *all the troops about nine miles east of the western extremity of Dauphin*
> *Island this afternoon at 4:00 o'clock, all the arrangements having been per-*
> *fected for such purpose. The tug-boat* Perry *with the* Alliance *have not yet*
> *arrived and some little delay has been caused thereby. You will please hurry*
> *forward as rapidly as possible the remaining troops of my command, as*
> *their services are required. It is probable that the fleet will not attempt to pass*
> *the batteries until Saturday next [6th], and certainly not before Friday*
> *[5th]. It affords me pleasure to state that all is progressing favorably.*[27]

At 1:35 P.M. Acting Ens. William G. Jones, captain of the *Narcissus*, and John Robinson, the vessel's pilot, returned from a reconnaissance of landing sites on the Mississippi Sound side of the barren spit known as the West End. The site recommended was three miles closer to Fort Gaines than Granger had reported to Christensen earlier in the day.[28]

With the navy's gunboats covering the operation, a landing could be made there without molestation from the enemy—an important requirement when landing troops, artillery, and supplies on a hostile shore. At this location, six feet could be carried three hundred yards off the beach, and a hard, sandy bottom would facilitate the manhandling of artillery. Granger agreed with the recommendations and ordered the landing to be executed.[29]

Six miles to the northwest, Lt. Col. James M. Williams, commander of
Fort Powell, longed desperately to see his wife and child before the battle
began. Although aware that an attack was imminent, he did not think it
would start for another four or five days. In a letter to his wife dated 3
August, he wrote:

*Mahomet [sic] went to the mountain when it wouldn't come to him—can't
you make a trip to see me? the sooner the better—say the next day after you
receive this.*

*I'd give anything in reason for a sight of George and ... to kiss your
pretty face! ...*

*Maj. Johnston's moving his wife to the old camp of the 21st near Cedar
Point—my opinion is that he had better send her to the city than leave her
liable to outrage from the straggling Yankees that will soon infest that country if they succeed in establishing their fleet in the bay.[30]*

Williams, however, was concerned with his fort's lack of preparedness
and blamed Maury's staff for the problem. "The bay side of Fort Powell
had been left unprotected while our engineers were engaged in many
absurd works," he wrote, "and some which deserve a worse name—such
as the construction of batteries near Fort Morgan for no other purpose
than the protection of blockade runners in the swash channel. That the
staff of the commanding general was interested in this money-making
business was an open secret."[31]

Unloading his anger and frustration, Williams continued writing. While
at Fort Morgan a year earlier, he had "repeatedly called attention to the
fact that we could not successfully oppose an attempt to pass the fort
unless the channel was effectively closed with torpedoes," he wrote. "No
attention was paid to this as to do so would stop the blockade runners—
such torpedoes as were placed were carefully buoyed," thus disclosing
their positions. With the grim reality of battle bearing down on him,
Williams's outlook was not as rosy as two days earlier when he had written
his wife that another enemy ironclad had arrived outside, "the more the
merrier," and that Fort Powell was "fixed up to make a good fight."[32]

Williams's garrison would fight, just as it had done back in February
when they had repulsed an attack from Mississippi Sound by six mortar
boats and two gunboats. The fort's rear, or eastern front, however, had still
not been completed, thus exposing the magazine and the crews of three
guns to direct fire should the enemy fleet pass Fort Morgan and enter the

TOP: *Fort Powell*. DRAWING BY E. B. HOUGH.
BOTTOM: *Fort Powell as seen from Mississippi Sound*.
Frank Leslie's Illustrated Newspaper, 2 APRIL 1864.

bay. As such, the fate of Fort Powell was linked directly to Fort Morgan's defense of the main channel—as was, indeed, the entire Lower Defense Line.[33]

As Williams brought his letter to a close, the telegraph at Fort Morgan was crackling with two-way traffic. The presence of transports loaded with troops in Mississippi Sound and twenty-one vessels—including three ironclads off Fort Morgan—meant only one thing: the Lower Defense

Line was about to be attacked by both land and water. The latest telegram from Mobile came from Lt. Col. von Scheliha informing General Page that fifty-one torpedoes were on the way by boat with another fifty-one scheduled for Friday, 5 August.[34]

No sooner had the *Cowslip* returned to the *Hartford* from its reconnaissance of the enemy's defenses, than the admiral received an appalling message from Captain Jenkins in Pensacola: The *Tecumseh* was still at the navy yard and had just started to coal. If true, Farragut reasoned, the vessel could not possibly reach the fleet in time for battle the next morning, 4 August, although the door would be kept open if by chance she should arrive during the late afternoon or early evening. Farragut had been told that the *Tecumseh* would join the fleet on 1 August—and here it was midday, the third, and no sign of her. Angry and embarrassed, the admiral penned a second note to Granger, informing him that the navy would again be late. There would, however, be no more delays; the fleet would go in on the fifth, with or without the *Tecumseh*.[35]

CHAPTER 14

→→ ←←

The Army Lands

FARRAGUT WAS ANGRY. IN A LETTER TO JENKINS, WHO WAS IN PENSACOLA attempting to expedite the *Tecumseh*'s departure, he wrote:

> *I could have done very well without her, as I have three here without her, and every day is an irretrievable loss.*
>
> *The soldiers, by agreement, are landing to-day back of Dauphin Island, and could I have gone in this morning, we would have taken them by surprise. . . . I can lose no more days. I must go in day after to-morrow morning at daylight or a little after. It is a bad time, but when you do not take fortune at her offer you must take her as you can find her. I have had the wind just right, and I expect it will change by the time I can go in.*[1]

Farragut's letter to Jenkins, dated 3 August, was followed by one from Drayton, urging him to do everything possible to get the other vessels, including the *Tecumseh*, back to Mobile. "If you can get the *Tecumseh* out to-morrow, do so; otherwise I am pretty certain that the admiral won't wait for her. Indeed, I think a very little persuasion would have taken him in to-day, and less to-morrow. The army are to land at once, and the admiral does not want to be thought remiss." He added that if Captain Jenkins wanted to be in the battle, he too "had better come out."[2]

As soon as Farragut's and Drayton's letters were transcribed and signed, the admiral ordered Lt. Cdr. H. L. Howison to "proceed at once with the *Bienville* to Pensacola, and take the *Tecumseh* in tow as soon as she is ready and bring her out to me here. If it is possible, she must be got off early to-morrow morning, otherwise she will be of no use to me in my operations."[3] At the navy yard, Captain Jenkins had finally gotten a coal tender along-side the *Tecumseh*. The task, however, of topping off her bunkers with 150 tons of coal, sack by sack, would take time. To hasten the work, crewmen from the *Richmond* and the *Bienville* would help. Remembering his fight with the *Arkansas* and "how unequal the contest is between ironclads and wooden vessels in loss of life," Farragut did not want to enter the bay with-out the additional firepower of a fourth ironclad, despite his disclaimer to Jenkins, but he would not disappoint Granger a third time. He would go in on 5 August, without the *Tecumseh* if necessary. Embarrassed and angered, he sent a dispatch to Granger notifying him that the *Tecumseh* probably would not arrive until late in the afternoon tomorrow, 4 August. Accord-ingly, the fleet would not enter the bay until the fifth.[4]

Sensitive to possible criticism for postponing the navy's attack—first from the third to the fourth, then from the fourth to the fifth, Farragut wrote Granger a soothing letter, telling him that he might find the task of capturing Fort Gaines easier than expected. "I think you will find them unprepared for you at Fort Gaines," he predicted. "They appear to think only of the peninsula [Fort Morgan], and are doing everything to get ready for you in that quarter. I hope, if we are so fortunate as to get inside the bay, that you will then find force enough to land there also."[5]

On 3 August, at 2:40 P.M., the *Conemaugh*, flagship of the Mississippi Sound Flotilla, four gunboats, and a tinclad proceeded up the sound, fol-lowed by the *Laura* and six transports. When the convoy reached the landing site, marked by a tripod of timbers, Commander De Krafft, the naval officer in charge of the landing, ordered the transports to anchor and discharge the troops. The time was 5:15 P.M. Enos Reed, a soldier in the 34th Iowa, wrote his wife that the transports ran up within four hundred yards of the beach and anchored. "The ships could not get nearer shore on account of their heavy draught." The regiments that were aboard the *James Battle*—the 34th Iowa, the 96th Ohio, and the 96th U.S. Colored Troops—were the first to disembark and the first to move forward, with "skirmishers well advanced and extending from shore to shore."[6]

At the beachhead, Corporal Hart, a gunner with the 2d Connecticut Light Artillery, was having a "great time unloading" the unit's six 3-inch ordnance guns. "We could not get any nearer to the shore than about 100 yard[s]," he wrote his wife. Working in water four feet deep, the battery had to pull the guns and caissons ashore by hand, which took about three hours. "Of course, we was soaking wet," he playfully added.[7]

The heavy artillery, with its eight 4,800-pound Parrots was not so lucky. In a letter to his mother, Rufe Dooley, a soldier in the 1st Indiana Heavy Artillery, wrote that General Granger "finds it impossible" to land the four 30-pounder Parrots there. The same dilemma plagued the 2d Illinois Light Battery, which despite its "light" classification also manned four 30-pounder Parrots. The landing of these guns would require deeper water. Overall, however, the operation had been a success: The infantry, light artillery, and telegraph trains were ashore, and the steamer *Alliance* finally had arrived with two additional regiments. Seeing the infantry move down the peninsula, Commander De Krafft ordered the *J. P. Jackson* and *Narcissus* to steam inshore and shell the woods, now about two miles ahead of the skirmishers.[8]

In the fleet off Fort Morgan, preparations continued for entering the bay. Should the *Tecumseh* arrive that night, the fleet would go in the next day, but that was unlikely. J. C. Gregg, a marine aboard the *Brooklyn*, considered 3 August to be the most exciting day he had spent on the blockade. He wrote in his diary that during the morning an officer and three privates from the signal corps came aboard and told us "a large land force was coming and that the battle would commence tomorrow." "At 5 P.M.," he continued, "13 vessels were in sight from the top coming from the westward." Later, "heavy firing was heard from the direction of Forts Powell and Gaines, which led to the supposition that our folks were landing troops."[9]

As the rumble of distant guns reverberated across the waters of the Gulf, the monitor *Winnebago* left Sand Island Channel and steamed toward Fort Morgan. Commander Stevens did not want to take the *Winnebago* into battle without firing her guns and exercising the crew while she was under way. When about halfway up the channel, he fired a "shot or two" at the fort, turned 180 degrees, and steamed out to the fleet anchorage and back, just in time to miss a severe squall, the white caps and lightning making "a most impressive sight."[10] On Dauphin Island, Dr. J. T. Woods, a surgeon with the 96th Ohio, described the storm: "The howling hurricane lashed the waters that rushed and raved along either shore. The very clouds seemed shivered reservoirs as the rain came pouring from them on our defenseless heads—fit prelude to the terrible drama that must soon begin."[11]

WHILE IN MOBILE, GENERAL MAURY STILL HAD TO KEEP AN EYE ON Mississippi and North Alabama, where the enemy was preparing to launch attacks. During the day he also had written letters to the president and secretary of war informing them of the various threats facing the department, and what he was doing in response. Seldom critical of his officers, but now under increasing stress, Maury mentioned in a letter to Jefferson Davis that General Page, the commander at Fort Morgan, "was too despondent. He seems to see only the weak points of these forts. We need a buoyant man there." The morning edition of a Mobile newspaper agreed with General Maury: Fort Morgan was unassailable. "By direct fire the Fort is invulnerable, its walls being protected by a glacis of sand in which all the shot and shell in the world could be innocently buried. If he resorts to throwing shell over and dropping them inside the work nobody need be hurt."[12]

Although Maury did not elaborate further on his subordinate's lack of "buoyancy," it was well known that Page lacked confidence in Fort Morgan's ability to withstand a siege, as did his chief engineer, Lt. Col. Victor von Scheliha. In a report dated 9 July, von Scheliha stated that "Fort Morgan in its present condition, cannot withstand a vigorous bombardment. The guns on the west faces, if not dismounted by the reverse fire of the enemy, will fall with the casemates on which they are mounted. The high scarp-wall will be breached by curbated shot. The citadel will crumble to pieces from the effect of either shot or shell, direct or reverse fire. These facts have not escaped the attention of the engineers, yet for want of laborers little or nothing has been done toward remedying the defects of our old fortifications, constructed at a time when an 8-inch Columbiad was the heaviest ordnance known."[13]

All was not gloom and doom, however. By the end of July, von Scheliha reported that 46 Raines and 134 Singer torpedoes, echeloned in three rows, had been placed in the main channel between Fort Morgan and the west bank. On 3 August, he notified General Page that 51 more had been sent by boat that morning for the Lower Defense Line, and another 51 would follow on the fifth, two days hence.[14]

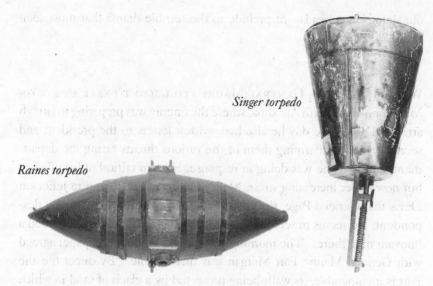

Singer torpedo

Raines torpedo

Confederate torpedoes used in Mobile Bay
U.S. MILITARY ACADEMY MUSEUM

The torpedoes were brought from Mobile to Fort Morgan where they were stored prior to being filled with powder. From there a party of several men, equipped with a large, wide-beamed launch, would plant them in the main channel or where circumstances required. The planting of a torpedo consisted of lowering a buoyant powder container attached to a chain and anchor. The length of the chain was cut so that the container floated under the surface, usually between two and four feet. Twenty torpedoes could be planted in one day.[15]

The Singer torpedo was made of light boiler iron and contained fifty-five to seventy pounds of powder. On top of the casing lay a heavy iron cap, connected by wire to a trigger. When the cap was dislodged by contact with a vessel, the attached wire would release the trigger, which in turn caused a plunger to ignite a fulminate substance, thus causing an explosion.[16] The Raines torpedo consisted of a large barrel filled with seventy to one hundred pounds of powder, leaving enough empty space to dispense with a buoy. Five or more sensitive fuses, containing a combination of fulminate of mercury and ground glass, protruded from the top and upper sides of the barrel. When these fuses were crushed by contact with a ship, their contents mixed with a solution of alcohol and liquid gunpowder, igniting the powder in the barrel.[17]

The torpedoes floated below the surface, attached by ropes or chains fastened to a heavy weight, such as a section of railroad iron or a mushroom anchor. The powder charges for the Singer and Raines torpedoes could sink an ironclad or a large sloop of war in a matter of minutes—a powerful new weapon that would go a long way toward offsetting the Union's superiority in vessels and firepower. There was, however, a nagging concern: When submerged, the torpedoes were prone to leak and corrode, thus rendering them harmless, in some instances within two weeks. In early June, Captain Fremaux, one of von Scheliha's engineers, reported that some of the torpedoes "are made of tin, and very indifferently lacquered; that the force of the current must rub the lacquer very soon and expose the tin to the corroding action of the sea water and that it takes a very short time to place them. If there is not an immediate necessity to have them placed this week, I would respectfully request that we wait for the last moment to place, to be sure of their efficiency."[18] There was, of course, merit to Fremaux's suggestion. But the risk of delaying was too great, his superiors reasoned. There would not be enough time to place the torpedoes once the enemy commenced an attack, particularly if the attack were made at night. They would be planted when delivered.

By 4:00 P.M. on 3 August, the long-awaited attack on Mobile's Lower Defense Line had begun. Two thousand enemy troops were advancing toward Fort Gaines, and a fleet of warships was preparing to fight its way into the bay, possibly that night or the next day. At Fort Gaines, Col. Charles D. Anderson, the garrison commander, had his hands full. Unfortunately, the fort's guns were useless against an enemy fleet entering the bay through the main channel: the range was too great. The guns bearing on the water could be used with good effect against shallow-draft vessels entering the bay through the channel between the fort and the western end of the pile obstructions. But Fort Gaines's primary mission was to prevent an enemy from using Dauphin Island as a base of operations against Fort Morgan and the city of Mobile. Earlier in the war, while on an inspection tour of Mobile's defenses, Braxton Bragg recognized this when he wrote that Fort Gaines is "of little or no importance except to prevent the enemy from using the island against us, being 2½ miles from the channel."[19]

Pondering his dilemma as darkness descended upon the island, Anderson knew that without reinforcements he would be unable to expel the enemy from the island. Excluding the troops at Fort Powell, his command

Fort Gaines, 1957
THIGPEN PHOTOGRAPHY

consisted of six hundred officers and men, enough to man the fort but not enough to counterattack a force three times larger. A little after sundown, Anderson learned that the enemy had stopped advancing and was camping in the woods about two and a half miles to the west. This was good; it would buy some time, but he knew they would resume the advance at daylight. He hoped reinforcements would arrive in time, and in sufficient numbers, to counterattack and drive the enemy off the island. In the meantime, he would continue as best he could to prepare the fort for a siege.[20]

Outside Fort Gaines, the timber had been felled for twelve hundred yards, providing the guns that bore on the land a clear field of fire; this also allowed the infantry to occupy advanced rifle pits to keep the enemy as far back as possible. Of the fort's twenty-six guns, eight bore on the land approaches; six, on the dry ditch that encircled the ramparts; and twelve, on the water.[21]

Thirty miles to the north, a relief force had been scraped together and was about to board a steamer for the four-hour run to Dauphin Island. Organized as a battalion under the command of Maj. W. R. Browne, an artilleryman, the force totaled 326 men and 20 officers. In addition, an infantry regiment stationed at Pollard in Escambia County, Florida, would follow as soon as transportation was available.[22]

Fort Morgan's seven-gun water battery.
NATIONAL ARCHIVES

Fifty years had passed since an invading army had attacked the lower Alabama coast. A handful of older people still remembered Gen. Andrew Jackson's thrilling communiqué to the secretary of war announcing the repulse of the British forces that had attacked Fort Bowyer on Mobile Point on 14 September 1814.

> *Sir—I have but a moment to spare to tell you since the departure of my letter of this morning, a messenger has returned from Fort Bowyer with the pleasing intelligence that Major Laurence has gallantly repulsed the enemy with great loss, blowing up a vessel of 36 guns—Only four of our men were killed and 5 wounded. The officer bringing the dispatches will be here in an hour, when I will be enabled to give you the particulars.*[23]

A half century later General Jackson's grandson, thirty-year-old Col. Andrew Jackson III, a graduate of West Point, was stationed at Fort Morgan as commander of the 1st Tennessee Heavy Artillery. His regiment manned Morgan's powerful water battery, which was located outside the fort a few hundred feet from the shoreline where Fort Bowyer had been.

Colonel Jackson, however, was not with the regiment on 3 August; he had been in Mobile attending to business but now was waiting to take the first boat leaving for Fort Morgan. In 1814, while Gen. Andrew Jackson was en route by schooner to inspect Fort Bowyer, he received word that the battle had already commenced and was therefore forced to hastily return to Mobile.[24]

The 170 men of the 1st Tennessee Heavy Artillery manned seven guns: four 10-inch and one 8-inch smoothbore Columbiads, and two rifled 32-pounders. Battle tested, most of the men had been at Vicksburg, where they received recognition for the "handsome manner in which their guns were handled" and for the gallant way in which they "bore the brunt of the labors and dangers of the siege." Paroled and then exchanged after the surrender of Vicksburg, the 1st Tennessee Heavy Artillery was reorganized into two companies, with Colonel Jackson as commander.[25]

From army headquarters in Mobile, Dabney Maury had sent Braxton Bragg an early morning dispatch, informing him of the developing situation in the department. "I arrived here this morning from Meridian," he began. "An important increase of the enemy's fleet has appeared off Morgan and Pascagoula. Raid reported advancing into North Alabama from Decatur. Column of enemy 14,000 strong moving down Mississippi Central road; advance at Holly Springs night before last. . . . Enemy concentrating at Morganza during the past three days. General Daniel Adams has been ordered to send Roddey's brigade to look after raid from North Alabama. I have ordered First Louisiana Artillery back from Mobile. Can you send back any other troops recently from here?"[26]

At 4:00 P.M., another dispatch followed: "The enemy have landed on Dauphin Island, seven miles below Fort Gaines. An attack against our outer line is no doubt mediated. Please send me back my heavy artillerists, the Louisiana Artillery and First Mississippi Artillery."[27]

CHAPTER 15

━┝> <┥━

The Navy Is Late

AT FIRST LIGHT THURSDAY MORNING, 4 AUGUST, THE UNION ASSAULT force—five regiments and a light artillery battery—broke camp and resumed the advance toward Fort Gaines: skirmishers ahead, the main body in column. A soldier in the 96th Ohio described the scene: "No enemy appeared to obstruct our way, but, within two hundred yards of where we had halted in the darkness, and just within the edge of the woods that had served the enemy as cover, we found a line of empty rifle-pits that, on the evening previous, had bristled with loaded muskets. Our halt had saved us a bloody reception. We could almost *feel* the guidance and protecting care of Providence."[1]

General Granger was pleased with the way the operation was progressing. He had assured Farragut that the army would shell Fort Gaines when the navy entered the bay, and he intended to keep that commitment. The heavy artillery had not yet landed, but the six 3-inch ordnance rifles of the 2d Connecticut Light Artillery should be within range of the fort.[2]

With the naval attack less than twenty-four hours away, the fleet was buzzing with activity. The vessels had been preparing for battle since the publication of General Order No. 10 in the second week of July, and the heavy work—the removal of nonessential spars and masts and the placing of chain armor and sand bags to protect machinery—had, for the most part, been completed. Much work remained, however: hanging splinter nets, shifting guns from port to starboard, lowering boats, placing projectiles in ready racks, and a multitude of other tasks essential to the next day's battle.

Sixty miles to the east, at the Pensacola Navy Yard, Captain Jenkins ordered the *Richmond* to weigh anchor and get under way for Mobile. Now satisfied that the *Tecumseh*'s bunkers would be topped off by mid-morning, he ordered the *Bienville* to stand by with steam up to tow her to Mobile. Craven, who wanted to participate in the battle as much as Jenkins, assured the captain that the *Tecumseh* would leave Pensacola no later than 10:00 A.M., which would enable her to reach the fleet by 4:00 P.M. This would give Craven plenty of time to pick up a pilot and report to the admiral for instructions.[3]

Off Mobile, the army steamer *Laura* had just entered Sand Island Channel and made fast to the *Chickasaw.* Aboard were General Granger and staff; Capt. Ernest A. Denicke, a signal officer; and several flagmen. They were there to establish communications with the army on Dauphin Island, which by now should have located a telegraph station on the Gulf beach opposite Pelican Island. Shortly after daybreak, black funnel smoke in Mobile Bay caught Denicke's eye. An hour later a rebel steamboat was seen disgorging troops at Fort Gaines's wharf, prompting Denicke's first message. Flagged at 7:30 A.M. and addressed to Colonel Myers, the message read: "I just saw 150 rebel infantry land at Fort Gaines from Mobile."[4]

To Granger, the arrival of rebel reinforcements—a battalion since day-light—meant that the enemy was serious about defending Fort Gaines, and there would be a long and costly siege. The landing of Union troops and light artillery yesterday had gone smoothly, but the shallow water and deep sand had so far prevented the heavy ordnance from coming ashore, without which a successful siege would be impossible. Considering these difficulties and Fort Gaines's lack of strategic importance, a siege, apart from keeping the garrison occupied, would not be practicable. Fort Morgan should be the objective. With its command of the main channel, Morgan's early investment would be of vital importance to the fleet. This, of course, would require additional troops, the availability of which, Granger understood, would depend on the rebel generals Kirby Smith and Nathan Bedford Forrest. In the meantime, he barely had enough troops on hand to keep the enemy from sallying out and attacking his lines, so he believed.[5]

THE OIL LAMPS HAD BEEN BURNING ALL NIGHT AT ARMY HEADQUARTERS in Mobile. General Maury, who had returned to Mobile from Meridian to be on hand when the attack came, had left Gen. Edward Higgins in tactical command of the District of the Gulf. Anxious to know if Major Browne's battalion had reached Fort Gaines, and if additional intelligence had been received concerning the enemy landing on Dauphin Island, Higgins wired Page, who answered, quoting a telegram from Colonel Anderson: "Major Brown[e] with reinforcements amounting to 276 muskets have arrived from Mobile. Enemy in lower bay of woods estimated by Lt. Col. Williams & scouts at 2000."[6]

Major Browne had wasted little time in reporting to Colonel Anderson once the *Natchez* reached Fort Gaines. The colonel welcomed Browne and told him that the enemy, estimated to be about two thousand, was now two miles from the fort and advancing; but even with the addition of his battalion, the garrison was too small to sortie out and attack the enemy. However, other reinforcements had been promised: the 22d Louisiana at Pollard, Alabama, and one of two 21st Alabama companies at Fort Morgan, both of which should be on the way. In the meantime, Anderson ordered Browne to have his battalion ready to relieve the picket line, eleven hundred yards west of the fort, at midnight.[7]

At Fort Morgan, General Page had ordered a boat to stand by, as he intended to cross the three and a half miles of open water and exhort the garrison of Fort Gaines to make a "protracted resistance." Upon arriving, he "encouraged the garrison" to stand by their guns, and Colonel Anderson assured him that the fort would hold out as long as it had the means to do so. On his way back to Fort Morgan, Page passed the steamboat *Dick Keys*, bound for Fort Gaines with Company I of the 21st Alabama. There was as yet, no sign of the 22d Louisiana, scheduled to arrive that day. But signs of the enemy were everywhere: Before reaching Fort Morgan, Page had counted twenty-five Union vessels, excluding the *Tecumseh*, *Richmond*, and several other vessels still at Pensacola.[8]

At 10:00 A.M., still aboard the *Laura* in Sand Island Channel, Captain Denicke flagged the relay station on Dauphin Island that "some eighty rebel infantry were just landed at Fort Gaines from Fort Morgan," bringing the total to about four hundred since 7:00 A.M. When Farragut learned that reinforcements had again reached Gaines unmolested, he ordered the *Winnebago* to "go up toward Fort Gaines and try and drive off the enemy's boats that are landing troops and supplies." He cautioned Stevens not to get closer than a mile and to get back to his anchorage before dark. He also directed him to try and make contact with the army on Dauphin Island, but not to "use up" his crew too much, since the fleet will "go in a little after daylight in the morning."[9]

As the *Dick Keys* was approaching the Fort Gaines wharf, a flurry of musket shots rang out from the picket line east of the fort: The enemy's skirmishers were finally in sight. A more ominous threat, however, soon appeared. One of the enemy's monitors had weighed anchor and was moving toward Fort Gaines. Observing the scene from Fort Morgan, Page knew exactly what was about to happen. "One of the double turreted monitors is now approaching Gaines by inside passage and will open directly on that Fort," he telegraphed Mobile.[10]

At Fort Gaines, Lt. John L. Rapier put his duties aside for a moment to watch the unfolding drama. Standing on the fort's ramparts, he saw the monitor fire "a dozen shell at the Fort, doing no damage." The fort returned the fire with three 10-inch Columbiads, but with "every discharge two of them would be dismounted." Rapier blamed the problem on the fort's officers, "as the guns were in no condition to fight. . . . Having remained as long as she saw fit," the monitor hauled around and returned to her anchorage.[11]

At 2:00 P.M. the gun duel between the *Winnebago* and Fort Gaines finally ended. Lieutenant Ely had watched the contest from a ringside seat in the channel, where his ironclad, the *Manhattan*, was anchored. The *Winnebago* "made most miserable shots," he wrote in his journal, and "the steamboats did not cast off a line, but continued to discharge until they had finished, and then quietly steamed away. Fort Gaines opened on the monitor, and after some rather wild shooting made more tolerable shots. None of them, however, struck the Monitor. About the middle of the afternoon she steamed to her anchorage, and this evening we hear that she has one of her turrets jammed and the other broken in two places. Consequently she will not participate in the engagement, which is to commence tomorrow at 4:00 A.M."[12]

Aboard the *Winnebago*, Acting Chief Engineer Simon Schultice blamed the problem on "bad management of the starting bar" in the forward turret, resulting in a broken tooth. In the aft turret there was more trouble. The outer rim of the main spur wheel was damaged. Schultice was convinced, however, that he could repair the defects in time for the next day's battle.[13]

A correspondent for the *New Orleans Times*, who had just joined the fleet, wrote the following inaccurate account of the *Winnebago*'s foray:

Contrary to expectations the land force under Gen. Granger . . . did not attempt the reduction of the forts today. But Captain Stevens, determined not to be balked of his share of the fight, steamed up in front of Fort Gaines, and at half-past 11 o'clock this morning threw his first shell at the transport Natchez, *which was unloading troops and ammunition at the landing in front of the fort. You should have seen her leave! In less than a minute after the shell burst in her neighborhood, the smoke of burning bacon and rosin was plainly visible. We gave and received about a dozen shots, but nobody was hurt on our side.*

Just inside the obstructions is lying the rebel's pride and hope—the ram Tennessee, *and three gunboats. Neither of these have dared to show themselves outside, while we were firing into the transports, but contented themselves with throwing a shot at us at long range, say about five miles, when they could have no hope of hitting us.*[14]

Ashore on Dauphin Island, Capt. Miles D. McAlester, Canby's chief engineer, moved with caution along the line of skirmishers. His first responsibility was to lay out a siege line across the island. Once this was done, trenches and gun positions would be constructed. In the meantime, Pvt. Charles C. Enslow of the 77th Illinois took advantage of the lull to write his wife a letter. He told her that if the troops were ordered to charge the fort, he feared "we will no doubt lose many of our boys." Although he had not yet been in a hard battle, he wrote that he would "take my chance like a man." He closed the letter by telling his wife that a monitor had opened fire on Fort Gaines.[15]

As cannon fire boomed across the water, General Page knew that an attack was imminent. Although many of Von Scheliha's recommendations for strengthening Fort Morgan had not been carried out due to a shortage of hands, much had been accomplished: The guns were protected by traverses; sandbags now reinforced the magazines and bastion casemates; and two strong outworks had been built east of the fort. Page was particularly pleased with Colonel Anderson's determination to hold out as long as possible, although the general was well aware of Fort Gaines's deficiencies. Now that the enemy had landed on Dauphin Island and a monitor had opened fire on Gaines, little time was left to further strengthen his defenses.

As signs of an attack grew more ominous, the hard work of preparing for battle gave way to speculation about its effectiveness. Many felt that the enemy's ironclads, as well as their wooden vessels, would pass the fort, which was of no comfort to Lt. Robert Tarleton and his hope for an autumn wedding. But opinions were widely varied concerning the wooden vessels. Lt. Hurieosco Austill, a friend of Tarleton's, later wrote: "Some agreed that their boats of all kinds would be able to pass with but little damage; others maintained that their wooden boats at least would certainly be destroyed."[16]

Learning of these apprehensions, a Mobile newspaper addressed the issue in an editorial. Beginning on an upbeat note, the article stated that

twenty-three Federal ships of war lie outside the harbor, including three ironclads which are reported to be in the lee of Sand Island, two and a half miles from the muzzles of the guns of Fort Morgan, and of course within range of their shot. The commander of the Fort has good reason for not opening on them at present.

The assemblage of this large fleet is not without its meaning, and the fortifications defending the mouth of the bay become points of great interest. That Admiral Farragut commands the fleet is an additional reason for believing that some military enterprise is on foot. Were it not known that the enemy has no land force disposable for a combined land and naval attack on Mobile, we should conclude naturally that this city's time of trial was at hand. What does the enemy mean to do with his fleet alone? We can but conjecture. First, he may mean to pen the batteries of his twenty ships on Fort Morgan and attempt to reduce it by fire. A similar attempt on little Fort Powell failed some months ago, and if there is the right kind of Fort Sumter pluck in Fort Morgan, Farragut may fire in vain until the end of the war. By direct fire the Fort is invulnerable, its walls being protected by a glacis of sand in which all the shot and shell in the world could be innocently buried.

If he resorts to throwing shell over and dropping them inside the work nobody need be hurt. The troops have only to keep away from the area, and they have no occasion to be there, for no fighting is to be done there. We take it therefore that in a stand-off fight of this sort, twenty wooden walls, even with the help of three ironclads will be no match for the heavy ordnance, the shot and shell, and gallantry of Fort Morgan. Our brave boys in that work have been waiting three long years in patient inactivity for the stirring scenes in which their comrades in arms, at other points, have participated. The Yankee Admiral seems disposed to gratify their desires for "fleshing their maiden swords," and testing their heavy artillery practice on real and living targets. They have been carefully and well instructed. They are commanded by an artillerist distinguished for scientific and practical skill and they have as pretty a chance for a beautiful fight, and for winning glory as could possibly be offered to gallant soldiers—Let them remember that the idea of the Yankee naval and gunboat invincibility has long since been exploded—that the forts in Charleston harbor whipped and disabled and drove off nine of the Yankee invincible monitors, and that one heavy shot, fairly hitting a monitor turret, jars it so that it will not turn, and its guns are thus rendered useless. As for the wooden ships, every encounter in this war has proved that a land battery well served can always whip them. Fifty men in a four gun battery at Sabine pass beat a Yankee squadron, sinking and capturing some, and taking more prisoners than double the number of the garrison. If any man feels any of that awe of the Yankee navy which used to be generally prevalent and which now has its depressing effects upon some of the officers who were brought up on its decks, let him remember Gen. Magruder in Galveston Bay who armed two or three old high pressure steamboats, made ramparts of cotton bales three deep, and then boldly sailed out and attacked, captured, sank and dispersed a Yankee squadron. Nor forget the glorious example of the lamented Villepique at Fort McCree in the harbor of Pensacola, who with a sand battery mounting two 3-inch guns whipped the Yankee steamships the Richmond *and the* Niagra. *The garrison at Fort Morgan should take courage from these examples, and if they serve their guns coolly and bravely, they have an opportunity of wearing the brightest laurels of this war.*

It may be the purpose of Farragut to attempt to run his iron-clads past Fort Morgan and lay siege to Fort Powell. This is a dangerous experiment in face of the torpedoes which lie across their path and the gauntlet of fire which Fort Morgan can open upon them, together with the not inconsiderable weight of ordnance with which Admiral Buchanan and his little navy can aid in disputing the passage. The commander at Fort Morgan is an old U.S. Navy officer, and our squadron is officered principally by members of the same old concern. They are true and tried men; and if they will just forget the past, and remember only to fight like Confederates, Farragut and his big fleet

*will be checked and Mobile Bay will be strewed with the wrecks of many a
Yankee man-of-war. A Fort Sumter commander and garrison would not
ask for a prettier opening for exemption and distinction.*[17]

The first to respond to the editorial was a soldier in the 1st Tennessee
Heavy Artillery who was stationed at Fort Morgan:

*An editorial in your paper of yesterday does injustice to the 1st Tennessee
Heavy Artillery, now a portion of the garrison at this place. They have not
"been waiting three years," but have [done] their part in the struggle now
going on for our independence. From Island No. 10, Tenn., to Vicksburg, we
have contended and have "fleshed our maiden sword" long since on the iron
sides of Porter's fleet on the Mississippi. We also gave Farragut a few shells
on the (28) of June, when he made his grand attack on Vicksburg. There are
two companies of the 21st Alabama Infantry here also, who are not novices
in the art of war.*

    *You will do an act of justice to both the Alabamians of the 21st regiment
and Tennesseeans at the post if you correct the statement.*[18]

Cdr. George W. Harrison, captain of the gunboat *Morgan*, also responded to the editorial by inviting the editors to volunteer as recruits
aboard the *Morgan* "when the expected en-gagement with the enemy's
fleet takes place. I promise that you shall have the most conspicuous position on board and the fullest opportunity to display your bravery and
naval knowledge."[19]

As the media battle raged, Admiral Buchanan was occupied with more
serious matters. Charged with keeping the Yankee fleet at bay, he did not
have many options. Less than a mile wide, the navigable entrance to
Mobile Bay left little opportunity for maneuver and the display of tactical
skill. Knowing Farragut, however, Old Buck reasoned that his opponent
would most likely attempt to enter close under the guns of Fort Morgan,
as he did when passing the forts below New Orleans. By doing so, the
enemy fleet would avoid the torpedo field and, at the same time, stand a
better chance of beating down Fort Morgan's fire with its broadsides.

The tactical plan devised by Buchanan placed the Confederate squadron in line ahead across the channel, with the *Tennessee* on the eastern
end opposite the safe channel. This formation would allow sixteen of the
squadron's guns to rake the enemy vessels as they steamed in, possibly

for three-quarters of an hour before their broadsides came into play. Furthermore, the *Tennessee* would be favorably positioned to ram the first vessel that entered the safe channel, thus blocking the way for those that followed. In the event the enemy chose to risk the torpedo field farther to the west, there would be plenty of time to intercept and sink the first vessel, causing confusion and chaos that might prompt the others to withdraw. Buchanan's plan was "well devised, and made probably the best use of the advantages of the ground possible to so inferior a force."[20]

At department headquarters in Mobile a mood of cautious optimism permeated the atmosphere. The long-awaited battle for control of Mobile Bay was now only hours away. With luck, the enemy would be repulsed. If so, another defeat would be added to the growing list of Northern military failures, assuring Lincoln's defeat in the November presidential election and paving the way for Southern independence. More and more Northerners, disgruntled with the war, "had abundant reason to project their resentments upon the Union President."[21]

Aghast at the carnage, and confronted with a call for "half a million more troops"—not to mention escalating taxes and dictatorial government—Northerners desperately wanted the war to end. Many believed that if Richmond, Atlanta, and Mobile, because of the latter's ties with Atlanta, could hold out through October, peace would follow. In Mobile, few were concerned about Richmond: Robert E. Lee would see to that. Atlanta, however, was a different matter: it was the Southern heartland's most im-portant city—a railroad hub "connecting Richmond with the deep South, the indispensable center of all heavy industries, cannon and powder factories, rolling mills and depots of supply."[22]

Sensing this concern, the commanding general at Atlanta, John Bell Hood, wrote an encouraging letter on 4 August to General Bragg, his immediate superior. "At present everything here looks well," he said. "I beg to assure you that I have no intention of abandoning this place, and that if no other recourse be left I shall certainly give the enemy battle before I leave it."[23]

In Mobile, optimism also prevailed concerning Atlanta. With the Georgia city still in Confederate hands and Kirby Smith threatening to cross the Mississippi with ten thousand infantry, the enemy would be reluctant to tie down fifteen or twenty thousand troops to besiege Mobile itself. Maury's immediate task, therefore, was to defend the Lower Defense Line, which was more vulnerable to attack than the city. But Maury and his staff were not the only ones pondering this problem. The navy had some ideas of its own.

In a letter to General Higgins dated 4 August, Lt. James Baker, a naval officer in the Mobile Squadron, requested permission to attack and capture Fort Pickens at Pensacola. In April, Baker had made a reconnaissance of the route and concluded that the mission was feasible. Starting at 5:00 P.M. from a point twenty miles east of Fort Morgan, Baker was certain that a force of "100 or 150 men in small boats" with arms and provisions for five days could land at Fort Pickens around midnight and enter through the sally ports or by scaling. About 100 men garrisoned the fort, which was usually guarded by only two sentinels. The time was opportune, he reasoned, because "the enemy have now withdrawn all their large vessels for an attack on Mobile, and their attention is wholly diverted from Pensacola. In the event of the capture of the fort, with the immense amount of ammunition, stores, etc., there and at the yard, the force of the blow here would be broken, as the enemy obtain all their supplies from that point. Having already reconnoitered the route, I feel confident in asserting its entire feasibility, and think it would greatly relieve Mobile."[24] With Higgins's and Maury's approval, Baker would be ready to make the raid as soon as the men and equipment were available. He hoped the mission would not get sidetracked by other concerns.

CHAPTER 16

✦➤ ◀✦

Tecumseh Steams In

WHEN THE *Hartford* HOISTED SIGNAL 2139, ORDERING THE CAPTAINS to report aboard for the second time in two days, the cannon duel between the *Winnebago* and Fort Gaines could be heard echoing across the water, adding a sense of urgency to the summons. William F. Hutchinson, an assistant surgeon aboard the *Lackawanna,* counted twenty-six ships anchored around the *Hartford,* while small boats with "blue jackets" and "gold-laced officers in the stern sheets" converged on the flagship.[1]

Once the captains were aboard and assembled in Farragut's cabin, Farragut wasted little time in getting down to business. The next day, 5 August, the fleet would go in. A final diagram was distributed showing the vessels that would make the attack. Some changes had been made since the previous day's briefing: The *Brooklyn* and *Octorara* would lead the wooden column, the *Octorara* having replaced the *Sebago,* which had damaged one of her side-wheels in an accident with the *Lackawanna* the evening before. With the admiral's reluctant approval, the *Hartford* and *Metacomet* would be second in line, and the *Seminole* would replace the *Lackawanna*'s consort, the *Conemaugh,* which would continue as flagship of the Mississippi Sound Flotilla.[2]

Twenty-four hours had passed since Jenkins reported that the *Tecumseh* had started to coal. If no problems were encountered, Farragut reasoned, she would reach the fleet in tow of the *Bienville* before sundown and would be on hand to lead the ironclad column into the bay. The *Richmond,* which was in Pensacola expediting the *Tecumseh*'s departure, would also arrive that afternoon. Since the ironclads were "slower than the wooden vessels," the admiral explained:

I desire that as soon as a signal is made from this vessel in the morning, or if a signal cannot be seen, you perceive any movement which shows that the fleet is about moving, you will get underway and proceed toward the fort, endeavoring to keep at about a mile distant until we are coming up and begin to fire, when you can move nearer, so as to make it certain that when abreast of the fort we have our ironclads as an offset to those, which otherwise might run us down.

The service that I look for from the ironclads is, first to neutralize as much as possible the fire of the guns which rake our approach; next to look out for the [enemy's] ironclads when we are abreast of the fort, and lastly, to occupy the attention of those batteries which would rake us while running up the bay.

After the wooden vessels have passed the fort, the Winnebago *and* Chickasaw *will follow them. The commanding officer of the* Tecumseh *and* Manhattan *will endeavor to destroy the* Tennessee, *exercising their own judgment as to the time they shall remain behind for that purpose.*

Also, if the situation permitted, the *Tecumseh* and *Manhattan* were to fire one round each at the water battery before engaging the enemy ram.[3]

Farragut was well aware of the value of these new engines of war; they comprised more than 20 percent of his fleet, but as one raised and trained in a world of wooden walls, he did not believe that men confined in iron fought their best. The admiral had often remarked that "the same officers and men taken from an iron clad and put on board . . . a wooden ship, would give a better account of themselves, and have a better chance in the latter than in the former." Or as he sometimes said, "Give me hearts of iron in ships of oak."[4]

Concerned that the rebels might have recently planted torpedoes in the clear channel following the departure of a blockade runner eight days earlier, the admiral wanted the area examined. After the briefing on 3 August, he ordered Lieutenant Watson to go in and examine the channel after dark. Working within a few hundred yards of Fort Morgan's seven-gun water battery, Watson's crew lowered a grapnel and dragged it between the black buoy and the shoreline. "My attempt to verify the fact that there were no torpedoes there," Watson explained, "was soon brought to an end by a heavy squall . . . and it was all we could do to get to the nearest blockading gunboat which was on the lookout for us." Although Watson did not complete his mission, enough was accomplished to convince the admiral that the channel probably was clear of torpedoes.[5]

The ships forming the battle line would anchor off the outer bar, as shown in the sketch distributed before the briefing. The first order of battle would form before dawn; the second and third, between dawn and sunrise. Shortly thereafter the fleet would be passing Sand Island. As the briefing ended, old friends shook hands and in hushed voices wished each other the best of luck. They hoped to celebrate a victory the next day, but now there was work to be done preparing for the attack.[6]

As Captain Marchand returned to the *Lackawanna*, he beckoned his executive officer, Lt. Thomas S. Spence, to his cabin, and "after a moment's conversation, the latter came forward, his face all aglow with excitement" and broke the news to the cluster of officers waiting on the quarterdeck: "Tomorrow at daylight, fellows, hurrah!"[7] But not everyone in the fleet was as exuberant about the attack, including Marchand. "What torpedoes or obstructions are in the ship channel we are ignorant," he wrote in his journal, referring to Watson's failure to locate anything during his foray. "An effort on our part to pass in will be made," he added, "but the result is in the hands of the Almighty, and we pray that He may favor us." The *Hartford*'s second assistant engineer, Isaac DeGraff, wrote in his diary: "All is now ready for the battle, and tomorrow morning is the time fixed upon [for it] to take place, and all are looking forward with more or less anxiety for the result. We hope and trust that it may be all that we could wish."[8]

As the afternoon wore on, Farragut finally found time to pen his wife a letter.

I am going into Mobile Bay in the morning if God is my leader as I hope He is, and in Him I place my trust; if He thinks it is the proper place for me to die, I am ready to submit to his will, in that as all other things. My great mortification is that my vessels, the ironclads, were not ready to have gone in yesterday. The army landed last night and are in full view of us this morning and the Tecumseh has not yet arrived from Pensacola. God bless and preserve you, my darling, and my dear Boy, if anything should happen to me and may His blessings also rest upon your dear Mother and all your sisters and their children. Your devoted and affectionate husband, who never for one moment forgot his love, duty, or fidelity to you, his devoted and best of wives.[9]

The ink was hardly dry on the letter when he was told that the *Richmond* had arrived from Pensacola. As the big sloop's anchor plunged downward, her lookouts read an interrogatory signal from the flagship, asking, "Has the *Tecumseh* left?" The return signal was: "About 10:00 A.M." Allowing six hours to cover the fifty-five miles between Mobile and Pensacola, the ironclad and her consorts, the *Bienville* and *Metacomet*, should join the fleet before sundown. This would give ample time for Craven and the consort captains to be briefed on the battle plan.[10]

ON THE EVE OF BATTLE, THE FORT GAINES GARRISON NUMBERED 818, and her armament, 26 guns, 8 of which bore on the land, 12 on the water, and 6 on both land and water. However, lacking adequate traverses to protect the gun crews and sand-filled timber cribs to reinforce the scarp walls and magazines, the fort was in no condition to withstand a prolonged siege.[11]

The beginning of August was a period of uneasiness and frustration for the North. If the war could be prolonged a little longer, victory would be within the South's grasp. General Maury's belief—that if Mobile and Atlanta could hang on for another month or so, the North would sue for peace—was becoming a reality. The need for Northern victories and the increasing dissatisfaction with Lincoln's war policies were accelerating the possibility of a negotiated peace. General Hood's predecessor, Joseph E. Johnston, believed that if Sherman could be held at bay, the Northern Peace Party would defeat Lincoln and bring the war to an end.[12]

In Atlanta, General Hood, was indeed "foiling" Sherman, although at great expense in casualties and suffering. The city was being sporadically shelled daily, causing the inhabitants to go underground as the people of Vicksburg did in 1863. Hood's lines, however, were holding—but the clock was ticking.

On the last day of July, Capt. Thomas Key of Gen. Pat Cleburne's division recorded in his diary what the fighting was like now that Atlanta was under siege: "Truly this morning appears like the Sabbath, for there is almost a perfect calm along the lines around the city." The quiet ended abruptly when musket fire broke out, and the Confederates opened with heavy artillery that had been sent to Atlanta from the fortifications at Mobile. Later in the day, a heavy rain drenched "the dirty and wearied soldiers in the entrenchments" against a backdrop of lightning and cannon fire. As night fell, the rain stopped and so did the fighting, to be replaced by the "sweet strains of music" of the 79th Pennsylvania band, "to cheer and comfort friends and foes alike."[13]

In Mobile, General Maury was convinced that the Yankee fleet would be repulsed or severely mauled when it tried to enter the bay; recent reports indicated that 46 torpedoes had been planted in the main channel during the last few days, bringing the total to 180. In addition, thirty-four guns, including those of the Confederate squadron, could be brought to bear on the main ship channel when the enemy attempted to enter the bay. Maury believed that "no vessel yet built could pass through that channel in daylight." He also believed that an attack on the city of Mobile was not imminent but could materialize in the near future. At present, about six thousand men were under arms in the district, of which only one thousand had been under fire. Of the total, about four thousand manned the city fortifications.[14]

At Fort Morgan, on the Lower Defense Line, the usually cheerful Lieutenant Tarleton found time to pen a quick note to his fiancée, Sallie Lightfoot, informing her that affairs at the fort were not encouraging. Yesterday the enemy landed "two to three thousand" troops on the west end of Dauphin Island. "This would seem to indicate that Fort Gaines is to be seriously attacked first and if this should prove to be the case I should not be surprised if we had no fight at all at this fort. For if the Yankees take Gaines and Powell this fort will fall, of course, by starvation in as short a time as they could reasonably hope to take it." But it was "useless to speculate about such matters," he continued.

We are in a position from which there will be no retreat and we shall have to do the best we can. Still it is possible the enemy may not run their iron-clads by us, for if they intend doing so at all, I can't see why they haven't done it already. They have been here now almost a week and could have passed us any night or day. I sincerely hope they will try to take us by an attack and not by cutting us off and starving us out.

*But whatever happens, unless the monitors run by us I shall not give up
the hope of our marriage in the fall or as soon after as possible. I have been
trying to persuade myself not to cherish hopes of it any longer—but it is no
use and I have determined not to give it up until I see the ironclads in the
bay. There is a great deal I have to say to you, but it would only make you
sad and so I will not say it. I fear you would think me unmanly were I to
write as I feel.*[15]

As soon as the *Richmond* had anchored, Captain Jenkins boarded a cutter and was rowed to the *Hartford*. Farragut and Drayton met him at the
gangway, exchanged greetings, then walked aft to the admiral's cabin.
There Farragut asked what had caused the *Tecumseh*'s delay. It was the
same old problem: a lack of organization at the navy yard and too much
concern for regulations and protocol. But the *Tecumseh* was now under way
and should arrive well before sundown.[16]

At 5:30 P.M. "Sail ho!" rang out from the *Hartford*'s maintop. To the
east the *Metacomet*, followed by the *Tecumseh* in tow of the *Bienville*, could
be seen steaming toward the fleet. At six o'clock the *Tecumseh* cast off her
hawser and came to anchor near the flagship. Within minutes, Commander Craven had reported aboard the *Hartford* to be briefed on his role in
the next day's battle.

The fleet would enter the bay through the channel opposite Fort Morgan, which was free of torpedoes, Farragut explained, and the *Tecumseh*
would lead the ironclad column. A black buoy marked the beginning of
the torpedo field, and the admiral stressed the necessity of keeping well
to the east. The mission of the *Tecumseh* and *Manhattan*, he reiterated, was
to destroy the rebel ram. The *Chickasaw* and *Winnebago* would stay behind
and fire on the water battery until the fleet had passed, then follow the
last vessel into the bay. Having received his instructions, Craven, accompanied by Lieutenant Watson and Martin Freeman, the *Hartford*'s pilot,
reboarded the *Tecumseh* and steamed for Sand Island Channel to join the
other three ironclads already anchored there. With the *Tecumseh* safely
moored in the channel, Watson and Freeman returned to the *Hartford*.[17]

Earlier in the afternoon, before the *Tecumseh*'s arrival, a heavy squall had
blown in from the northwest, but now the sky had cleared and a "gentle
breeze relieved the midsummer heat." By sundown, the vessels that
would form the battle line had anchored beyond the outer bar, ready to be
lashed together before dawn. Between dawn and sunrise, the battle line

would be formed, and by sunrise the column should be passing Sand Island.[18]

As darkness fell, an oppressive stillness hung over the water. By then, most officers and men had completed their duties and were tending to personal matters. Aboard the *Hartford,* the officers had gathered around the wardroom table, "writing what they knew might be their last letters to loved ones, far away, or giving to friends messages and instructions in case of death."[19]

In the *Richmond*'s wardroom, the same prebattle ritual was taking place: Letters and wills were being written and instructions given to friends should the writer be killed or wounded. Some left to store their belongings below the waterline; others had sent them ashore while the *Richmond* was in Pensacola. Second Asst. Engineer Absalom Kirby had put his wife's photograph in his dresser drawer under some clothes, "so that it would not be broken by the [jolt] of the guns." He also drew all his back pay and put it in his pocket should he be captured and sent to Libby Prison, "so I should have something to live upon, if the Rebels did not take it from me, which very likely they would do." As the *Richmond*'s deck officers relaxed in the wardroom, the engineers were hard at work in the engine room. "All fires were cleaned and built up, engines and everything inspected, so there could be no hitch or a moment's delay, for the Richmond was one of the best drilled ships afloat."[20]

STANDING ATOP THE *Tennessee*'s PILOTHOUSE, ADMIRAL BUCHANAN and Commander Johnston, the *Tennessee*'s captain, had watched the thick, black smoke of a fourth monitor join the other three in Sand Island Channel, a sign that an attack was imminent. For weeks, the crew of the *Tennessee* had suffered from the heat, making it impossible to sleep inside the iron casemate or belowdecks. The coming battle, therefore, "would soon be determined one way or the other, and everyone looked forward to it with a positive feeling of relief." Here and there, in the *Tennessee*'s casemate and on the afterdeck, crewmen could be seen scribbling last-minute notes to friends and loved ones. Aboard the gunboats, the same ritual was taking place, with one exception: The *Gaines*'s crew were being soothed "with music" from the vessel's quartet.[21]

Toward sundown, the enemy's sloops and gunboats could be seen coming together "nearly due south of the fort." Soon darkness closed in upon the scene "with the quiet and balmy stillness of a Southern mid-summer day." Ashore at Fort Morgan, Captain Whiting of the 1st Alabama Heavy Artillery was officer of the day. He had been on duty since 9:00 A.M. and would not be relieved until the next morning. As officer of the day, Whiting was responsible for alerting the garrison if the Yankee fleet began to move. Farragut had run by the New Orleans forts during darkness and might try it here, although negotiating Mobile's roadstead without beacons would be considerably more difficult than passing up the Mississippi River. Nevertheless, General Page was taking no chances: For several nights, gun detachments had remained on the ramparts should the enemy attempt to run in during darkness. Now an attack at daylight was almost a certainty.[22]

The *Red Gauntlet* had left Havana four days earlier. In twelve hours she would reach the Alabama coast somewhere east of Mobile Bay, where Captain Randal would assess the situation and decide how he would enter the bay. The vessel carried scarce supplies needed to sustain the Confederacy's war effort, the loss of which would be disastrous. Her sister ship, the *Ivanhoe*, had reportedly been intercepted and run aground while attempting to enter Mobile Bay a month earlier. As the *Red Gauntlet* knifed through the phosphorus-tinted waters of the Gulf, Randal continually adjusted the vessel's speed so that she would enter Mobile Bay before dawn on 5 August. With luck, he would catch the blockade's lookouts half asleep.[23]

CHAPTER 17

-»>- -«<-

Get Under Way

ABOARD THE *Red Gauntlet*, NOW FORTY MILES SOUTHEAST OF MOBILE BAY, Captain Randal had reason to be pleased; if his luck held, he would enter Mobile Bay just before sunrise. The vessel's cargo of lead bars, harness leather, salted beef, coffee, and stationery were needed to replenish the Confederacy's growing shortages of war material, finished goods, and food; her loss would be a major setback to the South's war effort, a fate Captain Randal would do his best to avoid.

Built in Scotland by John Scott and Sons, the *Red Gauntlet* was on her maiden voyage. She was a perfect example of the fast, shallow-draft, side-wheel steamer designed to evade the blockade; at sixteen knots, she could outrun almost anything in the Union Navy. Painted gray, and with her sleek lines and low profile, the vessel was nearly invisible, particularly on a dark night. By 4:00 A.M. she would be approaching the Alabama coast somewhere east of Mobile Bay. There, Captain Randal would slow the vessel to a crawl, hug the beach, and hope for the best. If all went well, she would be inside Mobile Bay by sunrise.[1]

In the Gulf off Fort Morgan, 5 August promised to be hot and sultry. At midnight, a mild southwest breeze did little to bring the temperature below 80 degrees. Aboard the *Brooklyn*, Lieutenant Blake awoke between 2:00 and 3:00 A.M., washed, dressed, and went on deck, where he found a number of officers already making preparations for the coming battle. Capt. James Alden wanted the *Brooklyn*, the lead vessel, ready well in advance of the order to get under way. On the *Hartford*'s berth deck, off-duty crewmen tossed and turned in their hammocks, trying to get a little sleep before the boatswains called "All hands!" and "Up all hammocks!" to the tune of their shrill pipes.[2] At three o'clock the *Brooklyn*'s crew were called and given coffee and sandwiches; breakfast would be served after the battle. While the crew was eating, a comet streaked across the sky—a good omen to some, a sign of impending doom for others.[3]

As the *Red Gauntlet* crept along the shore east of Fort Morgan, Captain Randal noticed that something strange was going on out in the Gulf: Lights were blinking; vessels were moving back and forth; and—strangest of all—the picket line appeared to be withdrawn. But whatever this meant, events were working in Randal's favor, for in another twenty minutes his vessel would be safely inside Mobile Bay, ending a voyage of seven thousand miles without mishap.[4]

By 4:00 A.M. the gunboats were coming alongside the larger vessels to be lashed onto the port side. Aboard the *Hartford* the anchor chain had been shortened to twenty fathoms, and the crew was standing by to receive the *Metacomet*, the flagship's consort. Having reluctantly agreed to let the *Brooklyn* lead the battle line, the admiral was still uncomfortable with the decision. But apart from his belief that "exposure is one of the penalties of rank," he could command as well in second place as in first.[5]

An hour earlier, learning that the wind was from the southwest, Farragut had ordered the attack to proceed as scheduled. He was at breakfast in his cabin with Captain Drayton and Fleet Surgeon James C. Palmer, who had come from the hospital in Pensacola to attend the wounded, when Lieutenant Watson came in at 5:30 to inform the admiral that the vessel pairings had been completed. Nodding to Drayton, Farragut told him to hoist Signal 1218: "Get under way!" Within five minutes, all vessels had answered, including the ironclads.[6]

By 5:40, the *Brooklyn* was under way, heading slowly for the outer bar. Behind, one by one, the vessels of the fleet followed in her wake. Aboard the *Lackawanna*, fourth in line, Assistant Surgeon Hutchinson described the scene: "At twenty minutes to six the line was formed, and we commenced to steam in slowly, the Admiral's order being to carry the lowest possible pressure, so as to avoid as much as possible the fearful scalding effect of steam, should the boilers be pierced. The ships were dressed from stem to stern in flags, as if for a gala day, and every man sprang to his station with a will when the long roll called all hands to general quarters."[7] As the drums rolled, the pulse of every officer and crewman quickened.

Guns were cast loose; shell rooms and magazines were opened; powder and shells were passed up; and everything was made ready for firing.[8]

In Sand Island Channel, the ironclads had beat to quarters and were awaiting Commander Craven's order to get under way. With the *Tecumseh* leading the way, they would steam out, cross the van of the wooden vessels, and proceed up the main channel on the starboard flank of the battle line. As instructed, when opposite Fort Morgan, the *Tecumseh* and *Manhattan* would attack the *Tennessee;* the *Chickasaw* and *Winnebago* would engage the fort's water battery.

At six o'clock, twenty minutes before sunrise, six vessels of the Mississippi Sound Flotilla, by prearrangement, steamed to positions off Fort Powell. Their mission: to shell the fort as the fleet entered the bay. At the same time, the six vessels of the Gulf Flotilla got under way, but fearful of shoals in their assigned area, took positions roughly two and a half miles southeast of Fort Morgan, a distance that would seriously affect the accuracy of their fire. The mission of these vessels would be to provide the battle line with fire support as it passed the fort.[9]

STANDING ON THE SOUTHWEST BASTION OF FORT MORGAN, CAPTAIN Whiting knew what was going on: the enemy was preparing to attack. Just before daylight, to his amazement, he watched a gray-hulled blockade runner enter the Swash Channel, round Mobile Point, and come to anchor near the *Tennessee*, where she was boarded by an officer from the ram, apparently to explain the situation at hand and give instructions for navigating the remaining thirty miles to Mobile.[10]

The fog that had blanketed the Gulf was now dissipating, revealing what was unmistakably the prelude to an attack. The Yankee fleet was crossing the outer bar, and the ironclads in Sand Island Channel appeared to be waiting to join the wooden vessels when they passed. Convinced that the attack had indeed begun, Whiting sent an orderly to General Page, who mounted the southwest bastion and confirmed that the Union fleet was indeed about to attack. However, since the enemy still had several miles to cover, he ordered the garrison to be fed breakfast before manning the guns.[11]

Across the channel at Fort Gaines, Major Browne's battalion was skirmishing on the picket line to recover the area that had been lost by

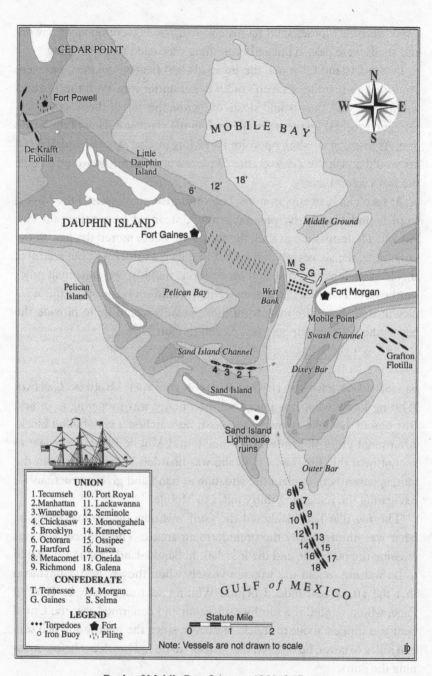

CEDAR POINT

Fort Powell

De Krafft
Flotilla

MOBILE BAY

Little
Dauphin
Island

6' 12' 18'

DAUPHIN ISLAND

Fort Gaines

Middle Ground

Pelican
Island

Pelican Bay

West
Bank

M S G T

Fort Morgan

Mobile Point

Swash Channel

Sand Island Channel

4 3 2 1

Dixey Bar

Grafton
Flotilla

Sand Island

Sand Island
Lighthouse
ruins

Outer Bar

UNION
1. Tecumseh   10. Port Royal
2. Manhattan   11. Lackawanna
3. Winnebago   12. Seminole
4. Chickasaw   13. Monongahela
5. Brooklyn   14. Kennebec
6. Octorara   15. Ossipee
7. Hartford   16. Itasca
8. Metacomet   17. Oneida
9. Richmond   18. Galena

CONFEDERATE
T. Tennessee   M. Morgan
G. Gaines   S. Selma

LEGEND
♦♦♦ Torpedoes   ⬟ Fort
○ Iron Buoy   ּיּ Piling

5
6 7
8
10 9
11
12 13
14 15
16 17
18

GULF of MEXICO

Statute Mile
0   1   2

Note: Vessels are not drawn to scale

Battle of Mobile Bay, 5 August 1864, 6:15 a.m.

Colonel Anderson's order to fall back. In the meantime, the colonel asked Capt. Charles C. Biberon, the engineer in charge, to post an officer on the fort's barbette battery to observe the Union fleet. As light began to spread across the water, Biberon described the developing scene:

> *I looked at the vessels as they changed their position with breathless interest, for it was apparent that some demonstration of importance was about to transpire. . . . In a little time I was convinced that such was the intention of the Commodore, and I watched the fleet with intense interest, calling to Col. Anderson and stating the intention of the enemy. They were now all in line— seventeen of them—and having crossed the bar, were bearing for the entrance of the bay near Fort Morgan. I turned my theodolite in the direction of that fort, and noticed that the water battery was manned and that the barbette battery was ready to receive the impending attack. From Fort Morgan I cast my eye along the shore and waters of the bay, and there was the iron monster, the* Tennessee, *lying at anchor a short distance below the fort, waiting to receive the approaching enemy.[12]*

About halfway between the outer bar and Sand Island, Captain Alden had all hands mustered on the *Brooklyn*'s quarterdeck and the *Octorara*'s wheelhouses. When all were assembled, he asked Lt. Cdr. Edward Sull, the *Brooklyn*'s executive officer, to read a short prayer, after which the captain said they had been selected to lead the fleet into Mobile Bay, and he expected them to give the rebels a rough fight. They then gave three cheers, "sending a flag to every masthead."[13]

At 6:35 the *Brooklyn* passed Sand Island; ahead, the *Tecumseh* was entering the main channel, followed by the *Manhattan, Chickasaw,* and *Winnebago.* Commander Craven, "although an experienced seaman," was not familiar with the approaches to Mobile Bay; John Collins, his pilot, however, "knew the bay like the palm of his hand," having fished its waters for years, but "knew little about conning a sluggish, 2,100-ton ironclad." Collins therefore found himself acting as "both pilot and helmsman for a vessel he had never conned."[14]

Ten minutes later, the *Tecumseh* was midway across the channel, followed by the *Manhattan* and *Winnebago*. The *Winnebago*, however, was lagging behind, having encountered problems getting under way; this, in turn, had delayed the advance of the wooden column. Nevertheless, now that Fort Morgan was within maximum range of the *Tecumseh*'s 15-inch

Dahlgrens, Commander Craven ordered the guns to be scaled, a procedure used to clean the bores by firing a round.

On the ramparts of Fort Morgan and in the lighthouse battery below, the guns were trained on the main ship channel south of the fort. General Page noticed that everyone was in "high spirits," waiting for the command to fire. At 6:47, as General Page, Captain Whiting, and Major Gee, the post commander, were standing on the southwest bastion sizing up the enemy's tactics, they saw a puff of white smoke erupt from the lead ironclad. The projectile became visible within seconds, growing larger and larger as it howled toward the fort. A moment later, a bright flash and an earsplitting crack sent 350 pounds of shrapnel smashing into the base of the fort's lighthouse. A second shell burst over the fort. Major Gee wanted to return the fire, but Page considered the range still too great and would not give the command.[15]

At 7:05 the *Tecumseh* was about two thousand yards from the fort; the van of the wooden column, nearly three thousand. Accuracy at these ranges was problematical, especially when the target was moving, but the morale of the garrison had to be considered. Ignoring for the moment the enemy ironclads, the general turned his attention to the more vulnerable wooden vessels. Looking at Captain Whiting, he said: "Open the fight, sir." Within seconds an 8-inch Brooke rifle sent a 100-pound projectile screaming toward the lead pair of wooden vessels, which was followed by a "soul-stirring cheer" from the garrison.[16]

When the Union fleet was observed crossing the bar, Admiral Buchanan had ordered Commander Johnston, the *Tennessee*'s captain, to signal the Confederate squadron to get under way and follow the flagship's motions. Within twenty minutes, the *Tennessee* and the gunboats *Morgan, Selma,* and *Gaines* were positioned in line ahead across the channel just north of the torpedo field, with the ram opposite the clear channel. The admiral then came down from the pilothouse to the gun deck and addressed the crew, "his snug, gray frock coat, gold braid, and sword imparting a deadly seriousness to his words: Now men, the enemy is coming, and I want you to do your duty; and you shall not have it to say when you leave this vessel that you were not near enough to the enemy, for I will meet them, and then you can fight alongside of their own ships; and if I fall, lay me on one side and go on with the fight, and never mind me—but whip and sink the Yankees or fight until you sink yourselves, but do not surrender."[17]

Returning to the pilothouse, Buchanan could see the dark hulls of four

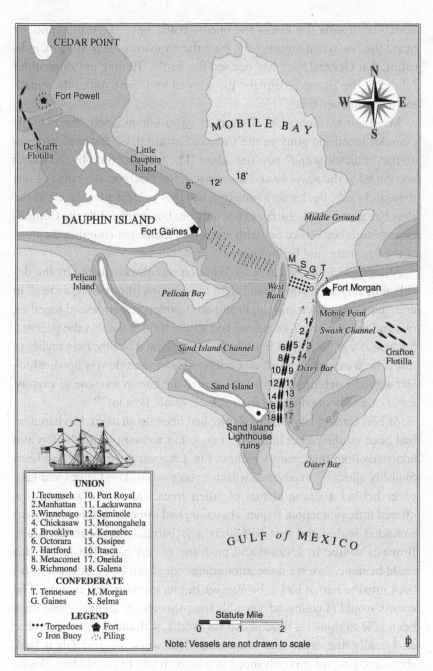

Battle of Mobile Bay, 5 August 1864, 7:10 a.m.

ironclads crossing the van of the enemy battle line. About this time, he heard the boom of a cannon echo from the ramparts of Fort Morgan, indicating that General Page had opened the battle. Turning to Commander Johnston, the *Tennessee's* captain, the admiral told him to order the squadron to commence firing.

Midshipman George S. Waterman, who commanded the two 32-pounder broadside guns on the *Gaines's* forward deck, fastened his eyes on the "majestic scene" now unfolding. The first shot fired by the *Gaines* was aimed at the *Brooklyn* and her consort, the *Octorara*, at a range of two thousand yards. Buchanan's squadron had the "perfect advantage"; as the *Brooklyn* approached, she could fire only her bow guns, while the Confederate vessels could rake her with sixteen of theirs, not counting the guns of the fort that could be brought to bear.[18]

Aboard the *Tennessee*, Lt. A. D. Wharton was also fascinated by the developing drama: "It was a grand sight to see when [the vessels] were all in line, the monitors leading singly and the wooden vessels lashed together, two and two. On the *Tennessee* we had ample time to witness the pageant, for such it was for half an hour, before it became a bloody, fiery reality of war. The water was smooth as a millpond, and the tide was flood, which fact argued a determination on the part of the enemy to come in anyway, for in case of being disabled their vessels would float in."[19]

At Fort Gaines, Lieutenant Rapier had been up all night. His battalion had been on the picket line since 1:00 A.M., 1,100 yards from the fort and 600 yards from the enemy's pickets. On 4 August the enemy "had been foolishly allowed" to advance within 1,700 yards of Fort Gaines and take cover behind a strong abattis of fallen trees. Occupying an area that offered little protection, Rapier's battalion had three men killed and eight wounded within the first half hour. His battalion commander, Major Browne, wanted to advance and push the enemy back, but before this could be done, "we rec'd the astounding order from Col. Anderson to fall back into the Fort, it had to be obeyed, but its stupidity was evident. The enemy would of course advance his sharpshooters & no one would have been able to show his head above the works, without at least being shot at. Luckily, the order was countermanded, when we had fallen back about 400 yds.; we then advanced to within 20 yds. of our old line. Whilst we were making these moves, like the 'King of France,' a most terrible bombardment had opened on Fort Morgan."[20]

DAUPHIN ISLAND'S TOWERING PINES, GLEAMING WHITE DUNES, AND exotic offshore scents presented to the Northern and western troops a spectacle straight from the pen of Herman Melville: romance, mystery, adventure, all in a South Seas setting. But once ashore, the vision vanished. The deep sands, thick underbrush, and insects—not to mention the threat of sudden death—had a profound impact on the young recruits.

General Granger, frustrated and embarrassed, planned to send a report to General Canby explaining why the heavy artillery would not be mounted in time to fire on Fort Gaines as the fleet entered the bay. "We are getting the 30-pounders into position slowly; the labor is severe, owing to the deep sand and the great distance; everything has to be hauled and packed on the men's backs," he wrote. "All the landings on this island are difficult and uncertain, owing to the wind and surf and shallow water, and nearly the whole of it is a quagmire of deep sand, hot enough during the day for roasting potatoes." The general did not think to tell Canby that if the army's big 30-pounder Parrots were not ready to fire on Fort Gaines when the fleet entered the bay the next day, two sections of the Connecticut Light Artillery would be in place with their 3-inch ordnance rifles elevated to pick off rebel gunners firing across the channel. Actually, an attempt to silence Fort Morgan's guns would be an exercise in futility, for the range was simply too great for effective results.[21]

Private Enslow of the 77th Illinois had written his wife on 4 August that the army was besieging Fort Gaines and would probably have to make a charge before it surrendered. If so, there would be many casualties, and he might be one of them. He would, however, take his chances like a man; and, should he fall, hopefully they would meet in a "Better World."[22]

Out in the channel, the monitors had crossed the van of the wooden column and now were within fifteen hundred yards of the fort. Several hundred yards aft, the fleet followed in close order, some already firing their chase guns. At this advanced range, the monitor *Chickasaw* and the *Hartford* had already been hit, evidence that the rebel gunners had zeroed in on every foot of the channel.

To the east, the six vessels of the Gulf Flotilla had opened fire on Fort Morgan, but with little effect. When firing, they had been ordered to keep well to the west of the fort and its outlying sand batteries, "but through some misunderstanding, perhaps on the part of their senior officer, Lieutenant-Commander Grafton, they were anchored at such a respectful distance from the shore as to render their fire useless."[23]

The Gulf Flotilla's failure to effectively bombard Fort Morgan during the fleet's approach was a bad omen so early in the attack; aboard the *Hartford*, however, other more serious matters were occupying Farragut's attention, such as keeping the battle line in close order and catching up with the ironclads, now a thousand yards ahead of the *Brooklyn*. This gap had developed when the *Chickasaw*, last in line, failed to keep up with the other monitors as they left Sand Island Channel, thus causing the wooden column to delay until she had crossed its van. The admiral now wanted the gap closed. On the *Hartford*'s poop deck with Farragut were Percival Drayton and other members of his personal staff: Flag Lieutenant Watson, responsible for signals; Alexander McKinley, his secretary; and two aides, A. R. Yates and H. H. Brownell.[24]

At 7:11 the *Hartford* fired her first shot from the starboard chase gun. At about this time, Farragut looked down from the poop deck and noticed that the two signal officers assigned to the flagship the day before—Maj. Frank W. Marston and Lt. John Coddington Kinney—were standing on the gun deck. He had issued an order that the army signalmen were to stay below during the fight. The officers, however, had decided to disobey the order and remain on deck. Seeing them below, Farragut sent a message to Lt. Cdr. Lewis A. Kimberly, the *Hartford*'s executive officer, to send them down to the cockpit to assist the surgeons. Since they would not be needed when passing Fort Morgan but would be wanted later to open communications with the army, it would be a misfortune if they were disabled. Lieutenant Kinney explained what happened next:

> In this [remaining on deck, we] were successful until shortly before passing Sand Island and coming within range of Fort Morgan. Then the lynx-eyed executive officer, Lieutenant-Commander Kimberly, who, as [we] afterward discovered, never allowed anything to escape his attention, came to [us] very quietly and politely, and told [us] the Admiral's order must be obeyed. We were satisfied from his manner that the surgeons had need of us, and, without endeavoring to argue the matter, made our way to the stifling hold, where Surgeon Lansdale and Assistant-Surgeon Commons, with their helpers, were quietly sitting, with their implements, bandages, and other paraphernalia spread out ready for use.[25]

At 7:21 a shot from Fort Morgan struck the *Hartford*'s foremast. Assessing the situation, Farragut observed that the *Brooklyn* was still too far behind the monitors. Motioning to Watson, he told him to signal the *Brook-*

lyn to "go on." According to the admiral's instructions, the *Tecumseh* and *Manhattan* would enter the bay though the clear channel and engage the *Tennessee*. Hugging the shore, the *Chickasaw* and *Winnebago* would remain stationary and fire at the water battery as the wooden vessels passed. Once the last pair of wooden vessels had entered the bay, the *Chickasaw* and *Winnebago* would follow and engage the rebel gunboats. When opposite the fort, the admiral wanted the fleet's firepower to be concentrated, and this could be accomplished only if the battle line passed the fort in "close order," which meant that the interval between vessels should not exceed 240 yards. However, with low steam and a strong incoming tide, it was nearly impossible for the big sloops to maintain the required interval.

By 7:25 the *Brooklyn* had overtaken the rear of the ironclad column, with the *Hartford* and *Richmond* close behind. The *Lackawanna*, followed by the *Monongahela*, *Ossipee*, and *Oneida*, however, was still five hundred yards behind the *Richmond*. Aboard the *Lackawanna*, Assistant Surgeon Hutchinson was on deck watching the drama unfold. As yet no casualties had been reported, and he wanted to see as much of the action as possible before being called to the cockpit, where he would remain until the battle was over. Standing on the forecastle watching Fort Morgan, he noticed a puff of smoke, then saw the shot, "looking exactly as if some gigantic hand had thrown in play a ball toward you. By the time it is half way, you get the boom of the report, and then the howl of the missile, which apparently grows so rapidly in size that every green hand on board who can see it, is certain that it will hit him between the eyes. Then, as it goes past with a shriek like a thousand devils, the inclination to do reverence is so strong that it is almost impossible to resist it."[26]

Lieutenant Batcheller, executive officer of the *Monongahela*, described this phase of the battle as "the beginning of the terrible portion of the action. From our station, being in the rear of the center of the line, we could watch the action, and with what interest you can imagine. In a few minutes we were to be in it ourselves."[27]

Next we began to sail up the narrow strait lamenting.
For on the one hand lay Scylla, and on the other mighty Charybdis.

HOMER, *The Odyssey*

Part Three

A STORM CLOUD ALL AGLOW

CHAPTER 18

➤➤ ◄◄

Catastrophe

AS THE UNION BATTLE LINE ADVANCED WITH FLAGS FLYING FROM EVERY peak, the spectacle "presented a scene worthy of the brush of an Angelo or Raphael." So far, only the *Hartford*'s starboard bow gun could be brought to bear on the fort and rebel squadron, but with her entire broadside firing, smoke was becoming a serious problem.[1]

Ahead, another problem was developing: the *Brooklyn* had stopped. By now she should be entering the channel east of the buoy. Beckoning to Watson, the admiral told him to signal the *Brooklyn* to go ahead. Within minutes, General Signal 665, "Go on," was fluttering from one of the *Hartford*'s fore-yards. The time was 7:24 A.M. on Friday, 5 August 1864, a date that would be long remembered by the officers and men of Farragut's fleet. Farragut had demonstrated at New Orleans, Port Hudson, and Vicksburg forts on land could not stop the passage of steam-powered wooden vessels as long as they continued to move and were handled with skill. Once they stopped, however, the advantage shifted to the fort—a vessel's wooden walls were no match for bricks and earth when it came to absorbing punishment.[2]

Captain Alden, also painfully aware that a crisis was at hand, opted to answer Farragut's signal by army wigwag, which was much faster than a navy flag hoist. The only persons aboard the *Hartford* who could read these messages were the army signalmen, still in the *Hartford*'s cockpit two decks below. "In the intense excitement of the occasion," Lieutenant Kinney said, "it seemed that hours had passed, but it was just twenty minutes from the time we went below, when an officer shouted down the

Union fleet opposite Fort Morgan.
Harper's Weekly, 3 SEPTEMBER 1864

hatchway, 'Send up an army signal officer immediately: the Brooklyn is signaling.'" In the meantime, the flagship's entire starboard broadside had begun to fire, further hampering the admiral's vision. As smoke continued to accumulate, Farragut left the poop deck and climbed the port main rigging to the sheer pole, just above the hammock railing. There he could communicate with Lt. Cdr. James E. Jouett, commanding officer of the *Metacomet,* who was standing on his vessel's starboard paddle box. But as the wind fell off, the admiral's view became more obscured, due to the heavy cannonading, forcing him to climb higher, ratline by ratline, until he reached the futtock shrouds just under the maintop, fifty-eight feet above the *Hartford*'s gun deck.[3]

In the words of Lieutenant Watson, Farragut could "lean either backward or forward in a comfortable position, having the free use of both hands for his spyglass, or any other purpose. Captain Drayton . . . becoming solicitous . . . that a slight wound, a blow from a splinter, or the cutting away of a portion of the rigging, might throw the admiral to the deck, sent the signal-quartermaster aloft with a small rope, to secure him to the rigging. The admiral at first declined to allow the quartermaster to do this,

Farragut in Hartford*'s rigging.*
DEAN MOSHER

but quickly admitted the wisdom of the precaution, and himself passed two or three turns of the rope around his body, and secured one end while the quartermaster . . . fastened the other."[4]

> *Bind me*
> *Hand and foot upright in the mast-step*
> *And tie the ends of the rope to the mast.*
>
> HOMER, *The Odyssey*

Although smoke was still a problem, Farragut's view of the battle was much improved. In addition, he could communicate with Pilot Freeman, who was in the maintop, and also with the deck, by transmitting messages through Freeman, who had a speaking tube connected to the deck. In addition, both could communicate by hand signals with Jouett, who was still on the *Metacomet*'s paddle box.

When Kinney reached the gun deck, he was directed to the forecastle where he saw that the *Brooklyn* had indeed stopped. A quick assessment revealed the problem: for some reason, the *Tecumseh* was approaching the channel on a course too far westward, thus crowding the *Brooklyn* away from the clear channel. Within seconds he had deciphered the *Brooklyn's* wigwag: "The monitors are right ahead. We cannot go on without passing them. What shall we do?" The time was 7:25.[5]

Scribbling the message on a sheet from his notebook, Kinney handed it to Lieutenant Yates for delivery to the admiral. Reading the message, Farragut told Yates to tell Kinney to signal Alden to "order the monitors ahead and go on."[6]

Aboard the *Tecumseh*, Commander Craven was doing his best to assess his next move. Squinting through the narrow observation slits in the *Tecumseh's* pilothouse, he could see the ram *Tennessee* six hundred yards ahead on the far side of the torpedo field, bucking the current; astern a hundred yards, the *Manhattan* was following in the *Tecumseh's* wake; and farther back, closer to the shore, the *Winnebago* and *Chickasaw* were approaching the water battery. To the southeast, three hundred yards off his port quarter, he could see the *Brooklyn*—but what worried him most was the enemy ram and the admiral's order to keep her away from the wooden vessels.[7]

Craven and Cdr. James Nicholson, the *Manhattan's* captain, had been given special instructions by the admiral to keep the enemy ram away from the wooden ships when they were passing the fort, then to stay behind long enough to destroy her. This was the opportunity Craven had been waiting for, "a regular iron clad fight." It was now 7:30.[8]

Moving ahead cautiously, oblivious to the problem he was causing, Craven was not convinced he could engage the *Tennessee*, as he had been ordered to do, before the *Brooklyn* entered the clear channel. Peering through one of the four observation slits in the pilothouse, he said to Collins: "The Admiral ordered me to go inside that buoy, but it must be a mistake." Assuming that Craven was concerned only with the depth of water, Collins told him there was plenty of water between the buoy and the shore.[9] Water, though, was not the problem. The *Tecumseh's* turning radius was too great to pass east of the buoy, turn, then engage the ram before the *Brooklyn* entered the bay. She also steered badly, particularly when going slowly. To compound the problem, Pilot Collins was still in the process of getting a feel for the *Tecumseh's* helm.[10] As Craven pondered his dilemma, the ram began to move farther to the west, as if coaxing him to cross the torpedo field. Noticing this, Craven decided to act: his mission was to engage the ram, not blindly follow an order that could not be executed. He commanded Collins: "Hard-a-starboard" and steer for the *Tennessee*.[11]

Aboard the *Hartford*, the crew of her starboard bow gun, a 100-pound Parrott rifle, was firing at the ram, now only a few hundred yards off the starboard bow. Soon the forecastle was clothed in smoke, obscuring Lieutenant Kinney's view of the *Brooklyn*, making it impossible to send and receive messages. Since the smoke was hanging low, Kinney's impulse was to get above it. Within minutes he had climbed to the *Hartford*'s foretop where a howitzer was firing, making it as difficult for him to signal as on the forecastle. Continuing to climb, he finally reached the topgallant crosstrees, ninety-six feet above the deck, where there was just enough room to sit and wrap his left arm around the peak of the topmast. Here signaling would be difficult, but at last he was above the smoke. Somehow he would get the job done.[12]

From his new position, Kinney had a panoramic view of the unfolding drama. What he saw was a major catastrophe in the making. Turning around, he could see the admiral in the rigging under the maintop, where he had climbed as the smoke had grown thicker—and beyond, off the *Hartford*'s starboard quarter, the *Richmond*, lying at an angle with her stern close to the shore. Farther out, he noticed that the rest of the fleet had stopped and were drifting with the current.[13]

Standing on the *Lackawanna*'s poop deck with a chart in his hand, Captain Marchand was piloting his own vessel. He had taken on this additional responsibility because the vessel's regular pilot was drunk, so it was rumored. Laughing as the enemy's projectiles whistled by, Marchand was an inspiration to the crew, who marveled at his composure. For the next quarter of an hour, the crew of the *Lackawanna*'s number two gun, a 150-pounder Parrott located on her forecastle, exchanged shots with the fort, which as yet had not scored a hit on the big sloop. This, however, would not last for long.[14]

From his position on the *Lackawanna*'s poop deck, Marchand described the scene from where he stood. "Although shot and shell were flying around," he explained, "none struck the *Lackawanna*'s hull doing serious injury till we were within 400 or 500 yards of Fort Morgan, when a heavy elongated shot from the fort passed through the ship's side, killing and wounding 16 men at the 150-pounder rifle, where it carried away two stanchions of the fife rail, passed through the foremast, carried away the head of the sheet cable bits, and passed through the other side of the ship, falling into the water. Blood and mangled human remains for a time impeded the working of the 150-pounder."[15]

Jesse Sweet, a member of the crew, described what it was like when the projectile hit. "We got a shot through us, one of them came in on the after side of the no. 2 gun (the gun which I belonged to) and wounded all of the men on that side of the gun except one. It also killed the Captain and one man on the other side. The shot itself hit 2 men, it blowed [off] both of one . . . [man's] legs and the left side of the left leg of the other one. All the rest of us was wounded by splinters. I was wounded slightly in the left leg above the knee. We had four men killed and two died from [their] wounds."[16]

Realizing that something had gone wrong at the head of the column—the van had ceased advancing—Captain Marchand stopped the *Lackawanna*'s engines to prevent further congestion. Aboard the *Monongahela*, next in line, Lieutenant Batcheller described the scene just before the *Lackawanna*'s engines were cut:

> At 7:30 the three leading vessels were fully engaged and the Lackawanna, our immediate leader, had just opened with her bow gun. If the scene when we formed in line of battle was magnificent, this was grand . . . too grand for my poor pen.
>
> Now our bow guns bear on the fort, and a 200 pdr. shell with our morning compliments is landed in the fort, and a few seconds afterwards the unpleasant "wher i-s-s-s y-e-e wher i-s-s-s y-e-e" of a rifle shell overhead told us the enemy had received [our] message and returned [their] answer in the same spirit.[17]

Fort Morgan's water battery was now fully engaged. Lt. Joseph Biddle Wilkinson, commissioned in the Confederate Army from Virginia Military Institute and a descendent of James Wilkinson, soldier and adventurer of the early republic, ordered the guns under his command to open when the enemy was about a mile distant. Within minutes, the fire was returned and soon "broadside after broadside shook the very earth."[18]

On the fort's ramparts, the gunners had been instructed to fire steel bolts at the ironclads and shells at the wooden vessels. Although the ironclads appeared to be immune from damage, the wooden vessels were taking a terrible pounding. From his post on the southwest bastion, Captain Whiting noted that the "roar from the guns was terrific, so much so that orders had to be screamed to the gunners who were within three feet. The hulls of the wooden ships could not be seen on account of the dense smoke."[19]

Lieutenant Wharton, commanding the first division of guns on the *Tennessee*, personally relieved the captain of the bow gun, a 7-inch Brooke rifle, loaded with a 140-pound bolt: He did not want anything to go wrong and was taking no chances. From the enemy ironclad's motions, now only two hundred yards away, she intended to grapple with the *Tennessee*. Buchanan had ordered Wharton to aim at the enemy's gun ports, or the base of the turret where it joined the deck—whichever offered the best target—and to wait until the two vessels touched before pulling the lanyard. With the *Tecumseh* now only a hundred yards away, Wharton sighted his gun on her turret, which was slowly revolving to bring its two 15-inch Dahlgrens to bear on the *Tennessee*. Suddenly, the Union ironclad shuddered and careened to port, her bow knifing below the surface.[20] The time was 7:40 A.M.

In the *Tecumseh*'s pilothouse, there was little Craven could do: The monitor had struck a mine and was sinking. In the turret below, the gun crews were already leaving their duty stations, some by the roof hatches and others through the gun ports; fortunately, the guns had not yet been run out. Lifting the floor hatch of the pilothouse, Collins and Craven descended into the turret, which by now had been abandoned. Meeting at the foot of a ladder, which led to one of the roof hatches, Craven, with water up to his waist, stepped back and said to Collins, "After you, pilot." Within seconds, the *Tecumseh* had heeled over 90 degrees, completely submerging the turret. Collins made it; Craven did not.[21]

Just two hundred yards astern, Asst. Engineer Harrie Webster was taking a turn of duty in the *Manhattan*'s turret to get away from the 150-degree heat of the engine room when the *Tecumseh* hit the torpedo. "A tiny white comber of froth curled around her bow, [and] a tremendous shock ran through our ship as though we had struck a rock." She then "reeled a little to starboard . . . and while we looked her stern lifted high in the air with the propeller still revolving, and the ship pitched out of sight like an arrow twanged from the bow."[22]

USS Tecumseh *sinking.*
SMITHSONIAN INSTITUTION

Still perched on the *Hartford*'s topgallant crosstrees, Kinney saw the *Tecumseh* heel over. Three minutes later, possibly less, she had disappeared from sight, leaving a cauldron of foam and steam bubbles on the surface, in which could be seen, here and there, bobbing heads and thrashing arms. From his elevated position under the maintop, Farragut also witnessed the tragedy. Seeing the struggling survivors, he yelled down to Jouett, still standing on the *Metacomet*'s paddle wheel, to send a boat and "pick up those poor fellows."[23]

Anticipating the admiral's order, Jouett had already dispatched a cutter in charge of Acting Ens. Henry O. Nields. Steering within a few hundred yards of the fort, through water churning with shot and shell, Nields picked up ten men, including Pilot Collins. His mission complete, Nields, unable to rejoin the *Metacomet*, boarded the *Oneida*, which was farther down the line. In addition to the sailors saved by Nields, seven survived in one of the *Tecumseh*'s boats, and four swam ashore and were taken prisoner. Ninety-four officers and men went down with the vessel.[24]

Land is a welcome sight to men swimming
For their lives, after Poseidon has smashed their ship
In heavy seas. Only a few of them escape
And make it to shore.

HOMER, *The Odyssey*

In the meantime, Kinney had received a message from Alden: "Our best monitor has been sunk." Again Lieutenant Yates delivered it to the admiral, and for a third time Farragut repeated his command to Alden: "Tell the monitors to go ahead and then take your place." But instead of going ahead, the *Brooklyn* started to back.[25]

When the *Tecumseh* sank, the *Brooklyn* was perilously close to the torpedo field. Learning that two buoys supporting torpedoes had been seen just ahead and that the water was shoaling rapidly, Alden gave the command to back hard, despite having been a member of the team that prepared the 1856 Mobile Bay hydrographic chart, which showed the depth at that location to be thirty feet, almost twice the *Brooklyn*'s draft. Aboard the *Hartford*, Kinney felt that a major disaster was in the making. "The advance vessels of the line were trying to back to prevent a catastrophe," he observed, "but were apparently not able to overcome the force of the current, and there was danger not only of collision, but of being drifted ashore."[26]

Alden was facing a dilemma with serious consequences. In General Order No. 11, the admiral had ordered the fleet to enter the bay east of the easternmost buoy, which was clear of torpedoes. This Alden had intended to do, but he had been blocked by the *Tecumseh* in her effort to engage the enemy ram. Craven had suffered the ultimate penalty for disobeying the admiral's order, and Alden was not going to commit the same blunder. The admiral's last signal, "Tell the monitors to go ahead, then take your place" was unmistakably an order to enter the bay through the clear channel, as originally planned—but now this could not be executed. The maneuver was too complicated.

The battle had now reached a crisis. As the *Brooklyn* backed, the *Hartford* stopped her engines but continued to drift with the flood tide, her bow approaching within a few yards of the *Brooklyn*'s port quarter. Astern 150 yards, the *Richmond*'s bow had swung to port, bringing her starboard broadside to bear on the fort. This compensated somewhat for the restricted fields of fire of the other two vessels, although the *Richmond*'s stern was dangerously close to the shore.[27] Half a mile astern, Lieutenant

Batcheller of the *Monongahela* observed that "all in advance was enveloped in a dense white smoke with nothing visible but the red flash of guns and bursting shells. At the center of the inferno, from his position on the *Hartford*'s topgallant crosstrees, Lieutenant Kinney looked down on the gun flashes and bursting shells: "Owing to the *Hartford*'s position, only a few bow guns could be used, while a deadly rain of shot and shell was falling on her, and her men were being cut down by the scores, unable to make reply. The sight on the deck was sickening beyond the power of words to portray. Shot after shot came through the side, mowing down the men, deluging the decks with blood, and scattering mangled fragments of humanity so thickly that it was difficult to stand on the deck, so slippery was it."[28]

When the Confederate ram *Tennessee* had been sparring with the *Tecumseh*, the Confederate gunboats had raked the cluster of vessels that had stopped on the other side of the torpedo field. The *Tennessee* had also been firing, but mostly from her bow gun. Buchanan wanted to keep the *Tennessee* pointed toward the enemy in case another vessel attempted to enter the bay. On the ramparts of Fort Morgan, amid the smoke and noise, General Page was moving from gun to gun encouraging the men and advising the officers. Occasionally he would stop and sight a gun, then move on to another position. The battle hung in the balance: no fleet could take indefinitely the punishment being meted out to the Yankees. A Confederate victory loomed—the cheers of the gunners confirmed it.[29]

THREE HUNDRED MILES TO THE NORTHEAST, SHERMAN WAS STYMIED in front of Atlanta, and in Virginia, Grant had been stopped cold outside Richmond and Petersburg. Over in the Shenandoah Valley, Sheridan had made little headway against Jubal Early. The Southern strategy of holding the Northern armies at bay until the presidential election, in order to deny Lincoln a major military victory, was so far a success. A peaceful conclusion to the fighting appeared to be possible.[30] If Buchanan could hold Farragut at bay off Fort Morgan for another hour, the Confederacy would be one step closer to independence.

In Mobile, the distant rumble of cannon fire told General Maury that the battle was still raging. As yet, however, he had not heard from General Page, indicating that the contest had not yet been decided. At her home on Government Street, two miles from army headquarters, Frances Mosby and a friend, Lou Mendenhall, were in the dining room eating breakfast when the Guard House bell rang out, stroke after stroke. Then the big market bell joined in, followed by the Cathedral bell, "forgetting its solemn swing in the sad chorus." Soon the clang of this bell was joined by every bell in town, "a pandemonium of sound." Putting on bonnets, the girls rushed outside and hailed a horse car. On the way to the river front, they saw "excited crowds gathering on the streets and sidewalks. Reaching the head of St. Francis Street . . . we girls locked arms and joined the crowd on the sidewalk. The confusion was indescribable, but we soon learned the cause. At sunrise that morning Admiral Farragut had formed his line of battle to attack the Forts."[31]

➤➤ ◄◄

CHAPTER 19

Go Ahead

THE SITUATION WAS BEGINNING TO UNRAVEL. ALDEN HAD IGNORED three orders to go ahead, enough to convince Farragut that he had no intention of doing so. Furthermore, the *Brooklyn* had cut loose the *Octorara* to prevent her from being sunk.[1] Nowhere was the deteriorating situation more apparent than from Lieutenant Kinney's vantage point high above the deck: "At one gun, all the crew on one side were swept down by a shot which came crashing through the bulwarks. A shell burst between the two forward guns in charge of Lieutenant Tyson, killing and wounding fifteen men."[2]

> *With crack on crack of thunder, Zeus let fly*
> *a bolt against the ship, a direct hit,*
> *so that she bucked, in reeking fumes of sulphur,*
> *and all the men were flung into the sea.*
>
> HOMER, *The Odyssey*

From his position in the rigging, Farragut could see the mounting chaos and realized that the time had come to act. Reaching up through the lubbers hole, he tapped Freeman on the foot and shouted, "What is the matter with the *Brooklyn?* She must have plenty of water there." "Plenty and to spare, Admiral," Freeman shouted back.[3]

The admiral knew that to cross the torpedo field would be risky; the *Tecumseh* had tried it and been blown up, but there was plenty of reliable evidence from refugees, deserters, and others, as well as his own experience with powder, that the risk was worth taking. Having been submerged in water for months, most of the torpedoes had almost certainly leaked and been rendered harmless. Many had also probably broken loose from their moorings and drifted away.[4]

Yet Farragut still hesitated. What should he do—cross the torpedo field or withdraw and admit defeat? Then, with no other way to turn, "the devout spirit that ruled his life" compelled him to ask for divine assistance. "Shall I go on?" he asked. "And it seemed," said the admiral, "as if in answer, a voice said, 'Go on!'" Motioning to Freeman, Farragut bellowed: "I will take the lead!" When Freeman asked about the torpedoes, he recalled, the admiral "told me to pick my way and go into the bay or blow up, so I started the ship ahead."[5]

> *If a moment's doubt be harbored—*
> *From the main-top, bold and brief,*
> *Came the word of our grand old Chief—*
> *"Go on!"—'twas all he said—*
> *Our helm was put to starboard,*
> *And the* Hartford *passed ahead.*

> HENRY H. BROWNELL, "The Bay Fight"

The fate of the battle was now in Freeman's hands. As the *Hartford*'s pilot, he was in virtual command of her movements, as well as those of the *Metacomet*. A speaking tube, connected to the deck, enabled Freeman to talk with the officer of the deck, who in turn passed on his commands to the helmsmen and bell-pull officers of both vessels. In a steam-powered vessel, the bell-pull officer was located on the quarterdeck and communicated with the engine room by the stroke of a bell: One pull meant "go ahead"; two, "stop"; three, "back"; and four, "go ahead at full speed." In addition, Freeman could communicate directly with the *Hartford*'s deck officer and with Jouett by hand signals, if visibility permitted. Written and oral messages, of course, could be delivered by messengers, but the din of battle prevented the human voice from carrying more than a few feet.[6]

By 7:50 A.M. the *Brooklyn*'s starboard quarter was perilously close to the *Hartford*'s port bow. Adding to the confusion, the *Richmond* had drifted with the current and was about to become entangled with the *Hartford*. Freeman shouted into the speaking tube, "*Metacomet*, back full!" followed by, "*Hartford*, hard a-starboard, four bells!" This pushed the flagship's

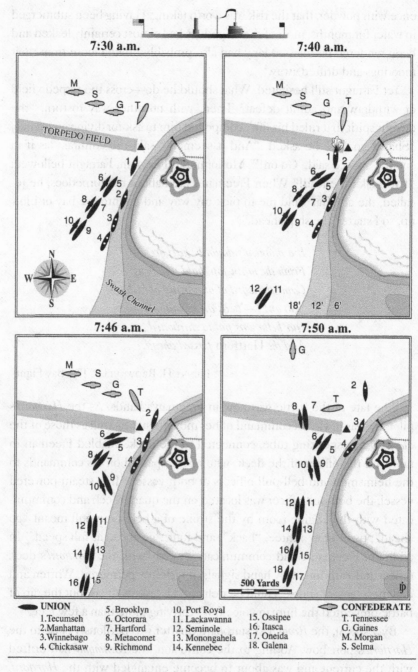

7:30 a.m.

TORPEDO FIELD

Swash Channel

7:40 a.m.

18' 12' 6'

7:46 a.m.

7:50 a.m.

500 Yards

UNION				CONFEDERATE
1.Tecumseh	5. Brooklyn	10. Port Royal	15. Ossipee	T. Tennessee
2.Manhattan	6. Octorara	11. Lackawanna	16. Itasca	G. Gaines
3.Winnebago	7. Hartford	12. Seminole	17. Oneida	M. Morgan
4.Chickasaw	8. Metacomet	13. Monongahela	18. Galena	S. Selma
	9. Richmond	14. Kennebec		

Battle of Mobile Bay, 5 August 1864, 7:30–7:50 a.m.

stern to starboard, causing her to pivot to port. The officer monitoring the deck end of the speaking tube, repeated the order, then transmitted it to the helmsmen and bell-pull officers of the two vessels. As soon as the *Hartford* cleared the *Brooklyn*'s stern, Freeman would have commanded, "*Metacomet*, stop your engine!" then to the *Hartford*, "Meet her!" which was an order to begin straightening out. "Metacomet, ahead full!" followed by "Steady as she goes!" to both vessels would be the order when on course. Passing close to the *Brooklyn*'s stern, 340 yards from where the *Tecumseh* had gone down, Freeman took the *Hartford* across the torpedo field a few degrees west of north.[7]

Standing on the *Hartford*'s poop deck observing the admiral, Lieutenant Watson knew he was going to cross the torpedo field, which he had forbidden the other vessels to do. "Some of us," he noted, "expected every moment to feel the shock of an explosion under the *Hartford* and to find ourselves in the water. In fact, we imagined that we heard some caps explode." And torpedoes were not the only problem. The enemy ram, now a hundred yards away, was steaming to intercept the *Hartford* should she get across the field unscathed.[8] As the big sloop, now recognizable as the *Hartford*, surged ahead, Captain Johnston put the ram's helm to port and rang four bells, "whereupon, all the speed that *Tennessee* could command was put forth," to sink the enemy's flagship should she succeed in crossing the torpedo field.[9]

Lieutenant Wharton had ordered the *Tennessee*'s 7-inch forward gun to be loaded with a percussion shell, convinced that at close range it would sink the *Hartford*. "This done," he believed, "the destruction of the remainder of the fleet seemed to be assured." As the enemy's flagship passed across the *Tennessee*'s bow less than two hundred yards away, Wharton "took the lock-string from the captain of the gun," adjusted the elevation for point-blank range, aimed, and fired. He was confident that the shell "would tear a hole in the *Hartford*'s side big enough to sink her in a few minutes.... It did tear the hole expected, but it was above the water line." As an afterthought, Wharton regretted that he had not let the gun captain fire the shot.[10]

Determined to sink the *Hartford*, Buchanan ordered Captain Johnston to follow her into the bay. There the *Tennessee* would have a better chance of ramming her, since she would be restricted to a small cul-de-sac four miles above Fort Morgan, the only area in the bay that had enough depth to accommodate the *Hartford*'s seventeen-foot draft.[11] In the meantime, the Confederate gunboats had swung around to starboard and straightened out ahead of the *Hartford*. Commander Harrison aboard the *Morgan*, the lead gunboat, was able to keep his vessel ahead and to starboard of the *Hartford*'s bow; and in the course of a few minutes had scored several hits on the larger vessel, one of which silenced the gun mounted on her forecastle.[12]

Following in the *Morgan*'s wake, the *Selma*'s stern guns were raking the *Hartford* with devastating effect, while maintaining a position the enemy's guns could not reach. Lt. Pat Murphey, her captain, had ordered his crew to go into battle dressed in their "best clothes," an old navy custom that not only boosted morale, but reduced the possibility of infection, if wounded. He was now doing his best to minimize casualties.[13] Last in line, the *Gaines* kept up a "deadly fire" along the *Hartford*'s decks. "We were now steering in nearly parallel lines with the enemy, at distances gradually lessening to within six hundred yards . . . for the guns of the enemy were too heavy, too numerous, and his crews too well trained to admit closer range. Our fire, directed at first against the bows of the Federal ships, now played along their decks with plunging effect. At no time in this action did our shot and shell pour in with greater accuracy."[14]

Farragut's decision to cross the torpedo field 340 yards west of the clear channel changed the mission of the *Manhattan*, which—together with the *Tecumseh*—had been to keep the *Tennessee* away from the wooden vessels as they entered the bay. This was now impossible. Therefore Commander Nicholson opted to remain with the other monitors and assist in suppressing the fort's fire, particularly that of the powerful water battery that commanded the channel. As a consequence, the *Manhattan* was "heavily pounded" by the enemy's rifled ordnance.[15]

Harrie Webster, an engineer aboard the *Manhattan*, described the sounds and sensations experienced by the *Manhattan*'s crew during this phase of the battle:

> *The sounds produced by a shot striking our turret were quite different from what I had expected. The scream of the shot would arrive about the same time [as] the projectile . . . and the air would be filled with that peculiarly shrill singing sound of violently broken glass, or perhaps more like the noise made by flinging a nail violently through the air. The shock of discharge by one of our own guns was especially hard on the hearing of those in the turret, and it seemed at times as though the very tympanum must give way. The sen-*

sations of the manipulator of the turning gear were not particularly pleas-
ant. In addition to the frequent shocks to his ears, his position was such that
the huge guns, as first one was discharged and then the other, recoiled to the
limit of the turret on either hand, and the space was so contracted that at
first it appeared certain that a shocking death would follow each round. But
it was really a place of perfect safety.[16]

During one of Webster's turns in the *Manhattan*'s turret, the guns were firing grape and canister, "and it was marvelous to note the effect of the small cartload of iron sent into the enemy's works by a 15-inch gun. In the first place, the noise of this mass of missiles tearing through the air was in striking contrast with the rushing roar of a smooth projectile, and its effect was even more marked. A cloud of dust, marked by flying debris, the sound of smashing and tearing coming back from the point of contact, and, as the smoke lifted, destruction and ruin."[17]

By now, back down the line, the *Monongahela* had been hit several times, one of which wounded Lt. Roderick Prentiss, the vessel's executive officer. He was struck by a shot from the fort that shattered both his legs and wounded two other crew members. Prentiss was not expected to live through the day. Amid the horror there was occasional humor. Aboard the *Ossipee*, a shot came through her side, sending splinters flying, one of which landed on the *Itasca*, the *Ossipee*'s consort, and hit Lt. George Brown on the leg. Fortunately it was small and inflicted only a bruise. Capt. William E. Le Roy, the *Ossipee*'s captain, saw him hopping around, and shouted, "Did one of those splinters hit you, Brown?" "Well, you might call it a splinter on board your big ship," Brown yelled back, "but over here it ranks as a log of wood."[18]

So far, the Confederate gunboats had not been seriously damaged. In fact, they had kept the initiative, but this was changing. The *Brooklyn* and *Richmond* had followed the *Hartford* across the torpedo field and now were close enough to provide the flagship with fire support—and soon there would be others. Midshipman Waterman, aboard the *Gaines*, described the turn of events: "A shell from the *Hartford* burst near the wheel . . . wounding the two helmsmen most fearfully and [killing] Quarter-Gunner Aherne; while the wheel ropes were cut and the helm splintered to pieces." Then "[a] 9-inch shell came through the side forward of my gun, extinguishing its fuse while passing through the woodwork and lodged on the berth deck. The Brooklyn sent a shot under our port counter and a shell from the Richmond struck near the same point on our starboard side, exploding below water. This started a little flood in and about our magazine and the *Gaines* now showed signs that her strength and speed were being sorely tried."

At this point, Waterman sensed that the end was near: "Our engineers and firemen battled their bravest but were at last compelled to send up word that the *Gaines* was approaching her doom; for the water in the engine room was nearly up to the grate bars and in a very short time would reach the fires and cause the steam to run down. The firemen were already ankle-deep in the water."[19]

By 8:00 A.M. the running fight between the *Hartford* and the rebel gunboats had reached the Middle Ground, three miles above Fort Morgan. Having shot past the *Morgan*, the *Selma* fired a shell at the *Metacomet*, still lashed to the *Hartford*, that exploded in her storeroom, killing one man and wounding another. Raging to get at the *Selma*, Jouett had asked the admiral three times to be cut loose, and each time he had been told to "wait a little longer." At 8:05, the admiral waved his hand at Jouett, and with "three hearty cheers" from the *Metacomet*'s crew, she was cut loose to pursue the *Selma*. Within minutes, the *Morgan* had hauled around and was heading for Navy Cove and the shallow water four miles east of Fort Morgan. In the meantime, the *Gaines*, with water pouring into her hull, had disengaged and was attempting to reach Fort Morgan before she sank.[20]

By now all the Union vessels, except the *Oneida* and her consort, the *Galena*, had crossed the torpedo field, leaving behind a floating trail of tangled rigging, broken masts, and "splinters of all sizes." Stretched out in a straggling column, the Union battle line resembled a fleet in retreat rather than a victorious armada. Gunfire ahead told that the battle was still raging. With all but one pair of vessels in the bay, the monitor *Manhattan* had left its station off Fort Morgan and was steaming north on the fleet's starboard quarter. The *Winnebago* and *Chickasaw* had remained behind shelling the water battery. As soon as the last vessel had passed, they also would enter the bay.[21]

About this time, when passing the fort, the *Oneida* was hulled by a shell, which passed through her chain armor and exploded in the starboard boiler. Nearly all the firemen and coal heavers were either scalded to death or disabled by the steam. Almost immediately, another shell entered at her waterline and exploded in the cabin, cutting the wheel ropes. Assessing the damage, Commander Mullany ordered the relieving tackles to be manned and the connection between the vessel's two boilers to be shut off, thus enabling the *Oneida* to operate on one boiler, assisted by her consort, the *Galena*.[22]

Aboard the *Tennessee*, as she approached the Middle Ground, Admiral Buchanan realized that his vessel could not catch the *Hartford;* she was still half a mile ahead. Now opposite the Middle Ground, where he had hoped to sink her, the admiral ordered Commander Johnston to haul around and engage the enemy, one by one, as they passed up the bay. The first vessel and its consort, which had been uncoupled, were still a thousand yards away, "owing to the confusion into which they had been thrown by the sinking of the *Tecumseh*." This vessel and the one following were firing at the *Gaines* as she passed a mile to the east, striving to reach Fort Morgan before sinking.[23]

As gunfire echoed from within the bay, General Page was busy assessing the situation at Fort Morgan. Casualties had been remarkably light: A trooper of the 7th Alabama Cavalry had been killed by a shell while eating his breakfast at the stables, and five officers and men of the garrison were wounded. Page believed casualties were not greater due "to the fact that the guns of the fleet were too much elevated." In all, the fort fired 491 projectiles at the enemy's fleet and sank one of its ironclads, from which four survivors who swam ashore were now prisoners. He had no complaints with the spirit of the garrison. Page's foremost concern was his belief that the "whole naval and land forces of the enemy would be brought against Fort Morgan" once Forts Gaines and Powell capitulated. The key, of course, was Fort Gaines, for it was an open secret that Fort Powell was untenable.[24]

As Page pondered his predicament, five Union gunboats were approaching Fort Powell from Mississippi Sound, apparently with the intent of opening fire. Anticipating a bombardment, Lt. James M. Williams readied four guns bearing on the sound and waited for the range to close. This was his strongest front, and he was confident the attack could be repulsed. His worry, however, was the fort's defenseless rear. The enemy needed to secure possession of Grant's Pass in order to open communications with New Orleans and its supply and maintenance depots at Pensacola and Ship Island. An attack from the bay side, therefore, was only a matter of time.[25]

Six miles to the east, Admiral Buchanan had given up his attempt to catch and ram the *Hartford*. However, by pursuing her as far as the Middle Ground, he had positioned the *Tennessee* to engage, one by one, the other wooden vessels as they came up the channel. Hemmed in by shallow water on either side, the enemy had no choice but to pass the ram at point-blank range without the support of its own ironclads, which were still hovering off Fort Morgan. A slaughter was in the making.[26]

CHAPTER 20

Gauntlet

FAILING TO CATCH AND RAM THE *Hartford*, ADMIRAL BUCHANAN ordered Captain Johnston to haul around and head back down the channel. The *Hartford* could be dealt with later; soon she would be confined to the pocket of water known as the Lower Fleet, a small anchorage bounded by shallow water on three sides.[1]

The next pair of vessels, the *Brooklyn* and *Octorara*, could be seen about three-quarters of a mile ahead, steaming in the *Hartford*'s wake. The time was 8:00 A.M. As the distance closed, Buchanan realized that the *Tennessee* did not have enough speed to catch and ram the *Brooklyn*; so he ordered Johnston to sheer off and fire a broadside into her starboard beam, which did "great injury." In return, the *Brooklyn* fired a broadside at the *Tennessee* that bounced harmlessly off her casemate.[2]

Both Buchanan and Johnston knew that "catching a vessel going at a speed of twelve miles an hour with one utterly incapable of more than half that speed" was an impossible feat. But when forced to fight at close range in confined waters, the ram's armor and low profile offset its lack of speed, and Franklin Buchanan was about to convince his nemesis, David Farragut, that "nothing except a battle lost can be half so melancholy as a battle won."[3]

Having failed to ram the *Brooklyn*, the *Tennessee* made for the *Richmond* and her consort, the *Port Royal*, third in line. Aboard the *Richmond*, Captain Jenkins had ordered the guns to be loaded with solid shot and the heaviest powder charges authorized by the Ordnance Department. In addition, the forecastle gun crews were instructed to fire their small arms into the ram's gun ports; and if the vessels collided, powder charges should be thrown from the fore and main yardarms down the ram's smokestack. Also, when the vessels passed, there should be time for the *Richmond*'s eleven guns to "fire three full broadsides."

The *Tennessee* and the *Richmond* did not come in contact, but the three broadsides were fired and "were well aimed and all struck, but there were no indications of damage other than scratches." The musketry fire into the ram's two ports prevented the leveling of her guns, causing two shells to pass harmlessly overhead "except [for] the cutting of a ratline in the port main-shroud, just under the feet of the pilot." One of the shells "whistled unpleasantly close" to the head of an officer standing on the poop deck.[4]

Continuing down the line, Buchanan identified the fourth pair of Yankee vessels as the *Lackawanna* and her consort, the *Seminole*. The fifth pair, the *Monongahela* and *Kennebec*, however, caught his eye. Assessing the *Monongahela*'s position and speed, the admiral ordered Johnston to bypass the *Lackawanna* and ram the *Monongahela;* this time there was an even chance that contact would be made; anticipating this, Johnston ordered the crew to stand by for a collision. As the *Tennessee* bore down on the *Monongahela*, the *Lackawanna* fired a broadside, which did little to distract the ram from her intended victim.[5]

Aboard the *Monongahela*, Lieutenant Batcheller was wondering what had happened to the Union monitors. The *Winnebago* and *Chickasaw* were to remain off Fort Morgan until the last wooden vessel passed, but the *Manhattan* and *Tecumseh* had orders to engage the ram and keep her away from the wooden vessels. The *Tecumseh*, unfortunately, had been sunk, but where was the *Manhattan*? So far, the vessels ahead had managed to avoid the *Tennessee*, but the *Monongahela* was trapped: she either had to "ram or be rammed."[6]

The *Monongahela*'s bow had been strengthened with an iron prow that, her officers had often jokingly said, would get her in a "heap of trouble." The trouble had come. "Gaining a position, she made a rush on the 'Tennessee.' The shock was terrific, but the ram, not liking the prospect, had taken a broad sheer, and the blow was oblique. The two vessels swung side by side, the bow of one towards the stern of the other, with the little 'Kennebec' . . . sandwiched between them. In this position they hung for some moments, the bow of the 'Kennebec' having caught the ram's lifeboat and torn it from the davits. Whilst in this position, the 'Tennessee' fired her two broadside guns into the 'Kennebec's' lower deck, setting her on fire, and playing sad havoc in that confined space."[7]

When the *Monongahela* struck the *Tennessee*, the ram's momentum caused her to swing around counterclockwise and emerge once again on the enemy column's starboard flank. With two pairs of vessels still ahead, Admiral Buchanan was relieved to be free of the entanglement with the *Kennebec*, a situation that would have denied him freedom of movement when the other remaining vessels passed.

As the *Tennessee* straightened out and headed down the channel, the sixth pair, the *Ossipee* and *Itasca*, were dead ahead less than three hundred yards. Several hundred yards beyond, still under fire from Fort Morgan, could be seen the last pair of vessels, moving slowly as if contending with some problem. So far, the *Tennessee* had failed to ram a single Union vessel, but her Brooke rifles had done considerable damage, while the enemy's fire had "made not the slightest impression" on her. For the last twenty minutes, Buchanan had been "master of the situation."[8]

As the rebel ram approached the *Ossipee* and her consort, the *Itasca*, Acting Ens. Charles E. Clark could not bring his guns to bear until she came farther aft. For the moment, however, his attention was focused on the huge rifled gun that was projecting from the ram's bow.

> *The hole in it look[ed] ominously large. The projectile, when it came, raked our berth deck and as the big ironclad was almost alongside by that time, we returned it with the muzzles of our guns depressed, but I imagine all our shot simply struck her casemate and bounced off. I was glad to see that she had a rammer in one of her broadside guns, and could therefore only give us one more in passing. It fortunately missed the boilers, going through just forward of them. Her stern gun, which could have raked us, was not fired. . . . Our narrowest escape was from a ten-inch shot that grazed our main steam pipe, tearing off the fearnaught and wooden battens in which it was encased.[9]*

Passing the *Ossipee*, the *Tennessee* headed for the seventh and last pair of vessels, the *Oneida* and the screw steamer *Galena*. Seeing the ram approaching, Lt. Charles Huntington, the *Oneida*'s executive officer, ordered the guns to be loaded with solid shot and maximum powder charges. As the ram passed, she attempted to fire her broadside guns, but the primers snapped and only one shot got off, which struck the *Oneida*'s aft 11-inch pivot gun. Four of the *Oneida*'s 11-inch and 8-inch smoothbore guns were now out of action, and the few that could be brought to bear were firing with little effect.[10] Meanwhile, powder boy David Naylor was doing his best to keep the vessel's 30-pounder Parrott in action. When returning from the passing-scuttle, something knocked his passing-box out of his hands and overboard into a boat that was being towed alongside. Without hesitation, he jumped into the water, recovered the box, and delivered it to the gun he was serving.[11]

Passing the *Oneida*, the *Tennessee* hauled around under her stern and crossed the T in reverse. "We were completely at her mercy," recounted Lt. Edward Kellogg, as the ram's shells went "raking & crashing through us mangling & wounding our men while they had no chance to return her fire. The carnage here was awful."[12] As the smoke cleared, Commander Mullany's left forearm was dangling from his elbow. He had been standing on the poop deck when a fragment of shell struck him. "He coolly took a handkerchief from his pocket, bound it round his arm, and remained for some time talking to his clerk," observed a correspondent for the *New York Daily Tribune*, who was aboard the *Oneida*, "His wound proved to be very serious, [and] he was compelled to go to the surgeon, where he suffered amputation of the limb below the elbow."[13]

After the *Tennessee* passed the *Oneida*'s stern, the ram continued to swing around to port as if intending to go back and attack her a second time. Seeing this, Commander Stevens, captain of the monitor *Winnebago*, decided to intervene. The other two monitors had already passed into the bay and were now several hundred yards up the channel. Either through a misunderstanding of orders or the belief that the wooden vessels now had room enough to maneuver and could avoid the ram, neither the *Manhattan* nor the *Chickasaw* attempted to engage the *Tennessee*. Commander Stevens, however, had a special reason for going to the *Oneida*'s assistance: until three days ago, he had been her captain.[14]

Commander Mullany, a friend of Stevens, came aboard the *Oneida* a few days before the battle and offered him a proposition. Farragut wanted to replace the captain of the *Winnebago* with a more experienced officer and had offered Mullany the command. Although experienced, Mullany had "seen but little fighting service" and had never served aboard a monitor. He therefore suggested that Stevens, who had previously commanded a monitor, take the *Winnebago*, and he in turn would take the *Oneida*. The admiral approved the swap, and the transfers were made.[15]

Attempting to guess what Buchanan had in mind when he circled to port after passing the *Oneida*, Commander Stevens steamed over and placed the *Winnebago* between the *Oneida* and the ram. Seeing their old captain, the *Oneida*'s crew "jumped upon the bulwarks and gave three heartfelt cheers." Standing on the monitor's deck directing fire, as was his custom, Stevens doffed his hat and bowed in acknowledgment.[16] But Buchanan had no intention of circling back and making another run past the *Oneida*, not because one of the enemy ironclads had intervened but because he wanted to assess the situation and plan his next move. Also, a heavy rain and wind squall, accompanied by dense mist, could be seen coming from the southwest, and he did not want to get caught in it while engaging the enemy.[17]

Ordering Commander Johnston to lay off Fort Morgan with the ram's screw turning just enough to buck the incoming tide, the admiral was anxious to feed the crew, examine the casemate for battle damage, and resume the fight, although he had not as yet revealed his intention to Captain Johnston or the ram's officers. As the *Tennessee* approached the fort, Fleet Surgeon D. B. Conrad left the cockpit and went topside for some fresh air. The time was 8:30 A.M. He was astonished to find that outside the casemate, "nothing [was] left standing as large as your little finger. Everything had been shot away, smokestack, boat davits, stanchions, and, in fact, 'fore and aft,' our deck had been swept absolutely clean. A few of our men were slightly wounded, and when the last vessel had passed us and been fought in turn, we had been in action more than an hour and a half."[18] An inspection of the *Tennessee*'s hull and casemate revealed that, except for perforations in the smokestack, she was still battle worthy. The smokestack damage, however, had seriously diminished her speed—but with the battle now over, there would be plenty of time to patch the holes, so he thought.[19]

By now the squall had passed a mile or so to the northeast, blotting out everything within the nine square miles it covered. About this time, the *Tennessee*'s lookout spotted the gunboat *Gaines* emerging from the mist, apparently heading for Fort Morgan in a sinking condition—a bad omen. At 8:40 hardtack and coffee were brought from the galley, the men going to the afterdeck to eat, the officers to the upper deck atop the casemate. Almost to a man, Buchanan's officer's believed that, although the ram's foray had severely punished the enemy, her future role would be defensive; when the enemy attacked Fort Morgan—it was only a matter of time—the *Tennessee*'s powerful battery would provide fire support.[20]

Buchanan, however, was not satisfied. "Grim, silent and rigid," he was "stumping" back and forth across the upper deck, lame from the wound received when he sank the *Cumberland* and *Congress* at Hampton Roads. Soon it became apparent that the admiral intended to steam out again and engage the entire Union fleet. Counting eleven Union vessels anchored, or about to anchor in the Lower Fleet, Dr. Conrad asked him, "Are you going into that fleet again, admiral?" "I am, sir," was his reply. Not meaning to be heard by the admiral, the doctor said to an officer standing nearby, "Well, we'll never come out of there whole!" Hearing the remark, Buchanan turned around and said sharply: "That's my lookout, sir!"[21]

The admiral reasoned that the *Tennessee* had only six hours of coal in her bunkers, and that would be expended attacking the enemy. "He did not mean to be trapped like a rat in a hole, and made to surrender without a struggle"—and when his coal was used up, he would return to Fort Morgan and assist General Page in its defense. Furthermore, "there were the chances that he might demoralize the Federals by ramming and sinking one or more of their ships; that a lucky shell in a boiler or magazine might have the same effect; or finally, that he might carry the *Tennessee* up to Mobile and save her for the eventual defense of the city."[22] As the admiral prepared to give the order to get under way, gunfire from the northeast told him that the *Selma* and, possibly, the *Morgan* were exchanging fire with the Union gunboats, evidence that the battle was not over.

Earlier, when the *Tennessee* had abandoned its pursuit of the *Hartford*, the Union flagship had just cast off the *Metacomet*, which went after the *Selma* and *Morgan*. Knowing that soon other gunboats would join in the pursuit, the two Confederate vessels steamed for the shallow waters of Bon Secour Bay, where a pilot unfamiliar with the shoals was likely to run aground. Hulled and taking on water, the third Confederate gunboat, the *Gaines*, was last seen heading for Fort Morgan.[23]

FOUR MILES UP THE BAY, ENS. JOSEPH MARTHON, WHO HAD BEEN IN charge of the howitzer in the *Hartford*'s maintop, had climbed up to the main topsail yard when the flagship had anchored and was now reporting the vessels as they cleared the Middle Ground and came up the bay, as well as the position of the *Tennessee*. By 8:45 the sloops *Hartford*, *Brooklyn*, *Richmond*, and *Lackawanna*, and the gunboats *Octorara* and *Seminole* had come to anchor in the Lower Fleet. The *Metacomet*, joined by the gunboats *Port Royal, Kennebec,* and *Itasca,* had been cast off near the Middle Ground and was now pursuing the rebel gunboats. The *Monongahela, Ossipee, Oneida,* and the latter's consort, the *Galena,* had yet to reach the anchorage.[24]

Except for the sound of gunfire off to the east, the roar of battle was over and preparations were being made to give the crew breakfast. Aboard the flagship, the officers had gathered in the wardroom to offer congratulations and compare experiences. Lieutenant Kinney, who by now had earned the respect and admiration of every man aboard, described the gathering. "Those of us who had been perched aloft came down on deck, and, as if by a general understanding, the officers of the *Hartford* who could be spared from immediate duty hastened to the wardroom to ascertain how it had fared with their messmates." There were only two casualties: Ens. William Heginbotham, of the admiral's staff, was mortally wounded, and Lt. LaRue P. Adams only slightly; all the rest had escaped unhurt. The *Hartford*'s crew, however, fared much worse. On the spar deck, "nineteen mangled bodies were lying in a ghastly row on the port side of the deck, and some thirty wounded were being cared for below."[25]

As yet, the captains of the anchored vessels had not come aboard the flagship to give oral reports and receive orders. Although the Union fleet was now in Mobile Bay—an objective that had eluded Farragut for the past two years—the cost, when counted, was going to be enormous—and the end did not appear to be in sight.

Ensign Clark of the *Ossipee* expressed the concern of his fellow officers when he said, "I believe the thought had come to many of us—and it was not a comforting one—that the *Tennessee,* which had proved that she could fight her way through our fleet from van to rear, might, when darkness fell, steam up into our midst, and while we were hampered by the fear of injuring our friends, she would feel free to ram and fire in any direction."[26]

Aboard the flagship, Farragut and Drayton were standing on the poop deck pondering the same possibility, when the fleet captain remarked, "What we have done has been well done, sir; but it all counts for nothing so long as the *Tennessee* is under the guns of Fort Morgan." "I know it," Farragut answered, "and as soon as the people have had their breakfasts, I am going for her."[27]

Farragut planned to personally accompany the three monitors, using the *Manhattan* as his flagship. He could wait until dark, but the advantage of attacking now would prevent Buchanan from making a foray into the confined area of anchorage. As they spoke, Drayton once again scanned the waters near Fort Morgan. It was too late; the ram was moving, apparently going outside to attack the vessels that had remained behind. "Then," said the admiral, "we must follow him out" but realizing that the southwest wind was blowing the ram's smoke to the northeast, he then exclaimed, "No! Buck's coming here. Get under way at once; we must be ready for him."[28]

As the *Tennessee* swung around to starboard and headed up the bay where the enemy vessels were anchoring, Captain Johnston ordered the crew to prepare for action. Ashore, seeing the *Tennessee* about to attack the entire Union fleet single-handedly, hundreds of soldiers, Confederate and Union alike, stopped what they were doing and turned to watch the unfolding spectacle. At Fort Gaines, a Confederate marine described the drama: "The skirmishing on land ceases by tacit agreement. Now comes a sight that throws all others in the shade."[29]

With her smokestack pierced in several places, the *Tennessee*'s speed had been reduced to less than six knots. It would take nearly an hour to cover the four miles between Fort Morgan and the Union fleet—but once there, in the confines of the anchorage, Buchanan would wreak havoc among the larger vessels, particularly the flagship, which he was intent on sinking. He also had the option of retiring to shallow water and firing at will on the larger vessels that were restricted to the anchorage because of their heavy draft.[30]

The enemy's three remaining monitors, however, had not yet reached the anchorage. After leaving Fort Morgan, they had continued up the bay on a course several hundred yards east of the wooden column and, having been signaled, were heading to intercept the ram. The monitors would bring the total number of Union vessels at or near the anchorage to eleven.

As the *Tennessee* steamed toward the enemy, cheer after cheer followed in her wake. The soldiers crowding Fort Morgan's ramparts had reason to be encouraged: not only was the most powerful warship afloat renewing the fight but also the rumble of gunfire from the northeast told them the gunboats were still in the fight. In addition, the Confederate battle flag was still flying at Forts Morgan, Gaines, and Powell. The fight was not over.

CHAPTER 21

✦➤ ✦◀

Gunboat Fight

As THE *Tennessee* HAULED AROUND AND HEADED UP THE CHANNEL TO single-handedly attack the Union fleet, now anchoring four miles up the bay, gunfire from the northeast could no longer be heard, indicating that the Confederate vessels had either withdrawn from the fight or been captured. During the past three-quarters of an hour, while the *Tennessee* was off Fort Morgan preparing to renew the attack, the *Selma* and for a while the *Morgan*, had been engaged in a running fight with four Union gunboats. The *Gaines*, however, was not involved in this action, having returned to Fort Morgan in a sinking condition earlier in the fight. But with the ram steaming for a showdown with the Union fleet, the soldiers and seamen of both sides knew that the battle was now entering its climax. Lieutenant Wharton, commanding the *Tennessee*'s bow gun, captured the essence of the moment when he said, "It was the beginning of a naval combat the like of which history has not seen."[1]

When Buchanan abandoned his first attempt to catch and sink the *Hartford*, the Confederate gunboats *Selma* and *Morgan* were several hundred yards ahead, and a point or two off, the Union flagship's starboard bow. Noticing that the *Metacomet* had been cut loose from the *Hartford*, a sign that other gunboats would soon follow, the two Confederate vessels sheered to starboard and headed eastward across Bon Secour Bay.

Hardly had the *Morgan* changed course when she turned and headed toward Pilot Town, a small fishing village four miles east of Fort Morgan. Cdr. George W. Harrison, the *Morgan*'s captain, explained his rationale for breaking off the engagement:

The enemy's fleet had now accomplished its purpose, being entirely within the bay and running up the "pocket" of deep water known as the "Lower Fleet." . . . *The* Gaines *had been disabled and forced out of action, and the course we were pursuing was taking us further and further away from the peninsula (which was our only place of refuge in case of being hard pressed), and thus the chances were continually increasing of our being cut off from all retreat by the enemy's gunboats, which I foresaw would soon be thrown off from the fleet in pursuit; so I sheered off to the starboard, the* Selma *doing the same, and (as I had anticipated) a double-ender, said to be the* Metacomet, *in a few moments after[,] started off from the* Hartford *and soon overhauled and engaged in action with my vessel, while the* Selma, *on our port bow, continued her retreat . . . in a direction to cross the mouth of Bon Secour Bay and reach the eastern shore of Mobile Bay. After a short cannonading between us the* Metacomet *slipped off and steamed rapidly in pursuit of the* Selma.[2]

Having abandoned the *Metacomet,* Commander Harrison continued his course to the southeast and the shallows off Pilot Town, now about three miles distant. Drawing less water than the Union gunboats, the *Morgan* would not be pursued there and his luck would hold, Harrison reckoned. So far, the *Morgan* had been "struck but six times, and only one of that number did any harm, and that entered the port wheelhouse and passed out of the starboard, destroying some muskets, boarding pikes, and stanchions in its progress over the deck. Only one person was wounded," he observed, "and he slightly, by a splinter. I owe this exemption from injury and loss, doubtless, in great measure, to the excellent position I was enabled to keep, generally, on the *Hartford's* bow."[3]

Three miles to the north, the fortunes of war had brought together two old friends in a desperate sea chase. James Jouett, commander of the Union gunboat *Metacomet,* and Patrick Murphey, commander of the rebel gunboat *Selma,* had served together in the old navy and were friends. Knowing that Murphey commanded the *Selma* and that he liked good food, Jouett had often remarked that "he intended to catch him, and that he always kept on hand some good wines and cigars especially for him." Two days before the battle, while the *Metacomet* was at Pensacola, Jouett directed his steward to purchase some crabs and oysters and put them on ice. As commander of the fleet's fastest gunboat, he would have a better chance than most to entertain his old friend.[4]

When Farragut ordered the *Metacomet* to be cut loose from the *Hartford*, three other gunboats—the *Port Royal, Kennebec*, and *Itasca*—were signaled to join the chase also, but due to the confusion caused by the *Tennessee* as she passed down the line a lapse of fifteen minutes transpired before the *Hartford's* hoist was made. The gunboats, however, were barely under way when the squall passed over, hiding both "pursuers and pursued from each other's sight."[5]

A mile and a half ahead, the *Metacomet* continued to pursue the *Selma* at top speed, although her leadsman was now reporting only one foot of water beneath the keel. With the *Metacomet* drawing nine and a half feet, compared with the *Selma's* six, Jouett was aware that he might be falling prey to a trap that would shift the advantage to his old friend, Pat Murphey, but still he pushed on. Soon the *Metacomet's* leadsman was crying out a foot less water than the *Metacomet* drew. Determined to capture Murphey, Jouett shouted to his executive officer, Lt. Henry J. Sleeper: "Mr. Sleeper, order that leadsman out of the chains, he makes me nervous!" Coming from one of the calmest officers in the fleet, this show of humor at such a time raised a hearty laugh from the men nearby.[6]

When within half a mile of the *Selma,* Jouett yawed two or three times to fire, but finding that the *Metacomet* lost way, he ceased and kept on. At the same time, Murphey appeared to be maneuvering to close on Jouett or, more likely, to lure him onto a shoal. Should the *Metacomet* run aground, Murphey could turn back and select a position from which to rake the *Metacomet* with his broadside guns.

"I had given my pilot to the gallant Craven, of the ill-fated *Tecumseh*," Jouett explained, "and having no time to consult the chart and knowing nothing of the channel, and as the admiral's instructions were imperative—not to allow any of the Confederate gunboats to reach Mobile—I abandoned the attempt to fight with my guns in this running chase." Instead, he would close the distance and fire on the *Selma* at point-blank range; which, Jouett was convinced, would "compel her to surrender."[7]

When the *Metacomet* was within five hundred yards of the *Selma,* the squall that had been moving from the southwest obscured everything in sight. Fifteen minutes later it was clear again, revealing the *Selma,* a few hundred yards off the *Metacomet's* port bow, and the other Union gunboats a couple of miles astern. The *Itasca,* the vessel closest to the *Metacomet,* was still almost a mile away.

USS Metacomet *chasing CSS* Selma.

NAVAL HISTORICAL CENTER

Lt. Cdr. George Brown, captain of the *Itasca,* described the unfolding scene. "As we passed out of range of the guns of Fort Morgan, we cast off from the vessels to which we were lashed. Jouett in the Metacomet was the first vessel to be cast off, and started after the Selma—Gheradi in the Port Royal followed as fast as his old tub would steam. Then the Itasca followed the Port Royal and soon passed her. I made sail, which increased our speed greatly. . . . The Metacomet was then engaging the Selma, and when I was within 1,400 yards of them, I ordered the helm put to starboard so that my guns would bear on the Selma."[8] In the meantime, the *Port Royal* had opened fire on the *Selma* with her 100-pounder rifle and was preparing to fire again when the *Itasca* arrived on the scene and began maneuvering for a shot. Astern, but out of range, the *Kennebec* had also arrived, giving the Union vessels a four-to-one advantage over the *Selma.*

Jouett's running fight with the *Selma* had taken him eight miles across Bon Secour Bay. If the chase were to continue, he reasoned, sooner or later the *Metacomet* would run aground, shifting the advantage to Pat Murphey. Jouett gives this account of the final minutes of the chase:

I was only about two hundred yards from her [the Selma*]; as she was running into shoal water, where the* Metacomet *could not go, I concentrated*

the entire battery upon her, giving the strictest orders not to fire a gun with-
out my command to fire. I directed the bow gun, a 100-pounder, to be fired;
this was enough. Had I fired the broadside, I knew but few would have sur-
vived, she was so close and at our mercy. I was not killing my countrymen
recklessly. I fired the one gun, and that was enough; it killed an officer,
wounded the captain and five men, I think. My men were mad to fire, but I
held their fire. I knew that as soon as the men on the Selma *could get to the*
flag, they would have it down, and they did. It would have been murder
to have fired the broadside.

Seeing the *Selma* lower her colors, Lieutenant Commander Brown of the
Itasca, ordered his guns not to fire on the stricken vessel. "I continued
on," he reported, "and passed between the *Metacomet* and *Selma* before
Jouett's boat reached the *Selma.* I asked Jouett if he wanted my assistance
and he said 'No.' I at once headed up the bay in chase of a [rebel] transport steamer."[9]

Several miles to the north, the transport carrying reinforcements for
Fort Gaines had finally reached the lower bay. The regiment, which had
been stationed at Pollard, Alabama, had been ordered the previous day to
reinforce Fort Gaines. However, the steamboat that had been sent to get
the regiment broke down and another was dispatched, arriving at the
river landing at 4:00 A.M. Five hours later, with the 22d Louisiana aboard,
it reached the lower bay, only to find that the Yankee fleet had passed the
forts and was anchored in the Lower Fleet. Learning this, the transport's
captain turned his vessel around, and headed back to Mobile.[10]

Eight miles to the east, six lifeless, mangled bodies lay sprawled across
the *Selma's* deck, one of which was Lt. John H. Comstock, the vessel's executive officer. In addition, Murphey and six others were wounded. Outnumbered and outgunned, Commander Murphey had defiantly "kept his
colors at the peak." Now it was time to surrender. "I perceived that the
Metacomet was about to rake me with grape and shrapnel," he reported,
"and that the *Port Royal,* of about the same class, was about to open on me
also, and as I did not believe that I was justified in sacrificing more of my
men in such an unequal contest, I gave the order, at about half-past 9
o'clock [*sic*], to haul down the colors. My wound was bleeding fast, and I
knew if I left the deck for one moment the vessel might be sunk."[11]

As the *Selma's* flag was being lowered, Murphey sent a boat to the
Metacomet to report that he was wounded, his executive officer had been

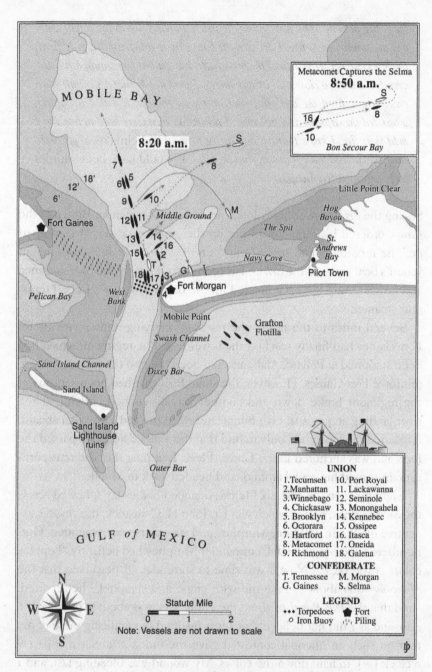

Battle of Mobile Bay, 5 August 1864, 8:20–8:50 a.m.

killed, and he was ready to surrender. With his arm in a sling and a midshipman carrying his sword, Murphey got in the boat when it returned and headed to the *Metacomet*. At sixty-five, Pat Murphey was an imposing figure. "He was 6 feet two inches in his boots, slender, wiry with stricking [*sic*] features and long, white hair hanging over his collar after the Southern fashion." The time was 8:50 A.M.[12]

Before Murphey reached the *Metacomet*, Jouett had sent the crew forward and the officers to the port side of the quarterdeck, to avoid embarrassing his old friend. The only people with him at the gangway were his executive officer, Lieutenant Sleeper, and the officer of the deck. When Murphey stepped on the *Metacomet*'s deck, his aide came forward and handed Murphey his sword. Drawing up to his full height, he handed it to Jouett and said, "Captain Jouett, the fortunes of war compel me to tender you my sword!" Grabbing it quickly and passing it to his executive officer, Jouett took Murphey's hand and shook it heartily. Smiling, Jouett replied: "Pat, don't make a d—d fool of yourself. I have had a bottle on ice for you for the last half hour!"

With this greeting, Jouett took his friend down into the cabin, where a sumptuous breakfast was spread—oysters, crabs, beefsteaks, wines, and so on. Sitting down, a "wan smile" came over Murphey's face, and he declared: "Look here, Jouett, if I had known that you had such a breakfast as this, I would have surrendered an hour ago; And champagne, too! But Jouett, your informal way of receiving my sword spoiled one of the best surrender speeches that ever fell from the lips of a Naval Officer."[13]

While Murphey and Jouett exchanged quips, the officers and men of the *Selma* were being transferred to the *Metacomet* and *Port Royal* as prisoners of war, giving way to a prize crew from both vessels. About this time, gunfire thundered across the water from the west, suggesting that Buchanan had renewed the action.[14]

As the *Tennessee* steamed toward the Union fleet, an event occurred off Fort Morgan that cost Farragut his finest dispatch boat, the 311-ton sidewheel steamer *Philippi*. Desiring to be of assistance if any of the vessels were disabled, her captain, Acting Master James T. Seaver, requested permission from Captain Drayton before the battle to follow the fleet into the bay. Drayton told him that "would be folly" and refused permission. The next morning, overwhelmed by a desire to participate in the battle, Seaver headed up the channel at 7:45, "keeping as far out of range of the fort as I could judge was necessary to clear the shoal. . . . At about 9:15, while going ahead slow, the quartermaster gave a cast, a quarter less three, and the steamer immediately struck. I rang three bells and tried to back her off, but she did not stir. I kept backing for ten minutes; had about thirty-five pounds of steam on."[15]

Atop Fort Morgan's southwest bastion, the gun crew of the 7-inch Brooke rifle stared with disbelief as the little steamer lurched to a stop; she had run aground. Noticing her dilemma, General Page ordered Capt. Wythe Whiting commander of the bastion, to commence firing. At two thousand yards, her destruction was certain. Seaver explained what happened next:

> *The fort then opened fire on us, and getting our range[,] every other shell did execution. The second shell . . . struck the rail about the starboard bow port, and immediately killed Frank Wilson, landsman. One shot passed through the boiler, entirely disabling us, and another burst in the engine room.*
>
> *The deck being full of steam and smoke, [an] indication of the ship being on fire[,] . . . and almost every shell, either direct or ricochet, striking the steamer, and the boiler being disabled, and my men, several of them, being almost paralyzed with fear, also the sight of the rebel steamer coming out, and the utter impossibility to . . . resist the enemy, I judged it best to abandon her.*[16]

Off Fort Morgan, the crew of the gunboat *Gaines* had been struggling for the past hour to keep her afloat. The ship had been hulled during the running fight with the *Hartford*, and Lt. John W. Bennett, her captain, described the dilemma he faced: "Finding the ship would sink in a short time, and thinking I might be able to reach the shore, now about two or three miles distant, I withdrew from action and made the best of my way toward the fort, steering the ship principally with the sidewheels, which position I reached without embarrassment from the enemy—thanks to an opportune rain squall which shut me from view."[17]

With seventeen shot holes in her hull and smokestack, two feet of water over the cabin floor, and her wheel ropes severed, the *Gaines* settled to the bottom. Before she sank, however, Lt. John Payne, the vessel's executive officer, noticed that the fort was firing at an enemy steamer on the west side of the channel. Not wanting to be left out of the action, he ordered the *Gaines*'s forward pivot gun to open fire. Noticing that the crew of the enemy steamer now appeared to be abandoning the vessel, Payne signaled the gunboat *Morgan*, which had just arrived from Navy Cove, where she had been stranded on a sand bar for the last three-quarters of an hour. "Come within hail," the *Gaines* flagged. As the *Morgan* approached, Payne informed her captain, Cdr. George W. Harrison, that the enemy was now abandoning the vessel and suggested that she should be burned.[18]

Young Lt. Thomas L. Harrison, a graduate of the Naval Academy, was ordered to command the boarding crew. An inspection from the *Morgan's* pilothouse convinced Commander Harrison that the vessel was indeed abandoned, at which time he and his crew cast off and boarded her. The vessel, identified as the *Philippi*, was a shambles; only one person was found, and his legs had been so shattered that he died while Harrison was aboard. Before the vessel was torched, however, he ordered the body to be thrown overboard—under the circumstances, an appropriate burial at sea.[19]

Three miles to the north, the *Tennessee* had passed the Middle Ground and was now within five thousand yards of the Union anchorage. Through the slits in the *Tennessee's* pilothouse, Buchanan could count eight wooden vessels and three monitors in the vicinity of the anchorage. For some reason, after entering the bay the monitors had kept far to the east of the wooden column and were just arriving at the anchorage. Although Admiral Buchanan was outnumbered eleven to one, no one who knew him could imagine his surrendering the *Tennessee* without making a final effort for the "honor and glory of his flag; nobody who understood the iron will and pertinacious courage of the man would have expected him to act differently."[20]

Having already engaged fourteen of the enemy's wooden vessels as they came up the bay, Buchanan was convinced that the *Tennessee* could hold her own with eleven, including three monitors. True, so far the ram had not engaged the Union monitors, but the protection that her armor had afforded the crew proved she was virtually unsinkable, even at point-blank range. Furthermore, after closing with the enemy, the *Tennessee* could fire in any direction, whereas the enemy's fire would be quite as likely to injure other Union vessels as the *Tennessee*. "Only in speed had she shown weakness, but this was now of less account as her opponents could not run away." The scene unfolding before the Confederate soldiers who "crowded the ramparts" of Forts Morgan and Gaines, and the Union soldiers atop the dunes on Dauphin Island "was such as has very rarely been furnished in the history of the world."[21]

Aboard the *Hartford,* Lieutenant Kinney had once again climbed into the flagship's rigging with his army signal flags. While the navy was preparing its signal hoists for a general attack on the approaching ram, Kinney flagged the admiral's first order to the *Monongahela,* "Run down the Ram." It took "less than twenty seconds" to convey, and before receipt had been acknowledged, "we could see the vessel slipping her cable and moving forward." An identical message was flagged to the *Lackawanna* and the monitors. Meanwhile a general signal, "Run down at full speed the enemy's principal vessel," had been hoisted to the *Hartford's* peak. Within minutes, Lieutenant Kinney noted, there was "a general slipping of cables and friendly rivalry to see which could quickest meet the foe." The time was 8:57 A.M.[22]

Clearly, the *Tennessee* was heading for the *Hartford;* with luck, the *Monongahela* would be able to intercept her before she reached the flagship. Admiring Buchanan's pluck, but fearful that he might be successful, Lt. Oliver A. Batcheller, aboard the *Monongahela,* described the unfolding drama: "With colors flying, [the ram] made directly for the flagship, ignoring all lesser fry. The perfect confidence which the commander of the *Tennessee* had in his vessel, and the absolute, imperative necessity which Farragut was under to capture or destroy her, rendered the fight which then took place, while it lasted, one of the most desperate on record. One side or the other must either surrender or be destroyed."[23]

CHAPTER 22

✦➤ ◄✦

Melee

HAVING MADE A WIDE SWEEP AROUND THE UNION ANCHORAGE TO GAIN "speed and position," the *Monongahela* straightened out and headed for the *Tennessee*. When she struck the ram, her chief engineer noted that the "engines were making 62 revolutions per minute, with 30 pounds steam and throttle valve wide open"—about 10 knots.[1] Just before the *Monongahela* struck the *Tennessee*, Captain Johnston yelled down from the *Tennessee*'s pilot platform: "Steady yourself when she strikes! Stand by and be ready! Below the gun deck, silent and rigid, the *Tennessee*'s crew awaited their fate. When the impact came, at 9:25 A.M., inflicting little damage, Johnston exclaimed: "We are all right; they can never run us under now!"[2]

From his vantage point aboard the *Hartford*, Lieutenant Kinney saw the *Monongahela* strike the *Tennessee* amidships, a blow that "inflicted not the slightest damage on the solid iron hull of the ram," largely due to the rebel commander's skillful handling of her helm. The *Monongahela*, on the other hand, emerged from the encounter badly damaged, including the loss of her iron prow and cutwater.[3] When the vessels scraped sides, the *Tennessee* fired two shots at the *Monongahela*, "piercing her through and through." In turn, as the *Monongahela* slid along the ram's side, she "fired one gun after another as they could be brought to bear, but the solid shot bounded off her side like peas from a shovel."[4]

As soon as the *Monongahela* had cleared the *Tennessee*'s stern, a second sloop, the *Lackawanna*, bore down on the ram's port side. Assistant Surgeon W. F. Hutchinson, who was aboard the sloop, described the moment of impact: "The *Lackawanna* was more fortunate and delivered a fair blow, going at the tremendous speed of 14 knots, just where the iron house joined the main deck, with a shock that prostrated every man on deck and tore to atoms [the *Lackawanna's*] solid oak bow for six feet as if it had been paper. No more damage was done the ram by this tremendous blow than if a lady had laid her finger upon the iron sheathing." The *Lackawanna*, however, had her "stem cut and crushed from three feet above the water-line to five below."[5]

Hutchinson then explained what happened next:

The Lackawanna *backed clear of the* Tennessee, *when the latter swung around on our port beam and delivered her broadside into us at three feet distance, at the same time receiving the fire of the only gun that could be sufficiently depressed to reach her, our deck being several feet higher out of water than hers. Her shell[s] . . . all exploded on the berth deck, just as they entered the ship, entirely destroying the powder division, with the exception of the officer in command . . . , who was wounded by flying splinters. The surgeon's steward and one nurse were torn into such small pieces that no part of either of them was ever identified.[6]*

The crew of the *Lackawanna* then experienced what seamen feared most: a fire in the magazine. On the berth deck, where the ram's shells had exploded, nothing was visible except thick smoke and blazing woodwork, and nothing could be heard but the thunder of exploding shells overhead, groans of the wounded and dying, and cries that the "magazine is on fire!" With seventeen tons of powder in the magazine, not a second could be wasted extinguishing the flames. Apparently, a trail of powder had been spilled along the passageway leading from the magazine to the gun deck ladder, which now was afire and flashing toward the main chamber.[7]

Responding to the cries of fire in the magazine, the *Lackawanna's* armorer, George Taylor, bolted down the ladder leading to the berth deck. In Hutchinson's words, he "sprang down into the passage and extinguished the fire with his naked hands, burning them to the bone in the process—but saving all our lives and the brave old ship." As the *Lackawanna* and *Tennessee* separated, the former's crew directed a heavy fire of musketry into the ram's gun ports, and the captain of the forecastle threw a holystone that struck a Confederate gunner who was using abusive language against the Union crew. Still full of fight, the *Lackawanna's* captain, John Marchand, pulled away to make another circle and continue the fight.[8]

Free of the *Lackawanna*, Buchanan now headed for the *Hartford*, and his nemesis, David Farragut. At this critical moment, "Buck" learned that the *Tennessee* was shipping water at the rate of six inches an hour, a result of being rammed by the *Lackawanna*. Ignoring the report, Buchanan ordered Johnston to stay on course, ram and sink the enemy flagship. Dead ahead, Farragut had accepted Buchanan's challenge and was now under way, the *Hartford*'s bow pointing at the *Tennessee*.[9]

At this moment, the *Tennessee* was beset by another threat far more formidable than the *Hartford:* she was about to be tested by the 15-inch guns of a twenty-one-hundred-ton monitor. While the two flagships were maneuvering for position, the *Manhattan* had worked its way between the vessels and was now a scant two hundred yards off the *Tennessee*'s port bow. Unbeknownst to the rebel admiral, however, only one of the *Manhattan*'s guns was operative. Early in the day, a flake of iron had dropped into the vent of her port gun and could not be removed. This, however, was not a problem; the other gun's 15-inch bore would compensate for the deficiency.[10]

Peering through the *Tennessee*'s forward gun port, Lieutenant Wharton watched the enemy monitor's turret revolve until its gun ports were pointed at the ram. Knowing that a 440-pound projectile was about to be fired, he shouted back to the gun deck: "Stand clear of the port side! . . . A moment after a thunderous report shook us all, while a blast of dense, sulphurous [*sic*] smoke covered our port-holes, and 440 pounds of iron, impelled by sixty pounds of powder, admitted daylight through our side, where, before it struck us, there had been over two feet of solid wood, covered with five inches of solid iron. . . . It did not come through; the inside netting caught the splinters, and there were no casualties from it. I was glad to find myself alive after that shot."[11] In the meantime, distracted by the *Manhattan*, the *Tennessee* had exposed her port bow to the *Hartford*, now only a few hundred feet away. However, as the *Hartford* approached, the *Tennessee* managed to turn toward her, thus lessening the angle of attack.

When the *Tennessee* and *Hartford* struck, the latter's port anchor had not been catted and was still hanging from the hawse-pipe. As such, it acted as a fender, causing the two vessels to scrape by with their port sides touching. Limited by the length and speed of the two vessels, moving in opposite directions, there would be time for either to fire one broadside, which consisted of seven guns for the *Hartford* and two for the ram. However, most of the *Hartford*'s main battery was still on the starboard side, having been moved there before passing Fort Morgan.[12]

Lieutenant Watson related what happened when the *Tennessee* rasped down the *Hartford*'s side: "We gave her a broadside of solid nine-inch shot, but they had not the slightest effect on her." In the meantime, Admiral Farragut had "jumped into the port mizzen rigging, above the poop deck, being eager to see the effect of the ramming. He laughed at my remonstrances as I seized the tails of his frock-coat and tried to prevent him from getting up there. I then caught up the end . . . of a small rope that happened to be handy, and, with his consent, secured him to the mizzen shrouds. I stood near him, just inside the rigging on the poop with a drawn revolver, ready to get the drop on anybody aboard the ram who might try to pick him off."[13]

As the two flagships were scraping hulls, a replay of sea battles in centuries past, officers and seamen on both vessels could be seen peering through the smoke, with pistols and muskets, searching for targets. Aboard the ram, a Confederate officer, crouching in a gun port with a revolver in hand, was seeking a target. He scanned the *Hartford*'s deck, which was enveloped in smoke, then looked aloft, and saw an officer in the rigging. "For an instant they gazed each other in the eyes, then, with a quick motion the Confederate raised his pistol to fire, but before he could fairly cover him[,] the smoke of a Dahlgren intervened, which so disturbed his aim that [the officer's] life was saved."[14]

Aboard the *Tennessee,* Engineer W. M. Rogers was not as lucky as the Yankee officer. While taking a break on the *Tennessee*'s gun deck, he received a pistol ball in his shoulder. As Surgeon Conrad was cutting the ball out, he asked whether the man, who was suffering terribly, wanted a shot of morphine. "None of that for me, doctor," the man replied. "When we go down I want to be up and take my chances of getting out of some 'port hole.'"[15]

At a distance of ten feet, the enemy's 9-inch Dahlgrens did little harm to the *Tennessee.* The ram's two broadside guns, however, inflicted considerable damage in return. Although one misfired several times, a shell from the other passed through the *Hartford*'s hull and exploded in her berth deck, causing heavy casualties. This was the last shot the *Tennessee* fired. The time was 9:35 A.M.[16] As the *Tennessee* scraped past the *Hartford,* the ram swung around to starboard and made a 180-degree turn to the south in an effort to engage her again, this time under more favorable circumstances. When turning, the ram exchanged fire with the *Brooklyn* and *Richmond,* both of which had been blocked from entering the melee by the arrival of the ironclads *Chickasaw* and *Winnebago.*

Lieutenant Perkins, the *Chickasaw*'s commander, described the scene: "Immediately after the *Hartford* gave the [*Tennessee*] her broadside, ... we closed with the ram, firing at her with steel and solid iron shot." However, while the *Chickasaw* had been off Fort Morgan, her smokestack had been pierced in several places, reducing the monitor's speed to a crawl; only by throwing tallow and coal-tar into the furnaces was enough steam raised to keep the vessel under way. Should this source of fuel be depleted before the fight ended, the *Chickasaw* would be in serious trouble. The *Winnebago* also had a problem—one that would dwarf the *Chickasaw*'s. She steered badly and neither of her turrets would rotate, requiring Commander Stevens to turn the vessel every time she fired.[17]

Steaming south, with the monitors trailing and the sloops jockeying for position on her flanks, the *Tennessee* was now subjected to a grueling fire from all quarters. Seeing an opening through which the *Hartford* might again engage the ram, Farragut ordered Drayton to make the attempt. Failing to notice that the *Lackawanna* was also heading for the *Tennessee*, the *Hartford* cut across the sloop's bow and was rammed by her just forward of the mizzenmast, where the admiral was standing. The blow was so great, the flagship's hull was crushed within two feet of the water.[18]

"For a time," Lieutenant Kinney remarked, "it was thought that we must sink, and the cry rang out over the deck: 'Save the Admiral! Save the Admiral!' The port boats were ordered lowered, and in their haste some of the sailors cut the 'falls,' and two of the cutters dropped into the water wrong side up, and floated astern. But the admiral sprang into the starboard mizzen-rigging, looked over the side of the ship, and finding there was still a few inches to spare above the water's edge, instantly ordered the ship ahead again at full speed, after the ram."[19]

Eager to destroy the *Tennessee*, Capt. John Marchand, the *Lackawanna*'s commander, backed off from the *Hartford* for another attempt to sink the ram. Turning to Lieutenant Kinney, Farragut asked: "Can you say 'For God's sake' by signal?" "Yes sir," Kinney replied. "Then say to the *Lackawanna*, 'For God's sake, get out of the way and anchor!'" In Kinney's haste to send the message, he brought the end of the signal flagstaff down on the admiral's head with considerable force. "It was a hasty message," Kinney explained, "for the fault was equally divided, each ship being too eager to reach the enemy, and it turned out all right, by a fortunate accident, that Captain Marchand never received it. The army signal officer on the *Lackawanna*, Lieutenant Myron Adams ... had taken his station in the foretop, and just as he received the first five words, 'For God's sake get out'—the wind flirted the large United States flag at the mast-head around him, so that he was unable to read the conclusion of the message."[20]

As the enemy's wooden vessels vied for positions from which to ram the *Tennessee*, the Union monitors were pounding away at her from distances of ten to fifty yards. With many of the *Tennessee*'s plates started, her smokestack perforated in numerous places, and both her aft quarter ports jammed, she was rapidly becoming unmanageable. Of the three ironclads, the *Chickasaw* was responsible for most of the damage. Firing shot after shot at close range, she "held on like a bulldog." At about 9:40 A.M., one of her solid shot jammed the *Tennessee*'s stern gun port, which now made it impossible for the ram to fire the stern gun at the ironclads trailing in her wake.[21]

From his station belowdecks, Surgeon Conrad could keep track of the deteriorating situation by the number of casualties reporting to him. "Soon the wounded began to pour down to me," he reported. "Stripped to their waists, the white skins of the men exhibited serious dark-blue elevations and hard spots. Cutting down to these [I] found that unburnt cubes of cannon powder, that had poured into the ports, had perforated the flesh, and made these great blue ridges under the skin. Their sufferings were very severe, for it was as if they had been shot with red-hot bullets." Unfortunately, injuries such as these were not considered wounds by the Confederate navy.[22]

For the past fifteen minutes, the *Tennessee* had not fired a shot. With her two aft quarter ports jammed, the enemy monitors were quick to take advantage of the ram's blind spots. Recognizing the seriousness of the situation, Admiral Buchanan left the pilothouse to superintend the gun deck. Shortly after he arrived, a shot struck the stern port-shutter, jamming it against the shield and providing the enemy with an unchallenged field of fire 180 degrees off the ram's stern.[23] Within minutes, John Silk, a machinist from the *Tennessee*'s engine room, had arrived to remove the pin from the bolt around which the port shutter revolved. Commander Johnston described the gruesome scene that followed: While Silk was removing the pin, "a shot from one of the monitors struck the edge of the port cover, immediately over the spot where the machinist was sitting, and his remains had to be taken up with a shovel, placed in a bucket, and thrown overboard. The same shot caused several iron splinters to fly inside of the shield, one of which killed a seaman, while another broke the admiral's leg below the knee."[24]

Notified that the admiral was wounded, Surgeon Conrad left the cockpit and went to the gun deck. There he found the admiral, grim and silent, lying on the deck, with one leg twisted under his body. He asked him if he was badly hurt? "Don't know," he answered. After Conrad had applied a temporary bandage, Buchanan sat up to read a report from Commander Johnston regarding the progress of the fight. Soon Johnston appeared in person, and was greeted by the admiral: "Well, Johnston, they have got me again," referring to his wound at Hampton Roads. "You'll have to look out for her now; it is your fight." "All right," Johnston answered. "I'll do the best I know how."[25]

Conrad then carried the admiral below. "I raised him up with great caution," he said, "and clasping his arms around my neck carried him on my back down the ladder to the 'cock-pit,' his broken leg slapping against me as I moved slowly along." Within half an hour, Commander Johnston again reported to the admiral that still not a gun could be brought to bear on the enemy and their "solid shot were gradually smashing in the 'shield.'" In addition, the "men were fast becoming demoralized from sheer inactivity, and that from the smashing of the 'shield' they were seeking shelter, which showed their condition mentally." "Well Johnston," the admiral replied, "fight to the last. Then, to save these brave men, when there [is] no longer any hope, surrender."[26]

Twenty minutes later, Commander Johnston went down to the cockpit and reported to the admiral that the *Tennessee*'s condition was now utterly hopeless. Four of her ten gun port shutters were jammed shut, the tiller chains and relieving tackle destroyed, and the smokestack knocked down, preventing the boilers from making enough steam to buck the tide, which was now running out of the bay at almost four knots. Furthermore, he had not been able to bring a gun to bear on any of the enemy's vessels for nearly half an hour. "Well, Johnston," the admiral replied, "if you cannot do them any further damage you had better surrender."[27]

Five miles to the northeast in Mississippi Sound, the Union gunboats had stopped firing at Fort Powell. During the morning, the fort had been shelled by five vessels at long range, none of which had inflicted any serious damage. However, anticipating that more was to come now that the Yankee fleet was in the bay, Lieutenant Colonel Williams ordered the seventy Negro slaves who had been working in the fort to return to Mobile by way of the shallows leading from Fort Powell to Cedar Point on the mainland.[28]

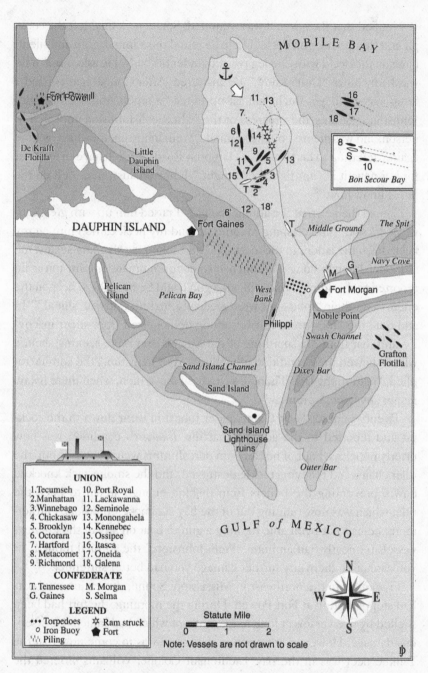

MOBILE BAY

⚓

16
17
18

Fort Powell

11 13
7
6   14
12   9
11   5   13
7
15   4   3
T 2

8
S
10
Bon Secour Bay

De Krafft
Flotilla

Little
Dauphin
Island

6' 12' 18'

DAUPHIN ISLAND   Fort Gaines

T

Middle Ground   The Spit

Navy Cove

M G

Pelican
Island   Pelican Bay

West
Bank

Fort Morgan

Mobile Point

Philippi

Swash Channel

Grafton
Flotilla

Sand Island Channel

Dixey Bar

Sand Island

Sand Island
Lighthouse
ruins

Outer Bar

GULF of MEXICO

UNION

1. Tecumseh   10. Port Royal
2. Manhattan   11. Lackawanna
3. Winnebago   12. Seminole
4. Chickasaw   13. Monongahela
5. Brooklyn   14. Kennebec
6. Octorara   15. Ossipee
7. Hartford   16. Itasca
8. Metacomet   17. Oneida
9. Richmond   18. Galena

CONFEDERATE

T. Tennessee   M. Morgan
G. Gaines   S. Selma

LEGEND

✦✦✦ Torpedoes   ✪ Ram struck
○ Iron Buoy   ⬟ Fort
〰 Piling

Statute Mile

0   1   2

Note: Vessels are not drawn to scale

N
W   E
S

Battle of Mobile Bay, 5 August 1864, 10:00 a.m.

Aboard the *Tennessee* Commander Johnston had returned to the gun deck for a final assessment of the situation—and to see if there was any chance of getting off a final shot at the enemy. Finding no targets in range, he then decided "with an almost bursting heart, to hoist the white flag, and returning again onto the shield, placed it in the same spot where but a few moments before had floated the proud flag for whose honor I would so cheerfully have sacrificed my own life if I could possibly have become the only victim."[29]

CHAPTER 23

➤➤ ◄◄

Surrender

STEPPING UP TO THE *Ossipee*'s PORT RAILING, CDR. WILLIAM E. LE ROY shouted to Johnston: "Do you surrender?" Shouting back, Johnston said, "Yes, we surrender. This is the Confederate States Ship *Tennessee*. I am the commanding officer. Admiral Buchanan is wounded." Commander Le Roy answered: "This is the United States steamer *Ossipee*. I accept the surrender for Admiral Farragut."[1]

When Commander Johnston raised the white flag, the *Manhattan* was fifty yards off the ram's port beam. "I was about to give the order 'Fire!'" said Acting Lt. Robert B. Ely, "which would have sent 870 pounds of cold iron fore and aft the whole length of her gun deck, when the Captain called out not to fire, that 'she had surrendered.' We all jumped out on deck, and sure enough the Rebel flag was down, much torn and the pale flag of truce in its place. We stopped the engines at once and just steamed clear of her, having been steaming after her at full speed with the intention of ramming her as we fired the last shot."[2]

With the *Tennessee*'s huge casemate blocking his vision, Commander Nicholson, the *Manhattan*'s captain, was not aware that the *Ossipee* was about to ram the *Tennessee* on her starboard beam. He did, however, see the white flag dangling from a boat hook on top of the ram's casemate. Believing that the *Tennessee* was surrendering to him, Nicholson left the pilot-house and went to the turret roof, where he yelled to the ram: "Who do you surrender to?" Amid the noise and confusion that followed, he heard a voice shout: "I surrender to you, sir; for God's sake, don't fire again; we are disabled." Shouting to Lieutenant Ely, who was in the turret below, Nicholson ordered him to board the ram and "take her colors," although he was not sure who surrendered the ram. According to Harrie Webster, an engineer aboard the *Manhattan,* Ely "stepped aboard the ram, now alongside, and, seizing the rebel flag lying in the starboard scuppers, brought it aboard the *Manhattan* and tossed it into the turret through a gun port." The 10:00 A.M. entry in the *Manhattan's* deck log read: "At 10 the rebel ram *Tennessee* surrendered to this vessel. Acting Master Robert B. Ely boarded her by order of Commander Nicholson and received her colors, which he brought on board this vessel."[3]

As soon as the enemy ceased firing, Surgeon Conrad had the *Tennessee's* wounded carried to the casemate roof where they could get some fresh air. "From that elevated place," he noted, "I witnessed the rush of the petty officers and men of the 'monitor' which was nearest to us to board the captured ship, to procure relics and newspaper renown. Two creatures dressed in blue shirts, begrimed and black with powder, rushed up to the wounded admiral and demanded his sword. His aide, [Masters Mate W. S. Forrest], refused peremptorily, whereupon one of them stooped as if to take it anyhow; upon which Aide Forrest warned him not to touch it, as it would only be given to Admiral Farragut or his authorized representative. Still the man attempted to seize it, whereupon Forrest knocked him off the 'shield' to the deck below."[4]

In the meantime, Commander Le Roy had sent Acting Lt. Pierre Giraud to accept Johnston's surrender and bring him to the *Ossipee.* Climbing aboard the *Tennessee,* he was approached by Surgeon Conrad who explained what had just happened, whereupon Giraud mounted the casemate, assumed command of the ram, and sent the man under guard to his boat, along with an accomplice who had seized the *Tennessee's* "smoke-stained and torn" ensign that was lying on top of the shield. When confronted with the theft, "amidst the laughter and jeers of his companions," he was forced to withdraw it from his "shirt bosom," where it had been "hastily concealed."[5]

With order restored, Giraud again ascended the shield, this time to inquire about the admiral's condition. Seeing him approach, and knowing his purpose, Buchanan instructed Forrest to give the officer his sword to be delivered to Admiral Farragut. Giraud then raised the American flag and, beckoning Commander Johnston to follow, boarded his boat and returned to the *Ossipee.*[6]

Circling around the *Tennessee's* stern, Giraud's boat headed for the *Ossipee,* which had backed off a few hundred yards, and edged up to her boarding ladder. As much as it hurt him, Johnston was convinced that he had

CSS Tennessee *surrendering.*
U.S. NAVAL INSTITUTE PHOTO ARCHIVE

done the right thing. Outnumbered nine to one, including three monitors, and unable to effectively return the enemy's fire, he had no choice but to surrender: His conscience was clear.

Climbing aboard the *Ossipee*, Johnston was met at the gangway by Commander Le Roy. "I'm glad to see you Johnston," Le Roy greeted him; "here's some ice water for you—I know you are dry; but I've something better than that for you down below." Johnston thanked him, but was in no mood for hospitalities, and quietly followed him to his cabin. Once there, Johnston said that Le Roy "placed a bottle of 'navy sherry' and a pitcher of ice-water before me and urged me to help myself." He then called his steward and told him "to attend to my wishes as if they were his own."[7]

At army headquarters in Mobile, a telegram from General Page had just been received. Sent at ten in the morning, it read: "The whole fleet of the enemy passed the fort and are now in the bay." An hour later another followed, with additional information: "Action commenced this morning between the fleet of the enemy and the Forts at 7 o'clock. They have passed us with three (3) iron clads and (14) fourteen ships. The monitor *Tecumseh* was sunk under guns of Water Battery. The *Tennessee* surrendered after a terrific single handed fight with Enemys [*sic*] fleet.

The *Gaines* is beached near the Hospital. The *Selma* was captured. The *Morgan*'s crew and Officers all safe."[8]

From her home on Government Street, Laura Pillans wrote in her diary: "Strange startling news. The Yankee fleet has destroyed or captured our fleet and is now inside of our port. Three monitors and fourteen gunboats. Rumors of all sorts afloat. The alarm bell summoned the citizens to arm. Mr. P[illans] and my beloved son away, nevertheless I feel a strange and solemn calm. Emotion so deep that not a bubble of excitement rises to the surface; noncombatants ordered to leave the city at once, but where to go! How can I go? I have not a cent in the world and will not borrow."[9]

At Battery Gladden, one of the water batteries opposite the city, Lieutenant Mumford made another entry in his diary, the second since daybreak: "Gen. Page telegraphed about 10 o'clock, A.M.[,] from Fort Morgan, saying the fighting was still going on." Continuing, he wrote: "One monitor was sunk under the guns of the fort. About 11 o'clock, A.M., another dispatch was received, saying the fleet had passed the Forts, our vessels had all been sunk, and the *Tennessee* after a gallant fight, was compelled to surrender. Admiral Buchanan was aboard. The dispatch created great excitement in town. The alarm bell was soon rung, and crowds turned out to receive arms. The vessels are reported off Point Clear, none having yet come within sight of the city."[10]

In the lower bay aboard the *Hartford*, Farragut learned of Buchanan's wound and sent him a message expressing his regret and offering anything in his power to help. Surgeon Conrad, who was standing nearby when Farragut's message was delivered to Buchanan, noted that the admiral accepted it "in the same kind spirit in which it was given." Buchanan's only request was that his "'fleet-surgeon,' and his aides might be allowed to accompany him wherever he might be sent until recovering from his wound."[11]

Dr. Conrad was asked to make this request in person. Boarding the *Hartford*, Conrad was forced to ascend by the "man-rope," as the gangway and

whole starboard side amidships . . . had been carried away by one of their own frigates having collided with the Hartford *after "ramming the Tennessee." Looking down from the hammock netting, the scene was one of carnage and devastation. The spar-deck was covered and littered with broken gun-carriages, shattered boats, disabled guns, and a long line of grim corpses dressed in blue lying side by side. The officer accompanying me told me that these men—two whole guns' crews—were all killed by splinters, and pointing with his hand to a piece of "weather boarding" ten feet long and four inches wide, I received my first vivid idea of what a "splinter" was, or what was meant by a "splinter."[12]*

Conrad continued his description: "Descending, we threaded our way, and, ascended to the 'poop,' where all of the officers were standing. I was taken up and introduced to Admiral Farragut, whom I found a very quiet, unassuming man, and not in the least flurried by his great victory. In the kindest manner he inquired regarding the severity of the admiral's wound, and then gave the necessary orders to carry out Admiral Buchanan's request." Before leaving, Dr. Conrad told Farragut that Admiral Buchanan's leg would probably have to be amputated that night or the next morning. Without hesitation, Farragut replied, "I have nothing to do with it; it is your leg now, doctor; do your best."[13]

Desirous of helping Buchanan in every way possible, Farragut asked Lieutenant Kinney to locate Fleet Surgeon James C. Palmer by signal and have him report to the *Hartford*. Aboard the steam launch *Loyall* at the time, Palmer was going from vessel to vessel visiting the wounded and giving advice, when the *Richmond* signaled that the admiral wanted him to report to the *Hartford*. Approaching the flagship, he was hailed by the admiral, and told to go aboard the captured ram and examine Admiral Buchanan, who was wounded.[14]

Because of the ram's slanting shield, getting on board the *Tennessee* from a small launch like the *Loyall* was difficult. "I had to make a long leap, assisted by a strong man's hand," Palmer explained. "I scrambled literally through the iron port, and threaded my way among the piles of confusion, to a ladder, by which I mounted to where Admiral Buchanan was lying." When introduced, the admiral said: "I know Dr. Palmer" and extended his hand, adding, "I am a Southern man, and an enemy, and a rebel." Palmer felt a "little offended at his tone, but rejoined carefully that he was at that moment a wounded person and disabled, and that I would engage to have his wishes fulfilled." After examining Buchanan's wound—a compound fracture below the knee—Dr. Palmer recommended that the operation not be performed. In his opinion, Buchanan's leg could be saved.[15]

By now the grim task of counting the dead and wounded was well under way. When first told of the slaughter, Farragut was aghast. He knew that casualties were heavy, but not to the extent reported. It was the bloodiest battle he had fought since he was a midshipman aboard the *Essex*, fifty years ago. So far, the number from only nine vessels, not counting the *Tecumseh*, totaled 129, with the final count estimated to be well over 300. The *Tennessee*'s casualties, as reported by Surgeon Conrad, were 2 killed and 9 wounded. The gunboats had not yet reported their losses.[16]

Recognizing that the seriously wounded could not be properly cared for aboard the vessels of the fleet, Surgeon Palmer suggested that the wounded of both sides be taken to Pensacola. Farragut concurred and sent a message to General Page requesting that a vessel be allowed to go to Pensacola under a flag of truce. "Admiral Buchanan is severely wounded," he wrote, "having lost a leg [*sic*]. There are in addition four or five others of the crew of the *Tennessee* who require more comfortable quarters than we can give them in the fleet. Will the commanding officer at Fort Morgan permit a vessel to take them to our hospital at Pensacola with or without our own wounded, the understanding being that the flag-of-truce vessel takes nothing whatever but the wounded and brings nothing back that she did not take out, and my honor is given for the above terms."[17]

General Page had no objection to Farragut's proposal, but requested that Admiral Buchanan, "having lost a leg [*sic*], be permitted to go to Mobile, where he can receive earlier and more prompt attention. If the latter request is granted," he added, "please inform me, and I will have a boat from town to take him up."[18] Mistaking Page's request as a condition for sending the wounded to Pensacola, Farragut wrote the general a scathing note, saying that "it is altogether out of the question that I should permit Admiral Buchanan to be sent to Mobile, but I will send him to Pensacola, where he will receive the same comforts as our wounded, which I apprehend are as good as they could be at Mobile. It was simply an act of humanity that I made the proposition I did to-day." He then added a statement that had no bearing on the subject at hand: "I would be glad to bury my dead on shore, but if there is any objection to it they can have a soldier's grave in the deep, honored by the heartfelt sighs of their shipmates."[19]

In no mood to remind Farragut that the subject of burying his dead had not been mentioned in his correspondence, Page sent him a simple, straightforward reply: "There is no objection to your burying your dead on shore. When they arrive near the wharf here, a point will be designated for the burial."[20]

Aboard the *Hartford* at her anchorage in the Lower Fleet, Farragut had just ordered Lieutenant Watson to hoist Signal 2139: "Captains repair on board." The time was 2:00 P.M. Farragut wanted to meet with his commanders to assess the situation—casualties, damage, ammunition expended, and so on—and to inform them that the *Metacomet* would be leaving for Pensacola under a flag of truce with the seriously wounded, both Union and Confederate, as soon as possible. The admiral also wanted to report that he had ordered the gunboats *Itasca*, *Kennebec*, and *Octorara* to reconnoiter the bay as far north as Dog River, seven miles south of Mobile. At 6:00 the *Itasca* returned, reporting that two fishing sloops had been captured; a steamer chased, which escaped; and the smoke of nine vessels had been observed near Dog River. The rebel ironclads *Huntsville* and *Tuscaloosa* had not been seen.[21]

At the moment Farragut was more concerned with the capture of Fort Powell. A fleet of eighteen vessels, including the captured *Selma*, could not remain inside Mobile Bay indefinitely without access to and from Mississippi Sound. He therefore ordered Lieutenant Commander Perkins to take the *Chickasaw* in and shell Fort Powell so that "troops and supplies might be brought into Mobile Bay from New Orleans, without undertaking to pass the guns of Fort Morgan." Thirty minutes later, the *Chickasaw* weighed anchor and stood toward Fort Powell, moving up within point-blank range of the work's rear face. The following entry in the *Chickasaw* deck log described the action: "At 2:45 P.M. got underway, and at 2:50 went to general quarters and stood within 350 yards of Fort Powell, taking the barge *Ingomar*, with shovels, pickaxes, and wheelbarrows on board. Fort opened on us and struck us once in the smokestack. We opened fire on the fort and expended 25 5-second shell[s], after which returned to our anchorage."[22]

Unable to adequately defend Fort Powell's eastern face, a weakness he had repeatedly brought to the attention of his superiors, Lt. Col. James M. Williams sat down and painfully wrote his after action report:

About 2:30 p.m. one of the enemy's monitors came within 700 yards of the fort, firing rapidly with shell and grape [twenty-five times]. I replied from the 7-inch Brooke gun on the southern angle. I succeeded in firing three shots from it while the iron-clad was in range, because there was no platform in the rear and a sponge head pulled off in the gun. The elevating machine of the 10-inch Columbiad was broken by a fragment of a shell. The shells exploding in the face of the work displaced the sand so rapidly that I was convinced unless the iron-clad was driven off it would explode my magazine and make the bombproof untenable. I telegraphed Col. Anderson that I would be compelled to surrender within forty-eight hours. His reply was, 'Save your garrison when your fort is no longer tenable.' I decided promptly that it would be better to save my command and destroy the fort than to allow both to fall into the hands of the enemy.[23]

Earlier in the day, General Maury had telegraphed James A. Seddon, the Confederate secretary of war, informing him that the long-awaited naval attack had commenced. Seddon immediately notified Jefferson Davis and Maj. Gen. Jeremy Gilmer, the Confederacy's chief engineer. By late afternoon, Maury had received an answer from both the president and General Gilmer. Davis's telegram began by encouraging him to hold the forts on the outer line "as long as possible. For that purpose, I hope they are adequately supplied. If there be deficiencies, they should, as far as practicable, be remedied promptly. Care is needed as to the character of their garrison. Reserves have, I suppose, joined you, and for the desperate defense of a work are, by pride and patriotism, fully reliable. You will have time, I hope, to make all needed additions to the works of the inner line. I have requested General Gilmer, Chief of Engineers, to present to you his views. May our Heavenly Father shield and direct you, so as to avert the threatened disaster."[24]

General Gilmer's telegram followed the president's: "By direction of the President I offer my views," it began. "Every effort should be made to hold Forts Morgan, Gaines, and Powell, with the hope of forcing the enemy to withdraw for supplies, or at least gain time to strengthen inner defenses. It is believed here that the outer works are supplied for two or three months. Can not torpedoes be placed in ship channel under guns of Fort Morgan? Impress labor for defenses, hurrying forward those of inner harbor and of the city. It is hoped you can prevent a lodgment on east of bay at Blakel[e]y and southward. Is it possible in darkness and fog to throw supplies into Fort Morgan in barges or rowboats? Put torpedoes and other obstacles in mouth of Dog River, also in Blakeley, Apalachee, and Tensas rivers. I will write."[25]

✦➤ ◄✦

CHAPTER 24

Aftermath

WITH THE CAPTURE OF THE *Tennessee* AND THE PENDING EVACUATION OF
Fort Powell, "the fate of Fort Gaines was decided, and its capture merely
a question of time," so believed Bernard Reynolds, an engineer officer at
Fort Gaines. In the meantime, Lt. John Rapier, commander of the fort's
marine detachment, was determined to make the enemy pay dearly for
such a victory. Following the surrender of the *Tennessee*, Rapier related that
Fort Gaines "plucked up courage to open on the woods with her 32s—
& though overshooting very far, [made] the enemy's battery keep respectable silence."[1]

At Fort Powell, Lieutenant Colonel Williams believed there would not
be another opportunity for his garrison of 140 men to escape. He had decided, therefore, that it would be better to save his command and destroy
the fort than to allow it to fall into enemy hands, which would probably
happen anyway within forty-eight hours. As yet, the enemy had not intercepted his communications with the mainland, and the garrison would
not have another opportunity to escape. Convinced that further resistance was impossible, Williams announced that the fort would be evacuated after dark.[2]

Across the channel, several hundred yards northeast of Fort Morgan's
wharf, the crew of the *Gaines* had been working since midmorning salvaging as much as possible from the vessel before she settled to the bottom. After the guns had been spiked, most of the remaining powder, shot,
and shell had been boated ashore and given to General Page. Lieutenant
Commander Bennett had also offered him the services of the *Gaines*'s 129

officers and men, but the general declined, saying that the garrison's complement was sufficient to defend the fort. Just before noon, the crew brought their dead and wounded ashore, and at "high twelve," Midshipman Waterman noted, "the *Gaines*, flying her battle flag, sank in two fathoms and we bade her adieu."[3]

Bennett now began making arrangements for taking the crew to Mobile. With six boats—four from the *Gaines* and two left behind by the *Tennessee*—he estimated that the *Gaines*'s crew should be able to row to Mobile under cover of darkness and arrive there at sunrise or a little after. Before leaving, however, Quarter Gunner Daniel Aherne and Seaman Michael Vincent were buried in Fort Morgan's little graveyard, "wrapt in the colors they had died for."[4]

A few hundred yards to the east, Cdr. George Harrison and his officers were discussing what was to be done with the *Morgan*. Two options were on the table: scuttle the vessel or attempt to evade the Union fleet and reach Mobile. "I felt exceedingly anxious to save her to the Confederacy," Commander Harrison explained, "by 'running the gauntlet' up the bay to Mobile. . . . But it seemed so impossible in a noisy, high-pressure steamer, making black smoke, to pass the enemy's fleet unobserved or to elude the vigilance of his gunboats, which were seen after the action to go up the bay, that I gave up the idea . . . as impracticable and made preparations to take to the boats, as the *Gaines* people intended to do when night should come."[5]

Following the discussion, Commander Harrison went ashore to inform General Page of his decision and arrange for landing the men. While he was gone, his executive officer, Lt. Thomas Locke Harrison (no relation to the commander), assembled the crew aft and told them that "the *Morgan* was the only vessel now left to the navy in those parts and she was more needed now than ever before, and that she was too valuable to give up." Continuing, he informed them that he "intended to take her to Mobile. Those who wanted to go with him could go to starboard; those who wanted to go ashore to port. All hands went to the starboard." When Commander Harrison returned and learned of the crew's desire to run the gauntlet to Mobile that night, he changed his mind, stating: "Upon reconsideration of the matter, . . . I determined to make the effort."[6]

As the crews of the *Gaines* and *Morgan* waited for darkness, Fort Morgan's garrison was hard at work preparing for the siege which was certain to follow. Lieutenant Wilkinson of the 1st Tennessee Heavy Artillery wrote in his diary that the fort "is in good fighting condition." He did not think, however, that it could hold out indefinitely. For the good of the service, therefore, the fort should be evacuated, he wrote; "but for the moral of the thing, we have determined to hold out to the last. I have been on my feet at work all day and am very weary—have as yet got no quarters fixed up— we are very cheerful and I only wish our loved ones could be as much . . . for I know they will be much distressed particularly as to the probable result of the siege—in peace is our only hope, as naught else can save us from capture."[7]

A fellow artilleryman in the 1st Tennessee, Sergeant R. B. Tarpley, also believed that, sooner or later, the war would end with a negotiated peace. He hoped that "some change will take place (not far off) for the best" and that "Peace would be glorious news to our little command provided it was on the right terms." But, he feared, "no such good news is in store for us yet awhile. I do not look for it for the next 8 months."[8]

As Wilkinson and Tarpley pondered the fate of Fort Morgan, the crews of the *Gaines* and *Morgan* prepared to depart for Mobile, Commander Harrison's men in the *Morgan*, Lieutenant Bennett's in boats. Now that enemy gunboats were roaming the bay, the attempt had become more hazardous, but preparations continued. At 8:00 P.M., the *Gaines*'s crew, with their "blankets, bags, small arms, pikes, and cutlasses," pushed off from the beach at Fort Morgan. The *Morgan* would follow at 11:40. In the words of Lt. John Rapier, a friend of Lieutenant Harrison, this was "the most daring action in the history of the Confederate Navy."[9]

Ninety minutes later, as the *Gaines*'s six boats were crossing Bon Secour Bay, Lieutenant Colonel Williams ordered the evacuation of Fort Powell. "The tide being low," he noted, "I marched my command to Cedar Point without interruption or discovery. In one narrow channel I found the water overhead, and in crossing it I damaged my ammunition and lost a few muskets (a special report of which will be made). Lieutenant Savage was left in the fort with orders to prepare a train and match to explode the magazine as soon as he discovered that I had gained the mainland. Lieutenant Jeffers, acting ordnance officer, was directed to spike the guns at the same time. The fort was blown at 10:30 P.M. Every man was brought off safely to Cedar Point, thence to the city."[10]

Eight miles to the east, the *Morgan* had weighed anchor and was steaming north into the darkness. Hardly had she left when the flash and whine of a projectile told that she had been detected. In the words of

Midshipman Waterman, the Union gunboats "joined in pursuit opening their guns furiously. The *Morgan* returned the fire with great rapidity. It was a regular conflagration of gunpowder all the way up the channel."[11]

SHORTLY AFTER MIDNIGHT ON 6 AUGUST, FROM THE *Winnebago*'s ANCHORage north of the Lower Fleet, her lookout reported a rebel steamer going up the bay, trailing black smoke. Cdr. Thomas H. Stevens immediately ordered the sluggish monitor to get under way, hoping to intercept the vessel as she passed. Failing to do this, he opened fire at long range, "expending 12 rounds from [the] forward turret" with little effect. About the same time, the *Itasca* joined in the chase, to be followed by the *Kennebec*, *Sebago*, and *Port Royal*. At 2:30 A.M., the *Kennebec* fired six rounds from her 11-inch gun and fourteen from her Parrott. Twenty minutes later the *Octorara* also opened fire.[12]

At 3:30 A.M., the following entry was made in the *Sebago*'s deck log: "A vessel's lights ahead, evidently crossing our bows to northward and westward. Went to quarters, but lost sight of her in a thick cloud." With lights burning, this was, no doubt, one of the Union gunboats.[13]

As the first rays of dawn spread across the bay, the *Morgan*'s lookout reported that the city's outer obstructions were in sight. In Commander Harrison's words, "fortune favored us, and although hotly pursued and shelled by the enemy's cruisers for a large portion of the way, we successfully reached the outer obstructions near Mobile at daybreak, having been struck but once slightly." However, much to Harrison's surprise, the "gap" through the obstructions was closed.[14]

Just below Mobile, the Confederate engineers had blocked the water approaches to the city with piles and sunken hulks filled with rocks, leaving a gap for vessels to pass in and out. When the *Morgan* was seen approaching, chased by several enemy gunboats, the officer in charge of the obstructions, believing that this was a federal *ruse de guerre*, proceeded at once to block the gap with rock-filled crates. By then, to further complicate the situation, Battery McIntosh had opened on the *Morgan*. In the meantime, fearful of torpedoes, the enemy gunboats had turned around and headed back down the bay.[15]

So far the *Gaines*'s boats had remained undetected. "It was a run of more than thirty miles," Midshipman Waterman reported. The *Morgan*, however, was "a source of constant anxiety to us, for the enemy, pursuing

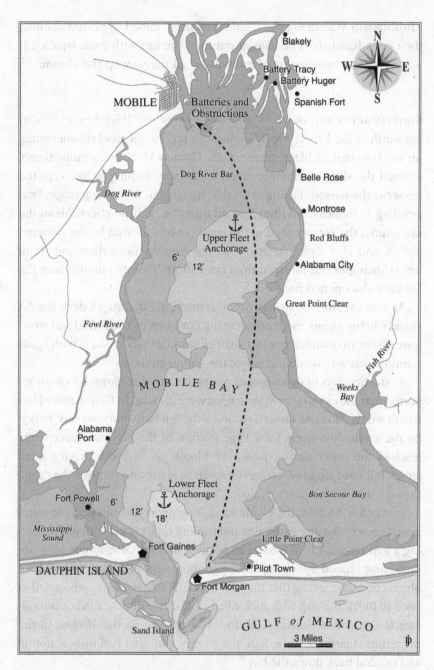

CSS Morgan *and boats of CSS* Gaines *escape to Mobile.*

her, might come upon us. . . . The lights . . . thrown out to detect the *Morgan* might betray us too. . . . At one time the enemy came [so] near us—yet unaware of our proximity, owing to our sitting low in the water—that Captain Bennett felt constrained to drop overboard the leaded 'signal code' [a lead-weighted signal book]. But fortune favors those who help themselves, and we reached Mobile Saturday morning at seven o'clock and reported for further service."[16]

As the crewmen of the *Gaines* were reporting to their new assignment, a water battery just south of the city, the *Morgan* and the steamer *Dick Keyes* were pushing aside the crate that blocked the channel. When the channel was clear, the *Morgan*—with her colors flying—steamed up to the city, the sole Confederate vessel to survive the battle, thanks to young Thomas Locke Harrison.[17]

Thirty miles to the south, the *Metacomet* had passed through the clear channel off Fort Morgan, a flag of truce fluttering from her forward mast. Aboard were the seriously wounded from both sides. Second Asst. Engineer John C. O'Connell, wounded in the shoulder by a musket ball, would later scribble an entry in his diary: "On the morning of the sixth at day light the Str. Metacomet proceeded to get under way. On going out of Mobile Bay we communicated with Fort Morgan. I embraced the opportunity of sending a dispatch to my father at Mobile. After communicating with the fort we stood out to sea."[18]

During the trip to Pensacola, A. T. Post, the *Tennessee*'s pilot, asked Commander Jouett, "Who commanded that Monitor that got under the ram's stern?" "George Perkins," Jouett answered. "D—n him!" Post replied. "He stuck to us like a leech; we could not get away from him. It was he who cut the steering gear, jammed the stern port shutters, and wounded Admiral Buchanan." Post was aboard the *Metacomet* to guide her through the clear channel opposite Fort Morgan.[19] Later in the day, aware of Lieutenant Commander Perkins's growing reputation as an aggressive fighter, Farragut sent him on another mission, this time to test the seaward defenses of Fort Gaines. At 4:00 P.M. the *Chickasaw* steamed up within two thousand yards of the fort; and by 5:00 had fired thirty-one shells, most of which fell within the fort. Fort Gaines returned the fire but failed to score a single hit.[20]

Over the past several days, the morale of the Fort Gaines garrison had plummeted. The capture of the *Tennessee* and the evacuation of Fort Powell, the stress of being under siege—and now the leisurely way in which the enemy monitor bombarded the fort, killing two men—all had worked to unnerve the garrison. It came as no surprise, therefore, when around midnight, 6 August, Colonel Anderson was handed a surrender petition signed by forty-three of his officers—all but a few who felt that honor required a more determined resistance. Agreeing with the petitioners, Anderson sent a message to Admiral Farragut the next morning at daylight. Dated August 7, it read:

> *Feeling my inability to maintain my present position . . . and feeling also the uselessness of entailing upon ourselves further destruction of life, I have the honor to propose the surrender of Fort Gaines, its garrison, stores, etc. I trust to your magnanimity for obtaining honorable terms, which I respectfully request that you will transmit to me and allow me sufficient time to consider them and return an answer.*
>
> *This communication will be handed to you by Major W. R. Browne.[21]*

At 7:00 A.M. Major Browne delivered Anderson's letter to Farragut and remained aboard the *Hartford* throughout the day while the admiral consulted with the army commander, General Granger. At dusk, Captain Drayton; Colonel Myers, the army's chief signal officer; and Browne returned to Fort Gaines and delivered Farragut's reply to Colonel Anderson. It read:

> *Sir: In accordance with the proposal made in your letter of this morning for the surrender of Fort Gaines, I have to say that after communicating with General Granger, in command of our forces on Dauphin Island, the only offers we can make are:*
>
> *First. The unconditional surrender of yourself and the garrison of Fort Gaines, with all of the public property within its limits.*
>
> *Second. The treatment which is in conformity with the custom of the most civilized nations toward prisoners of war.*
>
> *Third. Private property, with the exception of arms, will be respected.*
>
> *This communication will be handed to you by Fleet Captain P. Drayton and Colonel Myer, of the U.S. Army, who fully understand the views of General Granger and myself.[22]*

Believing that further resistance was hopeless, Anderson accepted Farragut's terms, despite pleas from Major Browne to withdraw the offer and continue fighting. "The ... condition and terms of surrender," Colonel Anderson wrote, "are agreed to by the undersigned, and the ceremony of turning over the prisoners of war, Fort Gaines, and all public property appertaining thereto intact, and in the same condition it is now in, will take place at 8 o'clock a.m., to-morrow, August the 8th."[23]

Having agreed upon the surrender terms, Drayton, Myer, Anderson, and Browne boarded the *Metacomet* and were taken to the *Hartford* to officially consummate the surrender. Waiting in Farragut's spacious day cabin were the admiral, Maj. Gen. Gordon Granger, Capt. Percival Drayton, and Maj. James E. Montgomery, assistant adjutant general and chief of staff of the 13th Army Corps, General Canby's representative.[24]

Anderson and Browne were very kindly received by the admiral. "Surrounded on three sides by my vessels, and on the fourth by the army," Farragut told Anderson, "you cannot possibly hold it." At this point, Major Browne objected and expressed his belief that the garrison should "fight it out." Getting this off his chest, he then agreed with the admiral that continued resistance was a "forlorn hope." With the matter settled, they took a glass of wine together, sealing the fate of Fort Gaines. The surrender ceremony would take place tomorrow morning.[25]

While Anderson was aboard the *Hartford*, General Page, his commanding officer, was rowed across the three and a half miles of open water between Fort Morgan and Gaines; he was concerned about the fort's failure to answer his signals and suspected that Anderson was negotiating with the enemy. Arriving at Fort Gaines, his worse fears were confirmed: Anderson was aboard the *Hartford* discussing terms of surrender. "I gave peremptory orders on his return, if the enemy did not return with him, all terms were annulled and he was relieved from command." Page needed Anderson to hold out as long as possible in order to strengthen Fort Morgan. Every day counted, for as soon as Gaines capitulated, Page was "confident that the whole naval and land forces of the enemy would be brought against Fort Morgan."[26]

As Page was returning from Fort Gaines, baffled by Anderson's premature surrender, General Maury, in Mobile, was reading a lengthy report written by Lieutenant Colonel Williams, defending his evacuation of Fort Powell. Also dismayed, Maury wrote: "This report is unsatisfactory. Colonel Williams should have fought his guns. They were not more exposed than those in every wooden ship, and vigorously served would probably have compelled the monitor to haul off. Fort Powell should not have been surrendered. Colonel Williams is relieved from command until full investigation can be had."[27]

At 7:00 A.M., 8 August, Fleet Captain Drayton and Colonel Myer left the *Hartford* for Fort Gaines to carry out the surrender, Drayton representing the navy and Myer the army. At 9:45 A.M., the Stars and Bars were hauled down and the Stars and Stripes were hoisted on the fort's staff. Absalom Kirby, an engineer aboard the *Richmond*, described the surrender in a letter to his wife: "I have just come from the deck to witness our troops march in Fort Gaines, and the Rebel flag hauled down and the glorious old stars & stripes go up. It was a beautiful sight to see all the vessels in the fleet giving three cheers to the flag as it went up. Fort Morgan will surrender in a few days. Then all our fighting will be over, for we cannot get further up the bay, for we draw too much water, but the gunboats can go some distance up."[28] Following the surrender, the Fort Gaines garrison was put aboard steamers for New Orleans, "while the Union troops, finding in the fort a large quantity of supplies, 'regaled themselves . . . with the best meal they had had since arriving on Dauphine [*sic*] Island,—corn dodgers, fried bacon, and coffee.'"[29]

During the afternoon of 8 August, Granger informed Canby that he would move his troops and artillery "without delay to Mobile Point near Pilot Town" and invest Fort Morgan, "leaving as small a force as possible to garrison and hold Fort Gaines." Reliable intelligence, he added, indicated that the garrison at Fort Morgan "already outnumbers my own force, and they are amply supplied to resist to the very last. Under these circumstances I respectfully request that my reinforcements may be forwarded without delay."[30]

With the enemy now landing four miles east of Fort Morgan, General Page ordered all structures—hospital, quarters, stables, and the redoubt twenty-seven hundred yards east of the fort—to be fired. While this was being done, "two monitors, three sloops of war, and some gun-boats engaged the fort for several hours—the wooden vessels at long range—with but little damage on either side. When the bombardment ceased, a boat was seen approaching with a flag of truce. The communication, dated 9 August and signed by Admiral Farragut and General Granger, read as follows. "Sir: To prevent the unnecessary sacrifice of human life which must follow the opening of our batteries, we demand the unconditional surrender of Fort Morgan and its dependencies."[31]

Page answered the enemy's surrender demand with an equally brief reply: "Sirs: I am prepared to sacrifice life, and will only surrender when I have no means of defense. I do not understand that while being communicated with under the flag of truce, the *Tennessee* should be towed within range of my guns." From then on, Page reported, Fort Morgan was engaged day and night by the enemy fleet, "sometimes in a brisk fight of several hours' duration, at others in desultory firing without any material damage being done to the fort, save a demonstration of the fact that our brick walls were easily penetrable by heavy missiles of the enemy, and that systematic concentrated fire would soon breach them."[32]

Granger's land forces completed their first parallel across the peninsula on 10 August and the second and third on 14 August. They were now within seven hundred yards of the fort. Lieutenant Austill wrote in his diary: "The monitors have just opened again. We were in hopes they would let the Sabbath pass quietly, but it seems such is not their intention. If we could only have twenty-four hours more of uninterrupted work, some of our case mates would be safe, as the traverses in front are nearly completed. The sharpshooters have been divided into five companies, one to each curtain. Oh, if we could only get them to attack us before our walls are battered down, what a glorious victory we would achieve."[33]

On the twenty-first Granger's sappers had approached to within two hundred yards of the fort's glacis. Such guns that could be brought to bear on these sappers, especially at night, retarded the work, but did not stop it. Lieutenant Austill entered the following comment in his diary: "The enemy have been almost silent today, replying but seldom to our guns. Which perplexes us some. They have received reinforcements of infantry today, and some are apprehensive of an assault."[34]

At first light the next day, Page was informed that the enemy fleet was "moving up and encircling the fort, the iron-clads and captured *Tennessee* included." The sun had hardly cleared the horizon when the fleet and land batteries "opened a furious fire, which came from almost every point of the compass, and continued unabated throughout the day, culminating in increased force at sundown; after which the heavy calibers and mortars kept it up during the night."[35]

On 23 August the garrison's company commanders reported that some of the casemates had been breached and that further bombardment would "bring down the walls." Sensing that the end was nearing, Page had no choice but to surrender the fort. At sunrise, the white flag was hoisted, and at 2:00 P.M., the garrison was marched outside the fort. Following a brief surrender ceremony, 572 officers and men were put aboard steamers and sent to New Orleans as prisoners.[36]

WITH THE DEFEAT OF THE CONFEDERATE SQUADRON AND THE CAPTURE of Forts Morgan, Gaines, and Powell, the Union navy now had full control of Mobile Bay, but as long as Mobile remained in Confederate hands, Farragut's victory fell short of its strategic objective—the capture of Mobile and access to the South's heartland, specifically Atlanta. A hoped-for by-product of the attack, which never materialized, was the diversion of troops from Sherman's front, a sign that the Confederates intended to try to hold Atlanta at all costs; thus increasing the possibility of a negotiated peace in November.

Four days after the surrender of Fort Morgan, Farragut wrote Gideon Welles and expressed his belief that the capture of Mobile was not feasible without sizable additions of ground troops. "I am now a little embarrassed by my position," he began.

> I consider an army of twenty or thirty thousand men necessary to take the city of Mobile and almost as many to hold it.
>
> The double-enders of the gunboats and the Mississippi monitors are the only vessels that can reach the defenses of Mobile. The larger vessels can not approach within 12 or 15 miles of the obstructions.
>
> It is evident that the army has no men to spare for this place beyond those sufficient to keep up an alarm, and thereby make a diversion in favor of General Sherman.[37]

The troops needed for the Mobile attack were fully occupied closing the noose on Atlanta 350 miles to the northeast. Heavily outnumbered and on the verge of losing his entire army, John Bell Hood evacuated the city on 1 September. This, together with Farragut's success at Mobile, assured Lincoln's reelection in the November presidential election. Elated with the news, the president issued the following proclamation on 3 September:

> The signal success that Divine Providence has recently vouchsafed to the operations of the United States fleet and army in the harbor of Mobile, and the reduction of Fort Powell, Fort Gaines, and Fort Morgan, and the glorious achievements of the army under Maj.-Gen. Sherman in the State of Georgia,

resulting in the capture of the city of Atlanta, call for devout acknowledg-
ments of the Supreme Being in whose hands are the destinies of nations. It is
therefore requested that on next Sunday, in all places of worship in the United
States, thanksgiving be offered to him for his mercy in preserving our
national existence against the insurgent Rebels who have been waging a cruel
war against the Government of the United States for its overthrow, and also
that prayer be made for divine protection to our brave soldiers and their
leaders in the field, who have so often and so gallantly periled their lives in
battling with the enemy, and for blessing and comfort from the Father of Mer-
cies to the sick, wounded, and prisoners, and to the orphans and widows of
those who have fallen in the services of their country, and that He will con-
tinue to uphold the Government of the United States against all the efforts of
public enemies and secret foes.[38]

Recovering from a sniper's bullet, incurred while steaming up the
White River in Arkansas, Canby now had orders to go ahead with the long-
awaited land attack on Mobile. During the remainder of 1864, Union
troops at Forts Morgan and Gaines staged small raids on both sides of the
lower bay. In December a combined force of several thousand men was
landed at Pascagoula in an effort to test the western approaches to Mobile.
Hardly had the column left Pascagoula when it was attacked and repulsed
by Confederate cavalry from Mobile. This convinced Canby that an attack
on Mobile from the west, where three lines of fortifications encircled the
city, would encounter "unequal resistance" and "a protracted siege." He
therefore decided to assault the city from the eastern shore of Mobile Bay,
and go in through the back door. At that time, Maury's total force numbered only nine thousand, "including 1,500 cavalry and all the available
fighting men for defence of Mobile, and all its outposts, batteries and dependencies."[39]

In March 1865, with an army of "fifty thousand infantry, seven thousand
cavalry, a very large train of field and siege artillery, a fleet of more than
twenty men-of-war, and about fifty transports, mostly steamers," Canby
attacked the eastern shore fortifications of Spanish Fort and Blakeley.
After a period of digging trenches, building bombproofs, and constructing
gun revetments, both works were captured—Spanish Fort on 8 April and
Blakeley the following day. With the abandonment of batteries Huger and
Tracy, two small works on the Blakeley River, the backdoor to Mobile was
wide open.[40]

Recognizing the impossibility of holding Mobile against Canby's army,

General Maury gave orders to evacuate the city. In the meantime, word reached Mobile that Lee had surrendered to Grant at Appomattox, Virginia. On 12 April, aware that the Confederacy's days were numbered, Maury left Mobile with forty-five hundred troops, remnants of the city's garrison, and headed for Meridian, Mississippi. There he planned to join the forces that were reporting to Lt. Gen. Richard Taylor, commander of all Confederate troops in the Department of Alabama, Mississippi, and East Louisiana.[41]

That afternoon, following Maury's departure, Union troops under the command of Maj. Gen. Gordon Granger crossed the bay and entered the city to the tune of *Yankee Doodle*. The next morning, Mary Waring, daughter of a prominent citizen, wrote in her diary: "The city is filled with the hated Yanks, who differ in the greatest degree from our poor dear soldiers—the commonest, dirtiest-looking set I ever saw. . . . To do them justice, however, I must admit, though reluctant to do so, that they are very quiet and orderly, and they entered the city with extraordinary order and quiet, so different from what we had anticipated, from the numerous accounts of their behavior in captured cities. We are thankful for it and hope such conduct will be preserved throughout their stay here."[42]

The exemplary conduct of the Union troops was due to General Canby, whose "liberality and fairness" was in stark contrast to the behavior of General Sherman's troops after the fall of Atlanta. General Taylor, who would eventually surrender to Canby, remarked that the "intelligent, comprehensive, and candid bearing [of General Canby] . . . entitle him to our highest respect and confidence."[43]

Arriving at Meridian, 120 miles northwest of Mobile, Maury received orders from General Taylor to move the Mobile troops to Cuba Station, Alabama, a day's march from Meridian, and prepare to "march across and join General Joseph E. Johnston in Carolina." While at Cuba Station, Maury learned that Taylor and Canby had been discussing surrender terms, and on 6 May, he received a copy of their deliberations, which included a statement by Taylor that Canby had accepted everything he "demanded."[44]

The next day, knowing that the war was over, Maury penned a message to his troops:

Soldiers—our last march is almost ended. To-morrow we shall lay down the arms which we have borne for four years to defend our rights, to win our liberties.

We know that we have borne them with honor; and we only now surren-
der to the overwhelming power of the enemy, which has rendered further
resistance hopeless and mischievous to our own people and cause. But we
shall never forget the noble comrades who have stood shoulder to shoulder
with us until now; the noble dead who have been martyred; the noble South-
ern women who have been wronged and are unavenged; or the noble princi-
ples for which we have fought. Conscious that we have played our part like
men, confident of the righteousness of our cause, without regret for our past
action, and without despair of the future, let us to-morrow, with the dignity
of the veterans who are the last to surrender, perform the sad duty which has
been assigned to us.[45]

EPILOGUE

→> <←

ALTHOUGH THE BATTLE OF MOBILE BAY FELL SHORT OF ACHIEVING ITS primary mission, the capture of Mobile, it was an important strategic success for the Union. In 1864 seven blockade runners accounted for twenty arrivals, bringing to Mobile much-needed war material, finished goods, medicines, and a variety of other scarce supplies. As long as the Confederacy had ports that blockade runners could use, the war would be prolonged, "but, once the seaports were captured, the [Confederacy] was destined to die."[1]

Farragut, however, paid dearly for his victory. He described it as "the most desperate battle I ever fought." With an advantage of eighteen to four in ships and an overwhelming superiority in firepower, the Union fleet suffered almost ten times as many killed and wounded as the Confederate fleet: 315 to 32.[2]

When the *Tennessee* surrendered around 10:00 A.M. on 5 August 1864, the Battle of Mobile Bay ended, a clear victory for the Union. The Confederacy, however, took solace in the damage and casualty comparisons: two Union vessels sunk (the *Tecumseh* and *Philippi*), totaling 2,411 tons, compared with the Confederate loss of one vessel sunk (the *Gaines*) and two captured (the *Tennessee* and *Selma*), totaling 2,456 tons—an even swap.[3] The advantages held by the Confederates were the torpedoes, even though one out of ten was harmless, and the character of the main ship channel, which enabled the Confederate squadron to rake the Union fleet for a full hour before receiving its broadsides. The Confederates also held the odds for about thirty-five minutes when the Union vessels were stalled opposite Fort Morgan.[4]

Apart from its pivotal role during the Civil War, the Battle of Mobile Bay "influenced the course of naval history for the next eighty years." Stephen R. Mallory, the Confederate secretary of the navy, observed in a report to the Confederate Congress that the Battle of Mobile Bay was the first fleet action in history to test the "modern and improved means of naval warfare, offensive and defensive." He was, of course, referring to those "emerging technologies that would dominate ship design and naval tactics in the years ahead: iron construction, steam propulsion, revolving turrets, sloping armor, twin propellers, rifled guns, explosive shells and mines."[5] But intermingled with the above were numerous carryovers from the Age of Sail: the full-rigged ship, smoothbore cannon, solid shot, black powder, and the line of battle, to name a few. The rum ration, however, had been abolished. Frank M. Bennett, a nineteenth-century authority on ship design and propulsion, wrote in 1897 that Mobile Bay was "the most sanguinary and important naval battle of the Civil War." As a naval engineer, Bennett, no doubt, had in mind Mallory's reference to "modern and improved means."[6]

Both Farragut and Buchanan could have stepped back in time and commanded at Trafalgar in 1805. But the pace of technological change foreshadowed at Mobile Bay would have made it difficult for them to have commanded at Tsushima during the Russo-Japanese War in 1905, where speeds of twenty knots, increased rates of fire, and gunnery ranges of eight thousand yards would have demanded new knowledge and new ways of thinking. Their leadership abilities, however, would have been as applicable then as they are today.[7]

THE COMMANDERS

Adm. David Glasgow Farragut, U.S. Navy

When describing the life of Admiral Farragut, Albert T. Mahan wrote: "There seems much to praise and very little to criticize in the tactical dispositions made by the admiral on this momentous occasion." Likewise, he praised Buchanan for his defense. "It was well devised," he wrote, "and made probably the best use of the advantages of the ground possible to so inferior a force."[8]

Following the Battle of Mobile Bay, Farragut was promoted to vice admiral; he was also offered command of the North Atlantic Squadron, which he declined. He was suffering from mental strain and fatigue and needed a rest. "Six months constantly watching day and night for an enemy; to know him to be brave, as skillful, and as determined as myself, who [had] pledged to his government and the South to drive me away and raise the blockade and free the Mississippi from our rule. While I was equally pledged to my government that I would capture or destroy the rebel."[9]

In July 1866 a law was passed by Congress creating the grade of admiral, which was immediately bestowed upon Farragut. A year later, he was appointed commander of the European fleet and, accompanied by his wife, sailed for Europe. During the next sixteen months, "he was the recipient of a series of public ovations and private marks of distinction such as no American had ever before received, and which have been paralleled since only by those of which General Grant was recently the object." Three years later, on 14 August 1870, while visiting the home of a friend in New Hampshire, he died at the age of sixty-nine. Immortalized by the apothegm "Damn the torpedoes, full speed ahead!" he has come down through the years as America's most popular admiral, John Paul Jones included.[10]

Capt. Percival Drayton, U.S. Navy

Capt. Percival Drayton, Farragut's fleet captain, remained with the admiral until the *Hartford* returned to New York, 12 December 1864. Prior to being detached from the *Hartford* and departing on leave, Drayton attended a formal reception honoring him and the admiral. On 28 April 1865 Drayton was made chief of the Bureau of Navigation. Three months later, on 4 August 1865, he died, exactly one day short of the anniversary of the Battle of Mobile Bay. J. T. Headley, author of *Farragut and Our Naval Commanders*, eulogized him when he wrote in 1867, "Captain Drayton, had he lived, would, doubtless, have received by this time a high rank. . . . In such high estimation was he held, that Farragut selected him to command his flag-ship—the *Hartford*—when he forced the entrance to the harbor of Mobile."[11]

Capt. James Alden, U.S. Navy

On 12 August, while anchored inside Mobile Bay, Farragut published General Orders No. 12, thanking the fleet for "following their commander in chief through the line of torpedoes and obstructions." Still angered that Farragut had taken the lead and crossed the field without signaling him that the original plan had been changed, Alden went to the admiral with a copy of the order and asked, "Is this so?" In his opinion, the admiral's explanation was not satisfactory, setting off a controversy that continued until Farragut's death in August 1870. This did not, however, prevent Alden from attaining the rank of rear admiral the following year, although it may have contributed to his being placed on the retired list after serving less than a year.[12]

Maj. Gen. Edward Richard Sprigg Canby, U.S. Army

In November 1864, following the surrender of Fort Morgan, General Canby was wounded by guerrillas while aboard a steamboat going up the White River in Arkansas. Recovering, he commanded the campaign that ended in the capture of Mobile, 12 April 1865. The following month, he "received the surrenders of Gen. Richard Taylor, May 4, and Gen. Edmund Kirby-Smith, May 26, who commanded the last Confederate armies in the field."[13]

In 1866 Canby was promoted to brigadier general in the regular army. In 1870, after various assignments, he was given command of the Department of Columbia, headquartered in Vancouver Barracks, in the state of Washington. At the time the Modoc Indians were "aroused by the intrusion of emigrants, settlers, and ranchers into their homeland on the Lost River along the California-Oregon boundary." On 11 April 1873, during negotiations between the Modocs and a peace commission, General Canby was shot and killed by an enraged chief known as "Captain Jack." Ironically, the general was a strong supporter "of fair treatment of the Modocs."[14]

On 24 May 1873 Edward Richard Sprigg Canby was buried in Indianapolis, the "first general officer of the United States Army to be killed by Indians." That morning, the Rev. Dr. J. H. Bliss delivered a sermon that summed up Canby's life, later so aptly defined in the title of Max L. Heyman's biography *Prudent Soldier.* "What we reverence after all, is character—broad, strong, noble character. We have ready applause for brilliant deeds, and are not slow to admire genius; and yet the thing which most commands our profound and abiding reverence is not the flash of some brilliant achievement, but the steady, strong, broad, progress of noble character. And this is the kind of power with which the memory of General Canby comes to us today. He was great in war and good, and equally so in peace. There are no private discounts to reduce the excellency and glory of his public record."[15]

Maj. Gen. Gordon Granger, U.S. Army

After the surrender of Spanish Fort and Blakeley, Canby ordered Maj. Gen. Gordon Granger to cross Mobile Bay with two divisions, occupy the city, and receive its surrender. After the war, he was mustered out of the volunteer service and commissioned a colonel of infantry in the regular army. No description of Granger surpasses that of Fairfax Downey's in his book *Storming of the Gateway:* "[A] West Pointer and Mexican War Veteran, 'a profane, bearded, rough-hewn regular-army type from the old days.' He was a fighter, the sort of general who marches to the sound of the guns with or without orders." He died 10 January 1876, in Sante Fe while commanding the District of New Mexico.[16]

Adm. Franklin Buchanan, Confederate States Navy

Under the care of Dr. Palmer and Surgeon Conrad, Admiral Buchanan spent three months in the hospital at the Pensacola Navy Yard while his wound healed. As Dr. Palmer had predicted, his leg did not have to be amputated. In November he was transferred to Fort Lafayette in New York and, five months later, was exchanged. Returning to Mobile via Richmond Buchanan had hardly arrived when the city was occupied by Union troops, making him a prisoner for a second time. On 17 May, a month after Lincoln was assassinated, he was paroled, giving his honor "never again to serve in the Confederate Navy or in any military capacity whatever against the United States of America."[17]

Returning to Virginia, Buchanan kept an eye on the family farm and "supervised the building of a new home" to replace the one that had burned down during the war. In the fall of 1868, now sixty-eight, he was "appointed President of the Maryland Agricultural College," which generated criticism from several Northern newspapers, among which was Horace Greeley's *New York Tribune:*

> *Com. Franklin Buchanan abandoned our Navy at the outbreak of the war, and became prominent in that of the rebels. He brought the* Merrimac *(alias*

Virginia*) out of Norfolk and destroyed several good vessels of the Union Navy at Fortress Monroe, but the* Monitor *at length drove him off.*

He fought us again in the ram Tennessee, *which did us great harm in Mobile Bay, where he had his leg broken; but Farragut at length captured her, with most of her associates. He has just been provided with a good office by the Maryland "Conservatives." We haven't heard of their giving any to a one-legged Union soldier or a sailor, but we hope they will all get along somehow. It is well that they don't depend for a living on the generosity or the loyalty of Maryland.*[18]

Following Greeley's editorial, the *Mobile Tribune* jumped to Buchanan's defense:

Democratic Maryland at last showed her appreciation of her old hero, by appointing him to the Presidency of the State Agricultural College, and she has the satisfaction of already reaping the rewards of her good deed, in the great impetus given to the progress of the college, which heretofore had been in rather a disorganized condition. Already the number of students [has] increased to 55 and more are on the way.

The institution has become popular, and the wholesome "man of war discipline" exercised by the gallant old admiral will cause it to continue so, for young people are always happier when they are governed with firmness and consistency.[19]

Under Buchanan's leadership, the college prospered. Enrollment increased from six to eighty, and in one year, "it managed to pay off its indebtedness out of its own revenues." But his days were numbered. He ordered the dismissal of a professor because he believed it would be for the good of the school. When the Board of Directors rejected his dismissal, Buchanan resigned. He then returned to Mobile and accepted a position with a life insurance company. He remained there for more than a year before returning to his beloved Maryland, where he died of pneumonia on 11 May 1874, at age seventy-four.[20]

Cdr. James B. Johnston, Confederate States Navy

After his capture Cdr. James B. Johnston, the *Tennessee*'s captain, remained at the navy yard in Pensacola for about three weeks, when he was put aboard a small ordnance steamer with Lieutenant Commander Murphey

and Lieutenants Bradford and Wharton of the *Tennessee* for transportation
to the Brooklyn Navy Yard. From there, the prisoners were taken in leg
irons to Boston by rail, then by boat to Fort Warren, which was located on
an island in Boston Harbor. "We remonstrated gently against this unprece-
dented mode of treating prisoners of war," Johnston would later write,

> *but to no purpose.*
> *When we reached the wharf at Fort Warren, the commanding officer,*
> *Major A. A. Gibson, inquired the cause of our being in irons, and upon*
> *being informed that they were placed upon us by order of Admiral Paulding,*
> *he made the further inquiry whether or not we had been guilty of any rebel-*
> *lious conduct as prisoners of war; this being answered in the negative, he*
> *replied that he had never heard of such treatment, and that we could not be*
> *landed on the island until the irons were removed.*[21]

Johnston and his companions stayed at Fort Warren less than a week,
for an order exchanging all prisoners had reached the fort's commanding
officer prior to their arrival. Johnston wrote that "after ten days we left for
City Point on the steamer *Assyrian*. We naturally supposed that on our
arrival at City Point we would be immediately forwarded to the landing on
the James River at which exchanges were usually made. But when General Benjamin F. 'Spoons' Butler, whose lines were between us and that
point, was advised of our presence he refused to allow us to pass through
them, on account of President Davis's declaring him an outlaw."[22]

When General Grant, who was in the vicinity, learned of Butler's spite-
fulness, he revoked the order and informed the prisoners that they would
be forwarded to Richmond and from there to Varina Landing where a
rebel steamer would be waiting with Union prisoners. The next day,
October 18, the swap was made to the tune of *Dixie*. "After a delightful
visit of five days at the house of Mrs. Stephen R. Mallory, the charming
wife of the Secretary of the Confederate Navy," Johnston noted, "I was
ordered to return to Mobile and report for duty under Commodore Ebe-
nezer Farrand, who had succeeded Admiral Buchanan in command of the
Mobile Station." Johnston surrendered with the Mobile naval contingent
on 4 May 1865 and was paroled six days later.[23]

After the war Johnston remained in Mobile for several years selling
insurance. He then moved to Savannah as representative of the Alabama
Gold Life Insurance Company. When the company failed, he was hired

by the Mutual Life Insurance Company of New York, where he worked until his death, 11 February 1886. At seventy-nine, he was the ranking surviving officer of the Confederate Navy.[24]

Maj. Gen. Dabney Herndon Maury, Confederate States Army

After bidding farewell to his friends and fellow soldiers, General Maury returned to Fredericksburg, Virginia, the town where he was born, and opened a school for boys. Two years later, he moved to New Orleans, where he worked for an express company and naval stores manufacturer. In his spare time, he founded the Southern Historical Society and served as its chairman for the next twenty years. He also served as a member of the executive committee of the National Guard Association. In 1885 the U.S. government appointed him its minister to Colombia. Four years later, when his term expired, he returned to the United States and moved to Peoria, Illinois, where his son was living. He died 11 January 1900, at the age of seventy-eight, and was buried in Fredericksburg.[25]

Brig. Gen. Richard Lucian Page, Confederate States Army

After the surrender of Fort Morgan, charges were brought against Brigadier General Page for destroying property after Fort Morgan had surrendered. During the trial, evidence was submitted that proved Page "had not violated any of the rules of war, and he was, consequently acquitted of the charges." He was, however, imprisoned at Fort Lafayette, New York, until September 1865, when he returned to Norfolk.[26]

While Page was in prison, he wrote a letter to the editor of the *New York Tribune,* saying:

> *Sir: In your issue of yesterday was the following paragraph: "The rebel General Page, captured near Fort Morgan, applied by letter lately to his old classmate, Commodore Rogers, for assistance in getting exchanged. The reply was: 'I can do nothing for you. You neither defended your post like a man, nor surrendered like an officer.'"*
>
> *It does me great injustice; and though a prisoner of war, in the hands of your government, I do not hesitate so far to presume on your sense of right as to solicit a correction of your misstatements. . . . Immediately after the capitulation of Fort Morgan, certain false and injurious reports were circulated,*

imputing irregularity and unfairness on my part in the surrender of the
work. By a council of war, ordered by Gen. Canby, and composed of officers
of the Federal army and navy, I was, after a most searching and protracted
investigation, promptly and entirely acquitted of all and every of the impu-
tations. The opinion and findings of this council were officially published in
the New Orleans papers; and it would have been agreeable to my desire to
have had the whole "proceedings" laid before the public, which I yet hope at
some future day may be done.[27]

From 1875 to 1883 Page served, with "marked efficiency" as Norfolk's
superintendent of schools. He died at the age of ninety-four in Blue Ridge
Summit, Pennsylvania, 9 August 1901. The next day, as a tribute to the
general, the *Norfolk Virginian* "laid before the public" the facts about the
surrender of Fort Morgan: "The defense of Fort Morgan under the command of General Page [was] one of the most celebrated instances of heroism in the history of the war."[28]

Col. Charles D. Anderson, Confederate States Army

Following the surrender of Fort Gaines, Colonel Anderson and the garrison were taken to New Orleans as prisoners of war, where they remained
for a brief time before being imprisoned at Fort Massachusetts off the
coast of Mississippi. Anderson's surrender brought scathing criticism from
his superiors. Learning that he had run up the white flag, General Maury
wrote the Confederate secretary of war that "it is painfully humiliating to
announce the shameful surrender of the Twenty-first Alabama Regiment.
. . . His conduct is officially pronounced inexplicable."[29]

Some people, however, supported Colonel Anderson. A letter to the
New Orleans Daily Picayune stated that "the fort was not in a condition to
be defended. After the fleet had passed into the bay every one of the
ditches could have been enfiladed, and the loss of life could have been
fearful. In one hour . . . , we would have been exposed to the most terrific
fire ever concentrated on one place from the front, from the rear and on
both flanks."[30]

On 6 January 1865 the Fort Gaines prisoners, having been exchanged,
were brought to Mobile Bay by a Union transport flying a flag of truce.
After the war, Anderson moved to Texas where he practiced civil engineering, including two years as the city engineer of Austin. He then

moved to Galveston as the keeper of the Fort Point Lighthouse. He died there 21 November 1901 at the age of seventy-four.[31]

Lt. Col. James M. Williams, Confederate States Army

Following his abandonment of Fort Powell, Lieutenant Colonel Williams was brought before a military court and acquitted of all charges. Maury, however, was still vexed with his failure to defend the fort and did not rush to give him a new command. In December, however, with the enemy preparing to attack Mobile, the general consented to give Williams command of the remnants of the 21st Infantry that were not at the fort when Gaines surrendered—a total of 210 men. As a result, Williams and his command were in the trenches at Blakeley when the order to withdraw was given. Returning to Mobile, they accompanied General Maury and the Mobile garrison to Cuba Station and then to Meridian, where they were paroled.

For the next thirty-eight years, Williams was employed in Mobile at various occupations, none of which enabled him to "achieve great economic success." He did, however, play a prominent role in the Alabama militia, achieving the rank of major; and in Confederate veteran affairs, as founder of the Raphael Semmes Camp Number 11 of the United Confederate Veterans. In addition, he was Southern copresident of the Blue and Gray Veterans Union and served a number of terms as president of the local camp. He was also president of the Can't-Get-Away Club, an organization that provided assistance for yellow fever victims. He died 21 January 1903 at the age of sixty-five.[32]

THE SHIPS

The *Hartford* made her final port in 1945, when she docked at the Norfolk Naval Shipyard and was left to rot, a mere shell of her former stateliness. In 1954 Congress introduced a bill to give the *Hartford* to the city of Mobile. The bill passed the House; the Senate never acted. Another bill was introduced in 1956, but before it could be considered, the end came: "At 4:30 A.M., November 20, the *Hartford* . . . resigned to her fate, listed to port and settled to the bottom of the Elizabeth River. Two years and two days more and she would have been one hundred years old."[33]

The monitor *Tecumseh* is the only remaining intact vessel that fought in the Battle of Mobile Bay. She lies three hundred yards west of Fort Morgan. When examined by the Smithsonian Institution in a series of dives begun in 1967, the *Tecumseh* was in excellent condition. Entombed in sand thirty feet under the water, she represents a "fully furnished" monitor, ready for battle. The bodies of ninety-four officers and crewmen lie buried with her.[34]

After her surrender, the ram *Tennessee* participated in the shelling of Fort Morgan, more for psychological purposes than combat effectiveness, for she was still in need of repairs. Following her final foray during the autumn of 1864, the ram was taken to New Orleans under her own power for repairs. When captured at Mobile Bay she was commissioned as a U.S. warship and then joined the Mississippi Squadron. She was decommissioned two years later and sold for scrap at public auction in New Orleans.[35]

THE FORTS

After the Civil War, Fort Morgan and Fort Gaines played an active role in three other wars: the Spanish American War, World War I, and World War II. Prior to the outbreak of hostilities in World War II, the Gulf of Mexico was considered to be a prime target for German submarines and surface raiders. Accordingly, both forts were garrisoned by contingents from the navy, coast guard, and coast artillery. Hardly had hostilities commenced than the assumption proved correct.[36]

Samuel Elliot Morison, in his history of the U.S. Navy in World War II, describes the "havoc wrought by [German] U-boats" in the Gulf of Mexico "during the first six months of the war.... One of the most fruitful hunting grounds in May and June 1942 lay off the passes of the Mississippi. This U-boat blitz gave the Gulf Sea Frontier the melancholy distinction of having the most sinkings in May [1942]... of any one area in any month during the war, and 55 percent of this was tanker tonnage, which made it all the worse. And it was wrought by not more than six submarines operating at one time."[37] Ironically, the threat that German submarines posed to the United States and its allies during World War II, had its genesis in Mobile in 1863, where the first operational submarine was built and tested prior to sinking a Union warship off Charleston, South Carolina. Little did the sub's builders suspect that enemy submarines—

descendants of the *Hunley*—would, in less than a lifetime, threaten the freedom of a reunited nation.[38]

Once the nation's first line of defense, coastal forts are now obsolete. The handwriting was on the wall as early as 1903, when the Wright brothers "gave notice that the sea was no longer the only approach to America." In 1944, when "Germany launched the first V-I rocket against England," the question was settled.[39] Today, Fort Morgan and Fort Gaines are managed as historic sites, Morgan by the Alabama Historical Commission, and Gaines by the Dauphin Island Park and Beach Board.[40]

In 1962 Fort Morgan was awarded National Historic Landmark status, the federal government's official designation of the "national significance" of a historic property. As trustee, the Alabama Historical Commission is "committed to the maintenance and long-term preservation of, not only the fort itself, but also of its historic support structures." The Dauphin Island Park and Beach Board is responsible for the upkeep and preservation of Fort Gaines, a state monument. The board's mission is to "protect and restore Historic Fort Gaines for the long-term education and enjoyment of the public, encouraging the performance of living history programs and promoting the Fort as a valuable community resource."[41]

THE NAVAL BATTLEFIELD

Today, no visible evidence of the Battle of Mobile Bay remains on the surface, although the wrecks of three vessels—two Union and one Confederate—lie on the bottom entombed in mud. However, if a sailor of the Union fleet were to return today, he would have no trouble identifying the naval battlefield.

From the outer bar, he would see the same line of dark pines and white dunes that he saw that fateful August morning in 1864. Sand Island is gone; but a lighthouse, built in 1872, marks its approximate location. Off to the west, Pelican Island still curves around from Dauphin Island and points an arm at Sand Island Channel, where the crew of the *Tecumseh* worked most of the night to get ready for the fight—and to the east, Dixie Bar continues to parallel the ship channel, ending at the Swash Channel, where the *Red Gauntlet* slipped in under the nose of the entire federal fleet just before daylight.

Approaching the fort, the old veteran might wince, for that is where

the Union fleet almost lost the battle. The water battery and lighthouse
are gone, but the massive walls of the fort still frown down on the channel, a reminder of the terrible pounding the Union fleet took while stalled
before the torpedo field. He would then see the buoy that marks the
grave of the *Tecumseh*—and beyond, the wharf that Craven feared would
prevent him from circling around and engaging the *Tennessee*, had he followed orders. Ahead, where the bay widens, he would be reminded of
Buchanan's gallant foray and the disbelief that rippled through the Union
fleet when they saw him coming out single-handedly. Turning his gaze to
the northeast, the old sailor would see Bon Secour Bay, where Lt. Peter
Umstead Murphey gave the Union gunboats a run for their money. But
most of all, he would remember the end:

> *Ended the mighty noise,*
> *Thunder of forts and ships*
> *Down we went to the hold—*
> *O, our dear dying boys!*
> *How we pressed their poor brave lips,*
> *(Ah, so pallid and cold!)*
> *And held their hands to the last*
> *(Those that had hands to hold).*

HENRY H. BROWNELL, "The Bay Fight"

NOTES

→> <←

ABBREVIATIONS USED IN THE NOTES

B&L   *Battles and Leaders of the Civil War*
NA   National Archives
NRC   Naval Records Collection, National Archives
NWC   Naval War College
ORA   *War of the Rebellion: A Compilation of the Official Records of the Union and Confederate Armies.* Series 1 unless otherwise indicated.
ORN   *Official Records of the Union and Confederate Navies in the War of the Rebellion.* Series 1 unless otherwise indicated.
RG   Record Group
SHC   Southern Historical Collection
UNC   University of North Carolina, Chapel Hill
USNA   United States Naval Academy
VHS   Virginia Historical Society, Richmond, Va.

PREFACE

1. John H. [Jack] Friend Jr., "Mobile Bay: First Strike for Grant's Strategy," *Mobile Register,* 24 April 1994.
2. Charles Lee Lewis, *David Glasgow Farragut, Our First Admiral* (Annapolis: U.S. Naval Institute, 1943), 2:280.
3. James A. Rawley, *Turning Points of the Civil War* (Lincoln: University of Nebraska Press, 1966), 174.
4. Ibid., 175; Clement Eaton, *A History of the Southern Confederacy* (New York: Free Press, 1954), 286; Richard M. McMurry, *Atlanta, 1864* (Lincoln: University of Nebraska Press, 2000), 55.

5. Rawley, *Turning Points*, 176; Wiley Sword, *Southern Invincibility: A History of the Confederate Heart* (New York: St. Martin's Press, 1999), 264–65.

6. Rawley, *Turning Points*, 185.

7. Grant to Halleck, 5 June 1864, *ORA*, 39, 2:79.

8. Friend, "Mobile Bay."

9. John H. [Jack] Friend Jr., "The Battle of Mobile Bay," *Great American Naval Battles*, ed. Jack Sweetman (Annapolis: Naval Institute Press, 1998), 157.

10. Foxhall A. Parker, *The Battle of Mobile Bay and the Capture of Forts Morgan, Gaines, and Powell* (Boston: Boston Stereotype Foundry, 1878), 5–136.

11. A. T. Mahan, *Admiral Farragut* (New York: D. Appleton, 1970), 263–65.

12. Ibid., 263; William B. Cogar, *Dictionary of Admirals of the U.S. Navy, 1862–1900* (Annapolis: Naval Institute Press, 1989), 1:3, 60.

13. Clausewitz cited in Gwynne Dyer, *War* (New York: Crown Publishers, 1985), 133.

14. Parker, *Battle of Mobile Bay*, 230; John C. Kinney, "Farragut at Mobile Bay," *B&L* (New York: Thomas Yoseloff, 1956), 4:391.

PROLOGUE

1. Mahan, *Admiral Farragut*, 123.

2. Ibid., 123–24.

3. Welles to Farragut, 20 January 1862, *ORN*, 18:8.

4. Ibid., 12 March 1862, *ORN*, 18:59.

5. Farragut to Welles, 6 May 1862, *ORN*, 18:159.

6. Ibid.

7. Farragut to Porter, 1 May 1862, *ORN*, 18:462.

8. Porter to Welles, 10 May 1862, *ORN*, 18:478; Arnold to Halpine, 10, 15 May 1862, *ORN*, 18:479–80.

9. Jones to Forney, 14 May 1862, *ORN*, 18:482–84; Mahan, *Admiral Farragut*, 196; Porter to Welles, 2 June 1864, *ORN*, 18:481.

10. C. Lewis, *David Glasgow Farragut*, 2:83–84; Autrey to Lee, 18 May 1862, *ORN*, 18:492.

11. C. Lewis, *David Glasgow Farragut*, 2:84.

12. Ibid., 2:87.

13. Ibid., 2:87–88.

14. Ibid., 2:88.

15. Ibid.; Fox to Farragut, 17 May 1862, *ORN*, 18:498–99.

16. Welles to Farragut, 19 May 1862, *ORN*, 18:502.

17. Farragut to Welles, 30 May 1862, *ORN*, 18:521.

18. C. Lewis, *David Glasgow Farragut*, 2:98–100.

19. Davis to Welles, 2 July 1862, *ORN*, 18:593; C. Lewis, *David Glasgow Farragut*, 2:105; Halleck to Farragut, 3 July 1862, *ORN*, 18:593.

20. Welles to Farragut, 14 July 1862, *ORN*, 18:595.

21. C. Lewis, *David Glasgow Farragut,* 2:112; Van Dorn to Davis, 14 July 1864, *ORN,* 18:652.

22. *Hartford* Abstract Deck Log, 26–28 July 1863, *ORN,* 19:707; Faxon to Farragut, 13 March 1863, *ORN,* 19:661; Mahan, *Admiral Farragut,* 196–97.

23. Farragut to Welles, 20, 21 August 1862, *ORN,* 19:164–65; Welles to Farragut, 19 August 1862 *ORN,* 19:161–62.

24. Fox to Farragut, 9 September 1862, *ORN,* 19:184–85.

25. Farragut to Welles, 30 September 1862, *ORN,* 19:242.

26. Farragut to Butler, 23 October 1862, *ORN,* 19:313.

27. Mahan, *Admiral Farragut,* 199; *Hartford* Abstract Deck Log, 7–9 November 1862, *ORN,* 19:708.

28. Farragut to Welles, 14 November 1862, *ORN,* 19:346–47.

29. Farragut to Bell, 30 November 1862, *ORN,* 19:386.

30. Palmer to Welles, 10 August 1863, *ORN,* 20:442; *Hartford* Abstract Deck Log, 1, 12 August 1863, *ORN,* 20:775.

31. Welles to Farragut, 20 January 1862, *ORN,* 18:8; Grant to Halleck, 18 July 1863, *ORA,* 24, 3:529–30.

32. Gustavus V. Fox, *Confidential Correspondence of Gustavus Vasa Fox, Assistant Secretary of the Navy, 1861–1865,* ed. Robert W. Thompson and Richard Wainwright (Freeport, N.Y.: Books for Libraries Press, [1918]), 1:336–37; Welles to Farragut, 30 December 1863, *ORN,* 20:751; Hurlburt to Halleck, 29 December 1863, *ORN,* 20:751; notebook of David Glasgow Farragut, 5 January 1864, Subject File HA, Entry 464, NRC, RG 45, NA.

33. Buchanan to Jones, 7 May 1864, *ORN,* 21:896–971; William N. Still Jr., *Iron Afloat: The Story of the Confederate Armorclads* (Nashville: Vanderbilt University Press, 1971), 188–91.

34. Still, *Iron Afloat,* 195; Maury to Cooper, 11 December 1863, *ORN,* 20:855; Davis to Maury, 9 January 1864, *ORA,* 52, 2:592.

35. Maury to Beauregard, 17 December 1863, *ORA,* 26, 2:510–11.

36. Von Scheliha to Buchanan, 15 January 1864, *ORA,* 32, 2:560–61.

37. Buchanan to Mitchell, 14 December 1863, John K. Mitchell papers, VHS.

38. Lee to Polk, 9 January 1864, *ORN,* 21:860.

Chapter 1. Ram Fever

1. Fox, *Confidential Correspondence,* 341–42.

2. Jenkins to Bell, 13 January 1864, *ORN,* 21:30.

3. Ibid., *ORN,* 21:31.

4. Bell to Welles, 14 January 1864, *ORN,* 21:32.

5. Farragut to Bell, 17 January 1864, *ORN,* 21:39.

6. Sherman to Banks, 16 January 1864, *ORA,* 32, 2:114; John S. Bowman, ed., *The Civil War Almanac* (New York: World Almanac Publications, 1983), 182.

7. Farragut to Welles, 7 February 1864, *ORN,* 21:90.

8. Farragut to Banks, 11 February 1864, *ORN*, 21:91; Marchand to Beers, 16 February 1864, *ORN*, 21:94; Farragut to Welles, 1 March 1864, *ORN*, 21:97–98; James Morgan Williams, *From That Terrible Field: Civil War Letters of James M. Williams*, ed. John Kent Folmar (University: University of Alabama Press, 1981), 174; Maury to Seddon, 3 March 1864, *ORA*, 32, 1:402–3; Farragut to Welles, 1 March 1864, *ORN*, 21:97–98.

9. Ives to Davis, 29 February 1864, *ORA*, 52, 2:631–32.

10. Kate Cumming, *A Journal of Hospital Life in the Confederate Army of Tennessee* (Louisville, Ky.: John P. Morton, n.d.), 123.

11. Craig L. Symonds, *Confederate Admiral: The Life and Wars of Franklin Buchanan* (Annapolis: Naval Institute Press, 1999), 201–2.

12. Loyall Farragut, *The Life of David Glasgow Farragut, First Admiral of the U.S. Navy* (New York: D. Appleton, 1897), 393; Farragut to Banks, 2 March 1864, *ORN*, 21:122.

13. Farragut to Palmer, 6 March 1864, *ORN*, 21:127–28.

14. Farragut to Welles, 9 March 1864, *ORN*, 21:130–31.

15. Farragut to Welles, 9 May 1864, *ORN*, 21:267.

16. Eggelston to Jones, 3 March 1864, *ORN*, 21:880; Symonds, *Confederate Admiral*, 201–2.

17. Buchanan to Mitchell, 13 March 1864, Mitchell papers, VHS.

18. *Tennessee* Abstract Deck Log, 3 April 1864, *ORN*, 21:934–35; Simms to Jones, 20 March 1864, *ORN*, 21:886; Buchanan to Jones, 14 April 1864, *ORN*, 21:892; William N. Still Jr., "Confederate States Navy at Mobile," *Alabama Historical Quarterly* 30 (1968): 138.

19. Buchanan to Jones, 14 April 1864, *ORN*, 21:892.

20. Buchanan to Mitchell, 11 March 1864, Mitchell papers, VHS.

21. John C. O'Connell, "The Journal of Mr. John C. O'Connell, C.S.N. on the C.S.S. Tennessee," in *Two Naval Journals: 1864*, ed. C. Carter Smith Jr. (Chicago: Wyvern Press, 1964), 18 May, 1; James D. Johnston, "Admiral Buchanan and the CSS Ram *Tennessee*," speech delivered to Georgia Historical Society, Subject File OO, NRC, RG 45, NA; James D. Johnston, "The Ram *Tennessee*," *B&L*, 4:401–2.

22. O'Connell, "Mr. O'Connell's Journal," 2.

23. Ibid.

24. Ibid., 2–3.

25. Ibid., 3.

26. Page to Jones, 26 June 1864, *ORN*, 21:903.

27. Charles Brother, "The Journal of Private Charles Brother, USMC on the USS Hartford," in *Two Naval Journals*, 31.

28. Farragut to Welles, 25 May 1864, *ORN*, 21:298.

29. Ibid.

30. Farragut to Bailey, 26 May 1864, *ORN*, 21:298–99.

31. Asboth to Levering, 24 May 1864, *ORN*, 21:296–97; Farragut to Asboth, 30 May 1864, *ORN*, 21:311.

32. Farragut to Welles, 4 June 1864, *ORN*, 21:316–17.
33. Grant to Halleck, 25 March 1864, *ORA*, 33:729.
34. Ibid.; Halleck to Grant, 25 March 1864, *ORA*, 33:729.
35. Welles to Nicholson, 7 June 1864, *ORN*, 21:323; Welles to Porter, 9 June 1864, *ORN*, 26:379–80.

Chapter 2. A New General in Chief

1. Rawley, *Turning Points*, 103.
2. Halleck to Banks, 8 November 1862, *ORN*, 19:340–41.
3. Grant to Halleck, 18 July 1863, *ORA*, 24, 3:529–30; Banks to Grant, 18 July 1863, *ORA*, 1, 24, 3:527–28.
4. Halleck to Grant, 22 July 1863, *ORA*, 24, 3:542.
5. Banks to Halleck, 30 July 1863, *ORA*, 26, 3:661–62.
6. Ibid., 1 August 1863, *ORA*, 26, 3:666.
7. Halleck to Grant, 6 August 1863, *ORA*, 24, 3:578; Jean Edward Smith, *Grant* (New York: Simon & Schuster, 2001), 260–61.
8. Lincoln to Grant, 9 August 1863, *ORA*, 24, 3:580.
9. Ulysses S. Grant, *Memoirs and Selected Letters* (New York: Library of America, 1990), 2:1030–31.
10. Bruce Catton, *Grant Takes Command* (Boston: Little, Brown, 1968), 101.
11. Lincoln to Stanton, 29 July 1863, *ORA*, 26, 3:659.
12. Shelby Foote, *Red River to Appomattox*, vol. 3 in *The Civil War: A Narrative* (New York: Random House, 1958–74), 25–26; Robert L. Kerby, *Kirby Smith's Confederacy* (reprint, Tuscaloosa: University of Alabama Press, 1991), 191; Returns of the Department of the Gulf, June 1864, *ORA*, 34, 4:610–11.
13. Grant to Halleck, 7 December 1863, *ORA*, 31, 3:349–50.
14. Dana to Stanton, 29 November 1863, *ORA*, 31, 2:72; Grant to Halleck, 17 December 1863, *ORA*, 31, 3:429–30.
15. Halleck to Grant, 21 December 1863, *ORA*, 31, 3:458.
16. Halleck to Banks, 4 January 1864, *ORA*, 34, 2:15–16.
17. Foote, *Red River to Appomattox*, 26–28.
18. Grant, *Memoirs*, 388.
19. Halleck to Grant, 8 January 1864, *ORA*, 32, 2:41.
20. Ibid.
21. Grant to Halleck, 15 January 1864, *ORA*, 32, 2:100–101.
22. Richard B. Irwin, "The Red River Campaign," *B&L*, 4:349; David D. Porter, "The Mississippi Flotilla in the Red River Expedition," *B&L*, 4:366.
23. Bowman, *Civil War Almanac*, 187–89.
24. Grant to Halleck, 25 March 1864, *ORA*, 33, 1:729; Irwin, "Red River," *B&L*, 4:350.
25. Grant to Banks, 31 March 1864, *ORA*, 34, 1:11.
26. Sherman to Banks, 3 April 1864, *ORA*, 34, 3:24.

27. Thomas O. Selfridge, "The Navy in the Red River, *B&L*, 4:366.

28. Rawley, *Turning Points*, 174.

29. Grant to Halleck, 25, 28 April 1864, *ORA*, 34, 3:279, 316.

30. Ibid., 29 April 1864, *ORA*, 34, 3:331; Halleck to Grant, 29 April 1864, *ORA*, 34, 3:331–32; Grant to Halleck, 29 April 1864, *ORA*, 34, 3:331.

31. *Webster's American Military Biographies*, (Springfield, Mass.: G. and C. Merriam, 1978), 58.

32. George B. Davis et al., *The Official Military Atlas of the Civil War* (Washington, D.C.: U.S. Government Printing Office, 1891–95); Halleck to Canby, 7 May 1864, *ORA*, 34, 3:491–92.

33. Grant, *Memoirs*, 129; Sherman to Halleck, 29, 30 May 1864, *ORA*, 38, 4:343, 351.

34. Grant to Halleck, 3 June 1864, *ORA*, 38, 4:185; Halleck to Grant, 4 June 1864, *ORA*, 34, 4:211; Grant to Halleck, 5 June 1864, *ORA*, 39, 2:79; Sherman to Smith, 4 June 1864, *ORA*, 39, 2:79.

35. Halleck to Canby, 6 June 1864, *ORA*, 34, 1, 4:240.

36. Max L. Heyman, *Prudent Soldier: A Biography of Major General E. R. S. Canby, 1817–1873* (Glendale, Calif.: Arthur H. Clark, 1959), 210; Special Order No. 39, Headquarters, Military Division of West Mississippi, 16 June 1864, *ORA*, 34, 1, 4:406.

Chapter 3. The Decision to Attack

1. *Hartford* Deck Log, 17 June 1864, Logs of U.S. Naval Ships and Stations, Entry 118, RG 24, NA.

2. Percival Drayton, "Naval Letters from Captain Percival Drayton, 1861–1865," *New York Public Library Bulletin* 10 (1906): 58–60; Heyman, *Prudent Soldier,* 211.

3. Farragut to Asboth, 24 June 1864, *ORN*, 21:343; Paul H. Silverstone, *Warships of the Civil War Navies* (Annapolis: Naval Institute Press, 1989), 108.

4. Sherman to Canby, 4 June 1864, *ORA*, 34, 4:212; Halleck to Canby, 6 June 1864, *ORA*, 34, 4:240.

5. Farragut to Fox, 14 June 1864, *ORN*, 21:335.

6. Farragut to Canby, 20 June 1864, *ORN*, 21:340–41; Canby to Halleck, 18 June 1864, *ORN*, 21:339.

7. *Webster's American Military Biographies*, 173; J. C. Gregg diary, 17 June 1864, Entry 392, RG 45, NA.

8. James J. Talbot, "Admiral David Glasgow Farragut," *United Service, A Monthly Review of Military and Naval Affairs* 3 (July 1880): 12–13; C. Lewis, *David Glasgow Farragut,* 2:2.

9. Page to Jones, 26 June 1864, *ORN*, 21:903; Buchanan to Jones, 14 June 1864, *ORN*, 21:902; Maury to Cooper, 14 June 1864, *ORN*, 21:902.

10. Harriet E. Amos, *Cotton City: Urban Development in Antebellum Mobile* (University: University of Alabama Press, 1985), 22–23, 92.

11. Gilmer to wife, 24 February 1864, Jeremy Gilmer collection, SHC, UNC.

12. Fitzgerald Ross, *Cities and Camps of the Confederate States*, ed. Richard B. Harwell (Urbana: University of Illinois Press, 1958), 241.

13. Hodge to Cooper, 13 April 1864, *ORA*, 32, 3:779.

14. Von Scheliha, Map of the Defenses of the City of Mobile, Drawer 121-15-3, NA.

15. U.S. Navy Department, *Civil War Naval Chronology, 1861–65*, vol. 2, part 6 (Washington: U.S. Government Printing Office, 1864), 202, 230, 251, 272, 275, 300, 312, 317; Still, *Iron Afloat*, 191–95.

16. A. T. Mahan, *The Gulf and Inland Waters* (1883; reprint, Freeport, N.Y.: Books for Libraries Press, 1970), 223; W. E. Geoghegan, "Confederate States Steamer 'Tennessee,' Lines, Outboard Profile, Deck Plan," USNM, 1961, Smithsonian Institution.

17. Jack Coggins, *Arms and Equipment of the Civil War* (Garden City, N.Y.: Doubleday, 1962), 142–44.

18. Mahan, *Gulf and Inland Waters*, 222; Geoghegan, "Confederate States Steamer," deck plans.

19. Cumming, *Journal of a Hospital Life*, 123.

20. D. B. Conrad, "What the Fleet Surgeon Saw of the Fight in Mobile Bay," *United Service: A Monthly Review of Military and Naval Affairs* 8 (1892): 269.

21. Charles Lee Lewis, *Admiral Franklin Buchanan: Fearless Man of Action* (Baltimore: Norman, Remington, 1929), 202.

CHAPTER 4. THE PLAN

1. Farragut to Welles, 4 June 1864, *ORN*, 21:318–19; Drayton, "Naval Letters," 57.

2. Drayton, "Naval Letters," 59; quoted in Heyman, *Prudent Soldier*, 198, 211.

3. Canby to Halleck, 18 June 1864, *ORN*, 21:339.

4. Farragut to Canby, 20 June 1864, *ORN*, 21:340–41.

5. Report to Welles, 9 August 1861, *ORN*, 16:618–30.

6. Special Order No. 39, 16 June 1864, *ORA*, 34, 4:406.

7. Drayton, "Naval Letters," 59.

8. Canby to Porter, 24 June 1864, *ORN*, 21:343–44.

9. Welles to Porter, 25 June 1864, *ORN*, 26:438; Welles to Porter, 9 June 1864, *ORN*, 26:379–80; Porter to Welles, 13 June 1864, *ORN*, 26:387–88; Welles to Farragut, 25 June 1864, *ORN*, 21:344.

10. William T. Sherman, *Memoirs of General William T. Sherman* (Bloomington: Indiana University Press, 1957), 60–61.

11. J. Thomas Scharf, *History of the Confederate States Navy* (1887; reprint, New York: Fairfax Press, 1977), 563; [Victor von] Scheliha, *A Treatise on Coast-Defence* (1868; reprint, Westport Conn.: Greenwood, 1971), 193–94.

12. Wayne P. Hughes, *Fleet Tactics: Theory and Practice* (Annapolis: Naval Institute Press, 1986), 58.

13. Canby to Sherman, 27 June 1864, *ORA,* 32, 2:149; Canby to Steele, 28 June 1864, *ORA,* 34, 4:579.
14. Mullaney to Welles, 28 June 1864, *ORN,* 21:350; Craven to Welles, 29 June 1864, *ORN,* 21:351–52; Porter to commanders of *Chickasaw* and *Winnebago,* 30 June 1864, *ORN,* 26:450–51.
15. Page to Garner, 5, 30 June 1864, Fort Morgan telegrams, Richard L. Page papers, SHC, UNC.
16. Robert Tarleton to Lightfoot, 22 June 1864, Robert Tarleton letters, Grace Bestor DuValle private collection, Mobile, Ala.
17. Ezra J. Warner, *Generals in Gray: Lives of the Confederate Commanders* (Baton Rouge: Louisiana State University Press, 1959), 226–27.
18. District Reports and Returns, 30 June 1864, *ORA,* 39, 2:677.
19. Scharf, *History,* 563.
20. Tarleton to Lightfoot, 30 June 1864, Robert Tarleton letters, Grace Bestor DuValle private collection.

CHAPTER 5. THE ATTACK IS CANCELED

1. Stephen R. Wise, *Lifeline of the Confederacy: Blockade Running during the Civil War* (Columbia: University of South Carolina Press, 1988), 178–79; Farragut to Welles, 2 July 1864, *ORN,* 21:353–54; Tarleton to Lightfoot, 3 July 1864, Robert Tarleton letters, Grace Bestor DuValle private collection.
2. Colby M. Chester, "Showing the Way," *Military Order of the Loyal Legion of the United States, Commandery of the District of Columbia, War Papers* 79 (1910): 6.
3. Drayton to Jenkins, 1 July 1864, *ORN,* 21:354.
4. Halleck to Canby, 24 June 1864, *ORA,* 34, 4:528.
5. Canby to Farragut, 1 July 1864, *ORN,* 21:357.
6. Farragut, to Canby, 7 July 1864, *ORA,* 41, 2:67; C. Lewis, *David Glasgow Farragut,* 2:381.
7. E. H. Hults, "Aboard the *Galena* at Mobile" *Civil War Times Illustrated* 10, no 1 (April 1971), 18.
8. Marchand journal, 6 July 1864, *ORN,* 21:817.
9. Page to Maury and Garner, 7 July 1864, SHC, UNC.
10. Maury to Cooper, 5 July 1864, *ORA,* 39, 2:687.
11. Ibid., 7 July 1864, *ORN,* 21:904–5.
12. Davis to Watts, 7 July 1864, *ORA,* 52, 2:687; Lee to Bragg, 6 July 1864, *ORA,* 39, 2:688–89; Lee to E. K. Smith via Gen. Walker, 6 July 1864, *ORA,* 39, 2:689.
13. Report to Maury, 9 July 1864, *ORA,* 39, 2:698.
14. Canby to Washburn, 2 July 1864, *ORA,* 41, 2:21–22.
15. Sherman to Canby, 7 July 1864, *ORA,* 38, 5:84–85.
16. Department of the Gulf Returns, District of West Florida, 30 June 1864, *ORA,* 35, 2:160.
17. Farragut to Welles, 8 July 1864, *ORN,* 21:366; Nicholson to Welles, 7 July 1864,

Letters Received by the Secretary of the Navy from Commanders, 1804–1886, Entry 23, NRC, RG 45, NA.

18. Robert B. Ely, "Journal of a Cruise in the Ironclad *Manhattan*," 10–11, Richard B. Ely private collection, Harrington, Del.

19. Farragut, *Life*, 402–3.

20. Tarleton to Lightfoot, 7 July 1864, Robert Tarleton letters, DuValle private collection.

21. Drayton to Farragut, 8 July 1864, *ORN*, 21:356–57; Miles M. Oviatt, *A Civil War Marine at Sea: The Diary of Medal of Honor Recipient Miles M. Oviatt*, ed. Mary P. Livingston (Shippensburg, Pa.: White Mane Books, 1998), 111.

CHAPTER 6. A NEW PLAN

1. Oviatt, *Civil War Marine*, 9 July 1864, 111; Canby to Farragut, 1 July 1864, *ORN*, 21:357.

2. C. Lewis, *David Glasgow Farragut*, 2:251; Farragut, *Life*, 403.

3. Ely, "Journal," 8 July 1864, 11, Ely private collection.

4. Brother, "Journal," 38; Canby to Farragut, 18 July 1864, *ORN*, 21:379.

5. McAlester to Delafield, 20 August 1864, *ORA*, 39, 1:408–10.

6. Fairfax Downey, *Storming of the Gateway: Chattanooga, 1863* (New York: David McKay, 1960), 176–77.

7. Christensen to Farragut, 9 July 1864, *ORN*, 21:368.

8. Marchand journal, 10 July 1864, *ORN*, 21:817–18.

9. Halleck to Grant, 13 July 1864, *ORA*, 37, 2:257–58; Carl Sandburg, *Abraham Lincoln: The War Years, 1864–1865* (New York: Dell Publishing, 1960), 554–55.

10. Albert D. Castel, *Decision in the West: The Atlanta Campaign of 1864* (Lawrence: University Press of Kansas, 1992), 343–44; Grant to Halleck, 5 June 1864, *ORA*, 39, 2:79.

11. General Order No. 10, 12 July 1864, *ORN*, 21:397–98. Quotations in the following paragraphs relevant to this order are also from this source.

12. Hults, "Aboard the Galena," 19; Marchand journal, 26 July 1864, NWC.

13. Notebook of David Glasgow Farragut, Entry 464, NRC, RG 45, NA; Hults, "Aboard the Galena," 20; Mahan, *Gulf and Inland Waters*, 228.

14. John Keegan, *The Price of Admiralty: The Evolution of Naval Warfare* (New York: Viking, 1989), 97–98; Spencer Tucker, *Arming the Fleet: U.S. Navy Ordnance in the Muzzle-Loading Era* (Annapolis: Naval Institute Press, 1989), 177.

15. Myer to Farragut, 13 July 1864, *ORN*, 21:371–74.

16. Farragut to Welles, 15 July 1864, *ORN*, 21, 374–75.

17. Farragut to Bailey, 16 July 1864, *ORN*, 21:376–77.

18. Farragut to Welles, 21 July 1864, *ORN*, 21:381.

19. Drayton, "Naval Letters," 63–64.

20. Jack Hurst, *Nathan Bedford Forrest: A Biography* (New York: Alfred A. Knopf, 1993), 202–7; Lee to Bragg, 10 July 1864, *ORA*, 39, 2:700.

21. Hurst, *Nathan Bedford Forrest*, 200–202.

22. Ibid., 203.

23. Withers to Cooper, 14 July 1864, *ORA*, 39, 2:712.

24. Lee to Bragg, 15 July 1864, *ORA*, 39, 2:714; Lee to Smith, 16 July 1864, *ORA*, 39, 2:714.

25. Davis to Lee, 14 July 1864, *ORA*, 39, 2:710; Lee to Bragg, 10 July 1864, *ORA*, 39, 2:700.

Chapter 7. More Delay

1. Joseph E. Johnston, *Narrative of Military Operations during the Civil War* (New York: Da Capo Press, 1959), 348–51.

2. Ibid., 363; Sword, *Southern Invincibility*, 264.

3. John G. Nicolay and John Hay, *Abraham Lincoln: A History* (New York: Century, 1914), 244–45.

4. Joseph Johnston, *Narrative*, 348–49.

5. Hood, Hardee, and Stewart to Davis, 18 July 1864, *ORA*, 52, 2:708–9; Foote, *Red River to Appomattox*, 421–22.

6. James M. McPherson, ed., *The Atlas of the Civil War* (New York: MacMillan, 1994), 176.

7. Castel, *Decision*, 411; Hood to Seddon, 22 July 1864, *ORA*, 38, 5:900.

8. Lee to Davis, 23 July 1864, *ORA*, 38, 5:903; Bragg to Davis, 25 July 1864, *ORA*, 38, 5:908.

9. Rawley, *Turning Points*, 180.

10. J. R. Gilmore, "Our Visit to Richmond," *Atlantic Monthly* 14 (September 1864), 379.

11. Mark E. Fretwell, "Rousseau's Alabama Raid," *Alabama Historical Quarterly* 18 (1956), 544–46.

12. Bragg to Sale, 20 July 1864, *ORA*, 38, 5:897; Davis to Bragg, 20 July 1864, *ORA*, 39, 2:719–20.

13. Tarleton to Lightfoot, 19 July 1864, Robert Tarleton letters, DuValle private collection.

14. Von Scheliha to Garner, 9 July 1864, *ORA*, 39, 2:706–7; Von Scheliha to Gallimard, 10 July 1864, *ORA*, 39, 2:707–8; Von Scheliha to Rives, 11 July 1864, *ORA*, 39, 2:704–5.

15. Maury to Lee, 10 July 1864, *ORA*, 39, 2:702–3; Don C. Seitz, *Braxton Bragg, General of the Confederacy* (Columbia, S.C.: State Company, 1924), 456.

16. E. B. Presley to Josephine Presley, 20 July 1864, Fort Morgan Museum.

17. Canby to Farragut, 18 July 1864, *ORN*, 21:379.

18. Kerby, *Kirby Smith*, 323–24; Canby to Halleck, 22 July 1864, *ORA*, 41, 2:325–26; Canby to Farragut, 18 July 1864, *ORN*, 21:379.

19. Christensen to McAlester, 18 July 1864, *ORA*, 41, 2:229.

20. Canby to Sherman, 20 July 1864, *ORN*, 21:380.

21. Asboth to Christensen, 20 July 1864, *ORA*, 35, 2:181.

22. Brother, "Journal," 20 July 1864, 41.
23. Charles F. Blake journal, 20 July 1864,.Manuscript Division, Library of Congress.
24. Ely, "Journal," 20 July 1864, 19–20, Ely private collection.
25. Brother, "Journal," 20 July 1864, 41; Farragut, *Life*, 403.
26. *Augusta* Deck Log, 20 July 1864, Logs of U.S. Naval Ships, RG 24, NA; Craven to Welles, 29 July 1864, *ORN*, 21:390; T. A. M. Craven to Gideon Welles, 11 July 1864, Entry 23, RG 45, NA.

CHAPTER 8. *Manhattan* JOINS THE FLEET

1. *Manhattan* Deck Log, 21 July 1864, Logs of U.S. Naval Ships, RG 24, NA; Tarleton to Lightfoot, 21 July 1864, Robert Tarleton letters, DuValle private collection.
2. Tarleton to Lightfoot, 21 July 1864, Robert Tarleton letters, DuValle private collection; Hurieosco Austill, "Fort Morgan in the Confederacy," *Alabama Historical Quarterly* (summer 1945), 255; Jones to Page, 25 July 1864, *ORN*, 21:908.
3. *Manhattan* Abstract Deck Log, 21 July 1864, *ORN*, 21:823.
4. *Manhattan* Deck Log, 21 July 1864, Logs of U.S. Naval Ships, RG 24, NA; Silverstone, *Warships*, 10, 36; Warren Ripley, *Artillery and Ammunition of the Civil War* (Charleston, S.C.: Battery Press, 1984), 99.
5. James Stokesberry, *How to Build a Monitor: A Study of the Construction of the USS Tecumseh* (Washington, D.C.: National Armed Forces Museum Advisory Board, Smithsonian Institution, 1966; revised, 1967), 30; Ely, "Journal," 21 July 1864, 21, Ely private collection.
6. Hults, "Aboard the Galena," 20.
7. *Bienville* Deck Log, 21 July 1864, Logs of U.S. Naval Ships, RG 24, NA; Farragut to Welles, 21 July 1864, *ORN*, 21:381.
8. Farragut to Newman, 22 July 1864, *ORN*, 21:381–82.
9. Asboth to Drake, 30 July 1864, *ORA*, 35, 1:416–17.
10. Ibid.
11. Ibid., 418.
12. Farragut to Canby, 25 July 1864, *ORN*, 21:386.
13. Canby to Halleck, 22 July 1864, *ORA*, 41, 2:325–26.
14. "A Successful Landing Party," *National Tribune*, 22 July 1864, Charles Stanhope Cotton papers, Manuscript Division, Library of Congress.
15. *Oneida* Abstract Deck Log, 23 July 1864, *ORN*, 21:837; C. T. Pope to wife, 13 July 1864, Fort Morgan Museum.
16. "Letter from Pollard, Alabama," *Mobile Evening News*, 1 August 1864.
17. William T. Mumford diary, 22 July 1864, Mobile City Museum; Maury to Cooper, 1 September 1864, *ORA*, 39, 1:429–31.
18. Page to Cluis, 22 July 1864, SHC, UNC.
19. Von Scheliha, Monthly Report of Operations for the Defense of Mobile, Ala., July 1864, *ORA*, 39, 2:739.

20. St. John Richardson Liddell, *Liddell's Record*, ed. Nathaniel Cheairs Hughes Jr. (Baton Rouge: Louisiana State University Press, 1985), 187; Lee to Liddell, 22 July 1864, *ORA*, 39, 2:721.
21. Lee to Liddell, 23 July 1864, *ORA*, 39, 2:724; Kerby, *Kirby Smith*, 326.

CHAPTER 9. *Tecumseh* REACHES PENSACOLA

1. Farragut to Canby, 25 July 1864, *ORN*, 21:386. Quotations in the following paragraphs relevant to this communication are also from this source.
2. Farragut to De Krafft, 27 July 1864, *ORN*, 21:388; De Krafft to Farragut, 6 August 1864, *ORN*, 21:502–3; Scharf, *History*, 560.
3. Farragut to Welles, 26 July 1864, *ORN*, 21:387; Ely, "Journal," 25 July 1864, 26, Ely private collection.
4. "A Journal of U.S.S. Cowslip," 27 July 1864, Entry 392, RG 45, NA; U.S. Navy Department, *Civil War Naval Chronology*, part 6, 92.
5. "Practical Observer" to Banks, 7 July 1864, *ORN*, 21:360.
6. C. Lewis, *David Glasgow Farragut*, 2:383; Canby to Farragut, 26 July 1864, *ORN*, 21:388.
7. Canby to Farragut, 26 July 1864, *ORN*, 21:388.
8. George Hamilton Perkins, *Letters of Capt. Geo. Hamilton Perkins, U.S.N.*, ed. George E. Belknap (Concord, Mass.: Ira C. Evans, 1886), 127–29.
9. *Eutaw* Deck Log, 28 July 1864, Logs of U.S. Naval Ships, RG 24, NA; *Augusta* Deck Log, 28 July 1864, Logs of U.S. Naval Ships, RG 24, NA; Craven to Welles, 29 July 1864, *ORN*, 21:390.
10. Mahan, *Admiral Farragut*, 273.
11. Drayton to Palmer, 28 July 1864, James C. Palmer Correspondence, Letterbooks of Officers of the U.S. Navy, Entry 395, NRC, RG 45, NA.
12. Bragg to Sale, 26 July 1864, *ORA*, 38, 5:911.
13. Samuel Carter III, *The Siege of Atlanta* (New York: Ballantine Books, 1973), 255–56; Maury to Forrest, 27 July 1864, *ORA*, 39, 2:731.
14. Fremaux to Maury, 2 June 1864, *ORN*, 21:899–901.
15. Jones to Page, 25 July 1864, *ORN*, 21:908.
16. Fremaux to Maury, 2 June 1864, *ORN*, 21:899–901; Report, July 1864, *ORA*, 39, 2:739–40; Meyer, Intelligence Report, 11 July 1864, *ORN*, 21:374.
17. Wise, *Lifeline*, 265–68.
18. Carter, *Siege*, 256; Bowman, *Civil War Almanac*, 217; Clifford Dowdey, *The Land They Fought For: The Story of the South as the Confederacy, 1832–1865* (Garden City, N.Y.: Doubleday, 1955), 396; Hudson Strode, *Jefferson Davis: Tragic Hero* (New York: Harcourt, Brace and World, 1964), 85.
19. James T. Gee to wife, 28 July 1864, James T. Gee papers, Fort Morgan Museum.
20. Tarleton to Lightfoot, 26 July 1864, Robert Tarleton letters, DuValle private collection.

21. *Eutaw* Deck Log, 28 July 1864, Logs of U.S. Naval Ships, RG 24, NA; Farragut to Palmer, 30 July 1864, *ORN*, 21:391–92.

22. John B. Marchand journal, 28 July 1864, NWC.

23. Craven Obituary, *Army and Navy Journal*, 20 August 1864, 850; John B. Marchand, Abstracts of Service, Records of Officers, Entry 193, NRC, RG 24, NA.

24. Hults, "Aboard the Galena," 20.

CHAPTER 10. GIRDING FOR BATTLE

1. *Augusta* Deck Log, 29 July 1864, Logs of U.S. Naval Ships, RG 24, NA; Ely, "Journal," 14 July 1864, 15, Ely private collection.

2. Oliver A. Batcheller, "The Battle of Mobile Bay, August 5, 1864," *Magazine of History* 14, no. 6 (December 1911): 222.

3. Smith to Welles, 1 July 1864, Letters from Commandants of Navy Yards and Shore Establishments, Pensacola Navy Yard, Entry 34, RG 45, NA; Farragut to Welles, 12 August 1864, *ORN*, 21:421.

4. Marchand journal, 29 July 1864, NWC.

5. Drayton to Jenkins, 1 August 1864, *ORN*, 21:394.

6. Ely, "Journal," 1 July 1864, 4, Ely private collection; Ernest W. Peterkin, USS *Tecumseh*, plans prepared for the National Armed Forces Museum Advisory Board, in author's possession.

7. Marchand journal, 28 July 1864, NWC.

8. Stokesberry, *How to Build a Monitor*, Smithsonian.

9. Peterkin, *Tecumseh* plans, in author's possession.

10. Stokesberry, *How to Build a Monitor*, Smithsonian; Ely "Journal," 2 July 1864, 5, Ely private collection.

11. Peterkin, *Tecumseh* plans, in author's possession; Ripley, *Artillery*, 99.

12. U.S. Navy Department, *Allowances Established for Vessels of the United States Navy, 1864* (Washington: Government Printing Office, 1865), 155.

13. Silverstone, *Warships*, 10, 38.

14. Drayton to Jenkins, 3 August 1864, *ORN*, 21:402.

15. Page to Garner, 29 July 1864, SHC, UNC.

16. Carter, *Siege*, 276.

17. Watts to Maury, 29 July 1864, *ORA*, 39, 2:734.

18. George Little and James R. Maxwell, *History of Lumsden's Battery, C.S.A.* (Tuscaloosa, Ala.: R. E. Rhodes Chapter, United Daughters of the Confederacy, 1905), 3; Watts to Maury (Maury Endorsement), 29 July 1864, *ORA*, 39, 2:734.

19. Von Scheliha to Garner, 9 July 1864, *ORA*, 39, 2:706–7; Von Scheliha, Monthly Report, July 1864, *ORA*, 39, 2:739–40.

20. Von Scheliha to Garner, 9 July 1864, *ORA*, 39, 2:706–7; Von Scheliha to Gallimard, 29 July 1864, War Department Collection of Confederate Records, RG 109, NA; Parthenia Antoinette Hague, *A Blockaded Family: Life in Southern*

Alabama during the Civil War (Lincoln: University of Nebraska Press, 1991), 38–39.

21. Barrett to Andrews, 20 August 1864 (Maury endorsement), *ORN,* 21:570.
22. Canby to Farragut, 29 July 1864, *ORN,* 21:390.

CHAPTER 11. THE TROOPS EMBARK

1. Henry W. Hart to wife, 28 July 1864, Special Collections, Emory University.
2. Orange Parret diary, 29 July 1864, Fort Morgan Museum; W. H. Bentley, *History of the 77th Illinois Volunteer Infantry, Sept. 2 1862–July 10, 1865* (Peoria, Ill.: Edward Hine, 1883), 318.
3. Canby to Farragut, 26 July 1864, *ORN,* 21:388.
4. Kerby, *Kirby Smith,* 323–24; Canby to Farragut, 26 July 1864, *ORN,* 21:388; Canby to Sherman, 20 July 1864, *ORN,* 21:380; Canby to Farragut, 29 July 1864, *ORN,* 21:390.
5. Rawley, *Turning Points,* 183.
6. *Winnebago* Deck Log, 29 July 1864, Logs of U.S. Naval Ships, RG 24, NA; *Chickasaw* Deck Log, 29 July 1864, Logs of U.S. Naval Ships, RG 24, NA; Farragut to Palmer, 30 July 1864, *ORN,* 21:391–92.
7. *Chickasaw* Deck Log, 29 July 1864, Logs of U.S. Naval Ships, RG 24, NA; Perkins to Palmer, 29 July 1864, *ORN,* 21:389.
8. General Orders No. 11, 29 July 1864, *ORN,* 21:398.
9. USS *Cowslip* Journal, 29 July 1864, Entry 392, RG 45, NA.
10. Ibid., 30 July 1864; Ely, "Journal," 30 July 1864, 31–32, Ely private collection.
11. Farragut to Palmer, 30 July 1864, *ORN,* 21:391–92.
12. *Winnebago* Deck Log, 29–30 July 1864, Logs of U.S. Naval Ships, RG 24, NA; *Chickasaw* Deck Log, 29–30 July 1864, Logs of U.S. Naval Ships, RG 24, NA.
13. Orange Parret diary, 30 July 1864, Fort Morgan Museum.
14. Tarleton to Lightfoot, 1 August 1864, Robert Tarleton letters, DuValle private collection; Ely, "Journal," 30 July 1864, 31, 32, Ely private collection.
15. Ripley, *Artillery,* 118.
16. Buchanan to Johnston, 30 July 1864, *ORN,* 21:909; C. Lewis, *Admiral Franklin Buchanan,* 218; Tarleton to Lightfoot, 1 August 1864, Robert Tarleton letters, DuValle private collection.
17. Joseph Johnston, *Narrative,* 363; Rawley, *Turning Points,* 174.
18. Kerby, *Kirby Smith,* 325–26.
19. Kirby Smith—Special Orders, 1 August 1864, *ORA,* 41, 2:1035.
20. Douglas Southall Freeman, *Lee's Lieutenants: A Study in Command* (New York: Charles Scribner's Sons, 1944), 3:571.
21. Lee to Seddon, 19 July 1864, *ORA,* 37, 2:346; "Trans-Potomac Raid," *New Orleans Times Picayune,* 10 August 1864.
22. Charles C. Osborne, *Jubal: The Life and Times of General Jubal A. Early, CSA, Defender of the Lost Cause* (Chapel Hill, N.C.: Algonquin Books, 1992), 297.

CHAPTER 12. RIVER MONITORS ARRIVE

1. *Chickasaw* Deck Log, 29–31 July 1864, Logs of U.S. Naval Ships, RG 24, NA; *Tennessee* Deck Log, 30 July 1864, Logs of U.S. Naval Ships, RG 24, NA; *Winnebago* Deck Log, 29–31 July 1864, RG 24, NA.
2. Perkins, *Letters*, 128–29; *Winnebago* Deck Log, 30 July 1864, Logs of U.S. Naval Ships, RG 24, NA.
3. Perkins, *Letters*, 127.
4. *Chickasaw* Deck Log, 31 July 1864, Logs of U.S. Naval Ships, RG 24, NA; *Winnebago* Deck Log, 31 July 1864, Logs of U.S. Naval Ships, RG 24, NA; Porter to Welles, 13 June 1864, *ORN*, 26:387–88.
5. Canby to Granger, 31 July 1864, *ORA*, 39, 2:216.
6. J. T. Woods, *Services of the Ninety-Sixth Ohio Volunteers* (Toledo, Ohio: Blade Printing and Paper, 1874), 82; Enos Reed to wife, 13 August 1864, Mobile City Museum; Oliver Batcheller to father, 31 July 1864, Oliver Ambrose Batcheller papers, Nimitz Library, Special Collections Dept., USNA; Hults, "Aboard the Galena," 20; Paul Henry Kendricken, *Memoirs of Paul Henry Kendricken* (Boston: Privately printed, 1910), 239.
7. *Metacomet* Deck Log, 31 July 1864, Logs of U.S. Naval Ships, RG 24, NA; Farragut, *Life*, 404.
8. Farragut, *Life*, 404; Batcheller to father, 31 July 1864, Batcheller papers, USNA.
9. Farragut to Jenkins, 1 August 1864, *ORN*, 21:395; Ely, "Journal," 31 July 1864, 32, Ely private collection.
10. *Chickasaw* Deck Log, 1 August 1864, Logs of U.S. Naval Ships, RG 24, NA; *Manhattan* Deck Log, 1 August 1864, Logs of U.S. Naval Ships, RG 24, NA; *Winnebago* Deck Log, 1 August 1864, Logs of U.S. Naval Ships, RG 24, NA.
11. Farragut to Jenkins, 2 August 1864, *ORN*, 21:401; Mahan, *Admiral Farragut*, 268; Drayton to Jenkins, 2 August 1864, *ORN*, 21:399.
12. USS *Cowslip* Journal, 1 August 1864, Entry 392, NRC, RG 45, NA.
13. Drayton to Jenkins, 2 August 1864, *ORN*, 21:399–400; Farragut to Jenkins, 2 August 1864, *ORN*, 21:401.
14. Granger to Farragut, 2 August 1864, *ORN*, 21:400.
15. Garner to Page, 2 August 1864, SHC, UNC.
16. Williams, *From That Terrible Field*, 135.
17. Maury to Seddon, 2 August 1864, *ORA*, 39, 2:747; Maury to Clark, 2 August 1864, *ORA*, 39, 2:747–48.
18. Maury to Seddon, 2 August 1864, *ORA*, 39, 2:747–48.
19. Maury to Clark, 2 August 1864, *ORA*, 39, 2:747–48.
20. Maury to Forrest, 2 August 1864, *ORA*, 39, 2:748–49.
21. Deas to Liddell, 1 August 1864, *ORA*, 39, 2:746; Maury to Adams, 2 August 1864, *ORA*, 39, 2:750.
22. Maury to Adams, 1 August 1864, *ORA*, 39, 2:746.
23. Maury to Cooper, 13 August 1864, *ORA*, 39, 2:773–74; District Returns, 3 August 1864, *ORA*, 39, 2:751; Maury to Bragg, 3 August 1864, *ORA*, 52, 2:716.

24. J. W. Whiting, letter to editor, *Mobile Register*, n.d., Whiting family private collection, Mobile, Ala.
25. J. L. J. Lear diary, 2 August 1864, Special Collections, Robert W. Woodruff Library, Emory University.
26. McAlester to Delafield, 20 August 1864, *ORA*, 39, 1:410; Williams to Garner, 7 August 1864, *ORA*, 39, 1:441–42.
27. Conrad, "What the Fleet Surgeon Saw," 261.
28. Page to Higgins, 2 August 1864, SHC, UNC.

CHAPTER 13. SO DARING A PLAN

1. USS *Cowslip* Journal, 3 August 1864, Entry 392, NRC, RG 45, NA; John C. Kinney, "An August Morning with Farragut," *Scribner's Monthly Illustrated Magazine* 22 (June 1881): 199–200.
2. Marchand journal, 3 August 1864, NWC.
3. Kinney, "August Morning," 200.
4. Ibid., 202–3, 207.
5. C. Lewis, *David Glasgow Farragut*, 2:382–83.
6. Farragut, *Life*, 401; Myer Report, 7 July 1864, *ORN*, 21:363; Myer Report, 9 July 1864, *ORN*, 21:372; Myer Report, 11 July 1864, *ORN*, 21:374.
7. Fremaux to Maury, 2 June 1864, *ORN*, 21:900; Marchand to Farragut, 18 February 1864, *ORN*, 21:105–6.
8. Wise, *Lifeline*, 268.
9. John Randolph Spears, *David G. Farragut* (Philadelphia: George W. Jacobs, 1905), 359; P. C. Headley, *Life and Naval Career of Vice-Admiral David Glascoe Farragut* (New York: William H. Appleton, 1865), 265; Von Scheliha, Monthly Report, 31 July 1864, *ORA*, 39, 2:739–40.
10. Mahan, *Gulf and Inland Waters*, 227.
11. Diagram of Line of Battle, 2nd and 3rd Order of Sailing, 3 August 1864, Museum of Mobile.
12. General Orders No. 10, 12 July 1864, *ORN*, 21:397–98.
13. General Orders No. 11, 29 July 1864, *ORN*, 21:398.
14. Farragut to Welles, 12 August 1864, *ORN*, 21:417.
15. Myer Intelligence Report, 11 July 1864, *ORN*, 21:373; Drayton to Jenkins, 22 May 1864, Mariners Museum Library; Von Scheliha, *Treatise*, 207; Mahan, *Admiral Farragut*, 260; F. von Ehrenkrook, *History of Submarine Mining and Torpedoes* (1878; reprint Berlin: Battalion Press, n.d.), 29; Scharf, *History*, 768.
16. Farragut to Stevens, 4 August 1864, *ORN*, 21:404.
17. Batcheller to father, 31 July 1864, Batcheller papers, USNA.
18. De Krafft to Farragut, 6 August 1864, *ORN*, 21:502–3; Edgar Stanton Maclay, *A History of the United States Navy from 1775 to 1901*, 3 vols. (New York: D. Appleton, 1898), 2:407.
19. Mahan, *Admiral Farragut*, 270; Farragut, *Life*, 430.
20. *Hartford* Abstract Deck Log, 5 August 1864, *ORN*, 21:799.

21. Kinney, "Farragut," *B&L*, 4:382–83.
22. Ibid., 381–82.
23. Ibid.
24. David D. Porter, *The Naval History of the Civil War* (Secaucus, N.J.: Castle, 1984), 569–71.
25. John C. Kinney, "Battle of Mobile Bay," speech delivered in 1891, Connecticut State Library.
26. USS *Hartford*, Plan 40-6-6-A, Bureau of Ships, RG 19, NA. Descriptions of the ship in the following paragraphs are also from this source.
27. Granger to Christensen, 3 August 1864, *ORA*, 39, 2:222.
28. *Conemaugh* Abstract Deck Log, 3 August 1864, *ORN*, 21:789.
29. *Narcissus* Deck Log, 3 August 1864, Logs of U.S. Naval Ships, RG 24, NA.
30. Williams, *From That Terrible Field*, 135.
31. Ibid., 177.
32. Ibid., 177, 135.
33. Williams to Garner, 7 August 1864, *ORN*, 21:560.
34. Von Scheliha to Page, 3 August 1864, Richard L. Page papers, SHC, UNC.
35. Farragut to Jenkins, 3 August 1864, *ORN*, 21:403.

CHAPTER 14. THE ARMY LANDS

1. Farragut to Jenkins, 3 August 1864, *ORN*, 21:403.
2. Drayton to Jenkins, 3 August 1864, *ORN*, 21:402.
3. Farragut to Howison, 3 August 1864, *ORN*, 21:401; C. Lewis, *David Glasgow Farragut*, 2:261.
4. Farragut to Welles, 9 May 1864, *ORN*, 21:267.
5. Farragut to Granger, 3 August 1864, *ORN*, 21:403.
6. *Conemaugh* Abstract Deck Log, 3 August 1864, *ORN*, 21:789; Enos Reed to wife, 13 August 1864, Mobile City Museum; A. A. Stuart, *Iowa Colonels and Regiments* (Des Moines: Mills, 1865), 505.
7. Henry W. Hart to wife, 10 August 1864, Special Collections, Robert W. Woodruff Library, Emory University.
8. Rufe Dooley to mother, 10 August 1864, Fort Morgan Museum; *Conemaugh* Abstract Deck Log, 3 August 1864, *ORN*, 21:789; *J. P. Jackson* Deck Log, 3 August 1864, Logs of U.S. Naval Ships, RG 24, NA.
9. J. C. Gregg diary, 3 August 1864, Entry 392, NRC, RG 45, NA.
10. Ibid.
11. Woods, *Services*, 86.
12. Maury to Davis, 3 August 1864, *ORA*, 52, 2:716; typescript of article from Mobile newspaper, 3 August 1864, in author's possession.
13. Von Scheliha to Garner, 9 July 1864, *ORA*, 39, 2:706.
14. Operations Report, 31 July 1864, *ORA*, 39, 2:739–40; Von Scheliha to Gallimard, 3 August 1864, War Department Collection of Confederate Records, RG 109, NA.

15. Myer Report, 11 July 1864, *ORN*, 21:373; Fremaux to Maury, 2 June 1864, *ORN*, 21:900.

16. Von Ehrenkrook, *History*, 33–34.

17. Ibid., 33.

18. Fremaux to Maury, 2 June 1864, *ORN*, 21:900.

19. Maury to Cooper, 1 September 1864, *ORA*, 39, 1:429–31; Seitz, *Braxton Bragg*, 52.

20. Reuben B. Scott, *History of the 67th Regiment, Indiana Infantry Volunteers* (Bedford, Ind.: Herald Book and Job Print, 1892), 79.

21. McAlester to Delafield, 20 August 1864, *ORA*, 39:410; John L. Rapier to Tom Rapier, 5 September 1864, John L. Rapier letters, Adelaide Trigg papers, private collection, Mobile, Ala.

22. Rapier to Rapier, 5 September 1864, Trigg private collection; Arthur W. Bergeron Jr., "The Twenty-second Louisiana Infantry in the Defense of Mobile, 1864–1865," *Alabama Historical Quarterly* (fall 1976): 207.

23. *Baltimore Patriot and Evening Advertiser*, 10 October 1814.

24. William S. Coker, *The Last Battle of the War of 1812: New Orleans! No, Fort Bowyer!* (Pensacola, Fla.: Perdido Bay Press, 1981), 51.

25. "Andrew Jackson Jr.," *Confederate Veteran* 13, no. 7 (July 1905), 329; Tennessee Civil War Centennial Commission, "Tennesseeans in the Civil War" (Nashville: Civil War Centennial Commission), 1:121.

26. Maury to Bragg, 3 August 1864, *ORA*, 52, 2:716.

27. Ibid.

CHAPTER 15. THE NAVY IS LATE

1. Scott, *History*, 79; Woods, *Services*, 86.

2. Canby to Halleck, 6 August 1864, *ORN*, 21:519.

3. *Bienville* Deck Log, 4 August 1864, Logs of U.S. Naval Ships, RG 24, NA.

4. Denicke to Myer, 4 August 1864, *ORA*, 52, 1:580.

5. Granger to Canby, 5 August 1864, *ORN*, 21:520–21.

6. Anderson to Smith, 4 August 1864, Anderson papers, SHC, UNC; Rapier to Tom, 5 September, 1864, Rapier letters, Trigg private collection.

7. Rapier to Tom, 5 September 1864, Rapier letters, Trigg private collection.

8. Page to Maury, 8 August 1864, *ORN*, 21:561; Page to Garner, 4 August 1864, SHC, UNC.

9. Denicke to Myer, 4 August 1864, *ORA*, 52, 1:581; Farragut to Stevens, 4 August 1864, *ORN*, 21:403–4.

10. Page to Garner, 4 August 1864, SHC, UNC.

11. Rapier to Tom, 5 September 1864, Trigg private collection.

12. *Winnebago* Steam Log, 4 August 1864, Logs of U.S. Naval Ships, RG 24, NA; Ely, "Journal," 4 August 1864, 34, Ely private collection.

13. Schultice to Stevens, 6 August 1864, *ORN*, 21:497.

14. "On Board Steamship Winnebago," *New Orleans Times*, 7 August 1864.

15. Charles Enslow to wife, 4 August 1864, Enslow letters, Charles C. Enslow private collection.

16. Austill, "Fort Morgan," 255.

17. Typescript of article from Mobile newspaper, 3 August 1864, in author's possession.

18. "Editor *Advertiser and Register*," letter, 4 August 1864, microfilm Z2 M715, University of Alabama.

19. Scharf, *History*, 583.

20. Mahan, *Admiral Farragut*, 265.

21. Rawley, *Turning Points*, 176.

22. Carter, *Siege*, 291; Rawley, *Turning Points*, 176; quote is from Fletcher Pratt, *A Short History of the Civil War* (New York: Pocket Books, 1960), 273.

23. Hood to Bragg, 4 August 1864, *ORA*, 52, 2:718.

24. Baker to Higgins, 4 August 1864, *ORN*, 21:917–18.

CHAPTER 16. *Tecumseh* STEAMS IN

1. William Hutchinson, "The Bay Fight: A Sketch of the Battle of Mobile Bay," *Personal Narratives of the Battles of the Rebellion* 8 (1879): 7.

2. C. Lewis, *David Glasgow Farragut*, 2:260.

3. Farragut to Howison, 3 August 1864, *ORN*, 21:401; Farragut to Stevens, 4 August 1864, *ORN*, 21:404; McAlester to Delafield, 17 August 1864, *ORN*, 21:532.

4. Hutchinson, "Bay Fight," 9.

5. Wise, *Lifeline*, 268; John C. Watson to A. T. Mahan, 4 May 1883, Entry 463, Area 6 (Union), NRC, RG 45, NA.

6. McAlester to Delafield, 17 August 1864, *ORA*, 39, 1:406–8; Diagram of Line of Battle, 2nd and 3rd Order of Sailing, 5 August 1864, *ORN*, 21:423.

7. Hutchinson, "Bay Fight," 8.

8. Marchand journal, 4 August 1864, NWC; journal of Isaac DeGraff, 4 August 1864, Entry 392, NRC, RG 45, NA.

9. Farragut, *Life*, 405–6.

10. *Richmond* Deck Log, 4 August 1864, RG 24, NA.

11. Granger to Christensen, 8 August 1864, *ORN*, 21:524.

12. Sword, *Southern Invincibility*, 264–65; Joseph Johnston, *Narrative*, 363.

13. Castel, *Decision*, 442–43; Joseph Johnston, *Narrative*, 363; quotes are from Castel.

14. Von Scheliha, Operations Report, July 1864, *ORA*, 39, 2:739; Barrett to Andrews, Maury endorsement, 20 August 1864, *ORN*, 21:570; Maury to Seddon, 12 August 1864, *ORN*, 21:566; Maury to Cooper, 9 August 1864, *ORN*, 21:564.

15. Tarleton to Lightfoot, 4 August 1864, Robert Tarleton letters, DuValle private collection.

16. Farragut to Welles, 12 August 1864, *ORN*, 21:420–21.

17. Farragut to Stevens, 4 August 1864, *ORN*, 21:404.
18. Kinney, "August Morning," 202.
19. Ibid.
20. Absalom Kirby to wife, 6 August 1864; Absalom Kirby, reminiscences, 7, both in Absalom Kirby papers, Naval History Division, Smithsonian Institution.
21. Conrad, "What the Fleet Surgeon Saw," 261; George W. Waterman, "Afloat-Afield-Afloat," *Confederate Veteran* 7, no. 1 (January 1899): 16.
22. Henry St. Paul, "The Attack on Mobile," *New Orleans Times Picayune*, 14 August 1864; Whiting, letter to editor, in author's possession.
23. Wise, *Lifeline*, 179.

CHAPTER 17. GET UNDER WAY

1. Wise, *Lifeline*, 317, 266; *Red Gauntlet* document, Eldridge Collection, Mariners Museum; *Red Gauntlet* vessel papers, Entry 159, War Department Collection of Confederate Records, NRC, RG 109, NA.
2. Charles F. Blake journal, 6 August 1864, Manuscript Division, Library of Congress; C. Lewis, *David Glasgow Farragut*, 2:263.
3. Kinney, "August Morning," 202; *Manhattan* Abstract Log, 5 August 1864, *ORN*, 21:824.
4. Blake journal, 6 August 1864, Manuscript Division, Library of Congress; James Johnston, "Ram *Tennessee*," *B&L*, 4:402.
5. Kimberly to Drayton, 8 August 1864, *ORN*, 21:428; Farragut, *Life*, 430.
6. Abstract of Notes of the Engagement of August 5, taken principally by Lt. John C. Watson, Entry 395, RG 45, NA.
7. Hutchinson, "Bay Fight," 13.
8. U.S. Navy Department, *Ordnance Instructions for the U.S. Navy*, 3d ed. (Washington. D.C.: U.S. Government Printing Office, 1864), 39.
9. Parker, *Battle of Mobile Bay*, 22.
10. James Johnston, "Ram Tennessee," *B&L*, 4:402.
11. Richard L. Page, "The Defense of Fort Morgan," *B&L*, 4:408.
12. Eyewitness, "Fort Gaines: Incidents of the 5th and 6th of August 1864, published 29 January 1873," unidentified Mobile newspaper, in author's possession.
13. J. C. Gregg diary, 5 August 1864, Entry 392, NRC, RG 45, NA.
14. Friend, "Battle of Mobile Bay," 161.
15. Page, "Defense," *B&L*, 4:408; Whiting, letter to editor, in author's possession; St. Paul, "The Attack on Mobile," *New Orleans Times Picayune*, 14 August 1864.
16. Benjamin Cox, "Mobile in the War between the States," *Confederate Veteran* 24, no. 5 (May 1916): 212; St. Paul, "Attack on Mobile," *Times Picayune*, 14 August 1864.
17. Scharf, *History*, 560; Friend, "Battle of Mobile Bay," 158–59.
18. George S. Waterman to John A. Payne, 6 August 1864, Battle of Mobile Bay, Subject File HA, NRC, RG 45, NA.

19. A. D. Wharton, "The Battle of Mobile Bay," *Nashville Daily American*, 13 September 1877.
20. John L. Rapier to Tom Rapier, 5 September 1864, Rapier letters, Trigg private collection.
21. Granger to Canby, 5 August 1864, *ORN*, 21:520–21.
22. Charles Enslow to wife, 4 August 1864, Enslow letters, Charles C. Enslow private collection.
23. Parker, *Battle of Mobile Bay*, 22.
24. Farragut to Welles, 12 August 1864, *ORN*, 21:415.
25. Kinney, "August Morning," 203.
26. Hutchinson, "Bay Fight," 13.
27. Batcheller to parents, 14 August 1864, Batcheller papers, USNA.

CHAPTER 18. CATASTROPHE

1. H[enry] Walke, *Naval Scenes and Reminiscences of the Civil War in the United States* (New York: F. R. Reed, 1877), 429.
2. Abstract of Notes of the Engagement of August 5, taken principally by Lt. John C. Watson, Entry 395, NRC, RG 45, NA.
3. Kinney, "Farragut," *B&L*, 4:387; Scharf, *History*, 563.
4. J. Crittenden Watson, "The Lashing of Admiral Farragut in the Rigging," *B&L*, 4:406.
5. *Hartford* Abstract Deck Log, 5 August 1864, *ORN*, 52, 1:575.
6. Kinney, "Farragut," *B&L*, 4:388.
7. Friend, "Battle of Mobile Bay," 162; A. T. Mahan, *Letters and Papers of Alfred Thayer Mahan*, ed. Robert Seager II and Doris D. Maguire (Annapolis: Naval Institute Press, 1976), 3:555.
8. Farragut to Stevens, 4 August 1864, *ORN*, 21:404; Mahan, *Admiral Farragut*, 273; Drayton, "Naval Letters," 66; Kinney, "Farragut," *B&L*, 4:388.
9. C. Lewis, *David Glasgow Farragut*, 2:267.
10. Alvah Folsom Hunter, *A Year on a Monitor, and the Destruction of Fort Sumter*, ed. Craig L. Symonds (Columbia: University of South Carolina Press, 1987), 50.
11. Parker, *Battle of Mobile Bay*, 26.
12. Kinney, "August Morning," 203.
13. Mahan, *Gulf and Inland Waters*, 232; Kinney, "Farragut," *B&L*, 4:392.
14. Sweet to his sister, 7 August 1864, Cultural History, No. 5, Brooklyn Children's Museum; Marchand journal, 5 August 1864, *ORN*, 21:819.
15. Marchand journal, 5 August 1864, *ORN*, 21:819.
16. Sweet to his sister, 7 August 1864, Brooklyn Museum.
17. Mahan, *Admiral Farragut*, 274–75; Batcheller papers, 14 August 1864, USNA.
18. Wilkinson diary, 5 August 1864, Fort Morgan Museum.
19. Cox, "Mobile in the War between the States," 212.
20. Jones to Buchanan, 2 February 1864, *ORN*, 21:873–74; Wharton, "Battle of Mobile Bay," *Daily Nashville American*, 13 September 1877.

21. Mahan, *Gulf and Inland Waters*, 231.
22. Harrie Webster, "Personal Experiences on a Monitor at the Battle of Mobile Bay," *California Commandery of the Military Order of the Loyal Legion of the United States* 14 (29 August 1894): 12.
23. Kinney, "Farragut," *B&L*, 4:388; Parker, *Battle of Mobile Bay*, 30; Robert G. Latour, University of New Orleans, School of Naval Architecture and Marine Engineering, personal communication; Kevin M. Lynaugh, Department of the Navy, Shipbuilding Technology Office, personal communication.
24. Parker, *Battle of Mobile Bay*, 30; Kinney, "Farragut," *B&L*, 4:388–89. Note: my research indicates 115 officers and men.
25. Alden to Farragut, 5 August 1864, *ORA*, 52, 1:575; Farragut to Alden, 5 August 1864, *ORA*, 52, 1:575.
26. Mobile Bay, Survey of the Coast of the United States, 1856; Silverstone, *Warships*, 35; John C. Kinney, "A Great Anniversary," *Hartford Courant*, 5 August 1889.
27. Mahan, *Admiral Farragut*, 274; Mahan, *Gulf and Inland Waters*, 232; Kinney, "August Morning," 204.
28. Batcheller, "Battle of Mobile Bay," 226; Kinney, "Farragut," *B&L*, 4:389.
29. St. Paul, "Attack on Mobile," *Times Picayune*, 14 August 1864.
30. Castel, *Decision*, 475–76.
31. William T. Mumford diary, 5 August 1864, Mobile City Museum; Mrs. Frances James Mosby, "Reminiscence," in *Mobile: 1861–1865*, ed. Sydney Adair Smith and Carter Smith Jr. (Chicago: Wyvern Press, 1964), 33–35.

Chapter 19. Go Ahead

1. Kinney, "August Morning," 204; *Brooklyn* Abstract Deck Log, 5 August 1864, *ORN*, 21:783.
2. Kinney, "Farragut," *B&L*, 4:389–90.
3. Farragut, *Life*, 416.
4. Farragut to Welles, 12 August 1864, *ORN*, 21:417; John C. Watson, "Personal Recollections of Admiral Farragut," Manuscript Division, Library of Congress; John C. Watson, "Farragut and Mobile Bay—Personal Reminiscences," U.S. Naval Institute *Proceedings* 53 (May 1927): 555–56.
5. Kinney, "Farragut," *B&L*, 4:391; quoted material from "the devout spirit" to "Go on!" in Mahan, *Admiral Farragut*, 277; remaining quotes in Martin Freeman, "The Mobile Naval Combat," 8 May [no year], Kingston, N.Y., newspaper article seen at the Naval Historical Foundation, Washington, D.C., now in possession of the Farragut Folklife Museum, Farragut, Tenn.
6. Kinney, "August Morning," 205; Kinney, "Farragut," *B&L*, 4:390–91.
7. Friend, "Battle of Mobile Bay," 165–66; Mahan, *Admiral Farragut*, 278; Von Scheliha Monthly Report, 31 July 1864, *ORA*, 39, 2:739–40; Waterman to Payne, 6 August 1864, Subject File HA, RG 45, NA.
8. John C. Watson, "Farragut and Mobile Bay," 555.

9. James Johnston, "Buchanan and the Ram *Tennessee*," Speech, Subject File 00, RG 45, NA.

10. Maclay, *History*, 2:428–29.

11. Batcheller, "Battle of Mobile Bay," 228.

12. Harrison to Buchanan, 1 October 1864, *ORN*, 21:583.

13. Murphey to Buchanan, 15 August 1864, *ORA*, 39, 1:448; Drayton to Farragut, 6 August 1864, *ORN*, 21:425.

14. Waterman to Payne, 6 August 1864, Subject File HA, NRC, RG 45, NA; Waterman, "Afloat," 19.

15. Webster, "Personal Experiences," 14.

16. Ibid.

17. Ibid., 13–14.

18. Journal of Carpenter's Mate W. M. C. Philbrick, vol. 3, Entry 392, RG 45, NA; Charles E. Clark, *My Fifty Years in the Navy* (Boston: Little, Brown, 1917), 53.

19. Waterman to Payne, 6 August 1864, Subject File HA, NRC, RG 45, NA.

20. C. Lewis, *David Glasgow Farragut*, 2:270; Kinney, "August Morning," 206; Bennett to Mallory, 8 August 1864, *ORN*, 21:589.

21. D.A.F. to father, 5 August 1864, Fort Morgan Museum.

22. Huntington to Farragut, 6 August 1864, *ORN*, 21:479; Hunt to Huntington, 6 August 1864, *ORN*, 21:481.

23. C. Lewis, *Admiral Franklin Buchanan*, 231; *Richmond* Abstract Deck Log, 5 August 1864, *ORN*, 21:847; Waterman to Payne, 6 August 1864, Subject File HA, RG 45, NA.

24. Maury to Davis, 6 August 1864, *ORA*, 52, 2:720; Page, "Defense," *B&L* 4:409; Page to Maury, 6 August 1864, *ORN*, 21:558.

25. *Conemaugh* Abstract Deck Log, 5 August 1864, *ORN*, 21:790; John Kent Folmar, "Lt. Col. James M. Williams and the Fort Powell Incident," *Alabama Review* 17, no. 2 (April 1964), 127–28.

26. C. Lewis, *Admiral Franklin Buchanan*, 231.

Chapter 20. Gauntlet

1. Kinney, "August Morning," 206.

2. Maclay, *History*, 2:432; Scharf, *History*, 564.

3. James D. Johnston, "The Battle of Mobile Bay," *United Service: A Monthly Review of Military and Naval Affairs* 6, no. 1 (January 1882), 105; T. N. Dupuy, *Understanding Defeat: How to Recover from Loss in Battle to Gain Victory in War* (New York: Paragon House, 1990), 3.

4. Jenkins quoted in Kinney, "Farragut," *B&L*, 4:393.

5. Kinney, "Farragut," *B&L*, 4:393; *Lackawanna* Abstract Deck Log, 5 August 1864, *ORN*, 21:808.

6. Batcheller, "Battle of Mobile Bay," 227.

7. Ibid.

8. Scharf, *History*, 564.

9. Clark, *My Fifty Years*, 54.

10. Huntington to Farragut, 6 August 1864, *ORN*, 21:479.

11. Maclay, *History*, 2:434.

12. Edward Kellogg to father, 7 August 1864, Area 6 (Union), Entry 463, NRC, RG 45, NA.

13. "Passage of the Forts," *New York Daily Tribune*, 2 September 1864.

14. Mahan, *Gulf and Inland Waters*, 238.

15. William N. Still Jr., *Ironclad Captains: The Commanding Officers of the USS* Monitor (Washington, D.C.: Marine and Estuarine Management Division, NOAA, U.S. Dept. of Commerce, 1988), 57.

16. Maclay, *History*, 2:435.

17. Scharf, *History*, 565.

18. Conrad, "What the Fleet Surgeon Saw," 263.

19. Parker, *Battle of Mobile Bay*, 34.

20. Conrad, "What the Fleet Surgeon Saw," 263.

21. Ibid.

22. Ibid., 264; Scharf, *History*, 567.

23. Mahan, *Gulf and Inland Waters*, 238–39.

24. Joseph Marthon, "The Lashing of Admiral Farragut in the Rigging," *B&L*, 4:407–8.

25. Kinney, "August Morning," 206.

26. Clark, *My Fifty Years*, 54.

27. Mahan, *Admiral Farragut*, 281.

28. Ibid., 281–82; Farragut, *Life*, 419–20; J. Crittenden Watson, "Lashing," *B&L*, 4:407.

29. Rapier to Tom, 5 September 1864, Trigg private collection.

30. Mahan, *Admiral Farragut*, 283.

Chapter 21. Gunboat Fight

1. Wharton, "Battle of Mobile Bay."

2. Harrison to Buchanan, 1 October 1864, *ORN*, 21:583–84.

3. Ibid., 584.

4. Alfred Pirtle, "Rear-Admiral James Edward Jouett, United States Navy," *United Service: A Monthly Review of Military and Naval Affairs* 6 (January 1897): 21.

5. *Hartford* Deck Log, 5 August 1864, Logs of U.S. Naval Ships, NA; Mahan, *Admiral Farragut*, 280; *Itasca* Abstract Deck Log, 5 August 1864, *ORN*, 21:804; *Kennebec* Abstract Deck Log, 5 August 1864, *ORN*, 21:806; *Metacomet* Abstract Deck Log, 5 August 1864, *ORN*, 21:828; *Port Royal* Abstract Deck Log, 5 August 1864, *ORN*, 21:844.

6. Pirtle, "Rear Admiral James Edward Jouett," 20.

7. Maclay, *History*, 2:437.

8. Brown to Mahan, 4 May 1883, Area 6 (Union), Entry 463, NRC, RG 45, NA.
9. Pirtle, "Rear Admiral James Edward Jouett," 20; George Brown to A. T. Mahan, 24 May 1883, Entry 463, NRC, RG 45, NA.
10. Bergeron, "Twenty-second Louisiania," 207.
11. Scharf, *History*, 565; Murphey to Buchanan, 15 August 1864, *ORN*, 21:587–88.
12. Admiral [James Edward] Jouett, "Fought in Mobile Bay," *New York Times*, 24 July 1897.
13. Charles E. Clark, *Prince and Boatswain* (Greenfield, Mass.: E. A. Hall, n.d.), 104; Jouett, "Mobile Bay."
14. H. D. Baldwin, "Farragut in Mobile Bay," *Scribner's* 13, no. 4 (February 1877): 541.
15. Farragut to Welles, 8 August 1864, *ORN*, 21:505–6; Seaver to Farragut, 6 August 1864, *ORN*, 21:506.
16. Seaver to Farragut, 6 August 1864, *ORN*, 21:506–7.
17. Bennett to Mallory, 8 August 1864, *ORN*, 21:589.
18. Payne to Bennett, n.d., *ORN*, 21:594.
19. Page to Maury, 6 August 1864, *ORN*, 21:557.
20. Scharf, *History*, 566–67.
21. Batcheller, "Battle of Mobile Bay," 228; Kinney, "Farragut," *B&L*, 4:395.
22. Kinney, "August Morning," 207; *Hartford* Deck Log, 5 August 1864, Logs of U.S. Naval Ships, Area 6 (Union), Entry 463, NRC, RG 24, NA.
23. Batcheller, "Battle of Mobile Bay," 229.

Chapter 22. Melee

1. Batcheller, "Battle of Mobile Bay," 229; Mahan, *Gulf and Inland Waters*, 240. Kutz to Strong, 5 August 1864, *ORN*, 21:473–74; Kellogg to father, 7 August 1864, Area 6 (Union), Entry 463, NRC, RG 45, NA.
2. Conrad, "What the Fleet Surgeon Saw," 264.
3. Kinney, "Farragut," *B&L*, 4:395.
4. First quote ("piercing her through") in Farragut, *Life*, 420; second quote in Batcheller, "Battle of Mobile Bay," 229.
5. Hutchinson, "Bay Fight," 20; Mahan, *Gulf and Inland Waters*, 241.
6. Hutchinson, "Bay Fight," 21.
7. Ibid., 21–22.
8. Ibid., 22–23; Marchand to Farragut, 5 August 1864, *ORN*, 21:466.
9. Scharf, *History*, 567–68.
10. *Manhattan* Abstract Deck Log, 5 August 1864, *ORN*, 21:825.
11. Scharf, *History*, 567–68.
12. Mahan, *Gulf and Inland Waters*, 241.
13. John C. Watson, "Farragut and Mobile Bay," 556.
14. Edwin B. Latch to Rush, 26 January 1897, Subject File HA, RG 45, NA.
15. Quoted in Conrad, "What the Fleet Surgeon Saw," 265.

16. Mahan, *Gulf and Inland Waters*, 241.
17. *Chickasaw* Abstract Deck Log, 5 August 1864, *ORN*, 21:786; Farragut to Welles, 12 August 1864, *ORN*, 21:420.
18. Maclay, *History*, 2:445–46.
19. Kinney, "Farragut," *B&L*, 4:397.
20. Ibid.
21. C. Lewis, *David Glasgow Farragut*, 2:277.
22. Conrad, "What the Fleet Surgeon Saw," 264–65.
23. James Johnston, "Ram *Tennessee*," *B&L*, 4:404; Scharf, *History*, 569.
24. James Johnston, "Ram *Tennessee*," *B&L*, 4:404.
25. Quoted in Conrad, "What the Fleet Surgeon Saw," 266.
26. Ibid.
27. James Johnston, "Ram *Tennessee*," *B&L*, 4:404.
28. Maury to Seddon, 12 August 1864, *ORN*, 21:566; Williams to Garner, 7 August 1864, *ORN*, 21:560–61.
29. Johnston to Buchanan, 13 August 1864, *ORN*, 21:581.

Chapter 23. Surrender

1. Clark, *My Fifty Years*, 57.
2. Ely, "Journal," 5 August 1864, 35, Ely private collection.
3. Webster, "Personal Experiences," 17; *Manhattan* Abstract Deck Log, 5 August 1864, *ORN*, 21:824.
4. Conrad, "What the Fleet Surgeon Saw," 266–67.
5. Ibid., 267; *Ossipee* Abstract Deck Log, 5 August 1864, *ORN*, 21:841–42.
6. Conrad, "What the Fleet Surgeon Saw," 267.
7. James Johnston, "Ram *Tennessee*," *B&L*, 4:404.
8. Page to Maury, 5 August 1864, *ORA*, 52, 2:719.
9. Elizabeth Pillans diary, 5 August 1864, in author's possession, courtesy of Mary Van Antwerp, Fairhope, Ala.
10. William T. Mumford diary, 5 August 1864, Mobile City Museum.
11. Conrad, "What the Fleet Surgeon Saw," 267.
12. Ibid.
13. Ibid., 267–68.
14. Farragut, *Life*, 427.
15. Maclay, *History*, 2:449; quotes from Farragut, *Life*, 427.
16. Farragut to Welles, 5 August 1864, *ORN*, 21:406; Buchanan to Mallory, 25 August 1864, *ORN*, 21:578.
17. Farragut to Page, 5 August 1864, *ORN*, 21:424.
18. Page to Farragut, 5 August 1864, *ORN*, 21:424.
19. Farragut to Page, 5 August 1864, *ORN*, 21:424.
20. Page to Farragut, 6 August 1864, *ORN*, 21:425.
21. *Richmond* Abstract Deck Log, 5 August 1864, *ORN*, 21:847; *Itasca* Abstract

Deck Log, 5 August 1864, *ORN*, 21:806; *Kennebec* Abstract Deck Log, 5 August 1864, *ORN*, 21:80; *Octorara* Abstract Deck Log, 5 August 1864, *ORN*, 21:835.

22. Scharf, *History*, 584; *Chickasaw* Abstract Deck Log, 5 August 1864, *ORN* 21:786–87.

23. Williams, *From That Terrible Field*, 136.

24. Maury to Seddon, 5 August 1864, *ORN*, 21:556; Davis to Maury, n.d., *ORN*, 21:557.

25. Gilmer to Maury, 5 August 1864, *ORN*, 21:556–67.

Chapter 24. Aftermath

1. Bernard A. Reynolds, *Sketches of Mobile* (1868; reprint, Bossier City, La.: Tipton Printing and Publishing, 1971), 55; Rapier to Tom, 5 September 1864, Trigg private collection.

2. Scharf, *History*, 584; Williams to Garner, 7 August 1864, *ORN*, 21:560.

3. Waterman to Payne, 6 August 1864, Subject File HA, NRC, RG 45, NA.

4. Ibid.

5. Harrison to Buchanan, 1 October 1864, *ORN*, 21:584.

6. John Rapier, "Brave Act of Harrison," *Mobile Register*, 5 June 1902; Harrison to Buchanan, 1 October 1864, *ORN*, 21:584.

7. Wilkinson diary, 5 August 1864, 1–2, Fort Morgan Museum.

8. Tarpley diary, 7 August 1864, Fort Morgan Museum, 33.

9. Waterman to Payne, 6 August 1864, Subject File HA, NRC, RG 45, NA; *Sebago* Abstract Deck Log, 6 August 1864, *ORN*, 21:850; Rapier, "Brave Act of Harrison."

10. Williams to Garner, 7 August 1864, *ORN*, 21:560–61.

11. Rapier, "Brave Act of Harrison."

12. *Winnebago* Deck Log, 6 August 1864, Logs of U.S. Naval Ships, RG 24, NA; *Itasca* Deck Log, 6 August 1864, Logs of U.S. Naval Ships, RG 24, NA; *Kennebec* Abstract Deck Log, 5 August 1864, *ORN*, 21:806; *Sebago* Abstract Deck Log, 5 August 1864, *ORN*, 21:850; *Port Royal* Deck Log, 6 August 1864, Logs of U.S. Naval Ships, RG 24, NA; *Octorara* Deck Log, 6 August 1864, Logs of U.S. Naval Ships, RG 24, NA.

13. *Sebago* Abstract Deck Log, 5 August 1864, *ORN*, 21:850.

14. Harrison to Buchanan, 1 October 1864, *ORN*, 21:584–85.

15. Rapier, "Brave Act of Harrison."

16. Waterman, "Afloat," 21.

17. Rapier, "Brave Act of Harrison."

18. O'Connell, "Mr. O'Connell's Journal," 7.

19. Perkins, *Letters*, 250.

20. *Chickasaw* Abstract Deck Log, 6 August 1864, *ORN*, 21:787.

21. John H. [Jack] Friend Jr., "The Controversial Surrender of Fort Gaines, August 1864," *Gulf Coast Historical Review* 2, no. 2 (spring 1987): 98; Anderson to Farragut, 7 August 1864, *ORN*, 21:414.

22. *Hartford* Abstract Deck Log, 7 August 1864, *ORN*, 21:801; Farragut, Granger to Anderson, 7 August 1864, *ORN*, 21:415.

23. Anderson to Farragut, Granger, 7 August 1864 *ORN*, 21:415.

24. Parker, *Battle of Mobile Bay*, 40.

25. Ibid.

26. Page to Maury, 8 August 1864, *ORN*, 21:561; Page, "Defense," *B&L*, 4:409.

27. Williams to Garner, 7 August 1864, *ORN*, 21:560–61.

28. Farragut to Welles, 8 August 1864, *ORN*, 21:414; Absalom Kirby to wife, 8 August 1864, Absalom Kirby papers, Naval History Division, Smithsonian Institution.

29. Parker, *Battle of Mobile Bay*, 41.

30. Granger to Christensen, 8 August 1864, *ORA*, 39:417.

31. Page, "Defense," *B&L*, 4:409.

32. Ibid., 4:409–10.

33. Austill, "Fort Morgan," 14 August 1864, 260–61.

34. Ibid., 21 August 1864, 264.

35. Page, "Defense," *B&L*, 4:410.

36. Ibid. (Fort Morgan prisoners, author's estimate.)

37. Farragut to Welles, 27 August 1864, *ORN*, 21:612.

38. Rawley, *Turning Points*, 191; Lincoln's proclamation, photocopy of article from unidentified New York newspaper, 6 September 1864, in author's possession.

39. Heyman, *Prudent Soldier*, 219–20; C. C. Andrews, *History of the Campaign of Mobile* (New York, D. Van Nostrand, 1867), 31; Dabney H. Maury, "The Defense of Mobile in 1865," *Southern Historical Society Papers* 3, no. 1 (January 1877): 4.

40. Maury, "Defense of Mobile," 6.

41. Ibid., 8.

42. Mary Waring, *Miss Waring's Journal, 1863 and 1865*, ed. Thad Hold Jr. (Chicago: Wyvern Press of S.F.E., 1964), 16.

43. R. Taylor, E. R. S. Canby, General Orders No. 54, 6 May 1865, *ORA*, 49, 2:1283.

44. Ibid.; Maury, "Defense of Mobile," 9.

45. Maury, "Defense of Mobile," 13.

EPILOGUE

1. Wise, *Lifeline*, 3.

2. C. Lewis, *David Glasgow Farragut*, 2:280; Friend, "Battle of Mobile Bay," 172.

3. Silverstone, *Warships*, 10, 86, 208, 219, 236; Jouett to Farragut, 8 August 1864, *ORN*, 21:443; Farragut to Welles, 27 August 1864, *ORN*, 21:489–90; Harrison to Mallory, 9 August 1864, *ORN*, 21:575; Buchanan to Mallory, 25 August 1864, *ORN*, 21:578–79; Harrison to Buchanan, 1 October 1864, *ORN*, 21:585; Murphey to Buchanan, 15 August 1864, *ORN*, 21:588; Bennett to Mallory, 8 August 1864, *ORN*, 21:590; Iglehart to Bennett, 9 August 1864, *ORN*, 21:590–91.

4. Mahan, *Admiral Farragut*, 265.

5. Friend, "Battle of Mobile Bay," 172; Mallory to Davis, 30 August 1864, *ORN*, Series 2, 2:632–33.
6. Frank M. Bennett, *The Steam Navy of the United States* (Pittsburgh, Pa.: Warren, 1897), 435.
7. Robert Gardiner, ed., *Steam, Steel, and Shellfire, the Steam Warship 1815–1915*, Conway's History of the Ship (Annapolis: Naval Institute Press, 1992), 132–33; Hughes, *Fleet Tactics*, 63.
8. Mahan, *Admiral Farragut*, 263–65.
9. C. Lewis, *David Glasgow Farragut*, 2:291.
10. Talbot, "Admiral David Glasgow Farragut," 19–20.
11. *Appleton's Cyclopaedia of American Biography*, ed. James Grant Wilson and John Fiske (New York: D. Appleton, 1887), 230; J. T. Headly, *Farragut and Our Naval Commanders* (New York: E. B. Treat, 1867), 575–76.
12. General Order No. 12, 6 August 1864, *ORN*, 21:438; Farragut to wife, Farragut papers, Farragut Folklife Museum; Clarence Edward Macartney, *Mr. Lincoln's Admirals* (New York: Funk and Wagnalls, 1956), 74–75; Cogar, *Dictionary of Admirals*, 1:85–86.
13. Heyman, *Prudent Soldier*, 219–20; *Webster's American Military Biographies*, 58.
14. *Webster's American Military Biographies*, 58; quotes in Robert G. Ferris, *Soldier and Brave* (Washington, D.C.: U.S. Department of the Interior, 1971), 96–98.
15. Heyman, *Prudent Soldier*, 383.
16. Downey, *Storming*, 18; *Webster's American Military Biographies*, 148.
17. Oretha D. Swartz, "Franklin Buchanan—A Study in Divided Loyalties," U.S. Naval Institute *Proceedings* (December 1962): 68–69.
18. Ibid.
19. Ibid.
20. Ibid.
21. James Johnston, "Ram Tennessee," *B&L*, 4:406.
22. Ibid.
23. Ibid.; James B. Johnston service record, ZB File, Naval Historical Center, Washington, D. C.
24. "Another Old Hero Gone," *Savannah Morning News*, 12 February 1886.
25. William C. Davis, ed., *The Confederate General* ([Harrisburg, Pa.:] National Historical Society, 1991), 168; Warner, *Generals in Gray*, 215–16.
26. S. R. Franklin, *Memories of a Rear Admiral* (New York: Harper and Brothers, 1898), 199; Richard L. Page service record in Confederate Navy/Marine Corps file, NA.
27. Scharf, *History*, 591.
28. Richard L. Page, Obituary, *Norfolk Virginian*, 10 August 1901; Warner, *Generals in Gray*, 227.
29. Maury to Seddon, 8 August 1864, *ORN*, 21:562.
30. "Fort Gaines," *New Orleans Daily Picayune*, 11 September 1864.
31. Williams, *From That Terrible Field*, 178; William T. Mumford diary, 6 January 1865, Mobile City Museum; "The Last Roll," "Col. Charles D. Anderson," *Confederate Veteran* no. 10 (2 February 1902): 31.

32. Williams, *From That Terrible Field,* xv–xvi.
33. Edwin M. Jameson and Stanford Sternlicht, *The Black Devil of the Bayous: The Life and Times of the United States Steam Sloop* Hartford, *1858–1957* (Upper Saddle River, N.J.: Gregg Press, 1970), 181–83.
34. John H. [Jack] Friend Jr., "Preliminary Considerations: The Salvage, Preservation, and Display of the USS *Tecumseh,*" typescript, 49.
35. Statistical Data of U.S. Ships, *ORN,* Series 2, 1:221.
36. Mike Henderson, executive director of Historic Fort Gaines, "Fort Gaines after the Civil War," letter to author, 6 December 2001; Mike Bailey, curator of Fort Morgan Historic Site, "Fort Morgan after the Civil War," letter to author, 21 February 1994.
37. Samuel Eliot Morison, *The Two-Ocean War* (New York: Ballantine Books, 1974), 96.
38. National Park Service, "H. L. Hunley" (N.p: National Park Service, Submerged Cultural Resources Unit, n.d.), 25–29, report in author's possession.
39. Harold L. Peterson, postscript to Emanuel Raymond Lewis, *Seacoast Fortifications of the United States: An Introductory History* (Annapolis: Naval Institute Press, 1979), 133.
40. Alabama Historical Commission, *Preserve Alabama: A Guide to Services and Resources* (Montgomery, Ala.: Alabama Historical Commission, 1998), 35–36; Fort Gaines, "History and Tour Guide," Dauphin Island Park and Beach Board.
41. National Park Service, "Guidelines for Completing National Register of Historic Places Forms," National Register, Bulletin 16 (N.p.: National Park Service, 1991), 68; Alabama Historical Commission, *Preserve Alabama,* 35; Henderson, letter to author, 21 May 2002.

BIBLIOGRAPHY

PRIMARY SOURCES

Archives

Brooklyn Children's Museum. Brooklyn Institute of Arts and Science Museum, Brooklyn, N.Y. Cultural History No. 5 Collection. Jesse Sweet, "The Battle of Mobile Bay, Letters Written by a Sailor-Participant, August–September 1864."

Connecticut State Library, Hartford, Conn. John C. Kinney, "Battle of Mobile Bay," speech delivered in 1891.

Emory University. Robert W. Woodruff Library, Atlanta, Ga. Special Collections, J. L. J. Lear Diary. Union Miscellaneous No. 99 Collection, Henry W. Hart Letters.

Farragut Folklife Museum, Farragut, Tenn. Farragut Papers. Martin Freeman, "The Mobile Naval Combat."

Fort Morgan Museum, Gulf Shores, Ala. D.A.F. Letter. Rufe Dooley Letters. James T. Gee Papers. Orange Parret Diary. E. B. Presley Letters. C. T. Pope Letter. Tarpley Diary (typescript). Joseph B. Wilkinson Diary.

Library of Congress. Manuscript Division. Charles F. Blake Journal. Charles Stanhope Cotton Papers. John C. Watson, "Personal Recollections of Admiral Farragut."

Mariners Museum Library, Newport News, Va. David G. Farragut Letters. Eldridge Collection, *Red Gauntlet* Document.

Mobile City Museum, Mobile, Ala. William T. Mumford Diary. Enos Reed Letters.

Mobile Public Library, Mobile, Ala. Iberville Historic Society Collection. Mrs. Frances James Mosby, "Reminiscence, Mobile: 1861–1865."

National Archives. Map of the Defenses of the City of Mobile. Drawn under the direction of Victor von Scheliha. Drawer 121-15-3.

————. Mobile Bay Map, Survey of the Coast of the United States, 1856.

————. Record Group 24. Logs of U.S. Naval Ships and Stations. *Augusta. Bienville. Chickasaw. Eutaw. Hartford. Itasca. J. P. Jackson. Manhattan. Metacomet. Narcissus. Octorara. Port Royal. Tennessee. Winnebago.*

————. Record Group 45. Naval Records Collection of the Office of Naval Records and Library. Entry 23, Letters Received by the Secretary of the Navy. T. A. M. Craven to Gideon Welles. James Nicholson to Gideon Welles. James Nicholson to David Glasgow Farragut.

————. Entry 34. Letters of Commandants of Navy Yards and Shores Establishments. William Smith to Gideon Welles.

————. Entry 392. Logs, Journals, and Diaries of Officers of the United States at Sea. Journal of Isaac DeGraff. John Marchand Journal. J. C. Gregg Diary. USS *Cowslip* Log/Journal.

————. Entry 395. Letterbooks of the United States Navy at Sea. Percival Drayton to James Palmer. James C. Palmer Correspondence. Abstract of Lt. John C. Watson's Notes.

————. Entry 463. Union Area File. George Brown to A. T. Mahan. Edward Kellogg Letter. J. W. Watson to A. T. Mahan.

————. Subject File HA. David Glasgow Farragut Notebook. Edwin B. Latch Correspondence. George Waterman to John A. Payne.

————. Subject File OO. James D. Johnston, Speech, "Admiral Buchanan and the CSS Ram *Tennessee.*"

————. RG 109. War Dept. Collection of Confederate Records. *Red Gauntlet* Vessel Papers. Victor von Scheliha to Franklin Buchanan. Victor von Scheliha to Gallimard. Victor von Scheliha to Page.

Naval War College, Newport, R.I. Naval Historical Collection. John Marchand Journal.

Smithsonian Institution, Washington, D.C. Naval History Division. W. E. Geoghegan, "Confederate States Steamer 'Tennessee,' Lines, Outboard Profile, Deck Plan," USNM, 1961. Absalom Kirby Papers.

Southern Historical Collection, University of North Carolina, Chapel Hill. Anderson Papers. Franklin Buchanan Letter Book, 1862–63. Jeremy Gilmer Collection. Richard L. Page Papers. Victor von Scheliha Papers.

U.S. Naval Academy, Nimitz Library, Annapolis, Md. Special Collections Dept. Oliver Ambrose Batcheller Papers.

Virginia Historical Society, Richmond, Va. John K. Mitchell Papers.

Private Collections

Ely, Robert. "Journal of a Cruise in the Ironclad 'Manhattan.'" Collection of Richard B. Ely.

Enslow, Charles. Letters. Collection of Charles C. Enslow.

Rapier, John L. Letters. Collection of Adelaide Trigg.

Tarleton, Robert. Papers. Collection of Grace Bestor DuValle.

SECONDARY SOURCES

Books and Articles

Alabama Historical Commission. *Preserve Alabama: A Guide to Services and Resources*. Montgomery: Alabama Historical Commission, 1998.

Amos, Harriet E. *Cotton City: Urban Development in Antebellum Mobile*. Tusca-loosa: University of Alabama Press, 1985.

"Andrew Jackson Jr." *Confederate Veteran* 13, no. 7 (July 1905): 329.

Andrews, C. C. *History of the Campaign of Mobile*. New York: D. Van Nostrand, 1867.

"Another Old Hero Gone." *Savannah Morning News*, 12 February 1886.

Appleton's Cyclopaedia of American Biography. Ed. James Grant Wilson and John Fiske. New York: D. Appleton, 1887.

———. *New Orleans Times Picayune*, 14 August 1864.

Austill, Hurieosco. "Fort Morgan in the Confederacy." *Alabama Historical Quarterly* (summer 1945): 254–68.

Baldwin, H. D. "Farragut in Mobile Bay." *Scribner's Monthly Illustrated Magazine* 13, no. 4 (1877): 539–44.

Batcheller, Oliver A. "The Battle of Mobile Bay, August 5, 1864." *Magazine of History* 14, no. 6 (December 1911): 217–30.

Battles and Leaders of the Civil War. Ed. Robert U. Johnson and Clarence C. Buel. Vol. 4, *The Way to Appomattox*. New York: Thomas Yoseloff, 1956.

Bennett, Frank. *The Steam Navy of the United States*. Pittsburgh: Warren, 1897.

Bentley, W. H. *History of the 77th Illinois Volunteer Infantry, Sept. 2, 1862–July 10, 1865*. Peoria, Ill.: Edward Hine, 1883.

Bergeron, Arthur W., Jr. "The Twenty-second Louisiana Consolidated Infantry in the Defense of Mobile, 1864–1865." *Alabama Historical Quarterly* (fall 1976): 207.

Bowman, John S., ed. *The Civil War Almanac*. New York: World Almanac Publishing, 1983.

Brother, Charles. "The Journal of Private Charles Brother, USMC." In *Two Naval Journals, 1864, at the Battle of Mobile Bay*. Ed. C. Carter Smith Jr. Chicago: Wyvern Press, 1964.

Brownell, Henry H. "The Bay Fight." *Harper's Monthly Magazine* (December 1864).

Carter, Samuel, III. *The Siege of Atlanta, 1864*. New York: Ballantine Books, 1973.

Castel, Albert. *Decision in the West: The Atlanta Campaign of 1864*. Lawrence: University Press of Kansas, 1992.

Catton, Bruce. *Grant Takes Command*. Boston: Little, Brown, 1968.

Chester, Colby Morgan. "Showing the Way." *Military Order of the Loyal Legion of the United States, Commandery of the District of Columbia, War Papers* 79 (1910).

Clark, Charles E. *My Fifty Years in the Navy*. Boston: Little, Brown, 1917.

———. *Prince and Boatswain*. Greenfield, Mass.: E. A. Hall, n.d.

Cogar, William B. *Dictionary of Admirals, 1862–1900.* Vol. 1. Annapolis: Naval Institute Press, 1989.

Coggins, Jack. *Arms and Equipment of the Civil War.* Garden City, N.Y.: Doubleday, 1962.

Coker, William S. *The Last Battle of the War of 1812: New Orleans. No, Fort Bowyer!* Pensacola, Fla.: Perdido Bay Press, 1981. Reprinted from *Alabama Historical Quarterly* 43, no. 1 (1981): 43–63.

Conrad, D. B. "What the Fleet Surgeon Saw of the Fight in Mobile Bay." *United Service: A Monthly Review of Military and Naval Affairs* 8 (1892): 261–70.

Cox, Benjamin B. "Mobile in the War between the States." *Confederate Veteran* 24, no. 5 (May 1916): 212.

Craven Obituary. *Army and Navy Journal,* August 20, 1864.

Cumming, Kate. *A Journal of Hospital Life in the Confederate Army of Tennessee.* Louisville, Ky.: John P. Morton, n.d.

Davis, George B., et al. *The Official Military Atlas of the Civil War.* Washington, D.C.: U.S. Government Printing Office, 1891–95.

Davis, William C. *The Confederate General.* [Harrisburg, Pa.:] National Historical Society, 1991.

Dowdey, Clifford. *The Land They Fought For: The Story of the South as the Confederacy, 1832–1865.* Garden City, N.Y.: Doubleday, 1955.

Downey, Fairfax. *Storming of the Gateway: Chattanooga, 1863.* New York: David McKay, 1960.

Drayton, Percival. "Naval Letters from Captain Percival Drayton, 1861–1865." *New York Public Library Bulletin* 10 (1906): 38–81.

Dupuy, Col. T. N. *Understanding Defeat.* New York: Paragon House, 1990.

Dyer, Gwynne. *War.* New York: Crown Publishers, 1985.

Eaton, Clement. *A History of the Southern Confederacy.* New York: Free Press, 1954.

"Editor *Advertiser and Register.*" Letter, 4 August 1864. Microfilm Z2 M715, University of Alabama, Tuscaloosa.

Farago, Ladislas. *The Tenth Fleet.* New York: Paperback Library, 1962.

Farragut, Loyall. *The Life of David Glasgow Farragut, First Admiral of the United States Navy.* New York: D. Appleton, 1879.

Ferris, Robert G. *Soldier and Brave.* Washington, D.C.: U.S. Department of the Interior, 1971.

Folmar, John Kent. "Lt. Col. James M. Williams and the Ft. Powell Incident." *Alabama Review* 17, no. 2 (1964): 123–36.

Foote, Shelby. *Red River to Appomattox.* Vol. 3 in *The Civil War: A Narrative.* New York: Random House, 1974.

"Fort Gaines." *New Orleans Daily Picayune,* 11 September 1864.

Fowler, William M., Jr. *Under Two Flags.* New York: W. W. Norton, 1990.

Fox, Gustavus V. *Confidential Correspondence of Gustavus Vasa Fox, Assistant Secretary of the Navy, 1861–1865.* Ed. Robert W. Thompson and Richard Wainwright. Vol. 1. Freeport, N.Y.: Books for Libraries Press, [1972].

Franklin, S. R. *Memories of a Rear Admiral.* New York: Harper and Brothers, 1898.

Freeman, Douglas Southall. *Lee's Lieutenants: A Study in Command.* Vol. 3, *Gettysburg to Appomattox.* New York: Charles Scribner's Sons, 1944.

Fretwell, Mark E. "Rousseau's Alabama Raid." *Alabama Historical Quarterly* 18 (1956): 544-46.

Friend, John H. [Jack], Jr. "The Battle of Mobile Bay" In *Great American Naval Battles.* Ed. Jack Sweetman. Annapolis: Naval Institute Press, 1998.

———. "The Controversial Surrender of Fort Gaines." *Gulf Coast Historical Review* 2, no. 2 (spring 1987).

———. "Mobile Bay: First Strike for Grant's Strategy." *Mobile Register,* 24 April 1994.

———. "Preliminary Considerations: The Salvage, Preservation, and Display of the USS *Tecumseh.*" Typescript, June 1974, Mobile, Ala..

Gardiner, Robert, ed. *Conway's History of the Ship: Steam, Steel, and Shellfire, the Steam Warship 1815-1915.* Annapolis: Naval Institute Press, 1992.

Gilmore, J. R. "Our visit to Richmond." *Atlantic Monthly* 14 (September 1864).

Grant, Ulysses S. *Memoirs and Selected Letters.* New York: Library of America, 1990.

Hague, Parthenia Antoinette. *A Blockaded Family: Life in Southern Alabama during the Civil War.* Lincoln: University of Nebraska Press, 1991.

Headley, J. T. *Farragut and Our Naval Commanders.* New York: E. B. Treat, 1867.

Headley, P. C. *Life and Naval Career of Vice-Admiral David Glascoe Farragut.* New York: William H. Appleton, 1865.

Heyman, Max L., Jr. *Prudent Soldier: A Biography of Major General E. R. S. Canby, 1817–1873.* Glendale, Calif.: Arthur A. Clarke, 1959.

Hughes, Wayne P., Jr. *Fleet Tactics: Theory and Practice.* Annapolis: Naval Institute Press, 1986.

Hults, E.H. "Aboard the *Galena* at Mobile." *Civil War Times Illustrated* 10, no 1 (April 1971): 12–21.

Hunter, Alvah Folsom. *A Year on a Monitor and the Destruction of Fort Sumter.* Ed. Craig L. Symonds. Columbia: University of South Carolina Press, 1987.

Hurst, Jack. *Nathan Bedford Forrest: A Biography.* New York: Alfred A. Knopf, 1993.

Hutchinson, William. "The Bay Fight: A Sketch of the Battle of Mobile Bay." *Personal Narratives of the Battles of the Rebellion.* 8 (1879): 7.

Irwin, Richard B. "The Red River Campaign." In *Battles and Leaders of the Civil War.* Ed. Robert U. Johnson and Clarence C. Buel. New York: Thomas Yoseloff, 1956.

Jameson, Edwin M., and Stanford Sternlicht. *The Black Devil of the Bayous: The Life and Times of the United States Steam Sloop* Hartford, *1858-1957.* Upper Saddle River, N.J.: Gregg Press, 1970.

Johnston, James D. "The Battle of Mobile Bay." *United Service: A Monthly Review of Military and Naval Affairs* 6 (January 1882): 104-8.

———. "The Ram *Tennessee.*" In *Battles and Leaders of the Civil War.* Ed. Robert U. Johnson and Clarence C. Buel. New York: Thomas Yoseloff, 1956.

Johnston, Joseph E. *Narrative of Military Operations during the Civil War.* 1874. Reprint. New York: Da Capo Press, 1990.

Jouett, Admiral [James Edward]. "Fought in Mobile Bay." *New York Times*, 24 July 1897.

Keegan, John. *The Price of Admiralty: The Evolution of Naval Warfare*. New York: Viking, 1989.

Kendricken, Paul Henry. *Memoirs of Paul Henry Kendricken*. Boston: Privately Printed, 1910.

Kerby, Robert L. *Kirby Smith's Confederacy*. Reprint, Tuscaloosa: University of Alabama Press, 1991.

Kinney, John C. "An August Morning with Farragut." *Scribner's Monthly Illustrated Magazine* 22 (June 1881): 199–208.

———. "Farragut at Mobile Bay." In *Battles and Leaders of the Civil War*. Ed. Robert U. Johnson and Clarence C. Buel. New York: Thomas Yoseloff, 1956.

———. "A Great Anniversary." *Hartford Courant*, 5 August 1889.

"The Last Roll." "Col. Charles D. Anderson." *Confederate Veteran* no. 10 (2 February 1902): 31.

Latorre, Robert G. "*Tecumseh* Sinking Time Study." University of New Orleans, New Orleans, La., January 1995.

"Letter from Pollard, Alabama." *Mobile Evening News*, 1 August 1864.

Lewis, Emanuel Raymond. *Seacoast Fortifications of the United States: An Introductory History*. Annapolis: Naval Institute Press, 1979.

Lewis, Charles Lee. *Admiral Franklin Buchanan: Fearless Man of Action*. Baltimore: Norman, Remington, 1929.

———. *David Glasgow Farragut: Our First Admiral*. Vol. 2. Annapolis: U.S. Naval Institute, 1943.

Liddell, St. John Richardson. *Liddell's Record*. Ed. Nathaniel Cheairs Hughes Jr. Baton Rouge: Louisiana State University Press, 1997.

Little, George, and James Maxwell. *A History of Lumsden's Battery C.S.A.* Tuscaloosa, Ala.: R. E. Rhodes Chap., United Daughters of the Confederacy, [1905?].

Lynaugh, Kevin. "*Tecumseh* Sinking Time Study." Professional Report. Department of the Navy, Bethesda, Md., March 1995.

MacArtney, Clarence Edward. *Mr. Lincoln's Admirals*. New York: Funk and Wagnalls, 1956.

Maclay, Edgar Stanton. *A History of the United States Navy from 1775 to 1901*. Vol. 2. New York. D. Appleton, 1898.

Mahan, A.T. *Admiral Farragut*. Great Commanders Series. New York: D. Appleton, 1970.

———. *The Gulf and Inland Waters*. 1883. Reprint. Freeport N.Y.: Books for Libraries Press, 1970.

———. *Letters and Papers of Alfred Thayer Mahan*. Vol. 3. Ed Robert Seager II and Doris D. Maguire. Annapolis: Naval Institute Press, 1976.

Maury, Dabney. "The Defense of Mobile in 1865." *Southern Historical Society Papers* 3, no. 1 (January 1877): 4.

McMurray, Richard M. *Atlanta, 1864*. Lincoln: University of Nebraska Press, 2000.

McPherson, James, ed. *The Atlas of the Civil War.* New York: Macmillin, 1994.

Morison, Samuel Eliot. *The Two-Ocean War.* New York: Ballantine Books, 1974.

National Park Service. "Guidelines for Completing National Register of Historic Places Forms." National Register. Bulletin 16. N.p.: National Park Service, 1991.

————. "H. L. Hunley." N.p.: National Park Service, Submerged Cultural Resources Unit, n.d.

Nicolay, John G., and John Hay. *Abraham Lincoln: A History.* 10 vols. New York: Century, 1914.

O'Connell, John C. "Mr. O'Connell's Journal." In *Two Naval Journals, 1864, at the Battle of Mobile Bay.* Ed. C. Carter Smith Jr. Chicago: Wyvern Press, 1964.

Official Records of the Union and Confederate Navies in the War of the Rebellion. 2 series, 30 vols. Washington, D.C.: U.S. Government Printing Office, 1894-1922.

"On Board Steam Ship Winnebago." *New Orleans Times,* 7 August 1864.

Osborne, Charles C. *Jubal: The Life and Times of General Jubal A. Early, CSA, Defender of the Lost Cause.* Chapel Hill, N.C.: Algonquin Books, 1992.

Oviatt, Miles M. *A Civil War Marine at Sea: The Diary of Medal of Honor Recipient Miles Morgan Oviatt.* Ed. Mary P. Livingston. Shippensburg, Pa.: White Mane Books, 1998.

Page Richard L. "The Defense of Fort Morgan." In *Battles and Leaders of the Civil War.* Ed. Robert U. Johnson and Clarence C. Buel. New York: Thomas Yoseloff, 1956.

————. Obituary. *Norfolk Virginian,* 10 August 1901.

Parker, Foxhall A. *The Battle of Mobile Bay and the Capture of Forts Morgan, Gaines, and Powell.* Boston: Boston Stereotype Foundry, 1878.

"Passage of the Forts." *New York Daily Tribune,* 2 September 1864.

Perkins, George Hamilton. *Letters of Capt. Geo. Hamilton Perkins, U.S.N.* Ed. George E. Belknap, Concord Mass.: Ira C. Evans, 1886.

Pirtle, Alfred. "Rear Admiral James Edward Jouett, United States Navy." *United Service: A Monthly Review of Military and Naval Affairs.* 6 (December 1896): 528.

Porter, David D. "The Mississippi Flotilla in the Red River Expedition." In *Battles and Leaders of the Civil War.* Ed. Robert U. Johnson and Clarence C. Buel. New York: Thomas Yoseloff, 1956.

————. *The Naval History of the Civil War.* Secaucus N.J.: Castle, 1984.

Pratt, Fletcher. *A Short History of the Civil War.* New York: Pocket Books, 1960.

Rapier, John. "Brave Act of Harrison." *Mobile Register,* 3 June 1902.

Rawley, James A. *Turning Points of the Civil War.* Lincoln: University of Nebraska Press, 1966.

Reynolds, Bernard A. *Sketches of Mobile.* 1868. Reprint. Bossier City, La.: Tipton Printing and Publishing, 1971.

Ripley, Warren. *Artillery and Ammunition of the Civil War.* Charleston, S.C.: Battery Press 1984.

Ross, Fitzgerald. *Cities and Camps of the Confederate States.* Ed. Richard B. Harwell. Urbana: University of Illinois Press, 1958.

St. Paul, Henry. "The Attack on Mobile." *New Orleans times Picayune,* 14 August 1864.

Sandburg, Carl. *Abraham Lincoln: The War Years, 1864-1865.* New York: Dell Publishing, 1960.

Scharf, J. Thomas. *History of the Confederate States Navy.* 1887. Reprint. New York: Fairfax Press, 1977.

Scott, Reuben B. *The History of the 67th Regiment, Indiana Infantry Volunteers.* Bedford, Ind.: Herald Book, 1892.

Seitz, Don C. *Braxton Bragg, General of the Confederacy.* Columbia, S.C.: State Company, 1924.

Selfridge, Thomas O. "The Navy in the Red River." In *Battles and Leaders of the Civil War.* Ed. Robert U. Johnson and Clarence C. Buel. New York: Thomas Yoseloff, 1956.

Sherman, William T. *Memoirs of General William T. Sherman.* Bloomington: Indiana University Press, 1957.

Silverstone, Paul. *Warships of the Civil War Navies.* Annapolis: Naval Institute Press, 1989.

Smith, Jean Edward. *Grant.* New York: Simon and Schuster, 2001.

Smith, Sidney A., and C. Carter Smith Jr. *Mobile: 1861-1865.* Chicago: Wyvern Press, 1964.

Spears, John Randolph. *David G. Farragut.* Philadelphia: George W. Jacobs, 1905.

Still, William N., Jr. "The Confederate States Navy at Mobile, 1861 to August, 1864." *Alabama Historical Quarterly* 30 (1968): 127-44.

―――. *Iron Afloat: The Story of Confederate Ironclads.* Nashville: Vanderbilt University Press, 1971.

―――. *Ironclad Captains: The Commanding Officers of the USS* Monitor. Greenville, N.C.: Marine and Estuarine Management, NOAA, U.S. Dept. of Commerce, 1988.

Stokesberry, James. *How to Build a Monitor: A Study of the Construction of the USS* Tecumseh. Washington, D.C.: National Armed Forces Museum Advisory Board, Smithsonian Institution, 1966. Revised 1967.

Strode, Hudson. *Jefferson Davis: Tragic Hero.* New York: Harcourt, Brace and World, 1964.

Stuart, A. A. *Iowa Colonels and Regiments.* Des Moines: Mills, 1865.

Swartz, Oretha D. "Franklin Buchanan—A Study in Divided Loyalties." U.S. Naval Institute *Proceedings* (December 1962): 61–69.

Sweetman, Jack, ed. *Great American Naval Battles.* Annapolis: Naval Institute Press, 1998.

Sword, Wiley. *Southern Invincibility: A History of the Confederate Heart.* New York: St. Martin's Press, 1999.

Symonds, Craig L. *A Battlefield Atlas of the Civil War.* Annapolis: Nautical and Aviation Publishing of America, 1983.

―――. *Confederate Admiral: The Life and Wars of Franklin Buchanan.* Annapolis: Naval Institute Press, 1999.

―――. *Joseph E. Johnston: A Civil War Biography.* New York: W. W. Norton, 1992.

Talbot, James Joseph. "Admiral David Glasgow Farragut." *United Service: A Monthly Review of Military and Naval Affairs* 3 (July 1880): 11-22.

Tennessee Civil War Centennial Commission. *Tennesseans in the Civil War.* Vol. 1. Nashville: Civil War Centennial Commission, 1964.

Tucker, Spencer. *Arming the Fleet: U.S. Naval Ordinance in the Muzzle-Loading Era.* Annapolis: Naval Institute Press, 1989.

Two Naval Journals: 1864 at the Battle of Mobile Bay. Ed. C. Carter Smith Jr. Chicago: Wyvern Press, 1964.

U.S. Navy Department. *Allowances Established for Vessels of the United States Navy, 1864.* Washington, D.C.: U.S. Government Printing Office, 1865.

———. *Civil War Naval Chronology, 1861-1865.* Part 6, Special Studies and Cumulative Index, Naval History Division. Washington, D.C.: U.S. Government Printing Office, 1966.

———. *Dictionary of American Naval Fighting Ships.* Vol. 3. Washington, D.C.: Office of the Chief of Naval Operations, Naval History Division, 1968.

———. *Ordinance Instructions for the U.S. Navy.* 3d ed. Washington, D.C.: U.S. Government Printing Office, 1864.

Von Ehrenkrook, F. *History of Submarine Mining and Torpedoes.* 1878. Reprint. Berlin: Battalion Press, n.d.

Von Scheliha, [Victor Ernst]. *A Treatise on Coast-Defense.* 1868. Reprint. Westport, Conn.: Greenwood, 1971.

Walke, H[enry]. *Naval Scenes and Reminiscences of the Civil War in the United States.* New York: F. R. Reed, 1877.

Warner, Ezra J. *Generals in Gray: Lives of the Confederate Commanders.* Baton Rouge: Louisiana State University Press, 1959.

Waring, Mary [Mary Douglass Waring Harrison]. *Miss Waring's Journal, 1863 and 1865.* Chicago: Wyvern Press of S.F.E., 1964.

War of the Rebellion: A Compilation of the Official Records of the Union and Confederate Armies. 4 Series, 128 vols. Washington, D.C.: U.S. Government Printing Office, 1880–1901.

Waterman, George S. "Afloat-Afield-Afloat." *Confederate Veteran* 7, no. 1 (January 1899): 18–21.

Watson, John Crittenden. "The Lashing of Admiral Farragut in the Rigging." In *Battles and Leaders of the Civil War.* Ed. Robert U. Johnson and Clarence C. Buel. New York: Thomas Yoseloff, 1956.

———. "Farragut and Mobile Bay—Personal Reminiscences." U.S. Naval Institute *Proceedings* 53 (May 1927): 551–77.

Webster, Harrie. " Personal Experiences on a Monitor at the Battle of Mobile Bay." *California Commandery of the Military Order of the Loyal Legion of the United States* 14 (29 August 1894): 12.

Webster's American Military Biographies. Springfield Mass.: G. and C. Merriam, 1978.

Wharton, A. D. "The Battle of Mobile Bay." *Nashville Daily American,* 13 September 1877.

William, James M. *From That Terrible Field: Civil War Letters of James M. Williams,*

Twenty-First Alabama Infantry Volunteers. Ed. John Kent Folmar. University: University of Alabama Press, 1981.

Wise, Stephen R. *Lifetime of the Confederacy: Blockade Running during the Civil War.* Columbia: University of South Carolina Press, 1988.

Woods, J. T. *Services of the Ninety-Sixth Ohio Volunteers.* Toledo, Ohio: Blade Printing and Paper, 1874.

Wukovitz, John L. "Decks Covered with Blood." *America's Civil War* (March 1992): 42.

Newspapers

Baltimore Patriot and Evening Advertiser, 10 October 1814.

Mobile Daily Register, 8 August 1864.

Mobile Evening News, 1 August 1864.

Mobile Paper, 29 January 1873.

National Tribune, 22 July 1864.

New Orleans Times Picayune, 14 August 1864.

New York Daily Tribune, 24 July 1897.

Richmond Examiner, 19 July 1864.

INDEX

>> <<

ABOUT THE AUTHOR

Jack Friend, a resident of Montrose, Alabama, graduated from Virginia Military Institute. Following graduation from VMI, he served as an aid de camp to the 5th Army chief of staff and as a tank company commander during the Korean War. After returning from Korea, he attended Dartmouth College, where he received a master's degree in business administration. When he returned to Mobile, Friend founded a market research company, which he ran for twenty-five years. He has also served on the Alabama Historical Commission and currently serves on the board of the CSS Alabama Association, an organization that funds the retrieval of artifacts from the famous warship. Friend is no newcomer to the Battle of Mobile Bay. He has previously written about the engagement for *Great American Naval Battles,* also published by the Naval Institute Press.